520
Os7m

92571

DATE DUE			
May 14 '76			
Oct 4 '76			
Mar 15 79			
Mar 16 '80			
Apr 30 '82			
OCT 1 0 1994			

modern astronomy

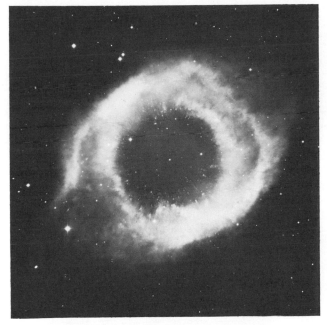

modern astronomy

Ludwig Oster
Joint Institute for Laboratory Astrophysics
University of Colorado

Holden-Day, Inc.
San Francisco

Düsseldorf   Johannesburg   London   Panama   Singapore   Sydney   Toronto

Cover: The η Carinae region. Photograph taken with the aid of an objective prism. The prism, placed in front of the lens of a refracting telescope, separates the light from each star into its component colors. *(University of Michigan Observatories.)*

Editors: Edward M. Millman and Sally Anderson
Designers: Sally Anderson and Gillian Johnson
Illustrator: David Strassman
Cover designer: Richard Forster
Production: Charles A. Goehring
Composition: Applied Typographic Systems, Inc. (Linofilm Optima)
Printing and binding: The Maple Press Company

MODERN ASTRONOMY

Library of Congress Catalog Card Number: 72–83247
ISBN: 0–8162–6523–2

234567890 MP 8079876543

Printed in the United States of America

preface

This text has been written for one- or two-semester courses in general astronomy. It is aimed specifically toward the student who is not fully familiar with mathematical techniques and has had little exposure to modern physics. Almost all quantitative statements are given in the form of simple graphs rather than complicated equations, and the background physics is explained to the point where the astronomical results and data follow readily. In addition, brief summaries of background material appear before they are used in the text, and a broader and more general survey is given in the appendices.

Throughout the text, the emphasis is on *why* we think certain statements are true, *how* we acquired our knowledge, and *why* we attempt to make certain new observations. Little is said about the technical details; but then no reader is likely to expect this text to serve as an operating manual for the 200-inch telescope. When I teach my students solar physics, I hope they will see why we think the sun's surface temperature is about 6000°, and not 3000° or 10,000°, and I usually don't mention that the presently accepted value is 5780°K. At the same time, I strive to make it clear that most of our results lie in the grey area between "almost 100% certain" and "probably correct."

Modern Astronomy is an attempt at a balanced description of all of astronomy as it presents itself in the 1970s. This emphasis on contemporary work is, I think, the main difference between this text and others; it includes most of the recent research, even areas whose origins go back no further than the last 5 or 10 years. About one-third of the text is devoted to the solar system including the sun, one-third to the stars and their evolution, and one-third to our galaxy and the universe at large. In my opinion, each of the three main parts should have about equal weight in a general survey course, and the book has enough material to fill a standard one-year course. Where astronomy occupies only a semester, say, in a multisemester science sequence, the instructor might either skip over those topics he considers secondary aspects or else choose particular topics to discuss in detail.

Chapter 1 is an introduction to historical and conceptual developments. I have tried there to stress two points of primary importance in understanding how astronomical knowledge was and is acquired. For one, astronomy was tied for centuries to the problems (and nonproblems) of people outside the realm of science as we understand it now. On the other hand, for the last hundred years or so, progress in astronomy has been achieved consistently by working out new approaches in the laboratory and applying them to the vast array of situations found in the universe.

Part I begins with a discussion of the earth as a celestial body. Here we talk about the conditions for life, and the geometric intricacies of rotation and revolution with their consequences for the earth-bound observer. The moon, the planets, and the minor members of the solar system are treated as physical bodies with specific structures and histories and as entities whose motion characteristics determine our ability to observe them. Our star, the sun, serves as a link to the larger units of the universe, and our detailed knowledge of its processes and structures is used as the primary example of how a star is built.

In Part II, stellar astronomy is introduced through observational facts and methods, such as the determination of distance, brightness, mass, radius, and surface temperature. The discussion of the observed distribution of stars among luminosities and temperatures—the H-R diagram—is immediately followed by its explanation in terms of stellar evolution, from the beginning condensation to the final white dwarf, neutron star, or black hole. A survey of the major classes of variable stars, some of which we understand and some of which we don't, concludes this part.

In Part III, we turn from the individuals to the great ensembles. A discussion of the distribution of uncondensed matter around us—the interstellar gas and its clouds—leads naturally to the organism we call our galaxy, its complex structures and its history. Other types of systems are then detailed, those close to "home" and those farther and farther away, out to where radio galaxies and quasars present us with a view into the distant past. The text ends with a description of current ideas about the universe as a whole, its past and its future, from the primordial fireball through the current expansion phase to the possible return.

More than the usual space has been allotted to auxiliary material, arranged in appendices. There is a short appendix on mathematical notation, graphical representation, and the little needed from geometry (I should hope that most of today's students will find this superfluous). It is followed by a survey of the facts and concepts of modern physics on which much of the text material is based. Here the sequence is from things commonly known to the less-often-treated subjects. There is a summary of astronomical instruments and a listing of objects in the sky that can be seen with the naked eye or a small back-yard telescope (after all, even the most radical theoretician, just once in a while, looks at the stars like everybody else). The tables include data on the various members of the solar system and stars and galaxies. Finally, there is a glossary of widely used words, with a special meaning in the sciences, which are not explained in detail in the text. Astronomical terms are, of course, listed in the general index.

At the end of each chapter, questions for discussion, designed to lead the student beyond what is in the book, exercises to test his knowledge or to make him compute some simple numbers of astronomical interest, and a few basic experiments and observations are listed.

This text owes much to E. M. Millman, Senior Editor of Holden-Day Inc., whose advice on style and presentation was invaluable to me. I have profited from discussions and correspondence with many friends and colleagues, notably W. Christiansen, C. Heiles, P. Hodge, R. Kraft, R. McCray, V. Trimble, and D. Wentzel. Finally, there were my undergraduates, whose responses inside and outside the classroom largely determined this presentation of modern astronomy.

Ludwig Oster

contents

III THE STAR SYSTEMS

APPENDICES

modern astronomy

1 astronomy: the history

More has probably been written on the history of astronomy than on the history of any other science. The reason is obvious: just look at the sky on any clear night. Astronomical observations gave man his first incentive to explore nature beyond his day-to-day needs, as well as the object of that exploration. Scientific methods as we understand them today were first applied to astronomy, and the results and theories of the astronomers appeal more than any others to the speculative mind. Thus, in a very real sense, the history of science begins with astronomy.

In this summary we shall make no attempt to record the history step by step, citing all the dates, names, places, and events. Instead, we shall show how early astronomy was interrelated with the general problems of its times, the thinking of philosophers, and the arbitrary will of authorities. We begin way back, when man, in spite of his daily fight for survival, still took the time to look up to the heavens.

1.1 THE BEGINNINGS

It is generally accepted premise that man had acquired significant intelligence long before civilizations, in the socioeconomic sense, had been formed. Thus we can assume that man tried to understand, or at least to classify, what he saw in the skies well before even the earliest dates indicated by archaeological evidence. But the very early evidence of astronomical undertakings is extremely sparse; it begins to show a pattern only in written records, first kept some time in the first millennium B.C. So our earliest indication of astronomical investigations must, in reality, be the product of hundreds and thousands of years of patient exploration.

There still exists one very striking example of early astronomy: the Stonehenge monument in England, dating from the middle of the second millennium B.C. It was clearly intended to serve astronomical needs, probably in some religious connection. The civilization that built Stonehenge (and a number of similar, but lesser monuments) must have been widespread, but we have no conclusive information as to its ethnic type, background, or other achievements. What we do know is that the stones of the monument are aligned to point to the extremes of the rising and setting of the sun and the moon on the horizon. No correlation has been found between the positions of the stones and any star or planet.

Let us pause to consider the implications of these findings. This earliest evidence of astronomical endeavors shows a preoccupation with the motion of the two most easily discerned bodies in the sky, the sun and the moon. To understand—or at least describe and predict—this motion seems to have been the concern of Stonehenge's protoastronomers. The configuration of the monument suggests that they

The Stonehenge monument, the oldest known astronomical observatory, near Salisbury, England. (*British Tourist Authority, New York.*)

went about their task by making many observations and trying to deduce a regularity that would ultimately allow them to predict motion and positions. It is possible that they even attempted to predict the occurrence of eclipses. At any rate, the Stonehenge evidence shows how the early astronomers tried to solve the most obvious (but, unfortunately, not the simplest) problem by the straightforward method of observation and deduction, nowadays the basis for all scientific work.

There were other beginnings: in China, in India, in the Mediterranean. All these civilizations must, at least initially, have worked the same way, and men must have thought the same thoughts—although we are now inclined to believe that many results were reported back and forth along the trade routes that spanned the ancient world. From our point of view, though, the question of mutual dependence is irrelevant. By the time the Greeks emerged as intellectual leaders, astronomers were able to predict the positions of the sun and the moon (and thus the likelihood of an eclipse), and the positions of the major planets. They had devised a rather accurate calendar based on their astronomical knowledge; it is the Babylonian division of the day into hours, minutes, and seconds that was inherited by the Greeks and left to posterity in all its splendid confusion.

All this occurred in a vast belt that we might call southern Eurasia. There, the climate is quite favorable to astronomical work: long periods of relatively cloudless skies make it possible to follow the motions of the celestial bodies to obtain meaningful data. Nature did not extend this "laboratory" to northern Europe, and so it is not surprising that little systematic knowledge was accumulated among, for instance, the Vikings. And it is all the more astonishing that Stonehenge was devised and built in the British Isles.

There were subtle differences in how the people, or at least the educated elite, looked upon the achievements of the "astronomers." The ancient cultures related the heavenly bodies to their religious beliefs to varying degrees, and with varying emphasis. Indian religions embraced very complex myths concerning the creation and destruction of the world; in China much of the information gained through astronomy was used to predict the (ominous) eclipses; the Babylonians practiced astrology more than astronomy. According to written accounts, the Babylonians' achievements were greatest, but it is difficult and not very fruitful to determine who discovered what and precisely when. Let us emphasize instead that much had been achieved by 600 B.C. in terms of observation, description, and interpretation, and that this was motivated by what might be called "spiritual needs."

However, there had been, from the very beginning, another more "down to earth" need. A society based on agriculture needs fairly accurate time keeping, something more than the rather trivial estimates of the time of day afforded by the apparent motion of the sun. In principle, one could deduce the length of a year, and perhaps some type of subdivision, from careful observation of seasonal changes in nature (if one wanted to forgo all help from astronomy), or from observations of the path of the sun at noon through the course of the year. The latter observations had actually been made quite early.

Fortunately, our solar system provides the earth with a much more elegant tool, namely, the moon, which, through its phases rather than its apparent motion in the skies, defines a "month" — probably the most useful time period for a primitive farmer. All that has to be done to devise a "calendar" is to count the number of full moons between, say, two consecutive summers. For this reason, as much as any other, early astronomy was directed toward the moon and the characteristics of its motion and, more generally, toward night-sky observations. Such observations must have included the planets, which also move across the sky, but in a much more complex manner. What would be more natural, once lunar and solar motion has been reasonably well described, than to attempt the same with the planets?

It must be noted here that several civilizations outside the main routes of Eurasia developed astronomy on their own, and with their own motivation. Among them were the Mayans, whose preoccupation with sun, moon, and planets (in particular, Venus) is documented in written records as well as in astronomical-religious monuments of eerie beauty. We mention them only in passing because they had no influence on the development of modern astronomy.

1.2 GREEK ASTRONOMY

Astronomy was well under way when, beginning about 600 B.C., the Greek astronomers began to make their contribution. Initially, we can be sure, their work was based on the thinking and observations of others, especially the Babylonians. But very soon they added their own emphasis; astronomy, and the natural sciences as a whole, were to become the basis on which were built meaningful (i.e., logical) chains of thought. Thus, it was neither socioeconomic interest nor a religious "need," nor even a fascination with collecting and ordering observations, that motivated Greek astronomers; they specialized in abstract models.

Hand in hand with this turn from "experiment" to "theory" came the increasing use of algebra and geometry. These disciplines had seen significant development earlier, particularly in Egypt, but only the Greek philosophers could turn the practical measuring tool of others into a preoccupation in itself. The expansion of a description of observed events into a deduced, more universal model is what made Greek thinking different from that of earlier civilizations. This deductive thinking introduced a new element into astronomy. It marked the first use of the methods of modern science, cautiously and tentatively on problems that were not beyond the grasp of contemporary abilities. To be sure, much of the Greek work overstated purely theoretical or speculative aspects, and it often left the realm of reality in search of abstract models. Nevertheless, out of it came a pressure to study more and more natural phenomena, and in particular those of astronomy.

The observed motions of the heavenly bodies caught the astronomers' fancy, and those of the sun, the moon, and the planets were carefully studied. Soon, astronomers realized that it is not self-evident that the "other" bodies move while the earth stands still. The hypothesis of a stationary earth could be removed, and other models constructed. Thus, the motion characteristics of our solar system became one of the central topics of research while Greek astronomy was at its peak. But there was much more: distances to the moon and the sun were measured; the relative orbits of the moon and the sun were estimated in an effort to understand eclipses; the diameter of the earth was obtained with surprising accuracy; and for the first time stars were catalogued and their differing brightnesses noted quantitatively.

Nevertheless, the main legacy of Greek astronomy was the unsolved problem of solar-system motions. The immediate consequence of the earth's revolution about the sun, the apparent motion of the "fixed" stars induced by this revolution, was not observed—indeed, it was not observable by contemporary means—and Aristarchus' explanation that these fixed stars were too far away was not accepted by everybody. The different viewpoints were written down, and encyclopedic summaries were published by many, most notably Aristotle in his *Organon* and later, specifically for astronomy, Ptolemy in his *Almagest*. Unfortunately for what was to come, both embraced an earth-centered system; and when all men believed that all original thoughts had been thought, when physicists merely wrote commentaries on commentaries and no new observations were made, this geocentric system had the majority.

1.3 THE MILLENNIUM IN BETWEEN

What shook Europe in A.D. 200 was not the excitement of scientific progress, but the economic and social decline of the Roman Empire, the wars, and the influx of foreign philosophies, in particular, Christianity. By the time the dust had settled, Christian authority was universal in civilized Europe, and the world of thought had been transformed. Intellect and faith were directed toward a unity beyond the senses and beyond human experience; and there was little place for a quest for independent knowledge through observation, deduction, and prediction. Instead, the combination of Aristotle and Ptolemy became the unquestioned source of truth in astronomy.

Indeed, the work of the Greek astronomers was not continued by the central Europeans but by the followers of Mohammed, who between A.D. 600 and 1000 conquered most of what was once the civilized world. They did not just build politically powerful satrapies, they also rebuilt the influence of the scientist and philosopher, and made them independent of the ruling religious authority. There are probably as many conflicting reasons as there are related reasons for this rebirth of science. Some have to do with the different outlook of the Moslem on God, life, and man. Some are accidental, such as the necessity of knowing the relative location of a garrison with respect to Mecca, the geographic center of the Islamic faith. And most quite simply resulted from the necessity to govern as vast a fiefdom as the Moslems had acquired by the end of the first millennium A.D.

At any rate, the Islamic culture produced a cast of scientists of very much the same stature as the classical Greek philosophers. And since the great centers of Greek achievement, notably Alexandria, were within the realm of their power, and most of the ancient writings and the later commentaries had been saved, Arab science was able to build upon a much broader basis than European science could have. The problems posed by the Greeks were inherited along with the Greek writings; the Arab astronomers became concerned with the motions of the planets, the distances to the stars, the shape and size of the earth.

As did some of the last great Greek astronomers, the Arab astronomers around A.D. 1000 realized that new and better observations were more important than the efforts of yet another genius. Some observations were made, notably of planetary and stellar positions, and of solar and lunar eclipses. But fate again decided against astronomy by reducing political and cultural expansion before any really significant progress was made.

The accomplishments of the Arabs, even those that were encyclopedic rather than original, did not remain unnoticed in the Christian lands. At the time when the Renaissance, the rebirth of arts and letters, swept over Europe, that subcontinent was neither politically isolated nor philosophically unwilling to listen to its colleagues of other religions. And many were at least intrigued by the opportunity of obtaining new translations of Greek works they knew existed but had never seen. Thus, through exchange with the new world, European interest in the real problems of astronomy was renewed. At first, much of this interest was concentrated on studying the authorities of old, so that once again Greek thinking and Greek problems became the starting point for discussions among the erudite.

1.4 THE BIRTH OF MODERN SCIENCE

When all the arguments had been weighed, the problems of astronomy simply required new observational data. The Greeks had just about come to this conclusion when the basis of their world collapsed. The Arabs had reached it too, although probably not quite so consciously, only to find their world recede into relative oblivion. When European Renaissance man had come to this point of departure, his world had barely begun to open up. What we call the rebirth of scientific thought is a rather late byproduct of the much more general internal upheaval that moved across Europe in the fifteenth and sixteenth centuries. Religion was the major area for study by the philosophers. The religious reformers probably had little sympathy or tolerance for scientists who wanted to explore the structure of the world independently of the great authorities, in spite of the fact that they themselves were interested in studying God without the restrictions imposed by these same authorities. Yet in jealously fighting for the right to unrestricted study, the reformers also liberated the exploration of nature. And only in the context of this new freedom, beginning with dispassionate analysis of observations, could the full impact of science be realized.

In the fifteenth century and through most of the sixteenth centruy there was little conflict seen between the endeavors of the astronomers to understand the motions of the heavenly bodies and the requirements of religious truth. We may speculate as to Copernicus' fears that his conviction that the earth orbits about the sun might lead to a confrontation with the Church; but rather little of this is evident in his writings. Tycho Brahe, on the other hand, rejected the heliocentric system of Copernicus. He carried out, without the aid of a telescope, the most accurate observations of his time. And throughout the rest of the sixteenth century, discussion of the relative motions of the earth, the sun, and the planets remained largely in the realm of astronomy.

Nevertheless, the problem was not just to establish precisely the orbits in the solar system, but as much to obtain the right to research nature independently of preconceived ideas. The man to force this larger issue was Galileo. At first he had little work of his own to offer in support of the Copernican system he so ardently defended. But after 1610, through his effective use of the telescope, which suddenly—almost overnight—made observations possible beyond anything attainable before, he took the center of the scientific stage.

The telescope permitted observation of the four brightest satellites of Jupiter in their orbits about the parent planet, a situation very suggestive of the motions of the sun and its planets. More important, the telescope permitted viewing of the phases of Venus, in support of the assumption that Venus is a body revolving about the sun inside the earth's orbit. These new discoveries were considered strong evidence in favor of the Copernican system by its adherents, while its opponents pointed to the absence of one conclusive observation: the apparent annual motion of the fixed stars. Even the best telescopes available in Galileo's day, and for almost two centuries to come, did not show any measurable annual stellar motion. The excuse that stars may be just too far away, which is the correct explanation, was not well received by the other side. (In addition, the Copernican system had from its conception one tremendous advantage over the geocentric Ptolemaic system: it could explain the available observations in a much simpler manner. The argument that nature almost always prefers the least complex solution is accepted by the modern scientist, as it was, to an extent, by Galileo and his friends.)

On the surface, the detractors won, even if the majority of astronomers may have sided with Galileo on the significant issues. He was incarcerated and died an unhappy old man. But the legacy of the battle was overwhelming: planetary motion became the burning issue of seventeenth century astronomy, and any scientist's first task was to demonstrate what really was the truth. For centuries to come, most

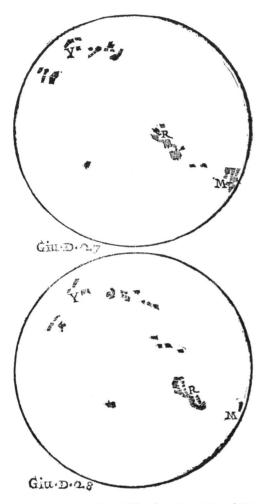

Sunspot drawings by Galileo from June 27 and 28, 1612. (*Reproduced in the 1718 edition of Galileo's works, Opere di Galileo Galilei.*)

European scientific thought was channelled toward the rather narrow field of celestial motions and the underlying problems of mechanics and gravitation. Astronomers lost almost all interest in phenomena that were not directly involved with motions in the solar system, in spite of the fact that the telescope had opened up much of the universe to study. For example, a Jesuit, Father Scheiner, faithfully made observations of the sun for many years. In particular, he found sunspots to be a rather regular event, and he followed their apparent motion across the solar surface. His voluminous report, entitled *Rosa Ursina*, came out in 1630, just in time to be banned by the Church together with the rest of the new astronomical works; solar physics had to wait almost 200 years until outsiders reopened this field of study.

1.5 THE CLASSICAL PERIOD OF ASTRONOMY

The remainder of the seventeenth century saw more and more accurate data collected by more and more independent observers. Any doubts about the Copernican system were silenced by the overwhelming evidence. Soon, the refined techniques were applied to secondary problems, in particular, the motions of planetary satellites, the moon, and comets.

The vast amount of accurate data now available made it possible for Johannes Kepler to extract the simple general laws governing the motion of celestial bodies. The search for universality and simplicity led scientists at least one step beyond Kepler's *descriptive* laws of planetary motion, to an *understanding* of the phenomena involved. In 1687, Newton derived his gravitational law, which not only gave the functional relationship between the masses of, and distance between, two attracting bodies, but also introduced the first "universal constant" into physics. Newton's law also claimed that the same force that causes the orbital motion of the earth about the sun also draws the notorious apple from the tree to the ground. It is remarkable how rapidly this concept was accepted only 45 years after Galileo's death; it is really a statement to the effect that there are no limits to man's ability to describe nature. There are no unobservables of any consequence.

The invention of needed mathematical techniques paralleled the development of physical insight. Newton's mechanics has to do with accelerations and velocities —in short, with rates of change in observable quantities. The problem of concisely describing rates of change was solved with the invention of the calculus by Newton and Leibniz. Of course, this new technique was immediately applied to a variety of problems, but its early triumphs all were concerned with mechanics, in particular, with the mechanics of celestial motions. In their turn, improved descriptions and predictions necessitated new and more accurate observations, and far into the nineteenth century the collaboration between celestial mechanics and applied mathematics was one of the most fruitful in the physical sciences.

In 1838, the first true parallactic motion of a fixed star was found by Bessel. This apparent annual motion was extremely small, but its existence was enough to prove the Copernican theory once and for all. Another milestone of the nineteenth century was the first observation of the minor planets. Their existence showed that the solar system comprises not only the planets proper, but also a large number of bodies whose size is only a fraction of that of the earth.

While the theorists in celestial mechanics became more and more involved in numerical computations, the observers turned to the field that seemed most germane to their preoccupation with positional measurements, namely, the cataloguing of fixed stars, and of other celestial entities that became loosely known as "nebulae." Thus we find the classical period of astronomy ending with the preparation of monumental star catalogues.

1.6 MODERN ASTRONOMY

Astronomy needed new ideas and new horizons if it was to keep up with the other rapidly developing sciences. The impulse had to come from the outside, and when it came it had no philosophical and little astronomical background.

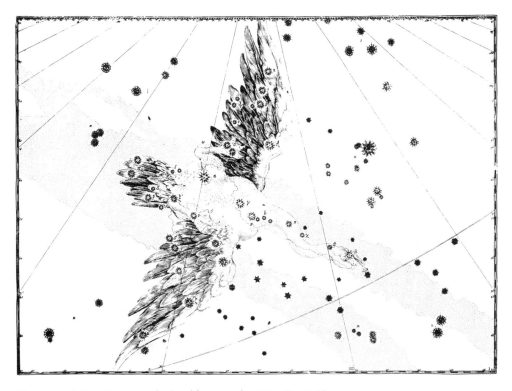

The constellation Cygnus as depicted by Bayer in 1655. *(Bayer, Ura-
nometria, courtesy of Yerkes Observatory.)*

While the laws of mechanics were being explored, other disciplines of physics grew with little interference, and even without much reference to each other. Huygens explained light phenomena in the framework of wave theory while Newton was trying to convince himself and his contemporaries of the corpuscular nature of light. The most consequential discovery for astronomy was that of the diffraction or separation of light into "colors." When an optician, Fraunhofer, did diffraction experiments with sunlight in 1814, he was surprised to find a large number of dark lines. Not too intently and, in fact, more often after hours than in their professional capacity, astronomers began to worry about these phenomena; after all, the sun was a celestial body. Sunspots were back in astronomical discussions, and the first scientific expeditions to observe total eclipses of the sun were organized.

At about the same time, that is, in the middle of the last century, photography was first used in astronomy to collect information on stars too faint to study with visual techniques. Methods developed for studying light sources in the laboratory were applied by Pickering, and from the work of the physicists Boltzmann, Kirchhoff, and Planck, it became clear that stars represent a wide range of temperatures. Thus, astrophysics, as we understand the word today, was born, and the question of what stars are and what physical processes occur within them became the central issue of astronomy.

After Einstein proposed his theory of general relativity, interest focussed on the universe at large, which until then had been thought to be the domain of a priori philosophy or sweet speculation. In practical terms, astronomers had to determine distances so that they might decide, for instance, whether the many known "nebulae" were simply amorphous masses of gas or unresolved very distant clusters of stars. That the latter proposition was correct became clear in the 1920s from studies with the 100-inch telescope, at that time the largest in existence. At that point it also became evident that the universe was much larger and more complex than had been thought before, and the search began for information relating to the size of the universe, its geometric structure, and its behavior in time. This search is still going on.

Meanwhile, nuclear physics had provided an explanation for the origin of the energy radiated by the sun and the stars. The electronic computer made it possible to carry out numerical computations of staggering proportions and helped shed light on the life of a star, from its birth out of gas and dust to its death, when all its energy sources are exhausted. Then, after World War II, as a consequence of the development of radar, radio astronomy began; besides providing immediate answers to a host of old questions, such as the structure of our galaxy, it led to new ones. Similarly, the ability via rocketry to observe the high-energy end of the spectrum from outside the earth's atmosphere opened up whole new areas of astronomy. One of the puzzles that turned up was the mechanism by which the sun and other stars suddenly release large amounts of energy in what we call "solar flares."

Almost every year brings a change in our view of astronomy. The discovery of quasars is just a few years old, and their distance from the earth is still the subject of some disagreement; so is the question of their energy source and their place in the evolution of the universe. Any one of the more recent discoveries could very well lead to a new chapter in the history of astronomy, reducing what we have called "modern astronomy" to just another by then "classical" period. Indeed, this could happen any day.

QUESTIONS FOR DISCUSSION

1. Most primitive societies looked upon astronomy as both a tool in everyday life and a basis for their religions. In what ways were these views of astronomy similar? In what ways were they dissimilar?

2. How did the preoccupation of the Greek astronomers with theoretical explanations of solar-system motions influence the historical course of astronomy?

3. What might have happened to the development of astronomy if the telescope had been invented in 1300 by an Arab scientist? Or if it had not been invented until 1700?

4. How closely do you think the goals of modern astronomers are allied with those of ecologists or ecology-minded laymen?

5. How does the physics of earthbound bodies influence astronomy, and vice versa?

FURTHER READING*

Dreyer, J. L. E., *A History of Astronomy from Thales to Kepler* (second ed.), New York: Dover Publications, Inc., 1953.

de Vaucouleurs, G., *Discovery of the Universe*, New York: The Macmillan Company, 1957.

Ronan, C., *The Astronomers*, New York: Hill and Wang, Inc., 1964.

Hodge, P. W., *The Revolution in Astronomy*, New York: Holiday House, Inc., 1970.

*The entries in this reading list and the similar ones following later chapters were selected on the basis of two criteria: that they enlarge significantly upon the material presented in this text and that their level be similar to ours. The latter restriction unfortunately removes a large body of astronomical literature from our consideration. It may be therefore desirable to point out some additional sources that are easily available, in particular, the *Annual Review of Astronomy and Astrophysics,* which, in book form and on a more-or-less technical level, reviews fields of current interest to astronomers. Then, reviews of astronomical problems appear regularly in such journals as *Scientific American* and, again on a more technical level, in *Science* and *Nature*. Finally, we must mention *Sky and Telescope,* which by monthly issues keeps its readers informed of current developments in astronomy.

THE SOLAR SYSTEM

THE INNER PLANETS

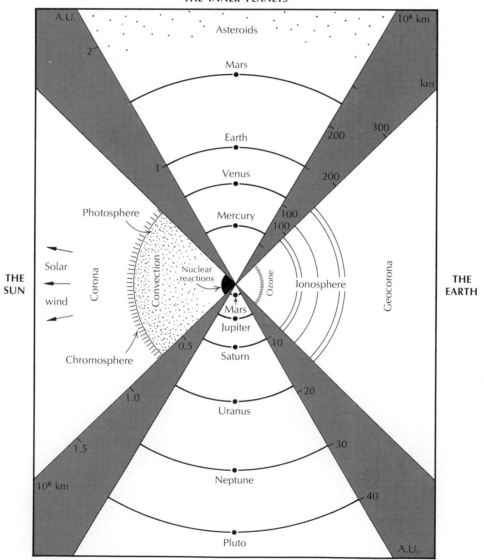

THE OUTER PLANETS

I the solar system

We begin our journey through the world of astronomy at home, on our earth, and explore from here our neighbors in space: the moon and the planets. All are members of what we call the solar system, the totality of things big and small that owe their existence, or at least their membership in the group, to our sun. This sun is our own star, the only one close by, and the primary testing ground for all our ideas about stars in general.

In the sections that follow, we shall discuss many details which would not even be of passing interest if we were concerned only with celestial bodies outside our solar system. The reason is not only our close proximity in space, which, for instance, allows us to substantiate some of the details with the naked eye, but also the conviction that what happens once near us will happen a billion times over, elsewhere in the universe.

2 the planet earth

The planet we live on is called the earth. During the great astronomical revolution of the seventeenth century, man finally became convinced that this earth is a ball-shaped thing, somehow suspended in the universe, in what appears as an endless void. If ultimate proof was necessary, it was obtained when man photographed the earth from space vehicles; the visual impression is very similar to the one we get from telescopic pictures of other planets. Thus, a feeling of proportion emerges from man's venture into space: in a universal framework the right way to look upon the earth is as just another of the sun's planets.

It is natural that we should have more information about our own planet than any other. Obviously, much of this information is in the form of details that would be irrelevant in a general discussion of planets; such material comprises the study of geophysics rather than astronomy. Nevertheless, there are wide areas of overlap, and where geophysics deals with the earth as a celestial body, we must take notice.

Newton's Law of Gravitation

Material bodies attract each other with a certain force. The strength of this *gravitational force* f_{gr} acting between two systems with masses m_1 and m_2 depends on the masses and on the distance r between them. The exact relationship is given by Newton's law of gravitation, which states that

$$f_{gr} = G\frac{m_1 m_2}{r^2}$$

where G is called the gravitational constant. If a force f acts on a body of mass m_2, the body experiences an acceleration a such that

$$f = m_2 a$$

Thus, through their mutual gravitational attraction, a body of mass m_1 gives a body of mass m_2 a gravitational acceleration of

$$a_{gr} = \frac{f_{gr}}{m_2} = G\,\frac{m_1}{r^2}$$

2.1   THE SOLID BODY

A photograph of the earth from space is reproduced in Fig. 2-1. It was taken by the Apollo 8 crew in orbit about the moon and shows, aside from the overall "ball" shape, mostly the ubiquitous cloud pattern in our atmosphere. Figure 2-2, taken at

FIGURE 2-1. View of the rising earth as seen from Apollo 8 coming from behind the moon in lunar orbit. Earth is about 5° above the lunar horizon. (*NASA.*)

closer range, indicates land and water areas, mountain structures, and again the cloud pattern. If this picture had been taken by an alien race, their astronomers could probably have deduced a bit more, perhaps the chemical composition and stratification of the atmosphere. If they had taken a time sequence of photos during an earth year, they would have deduced the existence of seasons and, with them, temperature fluctuations. And maybe, if they had come close enough, they could have distinguished some man-made patterns, such as the artificial lighting of our metropolitan areas. When we discuss the other planets later, we will find ourselves precisely in the position of these hypothetical space travelers, trying to glean as much information as we can from afar.

Size and Shape. We first note that the main bulk of the earth is a solid body. Its surface is not smooth, but covered with mountains, plains, and valleys; the large depressions are filled with water, mostly in the liquid form. The highest mountains and deepest trenches in the ocean differ only slightly in height, at least in comparison with the size of the earth, so it appears sensible to survey the gross features of a ''mean earth.''

FIGURE 2-2.   View from Apollo 8 of nearly the entire western hemisphere, from the mouth of the St. Lawrence River to Tierra del Fuego at the southern tip of South America. Almost all of South America, except the Andes mountain chain along the western coast, is covered by clouds. (*NASA.*)

Thus, we may begin, as Eratosthenes did in the third century B.C., by assuming the earth's shape to be a perfect sphere, and on this basis determine its **radius.** This can be done if we know the actual distance d between two points A and B on the earth in linear measure, say, in kilometers. If the same celestial object is observed from these two points at the same time, it appears at slightly different angles relative to the vertical (angles α and β in Fig. 2-3). It is important, though, that the observed object be far enough away so that we can safely assume its light reaches A and B in

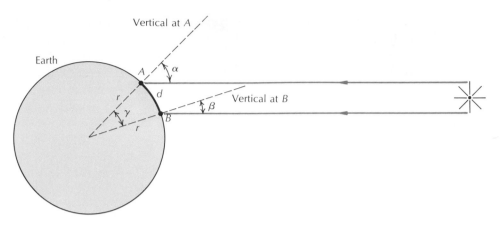

FIGURE 2-3. **Determination of the earth's radius. If the same celestial object is observed from two points *A* and *B* on earth at the same
time, it appears at slightly different angles relative to the vertical.
When $\alpha - \beta = \gamma$ is measured and the distance *d* between *A* and *B* is
known, the radius *r* can be calculated.**

parallel beams. Now, in Fig. 2-3, angle $\gamma = \alpha - \beta$. For very small angles γ, we have
$d = r\gamma$ (where γ is measured in radians). Knowing d and γ, we can calculate r, which
turns out to be about 6,500 km (4,000 miles). A little more precisely, the radius
of the earth is 6,378 km at the equator.

Mass.   Once we know the radius of the earth, we can use Newton's law of gravitation to obtain its mass. We need two things: the directly measured acceleration due
to gravity at the earth's surface, and the value of the gravitational constant. This
constant itself has to be measured. At any rate, the result is 6×10^{27}* grams (or about
1.3×10^{25} pounds) for the **mass** of the earth. By dividing the mass of the earth by its
volume, we find a mean density of 5.5 g/cm³.

  If the earth were really a perfect sphere and its matter distributed uniformly or,
at least, in concentric shells, the gravitational acceleration would be the same at each
point on its surface. Accurate measurements show that this is not the case. The most
recent measurements were made using artificial satellites; satellite orbits are determined by the gravitational attraction of the earth, and most irregularities in an orbit
are the direct result of variations in the earth's gravity. Most of the variation is due to
the fact that the earth is not spherical, but is slightly **oblate;** that is, the diameter from
pole to pole is smaller than the equatorial diameter by some 43 km.

Composition.   We really have direct information concerning only the very surface
of the earth, since even the deepest drillings merely scratch this surface. Most of what
we know about the composition of the interior is based on indirect evidence, gathered when possible during natural disturbances such as earthquakes, or during man-
made underground blasts. In either case, waves emanate from the site of the disturbance, and their properties (speed, strength, etc.) can be measured and fitted

*See Appendix A for a discussion of the scientific notation used for very large and very small numbers.

to theoretical models of the earth. The results, although by no means complete, indicate that there are several distinct shells, of which the uppermost, the **crust**, consists mostly of "common" materials such as granite (underlying the continents) and basalt (under the ocean basins). The deepest **core** seems to be in the liquid state and very dense, although it is possible that the very center is solid again. The most likely material comprising the core is molten iron, probably with an admixture of similar elements such as nickel and cobalt. If this is indeed the case, we conclude that the chemical elements have somehow become separated, even in the "solid" earth, in that iron, cobalt, nickel, and such are concentrated in the center, while the lighter metals, such as magnesium and silicon, sometimes combined with carbon and oxygen, are mostly concentrated in rock formations at the surface. Also at the surface, additional oxygen and most of the earth's hydrogen form the water in the oceans.

Temperature. The average **surface temperature** varies greatly, of course, from the equator to the poles. However, it is above the freezing point of water (0°C) in most areas, and below the boiling point (100°C) everywhere. This must have been the case for a long time (some 10^9 years) because even the oldest fossilized forms of life could not have existed under conditions drastically different from those now prevailing. Since the heat balance of the earth is completely dependent on radiation from the sun, this means that the solar radiation cannot have varied much in the last 10^9 years or so.

Compared to the energy received from the sun, energy sources remaining on the earth from primordial times are practically negligible, although sometimes, as during volcanic eruptions, the heat stored in the interior of the earth is the primary moving force. That there is some heat energy stored in the earth we know from the cited observations of volcanoes and hot geysers, and from such phenomena as the general temperature increase with depth in mines. However, how much energy is left and how fast it dissipates are less well known. Still other energy sources are the naturally radioactive elements left in the earth from the early days of the universe and now slowly being transformed into stable substances.

Atoms and Molecules

All matter is made up of *atoms*, or groups of atoms called *molecules*. They can be arranged in innumerable patterns, each pattern resulting in one specific material. Physicists and chemists have compiled a list of all the types of atoms, or *elements*; in this list, called the *periodic table*, elements are arranged in order of increasing mass or weight. The lightest element is hydrogen, the next is helium. The carbon, nitrogen, and oxygen atoms, those of primary concern to us here, are, respectively, about 12, 14, and 16 times as heavy as the hydrogen atom.

At the relatively low temperatures encountered in the earth's lower atmosphere, in the gaseous state, oxygen atoms exist in pairs as oxygen molecules (O_2).* Similarly, nitrogen atoms associate into nitrogen molecules (N_2), each consisting of two nitrogen atoms. If the temperature of the gas is increased, the molecules *dissociate*, and the atoms go their separate ways; the gas is then said to be *atomic*.

Atoms themselves are highly structured systems. The mass of an atom is almost totally concentrated in its center or *nucleus*, which is surrounded by a cloud of *electrons* of much smaller mass. Whereas the atom normally appears *electrically neutral*

*The shorthand notation for molecules is explained in Section C.3 and, in particular, in Table C-2.

to the observer, its two subparts are electrically charged; the nucleus is positive, and the electron cloud negative. Since electrical charges come in integer multiples of a basic unit, the *elementary charge*, there must be equal numbers of positively charged heavy particles—called *protons*—in the nucleus, and negatively charged electrons outside. In addition, the nucleus contains electrically neutral particles, called *neutrons*, each of almost the same mass as a proton.

2.2   THE ATMOSPHERE AT THE SURFACE

The atmosphere, bound by gravity to the solid body of the earth, is as much a part of our planet as the solid body. For that reason alone, its properties would belong in a survey of the earth as a celestial entity. But, in addition, the structure of our atmosphere is important in astronomy because it is the major factor that limits observations. We shall come back to this latter aspect presently.

Temperature and Density.   The average air density at sea level, that is, the average number of atoms or molecules per cubic centimeter is about 2.5×10^{19}. This number does not follow in any obvious way from other data, such as the size of the earth, its mass, or surface temperature, but is a consequence of several factors, most of them only partially understood. Let us, for the purpose of illustration, just consider how temperature might affect atmospheric density. The "temperature" of a body is a measure of the mean kinetic energy of its molecules which, in turn, expresses the mean speed of these molecules. Now, anything with a speed in excess of a certain critical value is able to escape from the gravitational attraction of the earth. Thus, if the temperature of the atmosphere were higher than it is, so that the mean speed of the molecules were close to this escape velocity, then most atmospheric molecules would actually escape from the earth, and we would lose a significant part of our atmosphere. This would, of course, decrease its density. In addition, the lighter molecules have greater speeds, so that at the same temperature the light atoms, such as helium, have a better chance to escape than the heavy molecules formed by oxygen or nitrogen.

Composition.   The atmosphere has a distinct **chemical composition** which, near sea level, amounts to approximately 80% N_2 and 20% O_2, with some He, CO_2, etc., and, unfortunately, a continually increasing amount of man-made "pollutants." This composition is remarkable for several reasons we shall discuss later. For now, we note that the other planets of the solar system do not seem to have free oxygen: the best explanation for this anomaly in the composition of our atmosphere is that the oxygen was produced by 10^9 years of plant life. On the other hand, no free hydrogen and very little helium are present in our atmosphere. We would expect to find both hydrogen and helium simply because these gases are present in the other bodies of the solar system. Indeed, they make up most of the matter throughout the universe, and we have no reason to believe that the earth was formed of some distinctly different material. We must therefore assume that, early in the history of the earth, the temperature was high enough to let the helium escape, and that this process continued through a time during which hydrogen combined with oxygen to form water vapor. In the very outer layers of the atmosphere, this primordial composition, including helium and hydrogen, actually still exists.

Atomic Energy States

The electrons of an atom can arrange themselves in a variety of ways about the nucleus. There is a certain energy stored in each of these arrangements, which we call the *energy levels* of the atom. In one of the levels the energy of the electrons will be minimal, and we call this the *ground state* of the atom. In all other possible arrangements, the internal energy content will be greater than that of the ground state. These *excited states* are discrete; that is, they occur at specific energy values rather than at all values. The particular excited states that are possible are characteristic of a given element.

Associated with each element is a limiting internal energy, its *ionization energy*. If an atom achieves its ionization energy, then one of its electrons has gained enough energy to leave the atom for good and become a *free electron*, not associated with a specific atom. If an electron escapes from an atom, we say the atom is ionized: the remaining nucleus plus electrons (whose number is now reduced by 1) is called the *ion*. Because a negative electron leaves the electrically neutral atom when an ion is formed, the ion becomes positively charged.

The ion can recapture a free electron in a *recombination process*, whereupon it becomes a neutral atom again. Depending upon the specific circumstances of the capture, the recombination may leave the atom in the ground state or in one of its excited states.

2.3 VARIATION OF THE ATMOSPHERE WITH HEIGHT

The molecules that make up the atmosphere are prevented from escaping into space by the gravitational attraction of the solid earth. If there were no other forces acting, all air molecules would crowd onto the surface. However, owing to the finite temperature and the corresponding speed of the molecules, there will always be some molecules flying away from the surface so that, on the average, we find a **height distribution**, that is, a smooth decrease in particle density with height. This is, of course, the reason why the air at the top of the Rocky Mountains is much thinner than that at sea level. In fact, at a height of about 15 km the number of air molecules per cubic centimeter is only one-tenth of the number at sea level.

The picture actually is not quite so simple. For example, there is a **temperature variation** with height. We have already seen that the temperature on the earth's surface and in the atmosphere close to it is maintained by the influx of solar radiation. More accurately, this temperature is the result of the solar radiation that seeps through the atmosphere. For the upper reaches of the atmosphere absorb a good deal of radiation; none of the sun's ultraviolet radiation and only a fraction of the infrared ever reach the ground. The energy acquired by absorption in the upper atmosphere results in an increase in temperature there. The actual variation of temperature with height is shown in Fig. 2-4, whose data refer to a so-called **standard atmosphere**—an average over the seasons—and a particular latitude. Just above the ground, the temperature is lower than at the surface; this has much to do with winds and the surface structure. It decreases with height up to about 100 km, above which the temperature begins to increase again, reaching a maximum at a height of about 300 km. Farther

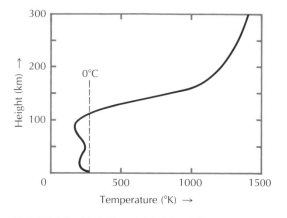

FIGURE 2-4. **Variation with height of the temperature of the earth's atmosphere.** (*I. I. Gringorten and A. J. Kantor, in Handbook of Geophysics and Space Environment, edited by S. L. Valley, Air Force Cambridge Research Laboratories, 1965.*)

up, the atmosphere has only a tiny fraction of its sea-level density, and we enter the realm of the exosphere or geocorona, discussed further in Section 2.4.

In moving upward from the ground, we not only pass through regions of ever-decreasing density and varying temperature, but we also encounter a change in chemical composition. The farther up we go, the more light elements we find on the average, since in a gravitationally bound atmosphere the heaviest molecules will be slowest moving, and therefore closest to the ground.

Photons and Their Spectrum

Light is energy, radiated in the form of "packages" we call *photons* which move through the universe at the *speed of light*. If they impinge on our eyes, they activate sensors which signal the sensation of light to the brain. If there are many photons arriving from a source, the source appears *bright* to us. To each photon we ascribe a specific energy. Among other things, the different photon energies are responsible for the different *color* impressions we obtain through our eyes, in the sense that, for example, blue photons are more energetic than red ones. It is the relative number of blue, red, and intermediate photons that determines the color of the source. The distribution of the number of photons of each energy or color arriving from a source is what we call its *spectrum*.

Instead of specifying a photon type by its energy, we usually ascribe to it a *wavelength*, inversely proportional to its energy. Because the wavelengths of the photons to which our eyes respond are rather small, we measure them in angstrom units (1 Å = 10^{-8} cm). "Dark" red light consists predominantly of photons of a wavelength around 6000 Å or 6×10^{-5} cm. The wavelength of blue light is about 4500 Å, and between 6000 Å and 4500 Å we find orange, yellow, and green in descending magnitude of wavelength. Photons with wavelengths outside the range of between about 3500 Å and 6500 Å are invisible to the eye.

Ionosphere. The portion of the solar radiation that is not absorbed by the atmosphere increases with increasing height: of this radiation, the high-energy photons are absorbed first. So with increasing height, an increasing percentage of high-energy photons is encountered. This explains the existence of the **ionosphere**, the region stretching above some 60 to 80 km (on the day and night sides of the earth) upwards into the geocorona. Here, high-energy photons radiated from the sun **ionize** the atmospheric molecules and atoms, that is, pry some of their electrons loose, so that a region is formed in which there are relatively large numbers of **free electrons.** The number of electrons present is, of course, greater on the day side than on the night side of the earth, although it is affected by horizontal motions ("winds"), conduction, solar activity, and the time lag between ionization and recombination. Many details of the ionosphere are currently being studied, among them the **stratification** or layering which indicates that particular photon energies are absorbed by particular types of molecules and atoms.

Other radiations, comprised either of material particles or of high-energy photons invisible to the human eye, are produced in the sun and the universe at large and fall onto the outer layers of the atmosphere. These **cosmic rays** never get through to the surface; nor do most **meteors,** small grains of cosmic dust. The atmosphere serves as a shield against these dangerous radiations and is thus a vital element in the conservation of life on the earth.

Atmospheric Balance.   One aspect of the physics of our atmosphere that has only very recently begun to concern scientists and laymen is the *extremely fragile* **balance** in its temperature structure and chemical composition. Most crucial is our almost complete ignorance of the workings of this balance. Atmospheric temperature changes, both upward and downward, which are suspected to be related to the burning of fossil fuel, have been well documented in this century. But to date, we have been unable to find a direct cause-effect relationship, and it is suspected that the real relation is exceedingly complex. We are at present increasing the CO_2 content of the lower layers of the atmosphere by a fraction of a percent per year, and this is, at least in terms of lifetimes, an irreversible change. Fortunately, society at large is becoming increasingly unwilling to accept such an irreversible degradation of our planet at a time when the consequences for us and our unborn children cannot be defined beyond the obvious statement that in most countries life conditions get worse every year.

2.4   THE GEOCORONA AND MAGNETOSPHERE

Geocorona.   The earth's atmosphere is a continuous gaseous envelope surrounding our planet; its density would eventually taper off to zero if it were not for the existence, everywhere in the universe and certainly in the neighborhood of stars such as our sun, of a low-density interstellar gas. Thus, there is actually a continuous transition from the relatively dense atmosphere at the ground to the region in which solar gravitational attraction takes over from that of the earth. Nevertheless, it is convenient to discuss the very outer layers of the atmosphere separately; we call them the **exosphere** or, in more recent terminology, the **geocorona.**

It has already been noted that the lighter gases are predominant at greater altitudes. Thus, we find atomic oxygen rather than molecular oxygen above some 150

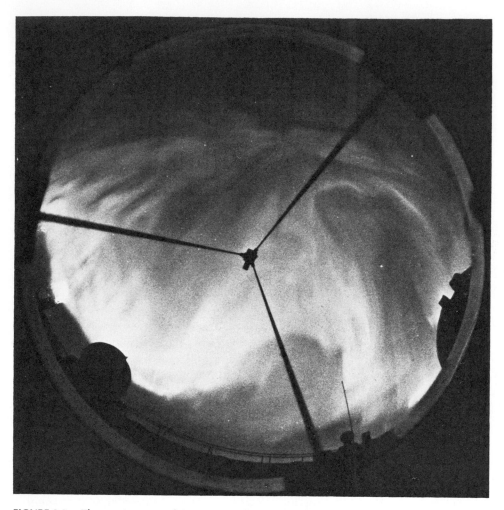

FIGURE 2-5.   **The great aurora of August 19 and 20, 1950, photographed with a wide-angle camera.** (*Yerkes Observatory.*)

km. Still farther out, helium and atomic hydrogen are prominent, even though these
gases are found only in small concentration. The presence of atomic hydrogen has
been known for many decades through **auroras** or **Northern (Southern) Lights** (Fig.
2-5). This phenomenon occurs when the sun emits a cloud of fast particles, probably
mostly protons and electrons, which enter the outer reaches of the earth's magnetic
field. They are guided by this field toward the Poles and occasionally collide with
oxygen atoms in the upper atmosphere. The excited oxygen atoms emit photons to
release the energy acquired by collison. The photons emitted (under the specific
circumstances of low temperature and density) have wavelengths either in the green
or in the red region of the spectrum, accounting for the often observed green and red
coloration of auroras.

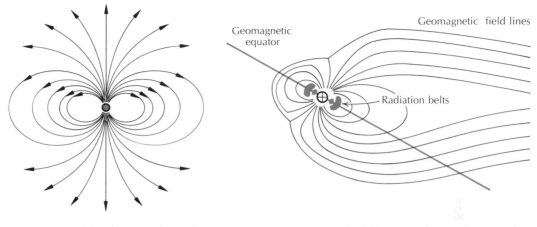

FIGURE 2-6. **Field of a magnetic dipole.**

FIGURE 2-7. **Geomagnetic field.** (*National Center for Atmospheric Research.*)

Geomagnetic Field. We have pictured interplanetary space, or at least the region between the earth and the sun, as comprising a transition from the earth's atmosphere to that of the sun. Actually, though, this transition is not smooth. Instead there is a discontinuity in the physical properties (including density) of the geocorona; it is called the **bow shock.** This phenomenon owes its existence to the fact that the solar atmosphere is not static near the earth, but moves outward (forms a **solar wind**) with a substantial velocity. The material comprising this solar wind is ionized; it consists mostly of free electrons and protons. This causes an additional complication, because it distorts the earth's magnetic field. Close to the surface, the field structure differs little from that of a common permanent magnet, whose **dipole field** is shown in Fig. 2-6 (the lines delineate the direction of the magnetic force). As a result of the interaction of the electrically charged solar-wind particles in the geocorona with the terrestrial magnetic field, the latter departs drastically from the simple dipole picture of Fig. 2-6. A recent compilation of how we think the **geomagnetic field** really looks is shown in Fig. 2-7.

Radiation Belts. While charged particles cannot enter a magnetic field at right angles to its lines of force, those essentially parallel to the earth's magnetic field can enter it. They are guided by the field toward the **geomagnetic poles**, that is, the poles of the earth's magnetic field. Most of them do not penetrate to the surface, but are deflected and *trapped* in a region of the geocorona called the **radiation belts** or **Van Allen belts.** Of greatest interest are those electrons whose velocities are close to the speed of light, in other words, whose energies are **relativistic.** They emit **synchrotron radiation** (Section C.7) of a type which has been observed in the Van Allen belts. The electrons whose radiation was actually measured were ''man-made,'' that is, they were produced in high-altitude explosions of nuclear warheads.

Figure 2-8 gives a schematic overview of the earth, based on the preceding discussions.

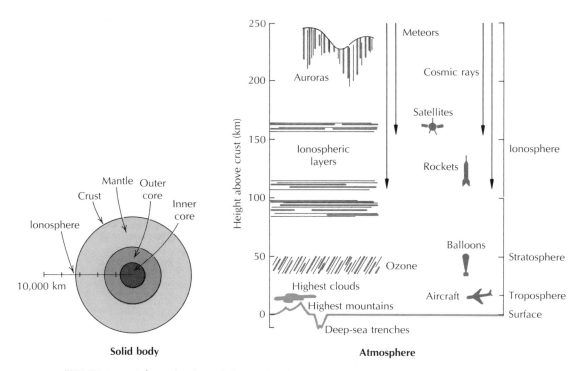

FIGURE 2-8. Schematic view of the earth: its solid body and its atmosphere.

Invisible Portion of the Photon Spectrum

There are photons with wavelengths below 4000 Å and above 7000 Å, that is, below and above the approximate response range of the human eye. Just above the high-energy (low-wavelength) limit are the *ultraviolet* photons that cause sunburn and that can be easily detected by photographic films. The ultraviolet region extends to higher and higher energies, merging with the region in which we find the *X-rays* of 10 Å to 100 Å wavelength. Here, the energy is some hundred times greater than the energy of visible-light photons. At still higher energies are the *γ-rays* which originate in atomic nuclei.

The photons whose energies are near the lower-energy (higher-wavelength) limit of the sensitivity range of the eye, the *near-infrared* photons, are detected by human skin as a sensation of heat. At still lower energies (or longer wavelengths) we have to rely solely on mechanical means of detection. Here are found the *far-infrared* photons of about 10^5 Å or 10^{-3} cm wavelength. Finally, above about 10^{-3} cm in wavelength stretches the *radio range*.

2.5 ATMOSPHERIC LIMITS ON GROUND-BASED OBSERVATIONS

Let us now return to the lower layers of the atmosphere and summarize their influence on the feasibility and quality of ground-based astronomical observations. In the last 25 years, rocket and, more recently, satellite technology has been perfected to the point where we can place major astronomical instruments outside the earth's atmosphere; however, the techniques are so expensive that for decades to come the main bulk of observations will be made from ground-based installations.

Climatic Limitations. Primarily, one would select as an observatory site a place where the lower layers of the atmosphere are not likely to be disturbed by climatic obstacles such as frequent cloud cover, sandstorms, high water-vapor content, and man-made pollutants, including scattered city light. Then, one would try to minimize **air turbulence,** a phenomenon that causes the twinkling of stars at night (**scintillation**) but is quite unwanted in astronomical work. The first requirement can usually be met by building on top of some mountain in a relatively dry area (southern California or Arizona in the United States, the Andes in South America, South West Africa, etc.). Air turbulence is not so easily predicted, and extensive site surveys are required before an observatory is actually built.

Spectral Absorption. The major limitations on ground-based observatories are due to the structure of the atmosphere itself, which absorbs almost all types of photons arriving from outer space, because it is the photons that give us our indication of what space is like. The energies of photons span many orders of magnitude (the specific designations, from γ-rays to visible and radio photons, are summarized together with the physical definitions in Fig. C-1). The various types of photons originate in different portions of a single source, and it often happens that information on a specific source comes to us only in a narrow range of wavelengths—not necessarily one that we can detect through our atmosphere.

Of all the photons falling on our atmosphere, none with wavelengths below 3000 Å get through to ground level; between 3000 Å and 3500 Å the atmosphere absorbs selectively, leaving occasional "windows" in the spectrum through which radiation filters down to the surface. The same is true for wavelengths above some 10,000 Å: only the visible and near-infrared regions are essentially unaffected by the atmosphere. Between 10,000 Å and 1 mm, there are again only occasional windows. Above 1 mm, in the radio range, no absorption of importance occurs, so that the skies are essentially open to exploration in that range. At the other end of the scale, at a wavelength of about 30 m or a frequency of about 10 MHz, the ionosphere reflects photons from space back out again. In summary, then, ground-based observations can only be made using visible and infrared radiation and the radio range.

As we have seen, the atmosphere is layered in the sense that specific molecules and atoms predominate at certain heights. An interesting example is the occurrence at a height of 30 km of **ozone,** O_3, which is formed from normal O_2 molecules with the aid of impinging ultraviolet photons, typically of 2500 Å wavelength. In the process, these photons are absorbed and are not available for ground-based observations—but neither are they available as a cause of skin cancer. In fact, one of the worries ecologists have about high-altitude pollution is the possibility of diminishing this ozone layer to the point where it is not sufficiently opaque to ultraviolet photons.

Other photons with wavelengths below 3000 Å are absorbed by other layers of the atmosphere—the particular layer, of course, depends on the particular wavelength. Thus, high-altitude rockets, that reach well above the layers where atmospheric absorption is strong, and satellites and space probes must be used to study celestial bodies whose radiation in this range is crucial for an understanding of their nature.

At very long wavelengths there is again a need for observations to be made from rockets or satellites, to overcome the influence of the ionosphere. Similarly, extending the radio window significantly downward into the **submillimeter range**, that is, toward wavelengths close to but less than 1 mm, requires that observations be made outside the atmosphere. Ultimately, astronomers hope to set up a permanent observing station either on the moon or in orbit about the earth; neither would be limited by our atmosphere, as are ground-based stations.

QUESTIONS FOR DISCUSSION

1. Where is the gravitational acceleration greater: at the earth's North Pole or at the equator, at sea level? Why?

2. Why may the gravitational acceleration be different at two points only 100 km away from each other?

3. The carbon dioxide content of our atmosphere has increased noticeably in the last few decades. Why?

4. If the atmosphere were removed, we would die very soon. What would kill us?

5. Many scientists fear that the exhaust of a fleet of supersonic aircraft in operation might threaten our health by destroying a particular chemical compound found predominantly some 30 km above the ground. Which compound is it, what is the health threat, and how would it come about?

6. Why would you not choose the coast of Florida, or the top of Mount Rainier in Washington, as the location of a large telescope?

EXERCISES

1. Find the equatorial circumference of the earth in kilometers and in miles.

2. With the aid of the radius of the earth given in the text and the formulas of Section A.4, calculate the volume of the earth in cubic kilometers, assuming it to be a perfect sphere.

3. What volume in cubic miles would correspond to your result in Exercise 2 (see Table H-1)?

4. Use the volume found in Exercise 2 together with the density given in the text to check the figure for the earth's mass.

5. Calculate the approximate mass of 1 cm^3 of air near the ground from the density given in the text, the mass of the proton given in Table H-1, and the fact that an average air molecule has a mass equal to about 30 proton masses.

6. The pressure p of N particles of a gas in a volume of 1 cm^3 at temperature T is given by the formula $p = NkT$, where k is Boltzmann's constant (see Table H-1). Calculate the atmospheric pressure p at sea level using the density and temperature data given in the text, and compare the resulting "average pressure of the earth's atmosphere at sea level" with the data given in your local weather report. Note that in the system of units employed in this text the pressure unit is the microbar, while weather reports list pressure in millibars (1 microbar = 10^{-3} millibar).

7. Use the data given in the text and in Section B.3 and Table H-1 to calculate the gravitational acceleration at the earth's equator.

8. Assume the earth to be a uniform sphere. By how much (in percent) does the gravitational force which the earth exerts on a jet plane differ from ground level to a height of 10 km?

9. Repeat Exercise 8 for the gravitational acceleration.

10. The weather reports given to passengers in jet planes often mention rather low temperatures outside the aircraft. Do these temperatures agree with the data in Fig. 2-4? What happens to the outside temperature of a spacecraft as it leaves the earth?

11. Name the major internal energy sources of our planet.

12. Which two elements would be most abundant if our planet still had the chemical composition of the gas from which it was formed?

13. Where is most of the element hydrogen concentrated on the earth?

14. What is the source of the energy which causes the temperature rise above about 100 km from the ground?

15. What type of particle is rather abundant in the ionosphere, but mostly absent in the atmosphere near the ground?

16. What causes the stratification of the ionosphere?

17. The properties of the ionosphere vary in time. Name a few reasons for these changes.

18. Why are auroras most often observed close to the Poles (North and South) on the earth?

19. Why don't solar-wind particles reach the earth's surface or, in fact, even the lower layers of the atmosphere?

20. If you are told that a light source emits synchrotron radiation, you are by implication told facts about this source: one has to do with the energy of the radiation-emitting electrons, the other with the presence of some entity. Specify both factors.

21. You are told that a certain type of photon is 100 times as energetic as another whose wavelength is 3000 Å. What is the wavelength of the more energetic one? What are the spectral ranges of the two types of photons called?

22. What are, approximately, the wavelengths (in angstroms and centimeters) of the two main types of photons that get through the atmosphere with little or no absorption?

EXPERIMENTS

1. Make observations of the scintillation of stars at various distances from the horizon under different weather conditions. Try to find a correlation between the amount of scintillation and the weather pattern.

2. Make a telescope by inserting an eye-glass lens of long focal length (say, +0.25 or +0.50 diopters) in a paper tube, and project a solar image on a screen. Of course, you could also use a field glass. Watch the "wobbling" of the edge of the solar image due to atmospheric turbulence. Observe the amount of wobbling at different locations: a black-topped parking lot, a lawn, the side of a lake. Explain any differences. Based on the results of this experiment, where would you erect a solar telescope? Correlate the daytime seeing conditions, that is, the amount of wobbling, with the nighttime conditions you estimated from scintillation measurements (Experiment 1).

3. If the sky is cloudy most of the time, telescopes stay idle. With the aid of weather maps of the United States, find regions with a very low frequency of cloud cover. How many of these regions are astronomical observation sites?

FURTHER READING

The Earth as a Planet, edited by G. P. Kuiper, Chicago: The University of Chicago Press, 1953.

The Earth in Space, edited by H. Odishaw, New York: Basic Books, Inc., 1967.

Takeuchi, H., S. Uyeda, and H. Kanamori, *Debate about the Earth* (rev. ed.), San Francisco: Freeman, Cooper and Company, 1970.

3 the motion characteristics of the earth

So far, we have discussed the constitution of our planet, its size and other physical data, and their influence on astronomical observations. We have yet to discuss the various motions of the earth in space. By themselves, they are not particularly noteworthy, say in the context of the planet's history or as indictions of the astronomical environment we live in, but, as we shall see, they profoundly affect our everyday life, and for this reason alone merit detailed investigation. In addition, the motion characteristics of the earth comprised the first scientific problem attacked and solved in a consistent manner by mankind. This has influenced the development of scientific thought up to the present time.

Leaving aside for the moment all details and complications, we recognize two main earth motions, which formed the basis of the Copernican system: first, the earth rotates about its axis with a period of one day (thus, stars "rise" in the east and "set" in the west), and second, the earth revolves about the sun with a period of one year (so that the stars which, in summer, rise in the evening and set in the morning, do the opposite in winter).

Energy and Momentum Conservation

The energy of a system is one of the most important of the parameters that characterize its physical behavior at any given time. A body can have a gravitational *potential energy* that can be converted into work: a falling weight can crush stone. Another form of energy is the kinetic energy of a body in motion. If its mass is m and its velocity v, then its *kinetic energy* is

$$E_{kin} = \tfrac{1}{2}mv^2$$

(Note that the velocity v includes both *magnitude* and *direction*; the velocity of a car moving north at 80 km/sec is not the same as that of a car moving south at that speed.) The kinetic energy of a moving body can also perform work on another body. If a car in motion hits another which is at rest, its kinetic energy performs work — in this case, damage. Other forms of energy are electrical and magnetic energy, and the internal energy stored in atomic systems.

The several forms of energy contained in a system may be transformed into each other by physical processes. However, the *total energy* of a system is *conserved*; that is, it does not change, provided that there is no loss or gain through interaction with anything outside the system. The fact that the energy of such a *closed system* is always conserved is one of the most basic properties of our universe.

The characteristics of the motion of a closed system are also conserved. The product of the mass and velocity of a moving body, its *momentum*, is conserved in a closed system. A body moving with constant speed in a straight line keeps moving with constant speed along the line as long as it does not interact with anything. Similarly, a body which is rotating and not interacting goes on rotating. Its rotational or *angular momentum* is conserved.

3.1 ROTATION. ASTRONOMICAL COORDINATES

That the earth **rotates** and the stars stand still, and not vice versa, can be shown directly by constructing a system which — ideally — is not connected physically with the postulated rotational motion of the earth. Such a system is a **Foucault pendulum,** an example of which hangs in the foyer of the United Nations Building in New York City. The basis for the experiment is the principle of **conservation of momentum**, which states that the motion characteristics of a system such as a pendulum cannot change by themselves. In order that the pendulum interact as little as possible with its immediate surroundings, that is, be as unconnected as possible with the earth's rotation, it is attached to the solid earth in such a manner that the frictional forces and, hence, energy and momentum losses at the point of attachment are minimal. Except for such small losses the pendulum has to conserve its energy and momentum once it is set in motion. This implies the conservation of its direction of motion in space. But, if the pendulum is started swinging in a certain direction and the earth does rotate, the pendulum should appear to change its direction relative to its surroundings, with a period related to the earth's rotational period. This is exactly what happens. At either Pole, the directional period of such a pendulum is equal to the earth's period, while at positions away from the Poles it is longer; at the equator it does not change direction with respect to its surroundings at all. In New York City the directional period of the pendulum is about 40 hours.

Earth Coordinates.   By again invoking the principle of conservation of momentum, this time with respect to the **angular momentum** of the rotational motion of the earth, we can determine the position of the line or **axis** about which the earth spins. We conclude that the position of the earth's rotational axis must be fixed in its solid body (although there are some very minor fluctuations, which, at least in part, have to do with changes in the interior structure of the planet). Thus, we now have reference points on the surface of the earth (which we take to be spherical), namely, the **North** and **South Poles,** where the rotational axis cuts the sphere of the earth, and the great circle halfway between them: the **equator**. Based on these reference points, we can build a grid, consisting of two independent sets of numbers, to specify all the points on that surface. The first set is obtained by drawing circles parallel to the equator (their radii get smaller as they move toward the poles), which we call the **latitude** circles; we number them from 0° at the equator to 90°N at the North Pole, and from 0° to 90°S at the South Pole.* The second set of numbers is derived for **longitude** circles, great circles through the Poles, starting arbitrarily with 0° for the great circle through the observatory at Greenwich in England. Longitudes are numbered up to 180°E (eastward) and 180°W (westward), so that longitude 180°E equals 180°W on a circle cutting through eastern Siberia and just missing New Zealand (see Fig. 3-1). We can now specify any point on the earth with its latitude and longitude, using decimals if necessary.

Again using an analysis based on momentum conservation, it can be shown that the rotational axis can be considered as always pointing in the same direction in

*The symbol ° is read "degrees" as in angular measure. The similarity is not accidental, for 90° of latitude sweeps out a central angle of 90° on a great circle.

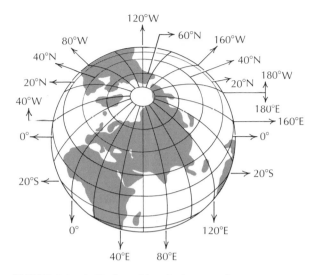

FIGURE 3-1. Latitude and longitude on earth.

space, at least for sufficiently small periods of time. If we are concerned with centuries or very accurate astronomical observations, then the phenomenon of **precession** must be taken into account. Because in reality the earth is not a perfect, uniform sphere, its reaction to the gravitational forces of the sun and the moon varies slightly along the rotational axis. As a result, the axis slowly turns in space, essentially describing a cone and taking about 26,000 years to complete one "sweep." The situation is shown in Fig. 3-2. At present, the axis points northward to a position close to the star Polaris in the constellation Ursa Minor or Small Dipper; in about 12,000 years it will point in the direction of the bright star Vega in the constellation Lyra. Precession can be observed in a toy top or its fancier cousin, the gyroscope. Once either is rotating, it tries to maintain the position of its rotational axis in space.

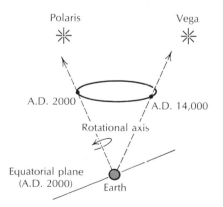

FIGURE 3-2. Precession of the earth's rotational axis. In 26,000 years, the axis completes one "sweep" along the cone.

If the top is pushed, that is, subjected to a force, the axis shifts at right angles to the direction of the force, so that it slowly sweeps out a cone, similar to the one depicted in Fig. 3-2 for the earth.

Celestial Coordinates. If we neglect the slow precessional motion of the earth and consider the sky as a hypothetical ball or **celestial sphere,** we can use the two points where the extended axis of the earth cuts the sphere to introduce a reference frame of **celestial coordinates.** At once, we have a *celestial north pole* and a *celestial south pole*. The former, as mentioned, almost coincides with the star Polaris, but there is no bright star close to the celestial south pole.

The next step in building a set of celestial coordinates is to draw a great circle around the celestial sphere halfway between the two poles, and call it the *celestial equator*. The angles (or parallel circles between celestial equator and poles are called the **declinations** δ and are numbered from 0° (at the equator) to +90° (at the north pole) and −90° (at the south pole). Thus, declination on the celestial sphere corresponds to latitude on the earth. As before, we need a second set of numbers for our celestial coordinate system, so we measure angles along the celestial equator and call them **right ascension** α. It is somewhat confusing to the uninitiated that α is usually measured in "hours" from 0^h to 24^h, instead of in degrees. The reason for this inconsistency is the relation between right ascension and sidereal time. At any rate, 0^h is placed at a certain point (called the **vernal equinox**) on the celestial equator, and right ascension is measured to the east. Figure 3-3 gives a view of the celestial coordinates from the fictitious point outside the celestial sphere.

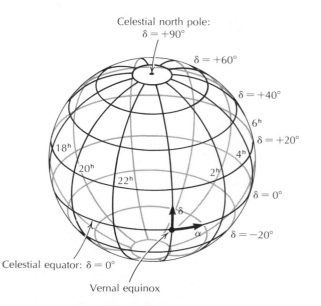

FIGURE 3-3. Celestial coordinate system viewed from a fictitious point outside the sphere.

It is worth emphasizing that the coordinate system of α and δ is strictly an *earthbound* one and, as such, completely arbitrary in the wider context of, say, the solar system. Of course, any spherical coordinate system that is unambiguously defined is as good as any other, but for the earthbound observer the right ascensions and declinations are the logical choice.

The Earth-based Observer.   We can now specify the exact position of any star in the sky by giving the appropriate values of α and δ and specifying the time of observation. Instead of the latter, one usually gives the **epoch,** say, 1950 January 1. Then, since the precession of the earth's axis slowly but predictably changes the right ascension and declination of any object in the sky, the change in α and δ for any object from year to year can be computed once and for all and collected in tables. Note, however, that a star's coordinates also change because of its individual or "proper motion" through space.

Suppose an observer is at a given point on the earth. His reference points are not α and δ which, after all, refer to abstract great circles on the celestial sphere, but rather the **horizon** and the point overhead, the **zenith.** (Opposite the zenith is the **nadir,** that is, the point directly underfoot.) To determine the position of a star, an observer will first measure an **altitude,** that is, an angular distance from the horizon, or, alternatively, an angular distance from the zenith (**zenith distance**), instead of a declination; then he will measure an azimuth angle along the horizon, instead of a right ascension. As a zero point for azimuth angles, the usual choice is the **meridian,** that is, the great circle on the sphere that cuts through zenith, nadir, and celestial poles. Figure 3-4 shows the various angles and great circles with reference to a particular star. While celestial objects have fixed α and δ (neglecting precession and proper motion), their altitudes and azimuths change continually and, in addition, depend on latitude and longitude of the observer. But again, these changes and differences can be calculated and compiled in tables.

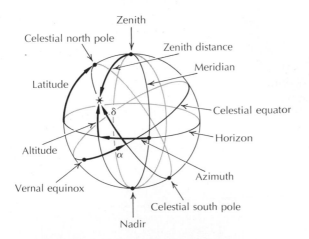

FIGURE 3-4.   Right ascension and declination, altitude, and azimuth, and their relation for a particular star. The observer is situated in the center of the sphere.

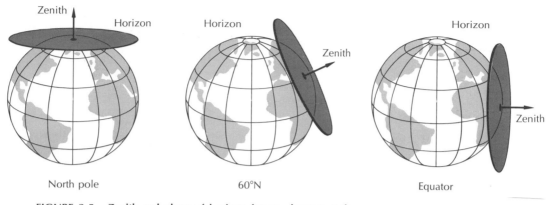

North pole   60°N   Equator

FIGURE 3-5. Zenith and plane of horizon for an observer at the earth's North Pole, at an intermediate latitude, and at the earth's equator. (Visualize the celestial sphere concentric with the earth.)

We now have introduced the three coordinate systems—the earth-specifying longitude-latitude system, the celestial α-δ system, and the horizon altitude-azimuth system for reporting celestial entities via earthbound observations. Figure 3-5 shows the relation between zenith and plane of horizon on one hand, and terrestrial latitude and longitude on the other, for observers at the earth's North Pole, at an intermediate latitude, and at the equator. For an observer at the earth's North Pole, the zenith and the celestial north pole coincide; at the earth's equator, the zenith is on the celestial equator, and the two celestial poles are in the plane of the horizon.

An observer at the earth's North Pole will never see any star in the southern celestial hemisphere (a star for which δ is less than zero), but he has a continuous view of all the stars in the northern hemisphere. They appear to move along circular paths parallel to his horizon. A person at the equator, on the other hand, sees half the northern stars and half the southern stars at any one time. During the course of 24 hours (if it were not for the light of the sun) he would be able to observe all the stars there are to be seen, but only half of them at a time. Between the equator and the Poles, say in New York, an observer sees some southern and some northern stars. Since he is in the earth's northern hemisphere, he "sees" all the northern stars during a 24-hour period. Moreover, some northern stars are *always* above his horizon; these are called his **circumpolar stars.** Stars close to the southern celestial pole, on the other hand, never rise above his horizon, and he has no chance ever to admire, for example, the Southern Cross (Crux). Figures 3-6 and 3-7 show his position.

Constellations

Originally, the brightest stars in each of several areas of the sky were grouped together and given the name of a mythological being or earthly object that their outline or configuration seemed to suggest. Such an area of the sky was then identified as a particular *constellation.* In modern astronomical usage the constellations are simply more or less gerrymandered areas on the celestial sphere. The brightest stars in a constellation are now named with letters of the Greek alphabet preceding the Latin designation of the

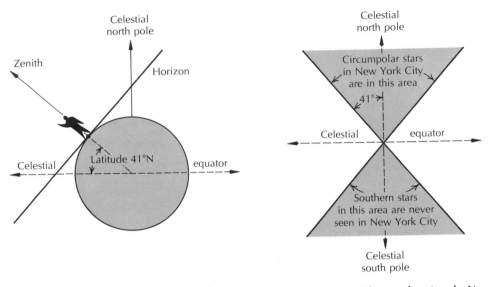

FIGURE 3-6. Coordinate systems for an observer in New York City. Both zenith and celestial equator, and horizon and celestial north pole form angles of 41° at a latitude of 41°N.

FIGURE 3-7. Circumpolar stars in New York City. The observer can see stars within 41° of the celestial north pole at all times, while stars within 41° of the celestial south pole never rise above the horizon.

constellation in the genitive form; for example, this is how δ Cephei in the constellation Cepheus gets its name. In addition, some stars have their own names, mostly badly mutilated Arab ones, such as Betelgeuse, otherwise known as α Orionis. Some of the stars of lesser brightness are identified by number and constellation name, such as 40 Eridani. Finally, a variable star is distinguished by a capital Roman letter preceding the constellation name, so we have T Tauri and RR Lyrae. Other naming schemes will be explained as we go along.

3.2 REVOLUTION

The second major motion of the earth in space is its **revolution** about the sun. This motion follows a periodic path, or **orbit**, which, although actually an ellipse, for all practical purposes is a circle with radius of about 150×10^6 km. This distance—or more precisely, the semimajor axis of the orbital ellipse—is commonly called the **astronomical unit** (A.U.). Proof that the earth moves about the sun is given by the **parallactic motion** of the stars which has already been alluded to in Chapter 1 and which we shall discuss in more detail in Section 9.1.

Plane of the Orbit. The earth completes one orbit about the sun in one year, all the while rotating about its own axis. The mean velocity of the earth in its orbit is almost 30 km/sec. The orbit of the earth defines a plane called the **ecliptic;** a line through the center of the earth at right angles to the ecliptic defines the **ecliptic poles.** The rotational axis of the earth is inclined at 23.5° with respect to the ecliptic

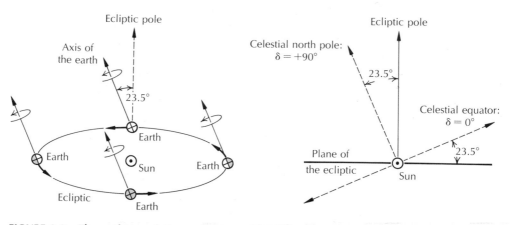

FIGURE 3-8.   The earth's revolution and rotation. The earth's axis is inclined by 23.5° with respect to the ecliptic pole. The position of the earth is shown at the solstices and equinoxes.

FIGURE 3-9.   Ecliptic (solid) and celestial (dashed) coordinates. Both ecliptic and celestial equator, and ecliptic and celestial poles form angles of 23.5°.

pole, and so is the celestial equator. The geometry is shown in Figs. 3-8 and 3-9. Thus, relative to the earth, the sun moves along a celestial great circle (also called the **ecliptic**) inclined 23.5° with respect to the celestial equator. These two circles intersect in two points, one called the **vernal equinox**, the other the **autumnal equinox**. The vernal equinox, remember, is the point from which we started to count right ascension along the celestial equator.

Solstices and Equinoxes.   Whereas the rotation of the earth marks day and night, its revolution about the sun gives us the **seasons.** Because the rotational axis is inclined with respect to the ecliptic, the sun is in the southern celestial hemisphere for half a year, and in the northern for the other half. When the sun is in the southern celestial hemisphere, it is summer in the earth's southern hemisphere, and winter in the northern; and vice versa. During summer, the sun appears higher in the sky than during winter; this seasonal difference is the more pronounced the closer to the earth's Poles the observer is situated, and the further the sun is into the particular celestial hemisphere. The days on which the sun reaches its maximum (positive or negative) declination, that is, when the sun is highest or lowest in the sky, are called **solstices**. They fall on or about June 22 (*summer solstice*, when $\delta > 0$, and the sun is in the northern celestial hemisphere) and December 22 (*winter solstice*, when $\delta < 0$, and the sun is in the southern celestial hemisphere). The times midway between the solstices, that is, when $\delta = 0$ and the sun crosses from one to the other of the celestial hemispheres, and consequently when day and night are just equal in duration everywhere on our planet, are called the **equinoxes** (*vernal*, March 22, and *autumnal*, September 22). Figure 3-10 shows a simplified version of the geometry of the solstices and equinoxes (using circular orbits). Note that, because the sun has the same celestial position at the same time each year, there is no contradiction in referring to equinoxes and solstices as times of the year and as positions of the sun.

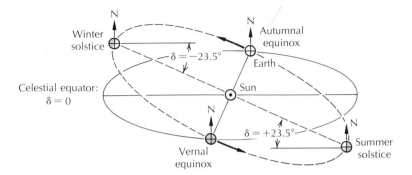

FIGURE 3-10. **Solstices and equinoxes. The earth's orbit, in the ecliptic plane, is shown by the dashed ellipse. The intersection of the ecliptic and the plane of the celestial equator defines the equinoxes; the extreme positions of the sun on the northern and southern hemispheres define the summer and winter solstices.**

Due to the fact that the sun's declination varies between $+23.5°$ and $-23.5°$ during the year, the azimuths of the points where the sun rises and sets, that is, their positions along the horizon, also change, from a maximum northern position at summer solstice to a maximum southern position at winter solstice. It is this seasonal change in the position of the rising and setting sun, as well as that of the moon, which the people of Stonehenge recorded in their monument.

We have seen that at the North Pole all objects with $δ > 0$ are always visible. Thus the sun must always be visible there between March 22 and September 22. Similarly, it will always be below the horizon there in the (northern) winter half-year. On the other hand, there must be latitudes at which the sun at summer solstice just touches the horizon. One can easily convince oneself that these latitudes are $23.5°$ away from the Poles. They define the **Polar Circles**; in the northern hemisphere, the Polar Circle runs through Alaska, northern Canada, and Scandinavia, and in the southern hemisphere it runs just outside the Antarctic continent. Between the Polar Circles and the Poles proper are the lands of the **midnight sun.**

At the equinoxes the sun passes through the zenith at the earth's equator. At the summer solstice, the sun is $23.5°$ to the north of the equator, at winter solstice $23.5°$ to the south. So there must be a latitude at which the sun just touches the zenith during each of the two solstices. In the northern hemisphere this happens in June at a latitude of 23.5°N, defining the **Tropic of Cancer** which runs through the Caribbean, northern Africa, India, and China. In the southern hemisphere this happens in December at 23.5°S, defining the **Tropic of Capricorn**, passing through Australia, Brazil, and South Africa. The names "Cancer" and "Capricorn" are derived from the names of the constellations in which the sun happened to be centuries ago on June 22 and December 22. They are 2 of the 12 constellations of the so-called **zodiac**, that is, constellations along the ecliptic which were held in high esteem by the astronomer-priests of the olden days (and their somewhat less influential modern counterparts, the astrologers).

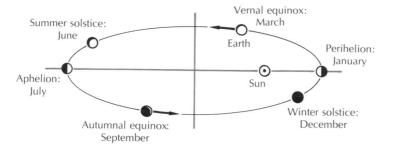

FIGURE 3-11. Aphelion and perihelion of the earth. The point at which the earth is closest to the sun (perihelion) is at present reached in January, the point of greatest distance (aphelion) in July.

We have noted that the earth's orbit, if measured very accurately, is an ellipse rather than a perfect circle, with the sun at one of the foci. The point at which the earth is closest to the sun (**perihelion**) is at present reached in January, the **aphelion** (point of greatest distance) in July. Precession will change the phase relation between perihelion and aphelion on the one hand, and the solstices on the other, so that 13,000 years from now (if nothing happens to the definition of our calendar) the perihelion will be reached in July. Figure 3-11 shows a vastly exaggerated view of the present situation.

3.3 THE ASTRONOMICAL DEFINITION OF TIME

The modern method of defining time and its unit of measurement, the second, is to relate it to some atomic quantity which we can be sure is constant and reproducible. However, since the first scientific endeavors, timekeeping was the most immediate application of astronomy, and thus our standard second is still related to an idealized motion of the earth. We are not so much interested in the details of the latest and most accurate astronomical definition as in understanding the relation between the earth's motions and the common time divisions—the day, the month, and the year.

The **day**, which we understand as the *sum* of daylight and night hours, or better, the time between two consecutive noons (when the sun crosses the meridian), is a fairly constant quantity. Any small variation is due to the inclination of the ecliptic with respect to the celestial equator and the fact that the earth's orbit is really an ellipse rather than a circle. If we average this noon-to-noon day length, called the **true solar day**, over the course of a year, we obtain the **mean solar day** of $24^h00^m00^s$ on which all practical time measurements are based.

The **month**, although extremely convenient for use by ancient farmers, does not fit into the scheme of solar time, since at least originally it referred to the moon's motion about the earth.* Physically, this has nothing to do with either the rotation or the revolution period of the earth. No wonder our modern "months" have such strangely varying lengths.

*The words for *moon* and *month* are indeed related in the Indo-European family of languages.

The **year**, although based on the motion of our own planet, bears no simple relationship to the rotation period. To be precise, the time difference between two consecutive vernal equinoxes (the **tropical year**) is $365^d05^h48^m46^s$, or just about a quarter of a day more than 365 days. Since our calendar is an attempt to give each year an integer number of days, while at the same time keeping the solstices at the same date of the year, we have the somewhat complicated system of extra days in **leap years** (with an exception when the number of the year is evenly divisible by 100). Astronomers who like to avoid these intricacies often simply count days, starting with 0 on January 1, 4713 B.C. (why not?), calling the number the **Julian Day.** We are now somewhere in the two millions.

Univeral Time.   So far, we have implicitly assumed that our calendar is the same all over our planet; this is indeed the case as far as astronomers are concerned. Their hours and days, called **Universal Time** (UT), now coincide with the standard time in Greenwich, England (where, as we have seen, longitude 0° is defined). Thus, "noon, Universal Time" is noon Greenwich Mean Time (GMT). But when it is noon in Greenwich, it is nighttime halfway around the globe. Because people everywhere would like 12 o'clock noon to be the time when the sun is high in the sky, a system of **time zones** has been devised. Every 15° of longitude, starting from Greenwich's 0° longitude (that is, every $\frac{1}{24}$ of the earth's circumference), the time is shifted back one hour (from 12 to 11) west of Greenwich, and forward (from 12 to 13) east of Greenwich. Since this is merely an arbitrary convention, some of these time zones are wider than 15° in longitude and some are narrower. At any rate, all these local times are securely tied to Universal Time, which in turn is anchored safely in astronomical observations.

Sidereal Time.   Our timekeeping is thus based on a combination of the earth's rotation (hours) and its revolution (years); this feature is the cause of such inconveniences as the difference between the mean and true solar days, and the need for leap years. However, the rotation of the earth, being quite constant, could be used by itself to define all time periods. To be precise, we could measure the time difference between two consecutive meridian passages of a selected celestial object (other than the sun). What we would obtain is the so-called **sidereal day** of $23^h56^m04^s$. This has actually been done, and every astronomical observatory has a clock running on **sidereal time**, gaining 3^m56^s each mean day, or exactly one full (sidereal) day every year.

The difference between sidereal and solar time is due to the difference between the **sidereal** and **synodic periods** of the earth's rotation. The observer who counts out a sidereal day measures the rotation period of the earth with respect to some remote object, a "point on the celestial sphere"; the observer concerned with the solar day measures the earth's rotation period with respect to the sun (the synodic period). However, with respect to the sun, the earth moves along its orbit during the day, so that, after a full sidereal day has elapsed, the sun is not yet in its original position relative to the background stars. (This is diagrammed in Fig. 3-12.) The

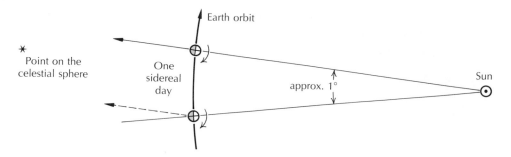

FIGURE 3-12.   Sidereal and synodic periods of the earth. The earth's motion along its orbit causes the sun, after a sidereal day, to be about 1° away from its original direction with respect to the earth.

difference must then be about $\frac{1}{365}$ of a rotation period per day, or 1 day out of about 365. Another way of stating this difference is by saying that the sun, after a sidereal day, is about $\frac{1}{365}$ of a full circle of—just about 1°—away from its initial direction relative to the earth.

QUESTIONS FOR DISCUSSION

1.   Why is it not very likely that one could construct a successful Foucault pendulum with a 1-kg weight, 2 m of household string, and a hook from the neighborhood hardware store?

2.   Compare longitude and latitude on the earth with right ascension and declination on the celestial sphere.

3.   You find many different objects close to your zenith during a night. Do they all have about the same declination? Right ascension?

4.   You find—to your surprise, we hope—an object which moves *exactly* along the ecliptic. What do you know concerning its orbit about the sun?

5.   You are told that somebody observed the sun at $\alpha = 12^h$ and $\delta = 0°$. What should be your comment?

6.   Is it true that winter always occurs when the earth is farthest from the sun? Explain.

7.   What do the signs of the zodiac, of vital importance in astrology, actually refer to? Why do they represent a somewhat inadequate system now?

8.   You are in Greenwich, England. The clock says it is 12ʰ00 GMT. Does this knowledge give you the *exact* azimuth angle of the sun? Explain.

EXERCISES

1.   Give two examples of conservation of momentum mentioned in the text, and one not mentioned.

2.   At what point or points on earth does a Foucault pendulum appear to rotate with the 24-hour period of the earth? Why there?

3. Is the relation 1:365 of the earth's rotation and revolution periods the result of a general law, such as the law of gravitation?

4. There are small, irregular changes in the direction of the earth's axis of rotation. What causes them?

5. Find the exact longitude and latitude of the community you live in.

6. Assume that your view of the sky at home is not limited by mountains or buildings. What is the declination of a celestial object which is visible all night and, on its apparent path, just touches the horizon? Of another object which is visible only for a short while and reaches a maximum altitude of 5° above the horizon?

7. Assume that there is a civilization on another planet which has defined its celestial coordinates α and δ in the same manner as we did. They give you the coordinates (in their system) of several celestial objects you can identify. For how many objects do you need coordinates in order to determine their planet's direction of rotation and its plane of revolution? Why would you have to know (at least approximately) the distance to this other planet?

8. Assume that you are on a spacecraft moving in a straight line through space, and that it has an observation window from which you can view a hemisphere of the sky. Assume further that the horizon plane as seen through the window is inclined by 30° with respect to the direction of motion of the spacecraft. Where on the earth would you find an equivalent situation? Describe the apparent motion of celestial objects across your hemisphere of view. Take into account a spin of the spacecraft about an axis which is exactly parallel to the direction of motion. Next, assume that the spacecraft spins about an axis inclined by an angle you can choose with respect to the direction of motion. What does this combination correspond to in terms of earthly observations?

9. It is not sufficient to know the altitude and the azimuth of a celestial object in order to find α and δ from tables. What else do you have to specify? Why?

10. We have introduced in the text three coordinate systems: their fundamental planes are determined by the earth's equator, by the celestial equator, and by the local horizon, respectively. What are the mutual relations among the corresponding six coordinates?

11. Where on the earth do stars appear to move parallel to the horizon? Explain the phenomenon.

12. Where on the earth do stars rise and set at right angles to the horizon? Explain.

13. Where on the earth does the celestial equator coincide with the zenith? Explain.

14. Where on the earth does the celestial north pole lie in the horizon? Where is it at 45° altitude?

15. Where on the earth are all stars with δ greater than 60° circumpolar stars?

16. Find the coordinates of Antares in Table H-9 and determine where on the earth it is a circumpolar star, and where it never rises above the horizon.

17. Assume the earth's orbit about the sun is a circle with a radius of 1 A.U. Verify the figure of about 30 km/sec for the orbital speed.

18. At what times of the year is the declination of the sun 0°?

19. You happen to be on the Tropic of Cancer on the day of the summer solstice. Where do you find the sun at noon?

20. How does your answer to Exercise 19 change if you move to the Tropic of Capricorn? If you go to either place at winter solstice?

21. Where is the sun as viewed from the earth's equator, at winter solstice?

22. How does the latitude of a polar circle relate to the inclination of the earth's rotational axis with respect to its orbital plane?

23. On what days of the year are day and night of equal length? What makes them equal?

24. Assume that the present calendar is kept in use for another 3,000 years. Approximately on what day of the year will the earth be closest to the sun 3,000 years from now?

25. Explain why the sidereal day is shorter than the mean solar day.

26. Calculate the difference between the sidereal and the mean solar day from the rotational and revolutionary periods of the earth.

27. What is the difference between Universal Time (UT) and Greenwich Mean Time (GMT)?

28. By how much does local mean solar time differ from Universal Time and from the standard time in Los Angeles? In New York? In Paris?

29. You want to telephone a person at a place that is at a longitude 120° west of your own town. It's high noon for you. What time is it, approximately, at the place you are calling?

30. Why does the mean solar day differ in length from the true solar day, that is, the time difference between two consecutive meridian passages of the sun?

EXPERIMENTS

1. Make a top out of a suitable piece of wood and some household matches. You will find that the top precesses, even if you just let it spin. Why?

2. What happens to a spinning top when you give it a push? Why?

3. Position a camera in such a fashion that it views the celestial north pole; open the shutter for a few hours on a dark night. Explain the picture you get.

FURTHER READING

The Earth in Space, edited by H. Odishaw, New York: Basic Books, Inc., 1967.

Tricker, R. A. R., *The Paths of the Planets,* New York: American Elsevier Publishing Company, Inc., 1967.

Minnaert, M. G. J., *Practical Work in Elementary Astronomy,* Berlin: Springer-Verlag, 1969.

4 the moon

The moon, our nearest neighbor in space, is a satellite of the earth in the sense that it is gravitationally bound to the earth. It is, moreover, the first celestial body on which man has set foot.

We have already discussed how the moon's phases were used in the early days of astronomy as convenient time units, and probably no celestial body has occupied poet's minds and pens more than the moon. Even with the naked eye we can make out some structural features—the "man in the moon." Once telescopes could be trained on this neighbor of ours, myriads of details were catalogued and given fancy names; after all, there are few areas in which an astronomer's fertile imagination is allowed to run loose. Nevertheless, to date we really know little more about many of these details than the names we have given them, and it is typical that until a few years ago (namely, before landing parties were able to see for themselves) some astronomers concluded from the data available that the moon might be covered with such a thick layer of dust that any spacecraft would simply be swallowed up. This, fortunately, was not the case. Even so, it will take many carefully planned landings before we can really say that we know our moon.

In this chapter we collect data of particular interest to us here on the earth, such as the phases and some of the more striking features of the moon's quite complicated motions in space, and of course the conditions necessary for the occurrence of eclipses. We also review some of the results of recent explorations from spacecraft, explorations aimed mostly at determining the physical nature of the moon, its surface structure, and a basis on which to reconstruct its history and development. Finally, we discuss the main points of space travel, acknowledging that the real problems are of a technological nature and hence outside the scope of astronomy.

4.1 THE MOON'S PHYSICAL CONSTITUTION

All the brilliant moonlight we admire on a clear night is borrowed from the sun—it is simply reflected light—since the moon's internal energy sources are insufficient to sustain any significant radiation mechanism. Thus, the fact that we can distinguish brighter and darker areas on the moon must mean that there are surface materials with higher and lower **reflectivity**, or **albedo**, as astronomers like to say. Before we were able to take samples right there, the problem of determining surface materials was largely one of guessing what mixture would yield the observed albedo values.

Distance and Radius. The average distance d of the center of the moon from the center of the earth is about 384,000 km, determined nowadays by bouncing a radar

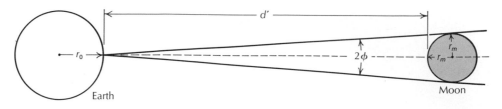

FIGURE 4-1.   Measuring the radius of the moon. The angular diameter 2ϕ, which can be measured, is related to the radius r_m and the
known distance d' by $\sin \phi = r_m/(d' + r_m)$.

signal off the moon's surface and measuring the time T the signal takes to go back
and forth. If d' is the distance between a point on the surface of the earth and a point
on the surface of the moon, then since distance equals speed times time of travel, we
have $2d' = cT$, where c is the speed of light (300,000 km/sec). Since it takes a radio
signal a little more than 2 seconds to go to the moon and back, d' is about 375,000
km. The center-to-center distance d is obtained from d' by adding to it the earth's
radius and the moon's radius r_m. The latter quantity is found by measuring the angular
diameter 2ϕ and relating r_m and ϕ to the known quantity d':

$$\sin \phi = \frac{r_m}{d' + r_m}$$

or

$$r_m = \frac{d' \sin \phi}{1 - \sin \phi}$$

as depicted in Fig. 4-1. (Of course, we have simplified our deduction by assuming
that the moon is a perfectly spherical body, and that the observation point on the
earth and the reflection point of the radar signal on the moon lie on the line connecting the centers of the earth and the moon; however, the real situation is treated
in approximately the same manner.) The result is a figure of about 1,750 km for the
moon's radius, or a bit more than one-quarter of the earth's radius; its volume is
about one-fiftieth of the earth's volume.

Mass.   The modern method of measuring the moon's mass involves careful study
of lunar **perturbations** of the motion of space probes. That is, we calculate what the
orbit of a satellite should be in the earth's gravitational field, and then relate certain
differences between this theoretical orbit and the actual measured orbit to the influence of the moon's gravitational field. Knowing the gravitational field of the moon,
we can determine its mass. The result is a lunar mass about one-eightieth of the
earth's mass, or about 7×10^{25} grams. From the values of the earth and moon radii
and their respective masses, we see that the average *density* of the moon is considerably less than the earth's—about 3.3 g/cm³. Finally, the *gravitational acceleration*
at the surface of the moon is only about one-sixth of that at the earth's surface.

The smaller gravitational acceleration has, of course, immediate consequences
for lunar exploration. For one thing, the weight of a certain mass on the moon is
less than on the earth; it is reduced by the ratio of the earth's gravitational accelera-

FIGURE 4-2. **Telescopic view of the full moon. Major surface features are identified in Fig. 4-3.** (*Lick Observatory.*)

tion to the moon's, or by a factor of 6. Thus, the same "effort" (in physical terms, the same force) applied against gravity, say in jumping up, has a much greater result on the moon: we would be able to jump six times higher on the moon. Similarly, much less rocket thrust is needed to leave the moon than to leave the earth.

Surface. A telescopic view of the full moon is reproduced in Fig. 4-2. The dark areas are called **maria** ("*seas*" in Latin) and are obviously smoother than the surrounding mountainous areas, although the maria certainly do not contain any water. The major surface features are identified in Fig. 4-3. A view through even a very low power telescope reveals the presence of countless **craters**; the larger ones have been named after an assortment of personalities. Figure 4-4 shows a telescopic picture of the area around the crater Copernicus. The typical features of large lunar

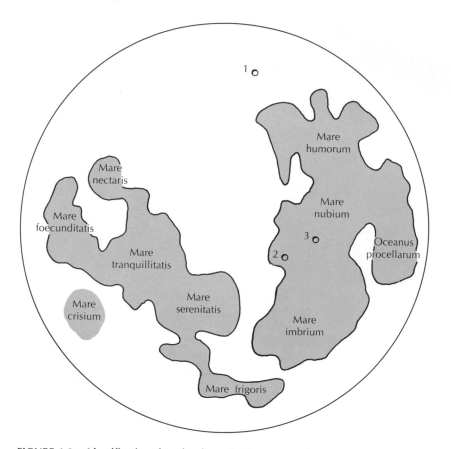

FIGURE 4-3. **Identification chart for the major features on the visible hemisphere of the moon. Craters shown are: 1, Tycho; 2, Eratosthenes; 3, Copernicus.** (*Lick Observatory.*)

craters—the terracing of the walls and the central peaks—are clearly seen in Fig. 4-5, a photograph of a large crater on the lunar farside, taken from a height of about 100 km by the crew of the Apollo 10. A close-up photo of the Apollo 14 landing site shows how the lunar landscape is littered with rocks and boulders of all sizes (Fig. 4-6). There are also the so-called **rilles**, deep valleys whose origin is not quite clear; Fig. 4-7 is a survey picture of the two branches of the Hyginus rille with the crater Hyginus in the center, taken by the Lunar Orbiter III spacecraft. Figure 4-8 shows astronaut Scott of the Apollo 15 crew with the Lunar Rover at the edge of Hadley rille. The rilles may have something to do with the flow of lava a long time ago. Also rather uncertain is the origin of the striking rays emanating from some craters, such as Copernicus (Fig. 4-4).

The farside of the moon is not within reach of earth-based telescopes because of the equality of its rotation and revolution periods. Pictures taken from spacecraft reveal a view which in some respects is quite similar to what we see on the visible

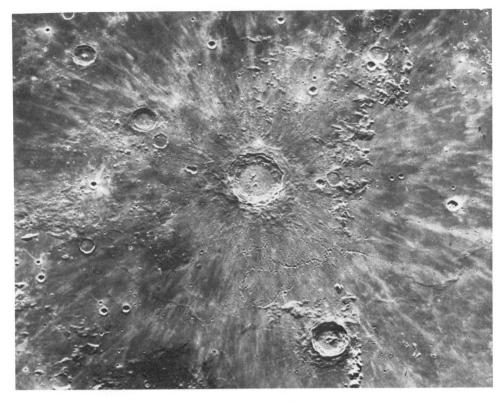

FIGURE 4-4. **Telescopic picture of the area around the crater Copernicus.** (*Lick Observatory.*)

hemisphere, in other respects not so similar. In particular, there are large and small craters, but it appears that the maria formations are much less prominent. Since the front and back of the moon are defined with respect to the position of the earth, and since this position does not change, similarities and dissimilarities between the front and back are important clues to the moon's history—and perhaps to that of the earth.

As to the origin of the most striking features, the craters, there are two theories: the first that they were caused by volcanic activity, and the second that they are due to meteoritic impact. Even now, with the results of the first manned lunar landings available, a choice either way is not possible, although it appears that meteoritic impacts are mostly responsible for the craters. On the other hand, the rather smooth maria are thought by many astronomers to be the locations of old lava flows. A knowledge of the amount of volcanic activity that has taken place on the moon in the past would permit reconstruction of its thermal history, and would allow for at least qualitative conclusions as to its internal structure. We have already seen that the mean density of the moon corresponds to the density of the relatively light, rocky material of the surface layers of the earth. Information on the interior structure might,

FIGURE 4-5.   Large crater on the lunar farside. The photograph was
taken from a height of about 100 km from the Apollo 10 command
and service modules. Note the terracing of the walls and the central
peaks. (*NASA.*)

in turn, make it possible to decide on the probable origin of the moon. We shall return to this latter problem presently.

Composition.   The chemical analysis of lunar rocks reveals that they are significantly different from earth specimens. As a consequence, we now feel that it is quite
probable that the moon and the earth had rather different histories, even in very
early times. This somewhat tentative conclusion is corroborated by the fact that the
moon rock formations, in their detailed structure, are not quite similar to anything
found on the earth.

As we now know directly from having been there, but had surmised previously,
the moon has no *atmosphere* beyond an infinitesimal gas density due to captured
interplanetary molecules and, possibly, occasional volcanic eruptions. The moon's

FIGURE 4-6.   Close-up view of a large boulder on the lunar surface, photographed by the Apollo 14 astronauts. (*NASA.*)

small gravitational constant results in a low escape velocity for particles that would otherwise constitute an atmosphere. Without an atmosphere there is no possibility of efficiently reducing the temperature difference between the sunlit and the dark hemispheres of the moon. Nor is there any way to keep a constant shower of cosmic rays and meteoroids from reaching its surface.

Also of interest is the fact that the moon does not appear to have a significant *magnetic field*, so that none of the complex phenomena we listed in relation to the earth, such as the radiation belts, exist at or around the moon.

Origin.   Let us now return to the question of the origin of the moon. What makes the problem difficult is the fact that the moon is very large for a planetary satellite, not in absolute size but in relation to the main planet. It is thus quite probable that its origin is unlike that of, say, the satellites of Jupiter. Among the theories put forth are a *common origin with the earth*, so that the earth and the moon would really be a system of twin planets, and a *catastrophic event* early in the history of the earth by which the moon was broken out of the earth's forming body (it would just about fit into the Pacific basin). Alternatively, the moon could have originated somewhere

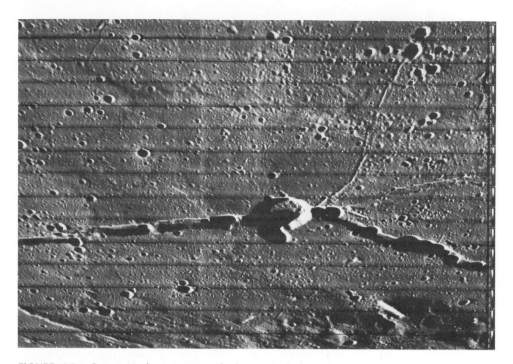

FIGURE 4-7.   Crater Hyginus (center of picture) and the two branches of the Hyginus rille. Photograph transmitted to earth by Lunar Orbiter III from a height of about 60 km. The crater Hyginus is about 10 km in diameter and 800 m deep. Note the innumerable smaller craters. (*NASA.*)

else in the solar system and been captured by the earth's gravity at some later time. None of these theories is at present backed by enough evidence to be considered as fact, although the chemical differences between earth and moon rock specimens seem to contradict the theory that proposes a relatively late breaking away of the moon from the earth.

4.2   THE MOTIONS OF THE MOON

Revolution and Rotation.   To the unaided eye, the most conspicuous feature of the moon is its **phases**: full moon, new moon, and the quarters in between, when the **terminator**, that is, the boundary line between night and day, moves through the middle of the apparent lunar disc. The time between two consecutive new moons is 29^d12^h. This is the **month of the phases**, or the **synodic month**, a result of the relative positions of earth, sun, and moon. Thus, the synodic month is the revolution period of the moon about the earth defined with respect to the **position of the sun**. As we saw in Section 3.3, there must also be a **sidereal period** defined with respect to a *fixed direction in space*. For the moon it is shorter than the synodic period by about $\frac{1}{13}$, or by the ratio of the moon's orbital time about the earth to the earth's

FIGURE 4-8. Astronaut Scott of the Apollo 15 crew with the Lunar Rover at the edge of the Hadley rille. The view is along the canyon. (*NASA.*)

orbital time about the sun. Figure 4-9 shows the geometrical relations; note the similarities with Fig. 3-12.

As the moon revolves about the earth, it always presents the same side to the earth. Thus, with respect to the celestial sphere, it rotates about its axis with precisely its sidereal period. We say that the moon's rotation period is *locked into* its revolution period; energy calculations show that such a situation is particularly *stable*. We mention in passing that, due to various perturbations, the moon actually moves back and forth slightly with respect to the earth, so that over long periods of time we can see a few degrees of the back of the moon. The main portion of this backside can only be observed from space probes, as we already pointed out.

At full moon, the sun and the moon are on opposite sides of the earth; we say that the full moon is at **opposition** to the sun. At new moon, the sun and moon are on the same side of the earth; they are at **conjunction**. The full moon rises when the sun sets, and then is in the sky all night; the (nearly) new moon sets and rises shortly before or after the sun sets and rises. Thus, we find the small **crescent** of the moon, a day or so after new moon, close to the western horizon just after sunset (**waxing** crescent). A day or so before new moon, it is seen close to the eastern horizon just before sunrise (**waning** crescent). The phase of the moon just before or just after

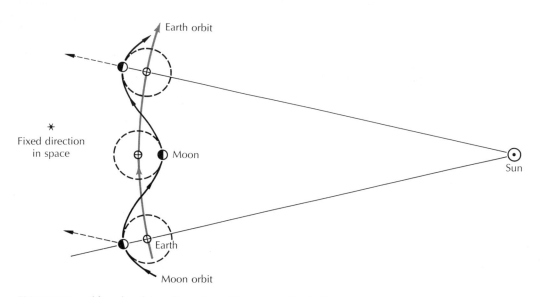

FIGURE 4-9. Sidereal and synodic periods of the moon. Due to the orbital motion of the earth about the sun, the moon completes one-thirteenth more than one sidereal revolution during its synodic period, the month of the phases.

full moon is called **gibbous** (waning or waxing). The positions of first and third quarters are called **quadrature**. The relative positions of the earth, the moon, and the sun in relation to the phases of the moon are shown in Fig. 4-10.

Orbital Plane.   The moon's orbit about the earth is almost circular. But its orbital plane does not coincide with the ecliptic, that is, the plane of the earth's orbit about the sun. Rather, it is inclined to the ecliptic by about 5°. During a month, the moon's position moves from 5° above the ecliptic to 5° below, and back again. Thus, the full moon may be higher or lower in the sky at midnight than the sun is at noon. The apparent motion of the moon on the celestial sphere is complicated by the fact that its axis of rotation, or its orbital plane, shows a *precession* with a period of 19 years. So, if in one year the winter full moon is higher in the northern sky than the summer sun, about 10 years later the summer full moon is higher in the sky than the winter sun.

Finally, at earth latitudes close to the Poles, the moon may never set, so that the sun and the full moon are in the sky at the same time, at least for a few days (i.e., 24-hour periods!). It is this complex movement that fascinated the men who built Stonehenge and is probably responsible for a great deal of the preoccupation of early civilizations with things astronomical.

4.3   ECLIPSES

Solar Eclipse.   A geometrical coincidence makes our planet rather unique in the solar system. The moon's size and distance from the earth, and the sun's size and distance from the earth make their *apparent* diameters equal. Owing to the inclina-

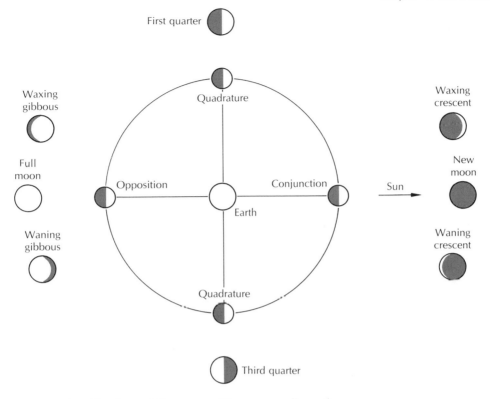

FIGURE 4-10. **The phases of the moon and the corresponding positions of earth, moon, and sun. The outermost drawings show the moon as seen from earth during its phases.**

tions of the orbits involved, once or twice a year (and not *every* new moon) the solar and lunar discs appear, to an observer somewhere on the earth, to coincide in a **solar eclipse** (Fig. 4-11).

In the eclipse position, the moon moves in its orbit in such a way that it passes in front of the sun (actually, it passes between the earth observer and the sun). Two observers, *A* and *B*, a few hundred kilometers from each other on the earth, might see the event as sketched in Fig. 4-12; these are **partial eclipses**. However, in a very narrow strip (typically, some 100 km wide) somewhere between positions *A*

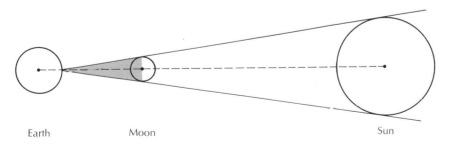

FIGURE 4-11. **Conditions for a total solar eclipse. Solar and lunar discs appear, to an observer somewhere on earth, to coincide in the position of a solar eclipse.**

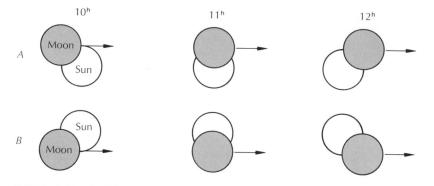

FIGURE 4-12. **Partial solar eclipse as seen by two observers** *A* **and** *B* **on either side of the totality strip; times shown are arbitrary.**

and *B*, an observer *C* sees a **total eclipse**; as seen from his position, the centers of sun and moon coincide *exactly*, and for several minutes the moon blocks out all the light emitted by the sun (Fig. 4-13). The positions of sun, moon, and observers *A*, *B*, and *C* are shown in a vastly exaggerated scale in Fig. 4-14. (Photographs of the sun taken during totality are shown in Figs. 8-10 to 8-12.)

Since the distances from the earth to the moon and sun vary slightly, the time of **totality** varies from zero to a maximum of some 8 minutes. Occasionally, the apparent size of the moon is smaller than the apparent size of the sun, so that at what otherwise would be totality the moon does not quite cover the sun. In this case, we have the **annular eclipse** of Fig. 4-15. Totality (or its annular phase) is seen on the earth only in very narrow strips that run from a location at which totality occurs at sunrise to a point where it occurs at sunset. The accurate prediction of where totality occurs, when exactly, and for how long—one of the main goals of ancient astronomy —is a very laborious task. Figure 4-16 is a world map with approximate locations of the totality zone for eclipses during the rest of this century.

A total solar eclipse is the most spectacular celestial event we can witness. The general illumination decreases from daylight to the level of a moonlit night—the residual brightness comes from photons scattered by the earth's atmosphere into the zone of totality. Around the main body of the sun (we shall call it the photosphere later in Section 7.4) there is the eerie bluish glow of the solar corona, the extended

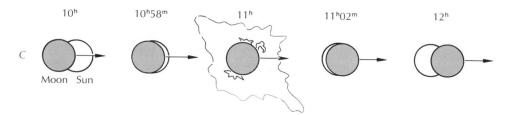

FIGURE 4-13. **Total solar eclipse as seen by observer** *C* **in the center of the totality strip; times shown are arbitrary.**

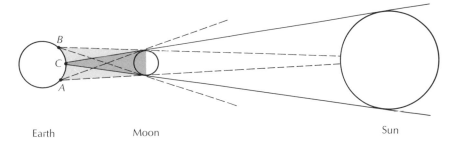

Earth   Moon   Sun

FIGURE 4-14. Relative positions of sun, moon, and earth during a
solar eclipse. At position *C* (and close to it) on earth, an observer
sees a total solar eclipse; at positions *A* and *B*, the eclipse is partial.
The intersection of the cone, indicated by the dashed lines, and the
sun determines the portion of the solar disc eclipsed by the moon.

outer atmosphere of our sun. Just at the beginning and at the end of totality, a thin
ring of red light, the chromosphere, appears around the eclipsed sun; often, weird
solar formations called prominences can be seen, glowing red and seeming to stretch
out from the edge of the moon.

A total eclipse is still the only possible occasion for studying certain important
details of the sun. Solar physics, and probably many other branches of astronomy,
would never have developed so quickly if astronomers had not been able to observe
the outer layers of the sun as directly as they can during total eclipses.

Lunar Eclipse.   When the earth is directly between the sun and the moon we have a
lunar eclipse, in which the moon is in the shadow of the earth; lunar eclipses always
occur at full moon. Owing to the relative sizes of the earth and the moon, the moon
often undergoes a total eclipse for almost all observers on the earth (compare Fig.
4-17 with the solar-eclipse sketch, Fig. 4-14). During totality (which may last for
an hour or so) the moon is not totally invisible but rather shows a faint reddish glow,
due to light scattered into the earth's shadow by our atmosphere.

4.4   MAN-MADE SATELLITES AND SPACE PROBES

While the moon is our only natural satellite, a decade of space exploration has seen
hundreds of artificial satellites placed into orbits about the earth. Once they had a
variety of more or less useful purposes, but by now they make up an ever-growing

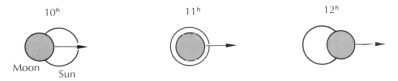

FIGURE 4-15. Annular eclipse of the sun; times shown are arbitrary.

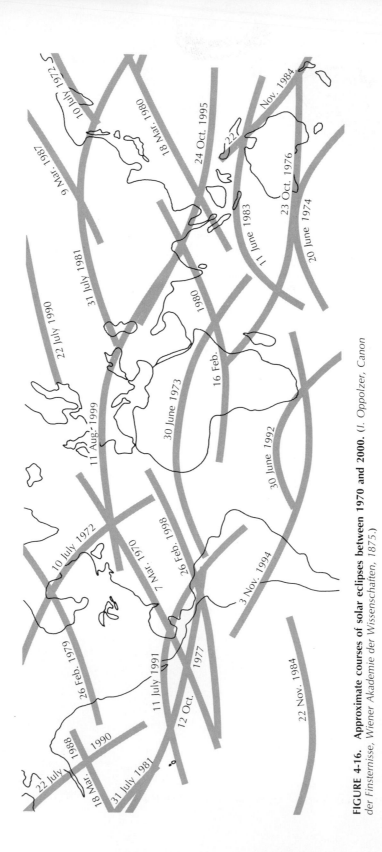

FIGURE 4-16. Approximate courses of solar eclipses between 1970 and 2000. (*I. Oppolzer, Canon der Finsternisse, Wiener Akademie der Wissenschaften, 1875.*)

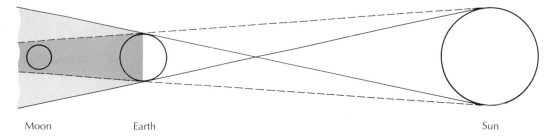

Moon   Earth   Sun

FIGURE 4-17.   Relative positions of sun, moon, and earth during a lunar eclipse. The shaded lines indicate the extent of the earth's shadow.

cosmic junkyard. Some satellites plunge into the earth's atmosphere and burn after a short enough period; however, others will stay with us for thousands of years.

Launch.   What are the conditions necessary for lifting a body permanently from the earth's surface? Let us first look at satellites proper, that is, objects in closed orbit about the earth, and for simplicity assume that we launch our satellite at some height *h* above the ground (for instance, by means of the second stage of a rocket, the first stage having lifted the satellite up to launching altitude). Assume further that the second stage turns so that the launch is in a direction parallel to the earth's surface. Now give the body a certain initial speed (**launch speed**). One of three things can happen: it can fall back to earth like a baseball, if its launch speed is not enough to carry it away from the earth as gravity pulls it toward the earth. It can "escape" the earth if its speed is high enough to pull it away from the earth's gravitational attraction forever. Or, it can orbit the earth, if its speed "balances" the pull of gravity; in a sense, the satellite "falls" around the earth. There is actually a range of launch speeds for which the last possibility occurs, each speed leading to a different orbit about the earth. The greater the speed, the farther from earth the orbit is.

Orbit.   We will see in Section 5.2 that gravitational theory predicts the path of the satellite to be an ellipse. The shape of the ellipse is determined by the launch speed *v* and such fixed quantities as the launch height *h*, the launch direction (parallel to the surface in our example), and the mass of the earth. Figure 4-18 shows orbits for three different velocities such that $v_1 < v_2 < v_3$. Note that there is one particular velocity (v_2 in Fig. 4-18) that results in a circular orbit; a circle is a special case of an ellipse. The value of v_2 can be calculated, and it turns out to be about 8 km/sec (5 miles/sec) or 29,000 km/h—that is, about 10 times the speed of our fastest supersonic aircraft. The points on the elliptic orbit at which the satellite is closest to and farthest from the earth's surface are called, respectively, its **perigee** and its **apogee**.

Escape.   If we increase the launch speed *v*, the apogee moves farther and farther out. The question arises as to the speed at which the apogee is at infinity, that is, the speed at which the satellite "escapes" from the earth. At that point, of course, the satellite is no longer a satellite, but rather a **space probe**. This **escape speed** v_0, has

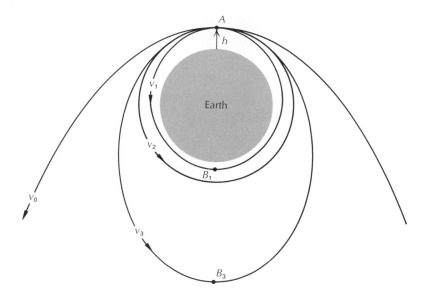

FIGURE 4-18.   Geometry of satellite orbits. The satellite is launched at point A **into an elliptic orbit at velocity** v_1 **(perigee** B_1**) or velocity** v_3 **(apogee** B_3**), and into a circular orbit at velocity** v_2**. At the escape speed** v_0**, the satellite leaves the gravitational field of the earth.**

been calculated and is approximately $\sqrt{2}\, v_2$, or 11 km/sec. If it is launched at a speed greater than that, the spacecraft leaves the gravitational field of the earth but is attracted by that of the sun. A launch speed v^* of about 41 km/sec is needed (at the distance of the earth) to escape the sun; then the body leaves the solar system forever in a hyperbolic orbit, a path whose geometric form is a hyperbola (Fig. 4-18). Note, however, that v^* is computed solely with respect to the sun. If we take into account and use the *orbital speed of the earth about the sun* (30 km/sec), we can launch at a much lower speed. Thus, launching in the direction of the earth's motion requires only the difference between v^* and the orbital speed of the earth, or 11 km/sec, for escape from the gravitational attraction of the sun. But another 11 km/sec, the escape speed from the earth v_0, must be added to this, so that altogether some 22 km/sec are needed to escape the solar system.

Interplanetary travel is, of course, much more complicated than has been shown here. In particular, the effect of the other members of the solar system must be taken into account. This is the realm of celestial mechanics, whose major areas of research are discussed in Section 5.2.

QUESTIONS FOR DISCUSSION

1.   Why is the back of the moon not visible from the earth?

2.   The revolution and rotation periods of the moon are equal. If this were not the case, would you still see phases of the moon? Explain.

3. Where in the sky do you find the full moon around midnight? Why?

4. Somebody claimed that the new moon was right in front of a rather bright star he had seen the night before around 11 P.M. What should your response have been?

5. Why does the moon rise about an hour later, on the average, every day?

6. Describe the phases of the earth as they might be observed from the moon.

7. Describe the solar eclipse as it would be observed from the moon.

EXERCISES

1. Calculate the time it takes light reflected at the moon's surface to reach the earth, given the distance and the speed of light noted in the text.

2. Compare your answer to Exercise 1 with the travel time of light from the sun to the earth.

3. Calculate the angular diameter of the moon with the aid of the formula $\sin \phi = r_m / (d' + r_m)$ and the values of r_m and d' given in the text.

4. How far away from your eye would you have to hold a quarter so that it would have the same angular size as the moon? Check your answer by fastening a quarter to a stick and holding it between you and the full moon.

5. How "large" (in angular measure) does the earth appear to a space traveler on the moon?

6. Check the number given in the text for the ratio of the earth's gravitational acceleration to the moon's by applying Newton's law.

7. Given the masses of the earth and the moon, determine where, on the line connecting the centers of the earth and the moon, the gravitational attraction of the earth just equals that of the moon.

8. Check the figures given in Table H-2 for the moon's synodic and sidereal periods, using the data given for the periods of revolution of the moon about the earth and the earth about the sun.

9. At what time of the day or night does the moon in its first quarter cross the meridian?

10. At what time of the day or night do you see the waxing crescent of the moon? Where is the moon then, with respect to your horizon?

11. Where on the earth can you see the full moon and the sun in the sky at the same time?

12. Why can you often see the outline of the whole moon during the crescent phase?

13. Why is there not complete darkness during a total solar eclipse?

14. Why does a total lunar eclipse last much longer than a total solar eclipse?

15. Why is the moon clearly visible during a total lunar eclipse?

16. Estimate the length of a solar eclipse from the orbital period of the moon and its angular diameter.

17. Some artificial satellites flicker markedly. What are possible reasons for the flickering?

18. In what direction would you launch a space probe that is to leave the solar system?

19. Why do satellites with large perigees "live" longer?

EXPERIMENTS

1.   Identify, during a full moon, the major features of the surface of the moon (Fig. 4-3) visible to the naked eye.

2.   Identify on the photograph of the full moon (Fig. 4-2) some landing sites of the Apollo Program.

3.   The heights of lunar mountains can be estimated by measuring the lengths of the shadows they cast on the surrounding plains when the sun is low above the lunar horizon. Set up an experiment, at least in principle, to measure the length of a stick stuck in the ground in your backyard solely by making observations from a window.

4.   Look up the times of sunrise and sunset, and of moonrise and moonset, in some almanac. Determine from the data for a few months the dates of full moon and new moon. Discuss some of the problems you encounter with this task.

5.   Try to observe one of the artificial satellites; their times of visibility are occasionally given in newspapers. Compare the visual impression with that of a high-flying aircraft and a shooting star.

FURTHER READING

Physics and Astronomy of the Moon (second ed.), edited by Z. Kopal, New York: Academic Press, Inc., 1971.

Whipple, F. L., *Earth, Moon, and Planets* (third ed.), Cambridge, Mass.: Harvard University Press, 1968.

Mitchell, S. A., *Eclipses of the Sun,* New York: Columbia University Press, 1951.

The Moon, Meteorites, and Comets, edited by B. A. Middlehurst and G. P. Kuiper, Chicago: The University of Chicago Press, 1963.

5 the planets

The motions of the planets have always fascinated man. They are prominent in every astronomical mythology, from the Greek identification of Mars with the war-god to the preoccupation of the Mayans with the planet Venus. And, as we have seen, out of the early study of planetary motion grew the scientific revolution and the basis for today's technological civilization.

The question of planetary motion now belongs to history, and what remains there in terms of details is of interest only to the specialist. By contrast, 350 years after the invention of the telescope we still know less about the *physical* nature of the planets than we do about many distant stars. And it is quite clear that we can increase our knowledge significantly only by going there, either to fly by and take readings or to make soft landings on the surface. The planets are next on the list of celestial objects to be visited by man or, at least, by man-made machines. Venus and Mars have already been visited by unmanned spacecraft, and the other planets will be too, provided society and its spokesmen continue to believe that this endeavor is worth the effort, the expense, and the frustration of the inevitable initial failures.

5.1 POSITIONS AND MOTIONS

There are nine known major planets in the solar system. We have already discussed the earth. Of the others, **Mercury, Venus, Mars, Jupiter**, and **Saturn** are visible to the naked eye and thus were observed by the ancient astronomers. Of the remaining three, **Uranus** is just barely visible without a telescope and was first identified as a planet in 1781; **Neptune** was found in 1846, and **Pluto** in 1930. Whether there are still more planets in the solar system — with orbits beyond the orbit of Pluto — is uncertain, since a complete telescopic search of the appropriate regions of the sky for a quite dim object such as a very distant planet is practically impossible.

The light of every planet is reflected sunlight. None of them now has a significant internal energy source; our discussion of stellar evolution in Chapter 12 will show even Jupiter, the largest and most massive of the planets, has never been a star. Thus, the relative brightness of the planets depends as much on their *albedo* or reflectivity as it does on their distances from the sun and their diameters. On the other hand, as we have seen in the case of the moon, the observed albedo offers valuable clues to the theoretician interested in deducing surface structure and composition.

The Inferior Planets. The orbits of Mercury and Venus are inside the orbit of the earth; because of this they are called the **inferior planets**. Their orbital planes are inclined only a few degrees with respect to the orbital plane of the earth. In fact, this feature is common to *all* the major planets save Pluto, which, as we shall see, is really a stranger to this group.

The intersection of the celestial sphere and the orbital plane of the earth, that is, the ecliptic, is a great circle which defines the apparent path of the sun in the sky. Since the major planets orbit the sun in planes very close to the earth's, the apparent paths of the planets are always very close to the path of the sun.

The orbits of the inferior planets are inside the earth's orbit, so that each of them is always seen from the earth as being within a certain angle from the sun. This angle is determined by the size of the orbit relative to that of the earth. The greatest angular distance of an inferior planet from the sun is called its maximum **elongation** (east or west). The geometry is sketched in Fig. 5-1, which is simplified in the sense that we have shown concentric circular orbits projected onto a common plane. Thus, the angles of greatest western elongation shown in Fig. 5-1 are smaller than the actual 28° and 47° which take into account the eccentricities of the orbits of Mercury and Venus, respectively (see Fig. 5-7). The positions marked with open circles, where the earth, the sun, and the planet in question are in line, are called **inferior conjunction** (planet between earth and sun) and **superior conjunction** (sun between earth and planet).

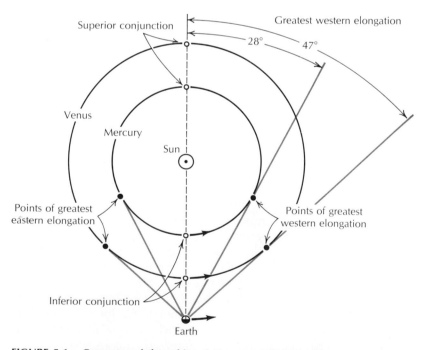

FIGURE 5-1. Geometry of the orbits of Mercury and Venus. The fictitious viewer is looking down on the planes of their orbits about the sun. As seen from earth, Mercury and Venus stay within 28° and and 47°, respectively, of the sun.

From the earth, then, Mercury and Venus may be seen west of the sun, at angular distances which may be as much as 28° and 47°. When they are west of the sun, as seen from the earth, they rise above the horizon *before* the sun does and appear as **morning stars** close to the eastern horizon. In the corresponding positions east of the sun, they set *after* the sun and appear as **evening stars** close to the western horizon. Since Mercury is always rather close to the sun, it is difficult to observe, and the poet's evening star is invariably Venus. In fact, most people have never seen Mercury in spite of its brightness. The orbit of Venus is almost exactly circular, while Mercury's orbit is somewhat more elliptical.

There are two effects we should consider now. The first is the appearance of **phases** similar to those of the moon, but unfortunately visible only through a telescope. Mercury and Venus present a **crescent** to the earth when close to it and on its side of the sun. At maximum elongation, they are half sunlit, half dark (**quarter** phase). At their greatest distance from the earth, they are almost full or, technically, **gibbous**. Figure 5-2 shows the positions of these planets during half their orbit (crescent, position *A*; quarter, position *B*; gibbous, position *C*). Note that we would see the planets in the positions west of the sun as morning stars. Figure 5-3 is a drawing of the appearance of an inferior planet to an earthbound observer.

The second effect is a *change in the apparent size* of the planet due to the fact that the distance between the earth and either Venus or Mercury varies greatly. For example, the distance from the earth to Venus is about 50×10^6 km in the crescent phase and about 250×10^6 km in the gibbous phase, so that the apparent size of the

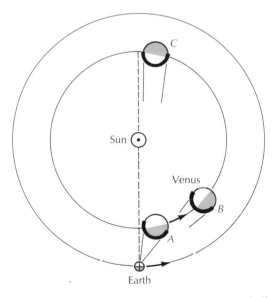

FIGURE 5-2. Illumination of Venus during one-half of its orbit about the sun. The fictitious viewer is looking down on the orbital plane. The night side of Venus is shaded. The planet is seen as a crescent around position *A***. Position** *B* **is the quarter phase. Near position** *C***, Venus is in its gibbous phase.**

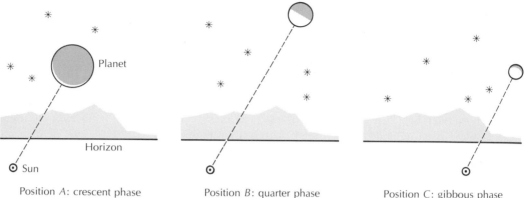

Position A: crescent phase   Position B: quarter phase   Position C: gibbous phase

FIGURE 5-3. **Venus as morning star in the crescent, quarter, and gibbous phases. Note the change in apparent size, position along the horizon, and altitude for the same position of the sun below the horizon.**

planet varies by a factor of about 5. Similarly, the apparent size of Mercury varies by a factor of about 8. This size difference relative to phase has been indicated in Fig. 5-3.

Sidereal versus Synodic Periods. The difference between the **sidereal period** of Venus (225 earth days) and its **synodic period** (about 580 days) is particularly noticeable. The latter, as we already saw in the case of the moon, is the **period of the phases**, that is, the time between two consecutive passages through a certain point of the orbit, say, the point of maximum western elongation, *as seen from the earth.* Thus, the portion of the orbit between *A* and *B* in Fig. 5-2 takes about 10 months, or more than the whole sidereal period of the planet.

Figure 5-4 shows, approximately to scale, the "race" between Earth and Venus. We begin with both planets at position 1 — inferior conjunction — which, for instance, occurred on June 17, 1972. After 71 days (on August 27, 1972) Earth and Venus have reached position 2, which is the greatest western elongation. All this time, Venus is the "morning star." It takes about 225 days to reach position 3, superior conjunction (on April 9, 1973). Venus has just completed a sidereal period in these 225 days, and it now emerges as the "evening star." After another 216 days, in position 4 (on November 11, 1973), it reaches its greatest eastern elongation. And finally, 73 days later (on January 23, 1974), we are at the next inferior conjunction, position 5, and Venus has finally completed one synodic period.

Superior Planets. The **superior planets** have orbits outside the earth's orbit. Thus, they may be seen near the ecliptic but at any angular distance from the sun. While the (sidereal) *revolution periods* of the inferior planets are shorter than the earth's, that is, less than a year, the periods of the superior planets are longer. They vary from almost 2 years for Mars to 250 years for Pluto.

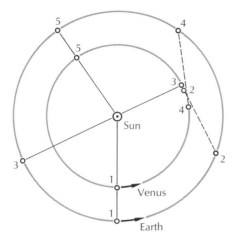

FIGURE 5-4. Motion of Venus and Earth in their orbits. The fictitious viewer is looking down on the ecliptic plane. Positions 1 and 5, inferior conjunction; position 2, greatest western elongation; position 3, superior conjunction; position 4, greatest eastern elongation. Venus is the morning star between positions 1 and 3, the evening star between positions 3 and 5.

The superior planets, revolving about the sun outside the earth's orbit, do not exhibit the distinct phase changes of the inferior planets. Nevertheless, they do have a **gibbous phase**, that is, a phase where a little of the surface turned toward us is in shadow and the rest is in sunlight, near the positions of quadrature (see Fig. 5-5). In actuality a gibbous phase can be *observed* only in the case of Mars. Also marked in Fig. 5-5 are the positions of **conjunction** and **opposition**, that is, the positions in which the earth, the sun and the superior planets are in line.

Planetary Orbits. The **relative sizes** of the inferior planetary orbits can be determined, in principle, by the method outlined in Fig. 5-6 for the simplified case of a circular orbit. From the known maximum elongation of the planet (an angle), the size of the orbit is obtained in units of the earth-sun distance (the astronomical unit), using the formula

Unknown distance = (A.U.) × sine of maximum elongation angle

From the actual value of the astronomical unit (150,000,000 km), we can find the size of the orbit. A similar consideration yields the sizes of the orbits of the superior planets. Actually, the absolute value of the astronomical unit itself is nowadays obtained by measuring the distance from the earth to a planet, say Venus, through the use of the transit time of radar signals and a very accurately calculated orbit of the planet, predicted on the basis of the *complete n-body problem* (see Section 5.2). At any rate, the result is the progression seen in Figs. 5-7 and 5-8, which show the

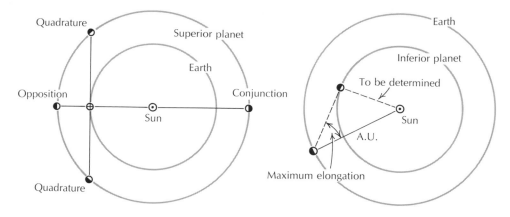

FIGURE 5-5. Geometry of the orbit of a superior planet. The fictitious viewer is looking down on the orbital plane. In the positions of opposition and conjunction, sun, earth, and planet are aligned; in the quadrature position, sun, earth, and planet form a right triangle.

FIGURE 5-6. Determination of orbital size of an inferior planet. The radius of the orbit is found from the observed maximum elongation angle and the known distance between earth and sun (the astronomical unit).

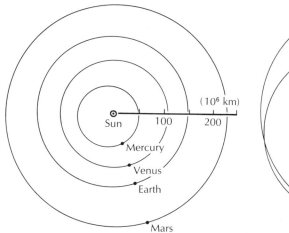

FIGURE 5-7. Orbits of Mercury, Venus, Earth, and Mars.

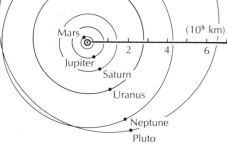

FIGURE 5-8. Orbits of Mars, Jupiter, Saturn, Uranus, Neptune, and Pluto.

actual orbits in a common plane. Note the eccentricity of the orbits of Mercury and, in particular, of Pluto, whose orbit even reaches inside that of Neptune. There appears to be a gap between Mars and Jupiter, as if there were a planet missing between the two. This is more clearly seen in Fig. 5-9, where we have shown the distances of the planets from the sun, that is, the semimajor axes of their elliptical orbits. We will return to this "missing planet" in Section 6.2.

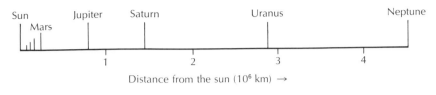

FIGURE 5-9. **Distances of the planets from the sun.**

5.2 KEPLER'S LAWS AND CELESTIAL MECHANICS

The mutual gravitational interaction among the members of the solar system determines the motion characteristics of the planets. In its most general form, analysis of this interaction is an **n-body problem** in that each planet is influenced by the sun and all the other planets. However, since the mass of the sun is so much greater than the combined mass of the planets, we can assume that the dominant influence on the motion of a planet is solar attraction; the other planets act as minor **perturbers**. In this approximation, planetary motion becomes a **two-body problem** (planet and sun), possibly requiring secondary corrections because of the perturbations.

The Two-Body Approximation. The procedure for analyzing planetary motion is to write, in mathematical language, the law that governs the gravitational interaction between sun and planet (**Newton's law of gravitation**) and to solve the resulting set of equations by standard methods. We would find that an object moves about the sun in a path which is a **conic section**, that is, either an **ellipse** or a **hyperbola**, with a **circle** or a **parabola** as a special case. The sun is at one of the foci of the ellipse or hyperbola, as is shown in Fig. 5-10. In that illustration, we have kept the perihelion, the distance of closest approach of the body to the sun, constant, and have varied the **eccentricity** e, a quantitative measure of the form of a conic section. Note from Fig. 5-10 that if $e = 0$, the orbit is a circle; if $0 < e < 1$ it is an ellipse; if $e = 1$ it is a parabola; and if $e > 1$ it is a hyperbola.

If the orbit is an ellipse, the planet is gravitationally bound to the sun and is thus a bona fide member of the solar system; if it is a hyperbola, the "planet" comes close to the sun once in its lifetime and then leaves forever. The form of the orbit depends on the "initial conditions," the planet's position and velocity at some given time. Thus, the planets are really bodies whose orbital velocities are too small to let them escape the sun's gravitational field: they describe elliptical orbits about the sun.

Barycenter. In the simplified description given here we have assumed that the sun is stationary in space. In reality, the sun is in motion with respect to coordinates outside the solar system. Aside from taking part in galactic rotation (Section 17.2) and having its own "proper motion" (Section 9.2), it reacts to the periodic motion of the planets by itself describing an elliptical orbit about the **center of gravity** or **barycenter** of the solar system. Since Jupiter, with its relatively large mass, is mostly responsible for the sun's barycentric motion, we can simplify our discussion of the barycenter to the two-body case.

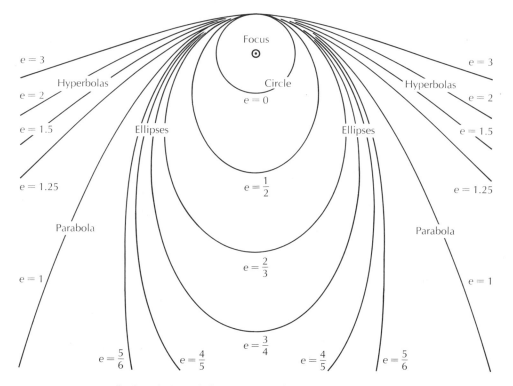

FIGURE 5-10. **Two-body solution of the gravitational equation: elliptic, parabolic, and hyperbolic orbits. The planets in elliptic orbits are gravitationally bound to the sun. A body on a hyperbolic orbit enters the solar system from the outside and leaves again forever. The parabolic orbit is the boundary case between elliptic and hyperbolic orbits.**

The barycenter of two bodies lies on the line connecting their centers. It is halfway between them if the two masses are equal; otherwise it is closer to the center of the more massive one. In general, it is located such that the mass of one body multiplied by its distance from the barycenter is equal to the mass of the other body multiplied by its distance from the barycenter. This is shown schematically in Fig. 5-11, where the area of the circle representing each body indicates its mass. The barycenter is marked by the letter B. Case (d) corresponds approximately to the actual situation in the solar system, with the barycenter positioned just outside the sphere of the sun.

Kepler's Laws. While we have introduced the main features of the two-body approximation to planetary motion as consequences of the universal law of gravitation, they were actually known as **Kepler's laws** *before* Newton formulated his law and (simultaneously with Leibniz) the mathematical methods needed to apply it. Kepler found them by trial and error from actual observation. In a version sufficient for our purposes, they state:

1. All planets revolve about the sun in ellipses, with the sun at one focus.

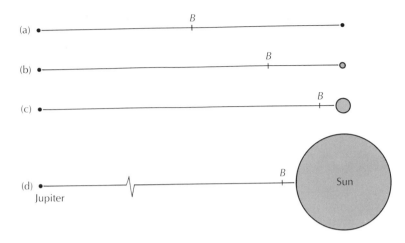

FIGURE 5-11. (a) to (c), two gravitating bodies and their barycenter *B*. **The larger the mass ratio of the two bodies, the closer is the barycenter to the more massive body; the simplified case of the solar system, represented by Jupiter and the sun, is shown in (d).**

2. The orbital speed of a planet becomes the greater the closer to the sun it gets; it attains maximum speed at **perihelion**, and minimum at **aphelion**.

3. The squares of the revolution periods of the planets are proportional to the third powers of their semimajor axes.

Figure 5-12 illustrates the second law in its quantitative form: the time behavior of a planet's motion is such that the line segment connecting the center of the planet with the center of the sun sweeps out equal areas in equal times. Thus, because the shaded areas in Fig. 5-12 are equal, the two time differences $t_2 - t_1$ and $t_2' - t_1'$ must be equal, so the speed of the planet must be greater at the left.

As we saw in Figs. 5-7 and 5-8, the orbits of the planets are very close to circular. *If* we approximate them as such, Kepler's first law simply says that the sun is at the center of the orbits, and his third law that the squares of the revolution periods of the planets are proportional to the third powers of their orbital radii. The second law would simply state that the planets move with constant speed along their orbits. The orbital speed itself is a function of distance from the sun, in the sense that it is the slower the greater the distance of a planet from the sun. It varies from about 50 km/sec in the case of Mercury to about 5 km/sec for Pluto, with the earth's mean orbital speed being about 30 km/sec.

The study of gravitational interactions among celestial bodies is called **celestial mechanics**; it has long since moved to problems much more complex than simple planetary motion in the framework of the two-body approximation. For instance, a typical problem of current interest is the analysis of perturbations of the earth's motion about the sun due to the other planets. Others are the exact motion of the moon and the satellites of other planets, and the time behavior of star clusters and the distribution of matter in the galaxy (Section 17.2). In recent years, the prediction of the motion of artificial satellites and space probes has become a major concern of celestial mechanicians and, at the same time, one of their great triumphs.

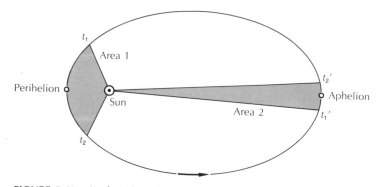

FIGURE 5-12. Kepler's law of equal areas: the two shaded areas are equal, so the speed of the planet is greater near perihelion because it must sweep out a larger arc of the ellipse in the time $t_2 - t_1$ compared to the equal time $t_2' - t_1'$.

Doppler Effect

The energy or wavelength of a photon, as detected by an observer, changes if there is a motion of the source with respect to the observer. This is the *Doppler effect.* Suppose three observers watch the same source; suppose further that the first observer is at rest with respect to the source, the second is moving toward the source, and the third is moving away from the source. Then the energy of the impinging photons appear greater to the second observer (he sees a *blueshift*) than to the first, and lower to the third observer (who detects a *redshift*).

To describe this change in energy or wavelength in quantitative terms, we write E_0 and λ_0 for the energy and wavelength of the photons as measured with source and observer at rest, and E and λ for the corresponding quantities measured by a moving observer. Then we have $E_0 > E$ or $\lambda_0 < \lambda$, that is, a redshift, if the motion of source and observer is away from each other; but we have $E_0 < E$ or $\lambda_0 > \lambda$, that is, a blueshift, if the motion of source and observer is toward each other. The absolute value of each difference is related to the absolute value of the relative velocity v by the formula

$$\frac{|E - E_0|}{E_0} = \frac{|\lambda - \lambda_0|}{\lambda_0} = \frac{|v|}{c}$$

where c is the speed of light and v is much smaller than c.

The Doppler effect is not limited to light. It is, for example, the reason for the increase in pitch of an automobile horn experienced when observer and horn are approaching each other at high speed.

Since a velocity is a *vector* quantity, it is completely determined only when we know both its numerical *absolute value* (say, in kilometers per second) and its *direction* of motion. These can be specified by recording its components v_r along the *line of sight*, that is, the line that connects the moving body with the observer, and v_p at right angle to the line of sight. The velocity v in the formula for the Doppler effect is actually the line-of-sight component; thus, if we use the Doppler effect to determine velocity, we obtain v_r, but not v_p.

5.3 THE INNER PLANETS

We turn now to the properties of the individual planets, discussing first Mercury, Venus, and Mars, which, with Earth, we categorize as the **inner planets** because of their positions with respect to the sun. We shall then discuss Jupiter, Uranus, and Neptune. Together with Pluto, which is something of a special case, they form the **outer planets**.

The solid bodies of the inner planets are more or less similar. There are, of course, minor differences in size, chemical composition, and the like; but they agree in one main aspect: their surfaces are all made up of **rocky material**.

Mercury. Mercury is closest to the sun and thus receives more solar energy per unit surface area than any other planet. It is the smallest of the major planets, just a bit bigger than our moon. Its diameter has been determined by the method outlined in Section 4.1 and is about 4,900 km. Mercury's surface structure seems to be very similar to that of the moon; it has, for example, mountain formations which cause small fluctuations in its albedo while it slowly rotates about its axis. There is no noticeable atmosphere, and while the sunlit hemisphere is scorched by solar heat, its dark side is cooled by radiation of the heat energy stored during the long "day." The temperature of the dark side, determined by measuring its level of radiation in the radio range, is of the order of 100° to 200° on the Kelvin scale (about −250°F). This temperature was somewhat of a surprise when first measured, since it turned out to be higher than was expected under the then current view that Mercury's revolution and rotation period are equal.

Measurement of Mercury's Rotation by Radar Reflection. The rotation of Mercury and Venus is measured by use of the Doppler effect; the method is outlined in Fig. 5-13. In practice, a radar signal (rather than visible light) is sent from earth to the planet, from which it bounces back to earth. Since the planet is rotating, one side is moving toward the earth, and the opposite side is moving away. Light reflected toward the earth from the edge of the planet moving toward us is blueshifted, whereas light reflected from the opposite edge is redshifted. The amount of blueshift or redshift is given by the formula

$$\frac{\text{Shift in wavelength}}{\text{Original wavelength}} = \frac{v}{c}$$

where v is the velocity of the reflecting surface with respect to us, and c is the speed of light. The "original wavelength" of the formula refers to a hypothetical measurement on the planet whose rotation is being measured; it has already been Doppler-shifted with respect to the source on earth. Thus, the signal received back on earth has actually been wavelength-shifted twice with respect to the signal originally transmitted.

Measuring the Doppler shift yields v, the rotational velocity of a point on the subject planet's equator. Such a point travels a distance of $2\pi r$ km (the planet's circumference) in one rotation. Its period of rotation is then the ratio of the planet's circumference to its rotational velocity, or $2\pi r/v$. For Mercury, the rotation period is 60 days, two-thirds of its (sidereal) revolution period of close to 90 days.

Mercury thus presents all of its surface to the sun during a revolution, and what we measure as the night-side temperature is mostly heat stored during the long hot "days." We noted, in the case of the moon, that equality of the rotation and revolution periods is a stable configuration, but this is true only for circular orbits. Where

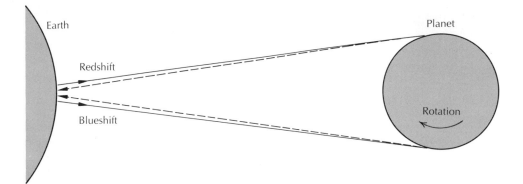

FIGURE 5-13.   Determination of planetary rotation by radar reflection. Photons reflected from the edge of the planet that is moving toward us are blueshifted; photons from the opposite edge (the one moving away from us) are redshifted. The amount of shift is a measure of the rotational velocity.

the orbit is rather eccentric, as is that of Mercury, the observed ratio of rotation and revolution periods (2:3) represents an equally stable system.

Venus.   Venus, very similar to the earth in size, had for a long time been thought of as a possible place where extraterrestrial life might flourish. However, by measuring the radio-frequency radiation given off by its surface during Venus night, its **surface temperature** was found to be about 400°C. This is close to the melting point of lead, and too high to support life as we know it.

The **chemical composition** of Venus' atmosphere has been measured recently via capsules parachuted onto the planet from Russian space probes. It is now clear that some 95% or so of the atmosphere is CO_2, with traces of other gases, such as oxygen, but very little, if any, water vapor, and it is quite obvious that the density of the atmosphere close to the surface is many times the density of our own atmosphere, although the exact value is unknown. The **pressure** at the surface should be in the neighborhood of 100 times the terrestrial value. By measuring radar reflections we have determined that there are mountain ranges on Venus, and in the superhot plains between these ranges we must expect winds of extremely high velocities, probably driving huge dust clouds over the barren land. Again, the atmosphere would seem to militate against life as we know it.

Telescopic studies, which have been confirmed by the Mariner flybys, reveal that Venus is covered at some altitude with a thick **cloud layer** impenetrable to visible light. Whether there are any permanent or temporary holes in this cloud layer is at present an open question. Even more fascinating is the fact that to date the composition of the clouds, as well as the mechanism that maintains them, are unknown. Suggestions range from frozen CO_2 and ice crystals to metal oxides and dust. It is clear, however, that the high surface temperature is at least in part due to the thick cloud layer, which prevents rapid cooling of the surface by radiation in the same manner as does the painted glass of a terrestrial greenhouse (the **greenhouse effect**).

Another peculiarity of Venus is its **rotation**. All early attempts to measure the rotational period using the Doppler principle in the visible spectral range, that is, with reflected sunlight, failed, for no value above a few meters per second could be ascertained. The possibility of a very small rotational velocity could not be excluded, of course, but it would have resulted in Doppler shifts too small to measure using visible light. Only with the perfection of the technique of radar reflection, which allows measurement of much smaller velocities, was the rotational period found. It is about 250 earth days, as compared to a sidereal *revolution period* of 225 days, but the interesting (and to date unexplained) fact is that the **direction of rotation** is opposite that of the sun and all other planets (except Uranus, whose rotational behavior is quite anomalous in other ways). Thus, on Venus the sun would move very slowly across the sky from west to east, if it could be seen through the clouds.

Finally, we mention that Venus appears to have only a very weak *magnetic field*, quite in contrast to that of the earth. Of course, an ionosphere has formed at levels where solar ultraviolet photons are absorbed by the major constituents of the Venus atmosphere.

Figure 5-14 shows a telescopic photo of Venus.

Mars. Mars is somewhere between Mercury and Earth in size, but because the mean density of Mars is less than the density of Mercury, their surface gravities turn

FIGURE 5-14. Telescopic view of Venus in the crescent phase, photographed with the 200-inch telescope. (*Hale Observatories.*)

out to be just about the same. Mars' *rotation period* is about the same as the earth's (and so is the orientation of its axis in its orbit), but its *revolution period* is about 2 earth years.

The Mars atmosphere is much thinner than the Earth atmosphere. Its exact composition is still not known, but it consists mostly of CO_2, as does the Venus atmosphere. The low mean temperature, together with the very **small density**, make it likely that during Martian night a significant fraction of this CO_2 gas simply freezes out and falls to the surface as "snow." In order to maintain an equal atmospheric pressure on day and night sides, gaseous CO_2 then rushes onto the night side, and we expect, again as in the case of Venus but for different reasons, storms of huge velocities.

Ever since large telescopes were available to resolve the Martian surface — apparently there are seldom any clouds — the quite varied features have intrigued astronomers and laymen alike. Figure 5-15 shows two overall views, one taken in red, the other in blue light. Visible are the **polar caps**, which appear to be a mixture of frozen water and frozen CO_2. Measurements made from the Mariner space probes yield a temperature of some $-60°C$, that is, close to the freezing point of CO_2. The polar caps follow the Martian seasons and are most prominent in winter; they almost disappear in Martian summer. As in the case of the earth, we distinguish an **equatorial belt**, which is of a yellowish-brown color and is agitated by storms that occasionally lift huge dust clouds into the thin CO_2 atmosphere, and the **temperate regions** between the equatorial and polar areas.

Details of the Martian surface were first recorded by Mariner 6. Figure 5-16, taken from a height of 3,500 km above the surface, shows a portion about 1,000 km across, in an area at latitude about 16°S. Most noticeable is the vast number of large and small **craters**, which make this particular portion of the Martian surface similar to the lunar surface. However, the results of the Mariner 9 mission show that Mars

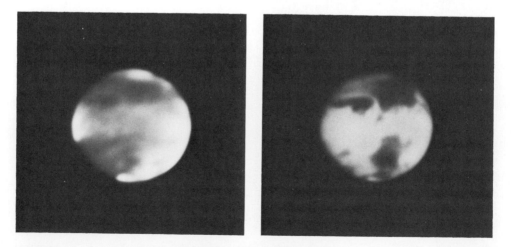

FIGURE 5-15. **Two telescopic views of Mars, taken with the 200-inch telescope in blue light (left) and red light (right). Note the polar caps at top and bottom of the left-hand picture, and the stark contrast in surface shading in the picture on the right.** (*Hale Observatories.*)

has a structure all its own, and only some portions—the older ones—can be compared to lunar structures. Of particular importance is evidence that points to a significant influence of **water** in shaping Martian surface features, even if not all of the recently detected "canyons" and "arroyos" are ultimately blamed on the action of flowing water. Figure 5-17 shows a sinuous valley amidst crater formations at 29°S latitude. Figure 5-18 is a picture of the now-famous **Giant Canyon**, a depression three times deeper than our own Grand Canyon, and ten times as long. Near the south polar cap, stair-step **terraces** have been found whose details lead to the speculation that they were formed by glaciers. Another exciting find was the existence of **volcanoes**. Finally, fields of **sand dunes** have been seen in several areas, of which Fig. 5-19 shows an example.

Is there life on Mars? We cannot decide either way at this time. The photographs sent back to earth by Mariner 9 are still too crude, and further detailed studies must be made. In principle, however, nothing has yet been seen that would exclude life, now or in the past.

Mars has two moons, which will be discussed in Section 5.5.

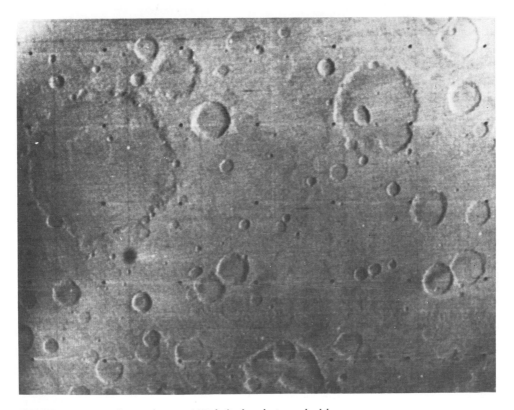

FIGURE 5-16. Martian surface at 16°S latitude, photographed by Mariner 6 from a height of about 3,500 km. Over 100 craters are visible; the large crater on the left is about 250 km in diameter. The small, regularly spaced black dots are reference points within the TV system. (*NASA.*)

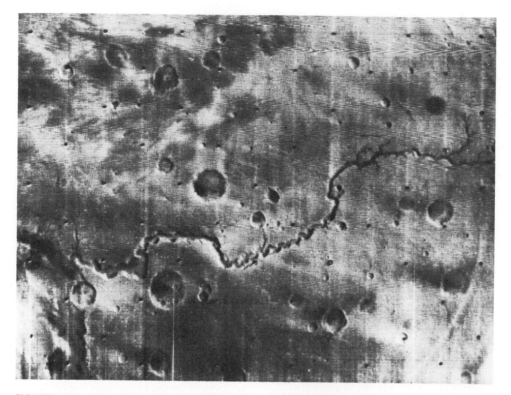

**FIGURE 5-17. Crater formations and sinuous valley at 29°S latitude
on the Martian surface. The valley — about 400 km long and 5 km
wide — resembles a giant "arroyo," but was probably not formed by
flowing water. Note the branching tributaries. Mariner 9 photograph
from a height of about 1,700 km. (*NASA*.)**

5.4 THE OUTER PLANETS

The outer planets are Jupiter, Saturn, Uranus, Neptune, and the ninth planet, Pluto,
which differs in all respects from the rest of this group. Whereas the inner planets are
relatively small (all about earth size), dense (composed mostly of rocky material),
and slowly rotating, the outer planets are large and of low density, and rotate
rapidly. Thus, in terms of physical constitution, there is a clear separation into two
groups which somehow must have had to do with the formation of the solar system.

Jupiter. Jupiter is the largest of the planets; its mass is about 318 times that of the
earth, or just about one-thousandth of the solar mass; as we shall see later, this is
within a factor of 5 or 10 of the masses of very small bona fide stars. However, it is
generally agreed that Jupiter never had any (nuclear) energy source; its energy is
derived from absorption of solar radiation and possibly a small contribution from
an internal heat reservoir — a situation thoroughly similar to that of the earth.

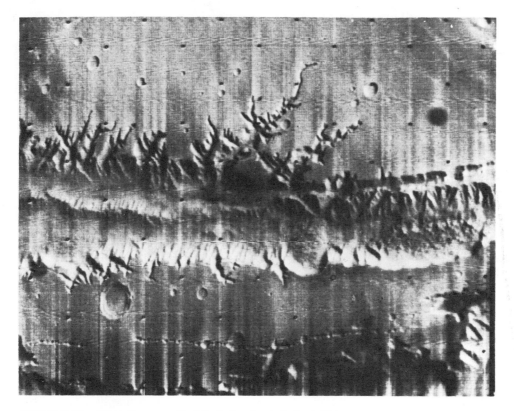

FIGURE 5-18. Giant Canyon with tributaries, located about 500 km south of the Martian equator. The photograph, taken by Mariner 9 from a height of about 2,000 km, covers an area of 379 by 480 km. (*NASA*.)

Jupiter's *radius* is about 10 times the earth's, and its *mean density* is 1.3, or just above that of water. Its *rotation period* is less than 10 hours, and the planet takes more than 10 earth years to complete a *revolution* about the sun.

On Jupiter, there is no sharp transition between the solid body and the gaseous envelope, as there is on the earth. The "surface" of the planet may be defined by the layer at which the gases of the atmosphere liquefy or freeze, owing to the high pressure and low temperature (below the freezing point of CO_2). The **constituents** of the atmosphere are mostly hydrogen compounds (water, ammonia, methane, etc.) and helium, and we suspect that Jupiter represents very much the element mixture of the sun and the primordial stage of the planets.

Jupiter's atmosphere is stratified, as can be seen from telescopic pictures; the distinct bands show up in Fig. 5-20, a reproduction of a telescopic view of Jupiter. Note also the so-called "Red Spot," whose origin at present is not quite clear, but which may signal an irregularity in the atmospheric circulation pattern above some internal obstacle. The relatively high rotation speed, together with the physical

FIGURE 5-19.   Mariner 9 photograph showing dune field of loose material on the floor of a great Martian crater, probably formed by strong winds blowing from a constant direction; the individual dunes are about 1.5 km apart. (*NASA.*)

and chemical constitution, have made the planet markedly **oblate**, that is, the polar radius is quite a bit smaller than the equatorial, much more so than is the case with the earth.

One most interesting feature of Jupiter is its **radio emission**, due to relativistic electrons (that is, electrons of very high kinetic energy) trapped into radiation belts in the planet's **magnetic field**. In addition, there are peculiar **bursts** of radio emission of short duration and within a very narrow wavelength range. The exact mechanism by which the radiation is produced is not completely understood at this time; however, it has been shown that the occurrence of the bursts is related to the motion of one of the planet's largest satellites, **Io**, through the vastly extended **ionosphere** of the planet. More recently it was found that another of Jupiter's satellites, **Callisto**, may even be a radio emitter itself, although the radiation mechanism in this case is even more of a mystery.

Saturn, Uranus, Neptune.   Saturn, Uranus, and Neptune are very much alike in their physical constitution, except that their surface temperatures become lower with increasing distance from the sun. Saturn has a *radius* of almost 10 earth radii, whereas Uranus and Neptune are only about three times as large as the earth. Their *mean densities* are in the neighborhood of that of water while their *rotation periods* are all shorter than the earth's. The sidereal *revolution periods* of Saturn, Uranus, and Neptune are approximately 30, 85, and 165 years, respectively.

Peculiar to Saturn is its **ring**, a collection of microscopic dust particles and ice

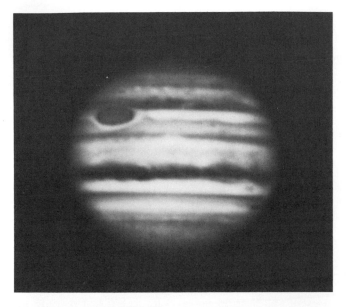

FIGURE 5-20. Telescopic view of Jupiter (200-inch telescope). Note the light and dark bands that exhibit the stratification of the atmosphere, and the great Red Spot. (*Hale Observatories.*)

crystals which have settled in the equatorial plane of the planet. Figure 5-21 shows the planet and its ring as they appear when viewed at an angle to the equatorial plane. Saturn's ring is a most beautiful sight, even when observed with only a very small telescope.

Uranus is outstanding in that its rotational axis lies within a few degrees of its orbital plane. The consequences, in terms of the properties of day and night and the seasons, are remarkable. Suppose, for simplicity, that the rotational axis were *exactly* in the orbital plane. Then, at the north pole, the sun would stand still at the zenith point at summer solstice. At the equinox it would disappear below the horizon for half a Uranus year. At the equator, on the other hand, the sun would stand still on the horizon at the solstices (in the north at summer solstice, in the south at winter solstice); at the equinoxes the sun would cross the sky in a great circle through the zenith. The actual situation on Uranus is close enough to this so that every part of the planet experiences the midnight sun.

Pluto. Pluto, the latest addition to the list of known major planets, is very different from its neighbors in that it is quite small (probably smaller than earth), and its orbit is both eccentric and markedly inclined (at 17°) to the ecliptic. It is difficult to understand how such an "outsider" could have been formed at the edge of the solar system. Possibly, Pluto was once a satellite of, say, Neptune, and by some unknown perturbation was pulled away from its planet and into an independent orbit about the sun.

FIGURE 5-21. Telescopic picture of Saturn with its ring system, photographed with the 100-inch telescope. Our view is at an angle to the equatorial plane, outlined by the rings. Note the stratification of the atmosphere. (*Hale Observatories.*)

Collected in Table H-4 are the more important data on the physical nature and orbits of the planets: radius and mass, rotation period, semimajor axis, eccentricity and inclination of the orbit, and the revolution period about the sun.

5.5 PLANETARY SATELLITES

We have already seen that the earth owns the largest satellite relative to its own size. Mercury and Venus do not have any satellites. Mars has two, **Phobos** and **Deimos**, which are remarkable because of their extremely small size (of the order of 10 km in diameter), high reflectivity, and orbits close to the surface. The lower one, Phobos, is less than 3000 km from the Martian surface. In addition, Phobos revolves with a period shorter than the planet's rotation period, so that it rises in the west and sets in the east more than once per Martian day-night cycle. Photographs radioed back by Mariner 9 show both Phobos and Deimos to be pieces of rock of irregular shape, covered with craters caused by meteoritic impact. Figure 5-22 shows a Mariner 9 picture of Phobos.

The outer planets, again excepting Pluto, each have several satellites. Jupiter has 12, Saturn 10, Uranus 5, and Neptune 2 according to the most recent count; some of them have been discovered only in the last few years. A number of satellites,

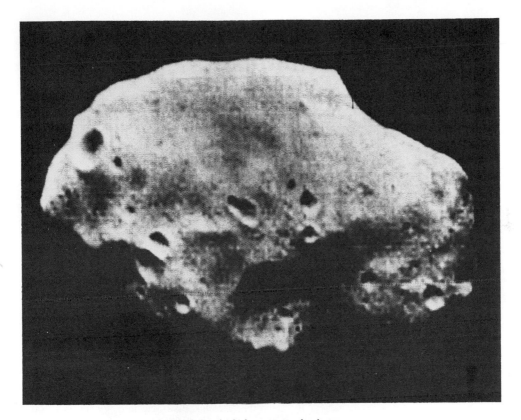

FIGURE 5-22. Mariner 9 photograph of Phobos. Note the large number of craters and the irregular shape, in particular, at the upper right, where an asteroid may have impacted on the body of Phobos. The terminator marks the lower edge of the picture. (*NASA.*)

for instance, the four largest moons of Jupiter (**Io**, **Europa**, **Ganymede**, and **Callisto**) and Saturn's satellite **Titan**, are approximately as large as Mercury. Thus, there seems to be a continuous transition of physical properties from the smaller planets proper to the satellites of the largest planets. Indeed, Titan is known to have an atmosphere.

The motions of the four largest moons of Jupiter about their parent plant are fascinating to watch with a small telescope or even a good field glass. Figure 5-23 shows a typical series of positions during a 12-hour period. Since Io completes a revolution in less than 2 earth days, and Europa in less than 4, their position changes can be noted and followed in a single night. The motions of Ganymede and Callisto, on the other hand, can easily be tracked during a week; a typical sequence of positions is shown in Fig. 5-24. The relative distances and Jupiter's radius are to scale, but the inclinations of the satellite orbits have been neglected, so that in reality the satellites will not appear lined up as they do in the figures.

A complete list of the presently known satellites of planets, along with some of the more important data on the satellites, is given in Table H-5.

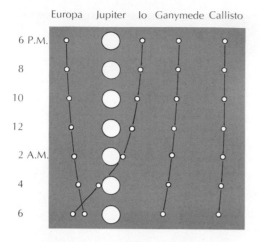

Europa   Jupiter   Io   Ganymede   Callisto

6 P.M.
8
10
12
2 A.M.
4
6

FIGURE 5-23. Typical changes in the positions of the four largest satellites of Jupiter during one night; the large circle represents Jupiter. (*The American Ephemeris and Nautical Almanac, U.S. Government Printing Office.*)

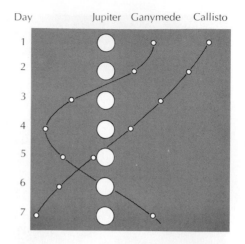

Day   Jupiter   Ganymede   Callisto

1
2
3
4
5
6
7

FIGURE 5-24. Typical changes in the positions of Ganymede and Callisto during one week; the large circle represents Jupiter. (*The American Ephemeris and Nautical Almanac, U.S. Government Printing Office.*)

QUESTIONS FOR DISCUSSION

1. Why would it be so difficult to search for another major planet beyond Pluto's orbit?

2. Somebody saw a bright object in the constellation Cassiopeia and speculated that it might simply have been the planet Venus. Would you agree? Why?

3. Why are different stars drawn in each of the parts of Fig. 5-3?

4. Why is the line connecting the sun and the planet in Fig. 5-3 drawn at different azimuths?

5. The farther away a superior planet is from the earth, the closer is its synodic period to the earth year. Why?

6. Which law is more basic, Newton's or Kepler's? Why?

7. Two bodies have the same perihelion distance; one is on an elliptic orbit, the other on a hyperbolic orbit. What do you deduce immediately as to the relative orbital speed at perihelion of the two bodies?

8. Contrast the main physical properties of the inner and the outer planets: size, rotation, chemical composition, surface structures, density.

9. When it first became probable that the temperature of the back of Mercury was higher than would be expected on the basis of equality of rotational and revolutionary periods and absence of an atmosphere, a reason different from the (correct) one given in the text was considered. What alternative do you think astronomers might have discussed, and why?

10. There are a large number of craters on the surface of Mars. Would you expect the same feature on Venus? Explain.

11. The polar caps of Mars recede very rapidly during Martian spring. From this observation it was argued that they, at least, cannot be thick layers of ice. Why?

12. Decide on the basis of simple geometric considerations how the ring of Saturn would look to an observer on the Saturnian equator at midnight.

13. How does Pluto differ from the other outer planets?

14. People who have argued (in earnest and otherwise) that Phobos and Deimos are deserted spacecraft produced by some unknown civilization have based their speculation on the decidedly unusual properties of the two Martian satellites. Name the relevant ones.

15. Look at the diagram for 6 P.M. in Fig. 5-23. One aspect of the relative positions of Jupiter and its satellites is not quite correct. Which one? What is the reason?

EXERCISES

1. If there is another major planet beyond Pluto, it may possibly be found in another 100 years or so. Why?

2. Which planets are called inferior planets? Which are called superior planets? Why?

3. Mercury's orbit is inclined by 7° with respect to the earth's orbit about the sun. What is the range of possible declinations of Mercury if its right ascension is 6^h0^m?

4. Why may the maximum elongation of Mercury be as much as 28°, rather than 23° as would follow from Fig. 5-1, in spite of the fact that the size of the planetary orbits is drawn to scale?

5. (See Exercise 4.) The angle drawn in Fig. 5-1 for the maximum elongation of Venus is about 47°. Why is that the correct figure?

6. Can you observe Mercury exactly at inferior conjunction?

7. If Venus is the morning star, is it west or east of the sun?

8. Which planets show distinct phases? Why don't the others show phases?

9. Using the orbital data for the planet, verify that the angular diameter of Mercury varies by a factor of about 2 between crescent and gibbous phases.

10. Does Fig. 5-3 refer to a place on the northern or southern hemisphere of the earth? Where is north in the pictures? For approximately what latitude are the pictures drawn?

11. From the dates given in the text for the conjunction and greatest elongations of Venus, construct a sequence of pictures similar to Fig. 5-3 for Venus as evening star.

12. Which is longer, the synodic or the sidereal period of Venus? Why?

13. Determine from the data given in the text when you will have a good chance to observe Venus as evening star and as morning star in 1977.

14. Do the superior planets show a crescent phase? Explain.

15. Approximately how many degrees does Pluto move across the star field in a year?

16. Which body of the solar system should be the major source of perturbations to the earth-moon system? Argue on the basis of Newton's law.

17. (See Exercise 16.) Now consider the system consisting of the sun on one hand, the earth and the moon on the other. Which body of the solar system is the major source of perturbations to the sun-earth-moon system?

18. What would be your weight on Mercury? Venus? Mars? Jupiter? Use the data of Table H-4 and Newton's law.

19. What is the geometric form of the orbit of a body gravitationally bound to another?

20. What determines the form of an ellipse? How do changes in its value affect the form?

21. Figure 5-11 shows the position of the barycenter of two bodies. Where would the barycenter be if the mass of one of the bodies were practically negligible?

22. If the earth's orbit about the sun were *exactly* circular, would there be a difference between true and mean solar time?

23. Check the value of the orbital speed of Mercury with the aid of the data given in Table H-4.

24. Calculate the rotational velocity of the equator of Venus and the corresponding Doppler shift (in angstrom units) for a spectral line at 5000 Å. Such a Doppler shift, as was stated in the text, is too small to observe.

25. Would you expect strong radiation belts around Venus? Why?

26. What is the cause of the marked oblateness of Jupiter, that is, the fact that the polar diameter is significantly smaller than the equatorial diameter?

27. Why is it that we sometimes see Saturn's ring at an angle, and sometimes almost edge-on?

28. Assume, as we did in the text for illustration, that the rotational axis of Uranus is *exactly* in its orbital plane. What is then the apparent path of the sun at summer solstice at a latitude of 45°N?

29. Actually, Uranus' rotational axis is inclined with respect to its orbital plane by an amount which is believed to be close to 8°. What consequence does this have for the apparent path of the sun to an observer standing on Uranus' north pole?

30. Why does Phobos appear to rise in the west and set in the east, as seen by an observer on the Martian surface?

31. Which were the first planetary satellites observed by man?

EXPERIMENTS

1. Try to find Venus as soon after sunset as possible. With a field glass you can see the planet against a still quite bright sky. Make several observations during the course of a few weeks, each time determining its position with respect to neighboring stars. Plot its apparent path on one of the star charts (Appendix G).

2. Repeat Experiment 1 for Mars or Jupiter and compare the results. What can you learn from this about the orbital motions of these planets?

3. Observe the moons of Jupiter with a good field glass and plot the change in relative positions over a period of a few hours. Repeat the procedure several nights in a row and compare the results with Figs. 5-23 and 5-24.

4. Compare the brightness and color impressions of Venus, Mars, Jupiter, and Saturn. In what ways are they similar? In what ways do they differ?

FURTHER READING

Neighbors of the Earth, edited by T. Page and L. W. Page, New York: The Macmillan Company, 1965.

Sandner, W., *Satellites of the Solar System*, New York: American Elsevier Publishing Company, Inc., 1965.

Abetti, G., *Stars and Planets* (second ed.), New York: American Elsevier Publishing Company, Inc., 1966.

6 the solar system: minor members and history

Before discussing the sun, the center of our solar system and the source of all its energy, we should survey some of its minor members, notably, the minor planets and the comets. In at least one theory, they represent what was "left over" after the sun and the principal planets were formed and had settled into their present patterns. In a sense, we may call them the construction debris of our solar system. This survey will complete our discussion of the population and dimension of the territory staked out by the gravitational field of our sun. Then in the last two sections of this chapter we shall touch briefly on the question of how the solar system came about and the possibility of life outside our planet.

6.1 METEOROIDS

As it travels in its path about the sun, the earth scoops up condensed grains of matter which we summarily call *interplanetary dust*. They range from microscopic particles to veritable chunks of matter; the latter are the **meteoroids**. Upon entering the terrestrial atmosphere, meteoroids collide with atoms and molecules. In the process, they convert their kinetic energy into ionization and excitation energy which is transferred to the air particles, and into heat which remains with the meteoroids themselves. Thus, a particle speeding toward the earth leaves a wake of ionized air molecules which then radiate the energy acquired during the collisions; the effect we see is a "shooting star" or **meteor**. The heating of the meteoroid body almost always leads to complete evaporation, and only a very few meteors ever reach the ground.

Meteorites.   Occasionally, the initial mass of a meteoroid is so large that some part of it survives the trip through the atmosphere and impacts on the surface; it is then called a **meteorite**. In most cases, the part that survives is only a small fraction of the original. Nevertheless, over the centuries enough of this material has been collected to give us a good idea of its chemical composition. Meteorites fall into two main classes: one corresponds closely to rocks (mostly silicates); the other consists of iron alloys with a peculiar crystal pattern. Age determinations by radioactive dating show meteorites typically to be as old as the earth and the sun.

Craters.   Only seldom is a meteorite large enough, when it falls onto the earth's surface, to form a significant crater. The best-known crater, and certainly one caused by a meteorite (because meteoritic material was actually found on the spot), is in Arizona. It is more than 1 km in diameter, is 200 m deep, and has a high rim, similar to many lunar craters. (See Fig. 6-1.) Many more suspected craters exist, suffering from varying degrees of erosion, but all of them taken together cover only a minute fraction of the earth's surface. Compared to what has been observed on the moon and Mars, our earth is very free of pockmarks. It may be that some craters formed here long ago have been smoothed over by the action of wind and water, whereas neither of these is present to efface craters on the moon, and on Mars erosion is at best inefficient. However, the main reason for the paucity of craters on the earth is our protective atmosphere, which prevents most meteoroids from reaching the ground in the first place.

Meteor Showers. At certain times during the year, so-called **meteor showers** occur; that is, a vastly increased number of shooting stars can be observed. At those times the paths of the particles seem to converge to a point on the celestial sphere, called a **radiant**, whereas the normally observed sporadic events show an essentially random distribution of paths. Among the better-known showers are the Perseid shower visible around August 12 (so named because the radiant is located in the constellation Perseus), and the Leonid shower around November 17 (with radiant in the constellation Leo). Aside from these periodic showers, the earth occasionally encounters an unexpected one. The origin of meteor showers is discussed in Section 6.3.

FIGURE 6-1. Aerial photograph of the great meteor crater near Winslow, Arizona. (*Yerkes Observatory.*)

6.2   ASTEROIDS

We have seen that the solar system contains, on the one hand, larger bodies that range from almost stellar mass, such as Jupiter, down to planetary satellites with diameters in the kilometer range. On the other hand there are the meteoroids, whose diameters vary from the microscopic to some 10 m or so. Between the two classes is a third one, made up of the **minor planets** or **asteroids**. Although the majority of these are concentrated near the ecliptic, and they revolve about the sun in the same sense as the principal planets, they can have almost any orbital ellipticity and inclination to the ecliptic. Thus, they differ from the major planets in both size and orbital characteristics. Their distance from the sun is in most cases about 3 A.U., which places them between Mars and Jupiter.

The largest asteroid and the first one to be discovered (in 1801) is **Ceres** with a diameter of about 800 km and an almost circular orbit halfway between Mars and Jupiter. Thousands of asteroids are known, most of them small and probably just pieces of rock, and one is tempted to relate the asteroids to a hypothetical planet that seems to be missing between Mars and Jupiter. However, they do not seem to be the remnants of a primordial planet, since their total mass is only a small fraction of the mass of an earth-type planet; besides, it is difficult to imagine how an originally solid planetary body could suddenly break up. It is more likely that, during the formation of the solar system, a break or instability occurred between the subcloud from which the inner small planets condensed, and the more distant portion of the cloud which gave rise to Jupiter and the other large planets, and that this instability was responsible for the asteroids. But even this hypothesis is far from generally accepted.

During their history, the asteroids have probably undergone countless mutual collisions and thereby continued the fragmentation process. In addition, they are constantly being perturbed by the gravitational fields of the nearest large planets, namely, Jupiter and Saturn. Indeed, detailed study of their orbits shows **families** of asteroids whose motions are related to these planets. Data on some of the better-known asteroids are collected in Table H-6.

6.3   COMETS

It is commonly believed that remnants of the cloud from which the sun was formed, and additional chunks of matter captured since, fill the neighborhood of the sun and are gravitationally held by it. The boundary of this neighborhood is approximately a sphere around our sun where its gravitational attraction is stronger than the attraction of neighboring stars. That is, if we moved away from the sun in any given direction, the gravitational pull of the sun would decrease until at some point it would be less than the pull from some other star; that point would be on the hypothetical sphere. If we repeated this for a number of directions, we would be able to determine the size of the boundary. In this sense, the boundary of the solar system is, on the average, some 10^{17} cm or 10^4 A.U. away. The comets are within that distance from the sun, and they can therefore be considered as members of our solar system.

These way-out members of the solar system move in elliptical orbits in this vast space and rarely come anywhere as near to the sun as the planets. One can argue, however, that when a comet is very close to the outer boundary of the sphere of solar gravitational influence, a neighboring star might just attract it enough to decrease the comet's orbital speed almost to 0. Then, the comet would start falling toward the sun with increasing speed and, after a trip of several hundred thousand years, it would arrive somewhere near the major planets. The comet would speed around the sun through what would become the perihelion of its highly elongated orbit, and then disappear again toward the boundary of the system.

Periodic Comets. If this were the whole situation, we would never see a comet twice, and indeed there are some comets that seem to follow such a motion pattern. However, in moving through the solar system, a comet may be deflected gravitationally by one of the large outer planets and be forced into a new orbit whose aphelion lies much closer to the sun. The result is a periodic comet such as **Halley's comet**, seen last in 1910 and due again in 1986.

Composition. When a comet is close to the sun, solar radiation heats it to the point where it can evaporate. The atoms and molecules freed by evaporation may be excited or ionized, thus allowing their identification through spectral analysis, the study of the specific types of photons emitted. From such analyses we know that cometary material typically consists of broken-up molecules (free radicals) such as CH, CN, and NH_2. This chemical composition is just what we would expect on the basis of our knowledge of interstellar material.

The Structure of a Comet. The most spectacular feature of a comet as observed from the earth is its **tail**, a stream of particles ("dust" grains, molecules, and atoms) pushed out from the comet's **head**, or main body when it is heated up by solar radiation near its perihelion. The tail particles collide with atoms and ions emitted radially by the sun (the "solar wind") and with photons of sunlight whose energy and momentum give them some of the properties of material particles. In each such collision, the tail particles are given a push radially away from the sun, so that the tail always points away from the sun (Fig. 6-2). Figures 6-3 and 6-4 show two of the more spectacular comets of recent years: comet Ikeya-Seki, 1965, and a sequence of photographs of comet Mrkos taken between 22 and 27 August 1957. Note the time variations in the fine structure of the tail.

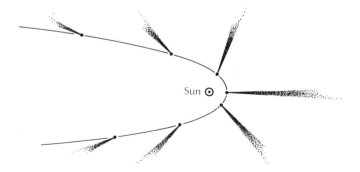

FIGURE 6-2. Positions of cometary tail near perihelion. The tail points radially away from the sun.

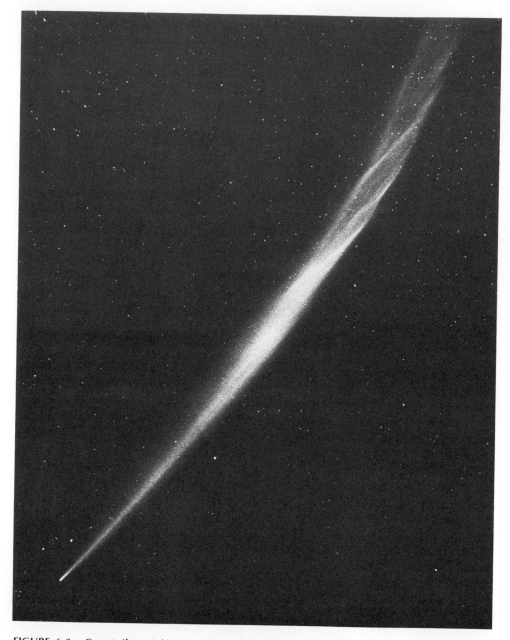

FIGURE 6-3. Comet Ikeya-Seki on October 29, 1965. Note the complex structure of the gases streaming from the head of the comet. (*Lick Observatory.*)

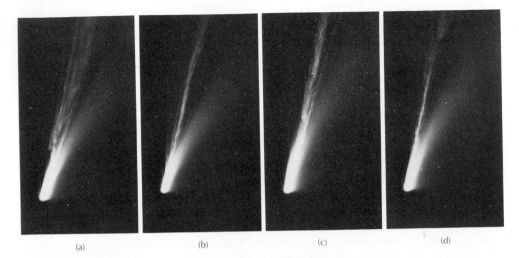

(a)   (b)   (c)   (d)

FIGURE 6-4. Comet Mrkos. Photograph taken with the 48-inch Schmidt telescope on (a) August 22, (b) August 24, (c) August 26, and (d) August 27, 1957. The changes in the tail structure are clearly visible. Note that, because of the daily motion of the comet, the star background changes completely from photograph to photograph. (*Hale Observatories.*)

Comets are brightest close to the sun; hence, they are most easily seen in the days before and after they pass through perihelion. This means that comets are best observed just after sunset in the western sky, and just before sunrise in the east. In either case, their tails point up at an angle defined by the observer's latitude and, of course, by the orbits.

Data on some well-known comets are collected in Table H-7.

Meteor Showers.   Since the head of a periodic comet loses a portion of its total mass each time the comet swings around the sun, it will last for only a number of passes. Eventually, most of the matter becomes scattered along the orbit; the head, getting smaller and smaller, finally breaks up. Whenever the earth crosses or even comes close to such an orbit, there is a vastly increased chance of encounters with meteoroids. This would explain the observation of meteor showers and their radiants, discussed earlier. In particular, some of the better-known showers correlate well with the orbits of comets that have broken up in recent centuries. In contrast, the more sporadic meteoritic events are probably just chance encounters with general debris in our solar neighborhood.

6.4   THE FORMATION OF THE SOLAR SYSTEM

We have a fairly good idea of how a star such as the sun is formed. We are less sure about the formation of the planets, and rather unsure about their satellites. The problem of star formation is, in a sense, simpler than the others since it involves better-known and probably less-complex physical processes. Details are always much harder to explain than broad general principles. Also, our ideas about star formation can be tested by observing a multitude of examples, whereas theories of planetary formation must rely for verification on the small and possibly not even representative sample provided by our own system. At the present level of astronomical technology, no planets outside our solar system are directly observable.

In brief, stars are thought to condense, under the influence of self-gravitation, out of the amorphous material that pervades space. In the process, two things happen. First, the star acquires rotation. At least part of the original cloud of material was likely to rotate very slowly. To conserve the angular momentum, the speed of rotation increases as the star condenses and contracts, becoming very fast by the time the star is formed. Anyone who has spun on skates with arms extended knows that he spins faster when he folds his arms back to his body; this is the same effect on a much smaller scale. Second, the star acquires a magnetic field, the beginnings of which must have been present also in the original material. In the condensation process the field is compressed along with the stellar matter. This originally un-ionized matter becomes ionized, and the electrons and atomic ions are then trapped in the magnetic field, a fact we have discussed with respect to the earth's radiation belts. From then on, the electrons and ions carry the magnetic field with them; as they contract toward the much smaller "final" size of the star, they compress the magnetic field as well.

Against this background, our best deduction is that planets are formed as sub-condensations of the main cloud of material from which the star was formed. It is commonly believed that the formation of planets is one of several processes by which some of the angular momentum of the original cloud is excluded from the protostar. The major planets of the solar system hold, in their orbital motions, all but some 3% of the total angular momentum of the solar system, the rest being vested in the slow rotation of the sun. But one may argue just as tellingly, although with fewer known details, that there is a tendency for a gas rotating along with a magnetic field to form blobs of the size and mass of our sun and planets. In that case, the formation of planets would have nothing to do with the angular momentum balance of the system.

At any rate, if the general picture is correct, and there is little doubt about that, then the formation of planets is a phenomenon that commonly accompanies the formation of a star. Consequently, one would expect a significant percentage of the existing solar-type stars to have planets.

For the reader who enjoys speculation, we offer the following: our sun has at least nine satellites, the major planets. Most of the planets have their own satellites, the moons. Since nothing in nature is unique, this satellite-to-a-satellite pattern might extend in both directions. That is, a moon may have its own satellites, and a sun could be a satellite of some other heavenly body.

6.5 LIFE IN THE UNIVERSE

Earlier, in discussing the earth, we mentioned in passing that one of the "unique features" of our planet is the existence of life. We shall now explore this "feature" in detail, against a more general background. The questions we shall attempt to answer are the following: first, is life on our planet really unique in the solar system? Second, to what degree can we consider our form of life as representative? And last—anticipating later sections of this text—what speculations can be made, on the basis of our knowledge of the solar system, about life in the universe at large?

Of course, as befits the astronomical view, we first must free ourselves from the tendency to marvel at our own greatness. There is no basis whatever for the a priori assumption that life is unique on our planet (or in the solar system, for that matter). The argument, if we can call it that, is quite simple. Every other known phenomenon in the universe occurs over and over again, billions and billions of times; it is therefore inconceivable that there is one and only one thing—the creation of life on our planet—that happened just once, in an incredible accident. This argument is more compelling than any other to an astronomer, and it is completely in line with the accepted view of the physical phenomena of our world. In a sense, it is nothing but a kind of "cosmological principle."

Life and Its Environment.   Now, in proceeding, we immediately encounter another problem: we are simply not able to define what we mean by "life" in any simple or straightforward manner. Fortunately, this is not crucial, and it is certainly excusable that we run into this difficulty; researchers in the life sciences seem to have much the same trouble, especially at the borderline between life and "nonlife." At any rate, the most basic life functions occur on the level of very complex molecules; it appears reasonable to assume that the more specialized life functions require increasingly more complex combinations of these basic units of matter. So probably more than anything else, complexity of construction is a sign of "life."

If we analyze life on our planet with the idea of extracting the most general conditions for sustenance, we must recognize several peculiarities. They all indicate that terrestrial life (and this is, after all, the only form we have been able to study) is confined to extremely narrow environmental limits. There is, first of all, a very limited range of temperatures that can be endured by life forms, from somewhere in the neighborhood of 50°C below the freezing point of water to about 60°C above it. While it is true that life can survive much lower and, on occasion, higher temperatures, its active range is about as given. Then there is the equally narrow range of chemical environments tolerated by most life forms, at least the highly developed ones. They are clearly restricted to the presence of free oxygen in the atmosphere and an ample supply (by astronomical standards) of water, combined with the availability of the solar radiation field as filtered through our atmosphere. Here, however, we must make note of the fact that for the most primitive bacteria such a rigidly specific chemical environment does not appear to be crucial. We will return to this important point presently.

Also, in a more general sense, we must realize that the life zone of our planet is a very thin shell at the surface of the solid body, including the oceans, and that all highly organized life forms make use of the particular properties of this shell. This includes, for instance, the use of gravity for moving about, feeding, etc. And it has not yet been shown that the more complex organisms such as mammals are able to forgo gravity for prolonged periods of time. On the other hand, the more primitive life forms are apparently not affected by a lack of gravitational force.

These then are some relevant aspects of life as we know it. The impression is that the very basic building blocks of living matter, the cells, do not really require such a carefully controlled environment, but the more complex, more specialized organisms have adapted to it.

The Solar System.   The next question is: under what conditions can life be supported in our solar system but outside the earth? Let us first consider present terrestrial forms. The main requirement is obviously the limited temperature range which, in principle, could at this time in the development of the sun and the planets be realized on Venus and Mars. Mercury, the only other possibility, is too close to the sun and thus too hot. But the surface of Venus, as we already saw, is also too hot, owing to several additive effects that tend to raise its temperature. Mars, on the other hand, is colder than we had thought for a long time; in addition, Mars has a very thin atmosphere, and its apparent lack of water makes it at present an unlikely home for higher life forms. On planets outside the orbit of Mars, temperatures are well below the level at which we think life can exist. Thus, our tentative first conclusion is that no life comparable to our own is found anywhere else in the solar system.

Has this been always the case? The answer is not necessarily yes. In the approximately 5×10^9 years our solar system has been in existence, many of the parameters that characterize planetary atmospheres and surfaces could have changed, and probably did. Hence, for instance, we think that the oxygen content of our own atmosphere is at least in part due precisely to the existence of life. Temperatures were different (usually hotter) in our early history, and it is quite conceivable that Mars at one time provided an environment close to what we have defined as that needed for the survival of earth-type life. As long as we have no definitive ideas about the time it takes to change initially inert matter into living matter, we cannot exclude the possibility of life on other planets in earlier days. But no real data are available to support a conclusion. The space probes that flew close to Mars, for instance, could have missed some manifestation of life, even on the scale of ours, let alone fossil evidence. Nor has any unambiguous evidence so far resulted from the study of meteorites and other cosmic debris.

In the same manner we must confess our inability to predict whether life may develop on some of the outer planets in the future. As we shall see in Section 12.5, it is expected that our sun will slowly expand, becoming more luminous and, at the same time, decreasing in its surface temperature but increasing that of the outer planets. This process is still billions of years in the future, but nevertheless it is conceivable that a planet such as Jupiter might get a ''second chance'' to develop life.

Other Systems.   If then, on balance, it is quite likely that at present our planet is the only one in the solar system to support life, the situation changes drastically when we turn to the planets of other stars. For it is almost certain that there are billions of planets elsewhere in the vast reaches of the universe, simply because, in a cosmological sense, the formation of planets appears to be a routine process. And by the very same reasoning, the development of life itself (whatever its definiton) from inert matter must be a common process. Until very recently, this statement would have sounded much more speculative than it does today. But recently radio astronomers have found, in interstellar space at positions of active star formation, traces of the chemical compounds that biologists consider necessary constituents of the first building blocks of life.

Other Forms.   Up to now we have based our arguments on what we know or think we know about earth-type life and on the probability of finding conditions similar to those prevalent during the early days of our planet. But there is no really good reason to assume that life processes, with suitably changed definitions, could not occur under very different circumstances. If reproduction or some form of growth is taken as a fundamental sign of ''life,'' then why could this not take place in interstellar space (where we already find the formation of quite complex molecules), free of the encumbrance of the gravitational field of a planetary surface? And why, we must ask, should all ''life'' (in its higher forms) be as attached to the concept of individuals as it is in our own and related species? Needless to say, this is an area of pure speculation; it will take science a long time just to compose the questions, so that we can attempt to find some answers.

If we are right in assuming that life is plentiful everywhere in the universe, then we also must conclude that ''intelligent'' life exists in abundance. Now, clearly, we are hard pressed to define what ''intelligent'' life means. To get around this difficulty we shall replace the somewhat suspect term with one which, in its connotations, may be even more suspect, but which is more open to an operational definition: life that manifests itself in terms of a technology, in terms of devices that are capable of, and intended to, alter its environment.

Interstellar Communication.   It is by no means clear that every life form will, in its development to higher organization, end up with a technological scheme, although it would appear strange for a highly developed life form to pursue knowledge simply for its own sake without technological by-products. At any rate, since technology has developed here, it must have done so elsewhere. The next step, then, is to speculate as to whether we could communicate with life that has developed in a fashion somewhat parallel to ours.

Since this would require a link with star systems so far away that their light would take decades or centuries to reach us, and since we are at present unable to decide what kinds of signals of our own to send, we have to concentrate on listening. But even this is dependent on our finding a civilization that, in its own progress, wants to announce its presence to the universe. Nevertheless, for a while radio telescopes were trained on the skies in the hope of picking up such stray messages.

No astronomer seriously believed that we would be successful right away, and we were not. The difficulties are formidable; for instance, we do not really know whether to scan the ultraviolet, visible, infrared, or radio spectrum or whether to concentrate on only part of one of these spectra. Then, for several reasons, an easily identifiable spectral line in the radio range became the primary candidate. Now we are not so sure, because we have found many more similar lines, and a simultaneous search on all wavelengths would be too expensive and time-consuming.

It is interesting to note that some people are doubtful about the whole idea of interstellar communication for another reason. They fear that technological civilizations may not last more than, say, 1,000 or 10,000 years, either because they destroy themselves in a nuclear holocaust for some utterly obscure reason, or simply because they poison themselves in their own pollution. These two alternatives are rather unnerving; somehow, it does not appear particularly sensible that self-destruction should be the inevitable end result of technological civilization. We could argue that this might be a uniquely human failing, but then we have maintained that what happens to us must occur many times in other places. And even if "reason" were to prevail, there is still one intrinsic and perhaps quite serious handicap built into the human race and other complex organisms on this planet: life is propagated by means of a chain of individuals who have little emotional and no physiological link with their forebears and progeny. Now, it is quite possible that our nearest partner in any interstellar communication is 50 or 100 light-years away so that, if we were able to send signals as well as to receive them, responses to our messages would come back to far-removed grandchildren. It is rather optimistic to believe that such communication would be of more than passing interest to people who seem unwilling to make the effort needed to leave their own children a planet worth living on. As far as interstellar communication is concerned, we might conclude that the human race just does not seem to be constructed to appreciate such an esoteric undertaking.

QUESTIONS FOR DISCUSSION

1.   Why was the discovery of the first asteroid hailed as great and exciting news?

2.   What would the visual impression of a comet be for an observer on Mercury? On Mars?

3.   What do our current theories on the formation of the solar system imply concerning the relative ages of the sun and the major planets?

4.   On what grounds can you reject a theory which postulates that the sun was twice as hot 500 million years ago as it is today?

5.   If life is to start from simple molecules under suitable conditions, does it have to begin with compounds such as O_2 and N_2?

6.   List the major factors that tend to complicate interstellar communication, and discuss the proposition that civilizations able to enter into such communication are also able to manufacture nuclear weapons.

7.   Why do you agree or disagree with the following statement: A major handicap in enterprises such as interstellar communication is the individualism built into the human race.

EXERCISES

1.   Draw a map of the solar system, including both major and minor planets.

2.   In traveling through space, the earth scoops up interstellar dust grains. Are they observable? Explain.

3.   What is the difference between a meteoroid, a meteor, and a meteorite?

4.   What is the origin of the energy vested in the photons emitted in a meteor trail?

5.   Why is it much easier to recognize an iron meteorite than a stone meteorite?

6.   List the members of the solar system that are known to be scarred by meteor craters, and comment on the reasons for the relative crater frequency.

7. What does the existence of a radiant for a meteor shower prove?

8. List some of the differences between asteroids and major planets.

9. Where in the solar system are the orbits of most asteroids located?

10. Using the data on nearby stars in Table H-10, determine whether our figure of 10^{17} cm for the extent of the solar system is reasonable.

11. The great majority of comets never come close to the sun. What causes some comets to enter the solar system?

12. What causes a comet whose aphelion is billions of kilometers from the sun to become a periodic comet?

13. Why does a comet's tail always point away from the sun?

14. Draw a picture of a comet as you would expect to observe it from New York City an hour before sunrise. How much variation can there be in the position of the tail?

15. Is the hypothetical comet in Exercise 14 east or west of the sun? Can you determine from this whether the comet is on its way toward the sun or away from it?

16. List some of the requirements of "life" as we know it on our planet.

17. List the physical and chemical properties that seem to prevent all major planets from harboring earth-type life at present.

18. Find, in Chapter 18, an estimate of the total number of stars in our galaxy. From that, deduce the number of planets in the galaxy, assuming only 1 of every 10,000 stars has planets associated with it.

EXPERIMENTS

1. If you are a reader of science fiction, try to find out what kind of conditions your favorite stories assume for extraterrestrial life. How do they compare with those given here?

2. Make observations of one of the great meteor showers. Plot the apparent paths of the meteors by relating them to bright stars.

3. Try to determine a radiant from the data collected from Experiment 2.

FURTHER READING

Roth, G. D., *The System of Minor Planets,* New York: D. Van Nostrand Company, Inc., 1962.

The Moon, Meteorites, and Comets, edited by B. A. Middlehurst and G. P. Kuiper, Chicago: The University of Chicago Press, 1963.

Richter, N. B., *The Nature of Comets,* London: Methuen & Co., Ltd., 1963.

Heide, F., *Meteorites,* Chicago: The University of Chicago Press, 1964.

Hoyle, F., *The Black Cloud,* New York: Harper & Row, Publishers, Incorporated, 1964.

Sullivan, W., *We Are Not Alone,* New York: McGraw-Hill Book Company, 1964.

The Origin of the Solar System, edited by T. Page and L. W. Page, New York: The Macmillan Company, 1966.

Shklovskii, I. S., and C. Sagan, *Intelligent Life in the Universe,* San Francisco: Holden-Day, Inc., 1966.

7 the sun as a star

In the center of the solar system is the sun, our star, the only one on which we can directly observe surface features. The sun is roughly spherical in shape, although it appears to us as a circular area, called the solar disc. All other stars appear as *point sources*, even through the largest telescopes. In fact, with ground-based equipment we can only distinguish details on the sun whose diameters are greater than about one two-thousandth of the solar diameter, or about 750 km in linear extent.

We have a wealth of detailed information about the sun, information that has helped astronomers greatly in understanding its mechanisms and history. Our sun is certainly not unique, and the physical processes that produce its energy and its radiation field, and that determine the temperature and density in the solar interior and near the surface must be similar to those in all stars. Thus, solar astronomy is one of the main guides to stellar astronomy.

For the most part, this chapter is concerned with the gross features of the sun, those properties that define the sun as a star.

7.1 THE GROSS FEATURES

Radius and Mass.* The **solar radius** $R_\odot$ can be obtained from the measurable angular size of the sun—about half a degree—and its known distance from the earth, the astronomical unit. More accurately, it is determined from the earth's orbit. The result is

$$R_\odot = 700,000 \text{ km}$$

Just as the astronomical unit is a convenient unit for expressing distances in the solar system, we use the solar radius $R_\odot$ as a referent for stellar radii and the like.

The **mass of the sun** $M_\odot$ is found by measuring the earth's acceleration in its orbit about the sun. According to Newton's law, this acceleration depends on the mass of the sun and the distance of the earth from the sun. Knowing the acceleration and the astronomical unit, we can calculate the mass of the sun. It turns out to be about 330,000 times the mass of the earth; that is,

$$M_\odot = 2 \times 10^{33} \text{ grams}$$

Again, the solar mass will serve as a unit with which to compare other stellar masses. As we shall see, *mass is the crucial parameter in the modern view of stellar evolution.*

*Radius, mass, luminosity, etc., of the sun are abbreviated by $R_\odot$, $M_\odot$, $L_\odot$, with the ancient sun symbol as subscript.

Note that at this point we can define a mean solar **density** by dividing $M_\odot$ by the volume of the sun, $\frac{4}{3}\pi R_\odot^3$. It turns out to be 1.4 g/cm³, just a little above the density of water.

Luminosity and Effective Temperature. Another parameter of primary importance is the amount of energy lost—or radiated—by the sun per unit time, that is, the **luminosity** of the sun. It is equivalent to an energy loss of

$$L_\odot = 4 \times 10^{33} \text{ ergs/sec}$$

or more than 10^{23} kilowatts. $L_\odot$ is found by measuring the total radiation falling on a square centimeter of the earth's surface, a quantity commonly called the **solar constant**. Multiplying this quantity by $4\pi d^2$—the surface area of a sphere where the radius d equals the astronomical unit—yields $L_\odot$. The original measurement is performed using a **bolometer**, a device that indiscriminately registers all photon energies. Then, corrections are made for the portion of the solar spectrum that does not reach ground level, but is absorbed in the earth's atmosphere.

The sun's energy loss doesn't look very large when written as 10^{23} kilowatts. It looks a bit larger written as 400,000,000,000,000,000,000,000 kilowatts, especially when we realize that the average household light bulb radiates less than 0.1 kilowatt. But it begins to attain its proper perspective when compared with world electric power output: The sun radiates 400 trillion times more energy than all the power plants on earth could generate if they were working at maximum capacity!

Dividing $L_\odot$ by the solar surface area, $4\pi R_\odot^2$, yields the energy emitted per square centimeter of solar surface per second. Instead of this figure, though, we usually quote the **effective temperature** of the sun, $T_\odot = 6000°K$. $T_\odot$ is obtained by equating $L_\odot/4\pi R^2$ with $aT_\odot^4$, where a is the *radiation constant* with a value of 5.7 $\times 10^{-5}$ erg/cm² · sec · degree⁴. The introduction of effective temperatures is convenient for several reasons. One is that most people have a better "feeling" for temperatures, even of a few thousand degrees, than for quantities expressed in such units as ergs per second. More important is the fact that the effective temperature has a physical meaning. It is rather close to the actual temperature of the body emitting the energy as photons. Strictly speaking, this is only approximately true, but it is quite sufficient for our qualitative purposes. We then conclude that the **surface temperature** of the sun is in the neighborhood of 6000°K.

Temperature and Density Variation. It is interesting to determine the variation with depth of the solar temperature and density, in particular their values at the center of the sun. Here, of course, we must rely on theory. The calculations are rather complex, but the basic idea is relatively simple: one invokes the principle of **hydrostatic equilibrium** which says that at any point in the star the internal pressure balances the gravitational force attracting the stellar material toward the center. Since the latter increases with increasing depth, the pressure must also increase toward the center of the sun. The results of the calculations are shown in Figs. 7-1 and 7-2. From central values of about $T_c = 16 \times 10^{6°}K$ and $\rho_c = 160$ g/cm³, both temperature and density fall off rapidly as we move radially toward the "surface." Thus, for instance, three-quarters of the solar mass is concentrated within about one-third of a solar

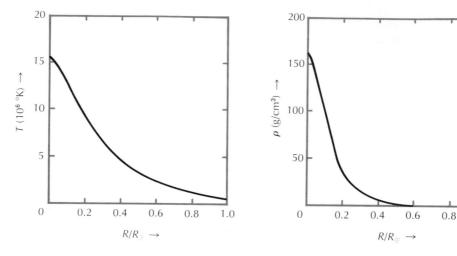

FIGURE 7-1. **Radial variation of temperature from the sun's center to the limb.** (*R. L. Sears, Astrophys. J., vol. 140, p. 477, 1964.*)

FIGURE 7-2. **Radial variation of matter density from the sun's center to the limb.** (*R. L. Sears, Astrophys. J., vol. 140, p. 477, 1964.*)

radius from the center, or within about 3% of the volume. Of greatest interest, however, are the values of central temperature and central density, since they determine the energy production that we are going to discuss in some detail in Section 7.2.

Rotation. There is one additional "gross feature" that should be mentioned, namely, the **solar rotation**. As soon as the first telescopes were available for detailed study of the solar surface, it was noticed that certain topographical features—the sunspots—appear to cross the solar disc in about 13 days. This was correctly interpreted as a rotation of the solar body rather than as a motion of the spots with respect to their surroundings. In fact, the sun rotates with an average period of 27 days about an axis inclined by a few degrees with respect to the ecliptic or, as we may say with more physical significance, with respect to the orbital planes of all the major planets. The rotation is not one of a *rigid body*, but rather **differential**; that is, at high solar latitudes the rotation speed is slower, while at the equator it is faster (24 days). Thus, a hypothetical observer standing at some middle solar latitude would overtake areas nearer the poles, but would be passed by areas closer to the equator.

Nuclear Reactions

The center portion of any atom, the nucleus, consists of positively charged *protons* and electrically neutral *neutrons*. The number of protons in the nucleus determines the element type; the total number of protons and neutrons together determine the mass. A given element may have various *isotopes* whose nuclei contain the same number of protons but different numbers of neutrons.

The protons and neutrons are held together in the nucleus by the *nuclear force*, but they can arrange themselves in various patterns, as can the electrons that surround the nucleus. Associated with each arrangement is a particular internal-energy content. Again we define the arrangement leading to the minimal internal energy as the *ground state*; the others are the discrete *excited states*.

The internal energy of a nucleus is changed when a proton is converted into a neutron, or a neutron into a proton. The process can occur *spontaneously*, provided the nucleus has a *lower* energy content after the conversion. This energy content is called the *binding energy* and is related to the total mass of the nucleus. In a proton-to-neutron or neutron-to-proton conversion, the total mass of the nucleus decreases by an amount *m* according to the formula

$$m = \frac{E}{c^2}$$

where E is the energy freed by the conversion and c is the speed of light.

A neutron can be transformed into a proton through β^- *emission*. The problem is to increase the total number of positive electric charges by one. This is accomplished by the creation of a pair of opposite charges, and emission of the negative one. The positive charge is retained within the nucleus, where it transforms a neutron into a proton. The negative charge is a conventional *electron* (in nuclear physics, normally called a β^- particle). For this process to be feasible, the nucleus must be capable of imparting to the electron its *rest energy* (mc^2, according to Einstein's formula) and some kinetic energy. For reasons that are not of concern here, another particle is emitted with the electron, a so-called *neutrino*, whose main properties are zero mass, zero electric charge, and some finite energy. Neutrinos almost never interact with other particles, so that the energy they remove from the nuclei is for all practical purposes lost forever.

A proton can be transformed into a neutron through the emission of a β^+ *particle* and a neutrino. This β^+ particle, the *positron*, has all the properties of an electron except that its charge is positive; we could call the positron the "mirror image" of the electron. Positrons (at least in our corner of the world) are extremely short-lived: As soon as one comes near an electron, the two combine in a so-called *pair-annihilation process* and transform themselves — rest mass, kinetic energy, and all — into radiation of very short wavelength (γ-rays).

Aside from these spontaneous conversions of proton and neutron, nuclei can be made to undergo *fusion* processes, in which two or more nuclei combine into one new nucleus. This process requires that the participating nuclei come very close to each other, and that the resulting compound nucleus be less massive than its parts. The mass difference is converted to energy of various forms.

7.2 THE SOLAR ENERGY BALANCE

The origin of the energy radiated by the sun was first discussed in the last century. At that time only *gravitational contraction* was considered to be capable of supplying such vast amounts of energy. If it is assumed that all the material of the solar system was originally scattered to infinity and was then gravitationally contracted down to the present size of the sun, the resulting energy could last for about 10^7 years. But the calculations based on the chemistry and physics of the earth gave the sun an age of the order of 10^9 years. Thus, it was concluded that gravitational contraction could not continuously yield the amount of energy radiated by the sun for a long enough time. However, we will see later that it is the process of contraction that *starts* star formation.

Nuclear Fusion.   Several other processes were half-heartedly proposed in the following decades, but it was only when nuclear physics had reached its present level of understanding in the late 1930s that the right answer emerged: The energy that the sun radiates through its surface is produced in its **core**, that is, its central region, by the conversion of hydrogen nuclei (protons) into helium nuclei in a ratio of four to one. Four protons are a bit heavier than the resulting helium nucleus; the difference in mass must be given off as energy. A mass Δm can be converted into an amount of energy $\Delta E = \Delta m \cdot c^2$, where c is the speed of light; conversion of the difference in mass between four protons and one helium nucleus yields an energy of about 27 MeV or 4.3×10^{-5} erg. Such a process has been shown to be capable of supplying the energy radiated by the sun.

The conclusion that the solar radiation loss is replenished by nuclear sources, and in particular by hydrogen-to-helium conversion, is based on a careful study of the probabilities of all conceivable types of nuclear reactions. Of these, the most probable process for the sun is the one just mentioned, which we shall discuss in more detail. Specifically of interest is the form taken by the energy surplus of 27 MeV per reaction.

Proton-Proton Chain.   The first step in the hydrogen-to-helium conversion or **proton-proton chain (pp chain)**, as we shall call it, is the combining of two hydrogen nuclei (protons). Both protons are, of course, positively charged, and thus repel each other according to the laws of electromagnetism. However, when they are very close to each other, the **nuclear force**, an attractive force, becomes stronger. Thus, if two protons are to combine, they must somehow overcome the electromagnetic repulsion (the so-called **Coulomb barrier**) until they are close enough so that the nuclear force can take over. We can visualize the situation by thinking of a ball we want to roll down an incline, but which we must first get up to the crest. We can do this by throwing the ball uphill with enough speed to reach and pass the crest. Similarly, our protons must be invested with enough kinetic energy to overcome the Coulomb barrier so that they can get close enough to each other to be attracted by their mutual nuclear forces. The kinetic energy is available to at least some of them if the gas they comprise has a high enough temperature, in the neighborhood of 10^7°K. The higher the temperature, the greater the average kinetic energy, and the larger the number of protons with enough energy to initiate the pp chain.

Once the two protons are under the influence of the nuclear force, they come together to form a compound nucleus. In order for this compound nucleus to be stable, one of the two positive charges must be removed; in other words, one of the positively charged *protons* must be converted into an electrically neutral *neutron*. This requires emission of a **positron** (β^+ **particle**), which has the same mass as an electron and thus much less mass than a proton, but carries a positive charge. Along with the positron, the compound emits a **neutrino**, a massless particle that carries a certain amount of energy. Since the neutrino does not interact much with other material, it removes its energy from the sun. Ejection of a positive charge in the form of a positron is not the only feasible conversion from proton to neutron, but it is the only one available to particles in the solar interior. The kinetic energy corresponding to the solar core temperature is insufficient to allow any particle other than a positron to escape.

Given the conditions prevalent at the core of the sun, it takes some 10^{10} years for the average proton actually to undergo the interactions just described. What this means is that—given the temperature and density conditions within the sun's core—an *average* proton moves about, colliding with other nuclei, being deflected here and there, etc., for 10^{10} years before its random movements bring it so close to another proton that the nuclear force between the two is strong enough to overcome the Coulomb barrier. Thus, relatively few such reactions take place. Obviously, though, there are enough protons in the solar core, and enough conversions do take place so that the sun is constantly supplied with energy by these reactions. At any rate, the result of the combination of two protons, and the emission of one positron and one neutrino, is a **heavy hydrogen nucleus**, H^2, an **isotope** of hydrogen consisting of one proton and one neutron. This isotope has the tendency to attract one more proton, with a very much higher probability than the original proton-proton reaction. The result of this second proton attraction is the nucleus of a helium isotope, He^3, containing two protons and one neutron. The mass difference between the original heavy hydrogen nucleus plus free proton and the resulting helium isotope is converted into energy within the He^3 nucleus; it is removed by the emission of γ photons, that is, photons of very high energy.

The more usual and more stable helium nucleus He^4 contains two protons and two neutrons. Formation of this particle is the last step in the conversion chain. Several reactions are possible, but the most probable is an interaction between two He^3 nuclei. Relative to the average of 10^{10} years that the first step takes, this interaction occurs almost "instantaneously," namely, in an average of only 10^6 years. The interaction of two He^3 nuclei yields a He^4 nucleus and two protons.

In equation form, the three steps read as follows:

$$H^1 + H^1 \rightarrow H^2 + \beta^+ + \nu$$
$$H^2 + H^1 \rightarrow He^3 + \gamma$$
$$He^3 + He^3 \rightarrow He^4 + H^1 + H^1$$

This notation will be used throughout the text; it is explained in Section C.3.

At this point, the chain stops, since the He^4 nucleus is stable under the conditions prevailing in the solar interior. The two protons are left to participate in other reactions. The 27 MeV energy mentioned at the beginning of this section and which represent the grand total of the energy production, reside mostly in the two β^+ particles, two neutrinos, produced in the two subchains that lead to He^3, and in γ photons. Of these, the neutrinos have virtually zero probability of interacting with solar material. The β^+ particles combine with the free electrons that are present in abundance in the solar interior, and their combined mass and kinetic energy is transformed into γ photons. Ultimately, then, taking into account the neutrino loss, some 25 MeV of energy are converted into γ photons in the center of the sun where the nuclear reactions take place.

Emission and Absorption of Photons

Since energy cannot be manufactured or destroyed, the electrons of an atom cannot change their internal energy, that is, undergo a *transition* from one state to another, without interacting in some fashion with their surroundings. If the transition is from a higher to a lower excited state, they must give off energy; if the transition is in the opposite direction, they must acquire energy. The amount of energy emitted or acquired is exactly the energy difference between the two atomic states involved.

The energy-exchange process of most importance in astronomy involves the *absorption* and *emission* of photons of precisely the right energy. If a photon is absorbed, the energy is used by the electron to undergo transition to a state of higher energy. When a photon is emitted, the electron falls back to a lower-energy state; the energy of the photon equals the energy difference between the two atomic states involved.

In a typical astronomical situation, photons of all possible energies abound, so that electrons are very seldom without photons suitable for absorption. However, whether an atom actually initiates such an absorption and, similarly, whether it actually emits a photon if it is in an excited state, depends on the structure of the atom and various other properties. We say that there is a specific *transition probability* associated with every possible transition between any two states of any atomic system; these transition probabilities vary by orders of magnitude.

In an *ionization process*, an electron can be freed from its atom if it receives an amount of energy greater than, or at least equal to, the appropriate ionization energy. The photon supplying the energy need not have exactly the required energy; any excess above the ionization energy simply becomes the kinetic energy of the freed electron. Similarly, if an ion captures a free electron with a certain kinetic energy in a *recombination process*, it emits a photon whose energy consists of the sum of the kinetic energy of the atom. Thus, while transitions among the various excited states within an atom involve discrete amounts of energy, ionization and recombination involve any of a continuous range of energies.

The photons emitted or absorbed in transitions among excited states have discrete wavelengths associated with their discrete energies; in the usual method for detecting these wavelengths, they show up as lines, and we say that the photons form *spectral lines*. On the other hand, the photons involved in ionization and recombination have a continuous distribution of energies and, therefore, of wavelengths; when detected, they form a *continuum* in the spectrum, with a fixed boundary corresponding to the ionization energy.

7.3 ENERGY TRANSPORT FROM CORE TO SURFACE

While γ photons are generated in the sun's core, most of the energy radiated through the solar surface is in the visible and adjacent regions of the spectrum. We assume that this situation is *stationary*, in the sense that every second the same amount of energy is produced in the center as is lost through the surface. The question we must then consider is the manner in which this energy is transported outward from core to surface.

Photon Transport. The transport process starts with a few very high energy γ photons which are broken up into an avalanche of low-energy photons during transport. This is essentially accomplished by many different nuclei in the solar interior, each of which can assume any one of a large number of discrete "excited" energy levels in the same manner as the electrons of an atom. A high-energy γ photon is absorbed by a nucleus, leaving the nucleus in an excited state in which the absorbed energy is temporarily stored. Eventually, the nucleus decays back to the ground state, the state of lowest possible internal energy. As it passes down through each energy level, the nucleus expels some of the excitation energy by emitting a γ photon of low energy. After many such processes, the original γ photon has effectively been broken down into lower-energy photons; at the same time, its energy has been moved by the nuclei outward toward the solar surface. Similarly, over the remaining distance to the surface, the photons are broken up by interaction with atomic and ionic electrons (Section C.5).

Radiation, Conduction, Convection. Although this picture is physically correct as far as it goes, it does not quite represent the actual energy transport. To see why, let us consider an energy-transport problem we are more familiar with, that of the heat of a fire in a fireplace. The heat generated as the wood burns moves outward into the surroundings. There, three processes occur. One is a **radiative** transfer of energy such as we have just discussed in relation to the sun; radiated heat is what warms one's face even when one looks at the fire from some distance. What happens is that infrared photons emitted in the fire are absorbed by our skin.

A second process, **conductive** energy transfer, involves the transfer of heat through the fireplace material. Here, the heat of the fire increases the kinetic energy of the molecules of the bricks near the fire. This energy is transferred to bricks farther out, which also heat up after a while. However, this is a slow process and, under most astrophysical conditions, negligible.

The third process, **convective** energy transport, is the most important one in the case of the fire. Air in the neighborhood of the burning wood is heated and expands, thus becoming lighter; it starts to rise toward the ceiling. As it does, it gives energy to the cooler air it meets, ultimately cooling itself to precisely the temperature of the surroundings. The warm air bubbles that rise and the cool air bubbles that descend to the fire are called **eddies**; the circulation of the air eddies is the process of **convection**. It is convection which is mostly responsible for the heat balance in our planet's atmosphere; convective eddies and their motions also show up in the scintillation of the stars and the apparent wobbling of a stretch of highway in the sunlight.

Granulation. Careful consideration of all the factors involved in energy transport within the sun have led astrophysicists to the conclusion that no convection takes place close to the center, where the nuclear reactions go on, but only radiative transport. Convection sets in some 10^5 km or so below the surface and becomes the predominant energy-transport mechanism out to almost the very surface. In the surface layers, the energy is again transported mostly by radiation. Nevertheless, some evidence of the original convection pattern appears in a mottling of the surface, called **granulation**; Fig. 7-3 is a photograph of the granulation taken from a high-altitude balloon to improve picture quality by avoiding air turbulence in the lower layers of the earth's atmosphere. This convection pattern also appears in a thin layer of liquid heated from below and cooled at the surface by the air above it. A granulation-type pattern can easily be produced by carefully adding a little cream to a freshly poured cup of hot coffee (to make the convection pattern more visible). The heat stored in the coffee is slowly lost through the surface and causes the obvious cell pattern of convective motion. The result of a more sophisticated experiment of this nature is shown in Fig. 7-4, where silicon oil is used instead of coffee, and the visibility of the convective pattern is increased by graphite flakes instead of cream.

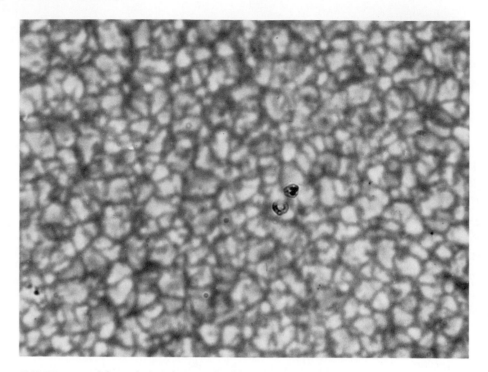

FIGURE 7-3. **High-resolution photograph of the solar photosphere, taken from a balloon about 30 km above the earth. The granulation pattern is clearly visible.** (*J. Bahng and M. Schwarzschild, Astrophys. J., vol. 134, p. 312, 1961.*)

In summary, then, owing to conditions within the sun there is a **convection zone** which stretches from layers just below the surface downward over a significant fraction of the solar radius. Below the convection zone, energy transfer is by radiation.

Temperature and Planck's Law

Any material body can be described as an assembly of atoms and molecules; the solid, liquid, and gaseous states differ in the amount of freedom the basic constituents have to move about. If the constituents do move about, they must have a certain kinetic energy. The *average* kinetic energy of all the atoms and molecules of a material body is described by its *temperature*.

In addition, some atoms and molecules will always be in excited states or even be ionized; the energy vested in excitation or ionization will also have an average value, and in most cases of astronomical interest the mean kinetic energy of the constituents and the mean internal energy of excitation or ionization will be the same. We say that they are in *equilibrium* and correspond to the same temperature. Thus, the percentage of the atoms of a body that are in excited states or that are ionized, that is, their *degree of excitation or ionization*, is described by the temperature of the body.

Excitation and ionization of atoms and the inverse processes involve photons, some being absorbed, some being emitted at all times. Thus, to a particular degree

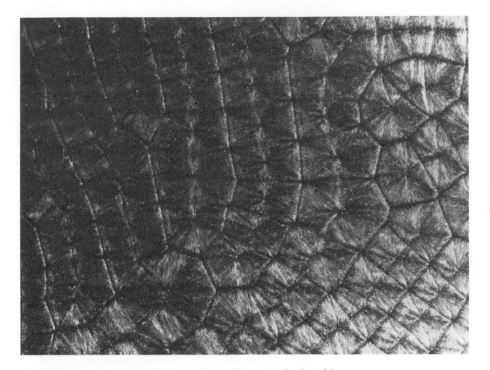

FIGURE 7-4. **Cell pattern of convective motion appearing in a thin layer of liquid heated from below. Note the similarity to the granulation pattern in Fig. 7-3.** (*G. E. Willis, National Center for Atmospheric Research.*)

of excitation or ionization there corresponds a particular average number of photons and a particular average of their energies, both quantities being described again by the temperature.

The quantitative expression of this dependence of photon number and photon spectrum on temperature is called *Planck's law*. It first states that the total energy of all photons present in a cubic centimeter is proportional to the fourth power of the temperature. It then follows that the photons that leave a surface held at temperature T carry away the energy proportional to T^4. Second, the spectrum, that is, the relative number of photons of each energy or wavelength, is given by the Planck curves shown in Fig. C-4, which express in a quantitative fashion the fact that the maximum number of photons tends toward shorter wavelength (higher energy) as temperature increases. Thus, we find that the higher the temperature, the larger the total number of photons, and the higher their mean energy.

7.4   THE PHOTOSPHERE

We have on several occasions used the term solar surface to mean the factual or imaginary boundary of the star. The photons we receive leave from this boundary, and the radius of the sun is measured from its center to this boundary. The concept of a well-defined boundary appears to make sense in the light of everyday experience, which shows the sun to have a sharp edge or, technically, a sharp **limb**;

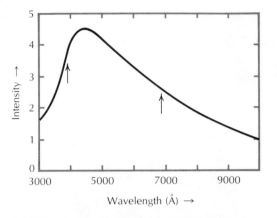

FIGURE 7-5. Mean solar intensity distribution between 3000 Å and 10,000 Å. The arrows indicate the extent of the high-resolution spectrum reproduced in Fig. 7-6.

even the best telescopic images obtained from the surface of the earth show this phenomenon. However, knowing that the sun is in reality a ball of gas, and recalling the earth's atmosphere which tapers off slowly into interplanetary space, we should suspect that the actual situation is somewhat more complicated.

Fraunhofer Lines. The information relevant to an understanding of the situation is contained in the **solar spectrum**, that is, the wavelength-resolved light of the sun. A rough plot of the total intensity of radiation given off as a function of wavelength would appear like Fig. 7-5, where most of the details have been omitted. Comparing Fig. 7-5 with the Planck curves reproduced in Fig. C-4, we have concluded—again roughly—that the sun radiates as if its "surface" had a temperature in the neighborhood of 6000°K.

On the other hand, a very detailed photograph of the spectrum, employing very high resolution of wavelength, would appear as in Fig. 7-6, which is a photographic reproduction of most of the visible range, between about 3900 Å and 6900 Å. Note the numerous **spectral lines**, each at a wavelength characteristic of a specific atom or ion (see Section C.5 for a detailed discussion). These spectral lines are dark against the background consisting of all wavelengths, the **continuum**; that is, fewer photons reach us at the wavelengths at which there are spectral lines. We say that the sun shows an **absorption spectrum**, or that **Fraunhofer lines** (or **absorption lines**) are superimposed on the continuum.

Modern detection methods make it possible to study intensity variations over minute fractions of the spectrum; Fig. 7-7 shows, as an example, a small region around 4861 Å, the location of a line characteristic of hydrogen atoms. In addition to the hydrogen line, the figure shows many weak Fraunhofer lines that can be identified with metals such as iron, nickel, chromium, vanadium, and titanium.

How does such a spectrum come about? The details are quite complex, and we shall here consider only the main features. Keep in mind that the simplified relations we shall give should be qualified in many respects, and that study of the solar

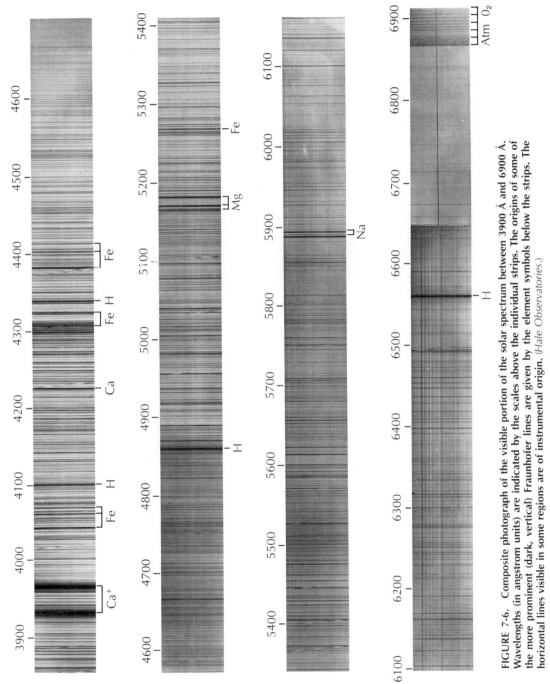

FIGURE 7-6. Composite photograph of the visible portion of the solar spectrum between 3900 Å and 6900 Å. Wavelengths (in angstrom units) are indicated by the scales above the individual strips. The origins of some of the more prominent (dark, vertical) Fraunhofer lines are given by the element symbols below the strips. The horizontal lines visible in some regions are of instrumental origin. (*Hale Observatories.*)

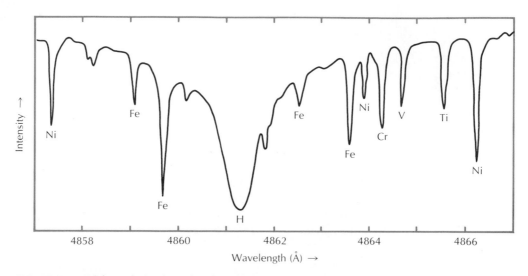

FIGURE 7-7. **High-resolution intensity plot of the spectrum in the neighborhood of the strong line of neutral hydrogen at 4861 Å. The weak narrow lines nearby originate from metals such as Fe, Ni, and Cr.** (*Photometric Atlas of the Solar Spectrum, Utrecht: Sterrewacht Sonnenborgh, 1940*)**.**

spectrum reveals innumerable details which, if taken together, amount to a wealth of data—much more than we know about any other light source.

Origin of the Solar Spectrum.   The main point is the existence of a **gradient**, that is, a continuous change in temperature and density through the layers of the sun from which we receive photons. Let us call these layers by their technical name, the solar **photosphere**; they are really quite thin, almost comparable to eggshells, a few hundred kilometers in extent. It is the photosphere which gives our eyes, whose resolving power is relatively low, the impression of a sharp boundary. The gradient is such that the farther away from the center, the cooler and less dense is the solar gas. Cooler now means, as we have seen earlier, that the atoms and ions not only have a lower average speed (kinetic energy), but also store less excitation energy in their electrons: Fewer atoms are excited; those that are, are excited in lower-energy states; fewer atoms are ionized.

Now suppose a photon is emitted somewhere inside the sun. Either it can be reabsorbed before it leaves the sun, or it can escape and, for instance, reach the earth. The *probability* of escape is high if the photon's energy does not fit into the scheme of energy states of the most abundant atoms and ions along its path. On the other hand, the photon will most probably be reabsorbed if its energy just equals the energy difference between two states of a very abundant species of atom or ion. Thus, these latter photons can escape only when their paths lead through very few atoms that can absorb them; that is, they can escape only from positions far out. The photons we receive will then most probably come from higher layers of the photosphere if their energies are such that they are likely to find atoms to absorb them in the outermost layers of the sun, which are known as the solar **atmosphere**.

There is an additional factor that determines the absorption probability for a photon, a quantity that depends intrinsically on the structure of the atoms. Some transitions from one energy state of the atomic electrons to another are more likely to be activated than others, so that photons whose energies fit the most likely transitions have a better change of being reabsorbed; again, if photons of this type are to escape, they must do so from the highest levels.

Study of the interactions between photons and atoms shows that the number of photons, and their energy distribution, adjust to the temperature or energy content of the atoms. In essence, this means that fewer photons are present at a lower temperature. (This is obvious in Fig. C-4, which shows the number of photons as a function of wavelength and temperature.) Thus, closer to the outside of the sun, the photon density is smaller, and the mean energy of the photons is at a lower value.

In light of the preceding discussion, we interpret the absorption or Fraunhofer spectrum of the sun as indicating that the photons that reach us at wavelengths coinciding with very strong atomic transitions, that is, transitions in highly abundant atoms and with high probability of taking place, come from farther out in the solar atmosphere, where the temperature is lower and where there are fewer photons. "Fewer photons" means less intensity; therefore, the intensity at the wavelengths of strong transitions must be lower, and we get *dark* lines denoting less light at these wavelengths.

Let us mention immediately that if the temperature gradient were reversed, that is, if the temperature increased outwards, we would find *emission lines*—lines whose intensity is higher than that of the surrounding continuum—at the strong transition wavelengths.

Abundances.   More detailed investigation of the Fraunhofer lines makes it possible to deduce not only the radial variation of temperature and density in the outer layers of the sun, but also the **chemical abundances**, that is, the relative amounts of the elements present in the sun. (The latter data are of particular interest in connection with the problems of stellar evolution and are discussed in Section 18.3.) Table 7-1 lists some important solar elements and gives a measure of the amounts present in relation to the most abundant element, hydrogen. No abundances are given for helium and neon, both seemingly rather abundant in the universe, because the photosphere is not hot enough to excite helium or neon. The numbers given are as accurate as present-day solar-abundance determinations can be made, that is, to within a factor of 2 or better.

The most prominent Fraunhofer lines in the visible portion of the solar spectrum are the lines of neutral hydrogen and some metals such as sodium and magnesium, various clusters of iron lines, and two very strong lines of once-ionized calcium (Ca^+). The continuum, on the other hand, is mostly produced by transitions of hydrogen, in particular, in an arrangement where a free electron is captured by the neutral hydrogen atom to form the **H^- ion**, actually a combination of a proton and

TABLE 7-1. SOLAR ELEMENT ABUNDANCES RELATIVE TO HYDROGEN

Element	Number of protons in nucleus	Abundance relative to hydrogen
Hydrogen	1	1.0
Carbon	6	5.2×10^{-4}
Nitrogen	7	1.0×10^{-4}
Oxygen	8	1.0×10^{-3}
Sodium	11	2.0×10^{-6}
Magnesium	12	2.3×10^{-5}
Silicon	14	2.8×10^{-5}
Calcium	20	1.4×10^{-6}
Chromium	24	2.3×10^{-7}
Iron	26	3.0×10^{-6}
Nickel	28	8.3×10^{-7}

Source: A. Unsöld, *Der neue Kosmos*, Berlin: Springer-Verlag, 1967.

two electrons. In the photosphere, hydrogen, the most abundant element, is essentially *neutral*. Only a small number of free electrons are present; these were separated from elements such as iron, which is mostly in the ionized state at the temperature of the solar photosphere. The more prominent transitions have been marked in Fig. 7-6.

The methods of this section can be applied to any star, except that variation in the spectrum across the disc, the so-called limb variation, can be studied only in the case of the sun, where surface details are observable. The limb variation can either take the form of **limb darkening** (corresponding to a temperature *decrease* as we move outward through the layers that emit photons) or of **limb brightening** (a temperature *increase*). Nevertheless, analysis of the photospheric spectra of stars is one of the most successful tools for understanding the physics of our universe.

7.5 CHROMOSPHERE AND CORONA

During a total solar eclipse, when the moon blocks out the photosphere completely, a very thin layer with a reddish glow appears just beyond the photosphere. This is the solar **chromosphere**. Still farther out, of irregular shape and visible to the naked eye for many solar radii, stretches the solar **corona**, whose light has a bluish-white quality. In absolute measure, the chromosphere is much brighter than even the innermost parts of the corona, but it is difficult to photograph owing to its limited radial extent. Figure 7-8 shows a typical corona configuration.

Even a very crude analysis of the spectrum of the corona shows that most of its light is photospheric in origin and **scattered**; that is, a small percentage of the photons emitted by the photosphere is always undergoing a change in direction without a change in energy, thus conserving the spectral distribution. We are all familiar with similar phenomena in the earth's atmosphere, for instance, when fog particles scatter photons emanating from the headlights of a car.

The crucial property of the corona is its temperature (understood as the mean

FIGURE 7-8. The solar corona as observed during the total eclipse of August 31, 1932. The rotational axis of the sun runs close to the vertical. Note the different radial extent of the bright inner corona at the poles and close to the equatorial plane, and the radial "streamers" visible in the outer portions of the photograph. (*Lick Observatory.*)

kinetic energy of its free electrons), which is in the neighborhood of $2 \times 10^{6\circ}$K. After it was possible to obtain solar spectra via rockets sent above the earth atmosphere's densest layers, emission lines due to highly ionized metals were found in the ultraviolet and X-ray regions of the spectrum. Such lines and related ones in the visible region of the spectrum, which had been known from eclipse observations for a long time, can only be formed at the very high temperature noted above. Analysis of the spectrum of the chromosphere shows that the solar temperature there reaches a minimum of some 4000°K. So the temperature actually decreases from the photosphere out to the chromosphere, and then increases again abruptly to the coronal value. Independent confirmation of this **temperature reversal** above the photosphere was obtained from the radio spectrum of the sun that passes through the earth's atmosphere. Once the high coronal temperatures are reached, very little change occurs farther out, so that even millions of kilometers above the photosphere the coronal temperature is still close to $10^{6\circ}$K. There, of course, the solar density decreases even further, and we believe now that the solar corona, the outermost portion of the atmosphere of our sun, simply tapers off into interplanetary space. In a sense, then, the earth orbits through outlying portions of this solar corona.

In addition to the hot gas, the solar corona has a component of dust, that is, of grains we find in interstellar material. Very low in the solar corona, this dust is evaporated by the intense solar radiation. However, farther out the **dust corona** is quite prominent and apparently concentrated toward the sun's equatorial plane which, as seen from the earth, is close to the ecliptic. This concentration of dust in the ecliptic scatters photospheric light (as does the electron component) and is responsible for the **zodiacal light**, a faint glow visible to the naked eye after sunset on extremely clear nights, near the horizon where the ecliptic ascends.

In summary, we can say that while the sun presents a spectrum with absorption lines in the visible range, the spectrum is dominated in the ultraviolet and X-ray ranges by emission lines. The complete solar spectrum consists of a photospheric continuum and superimposed absorption and emission lines, originating in the various colder and hotter layers above the photosphere. Theoretical studies show that the separation of absorption and emission lines in the various spectral ranges depends strongly on the temperature and density structure of the sun's atmosphere and that, consequently, under somewhat different conditions we could have absorption and emission lines side by side in the same spectral region. This indeed is observed in several classes of stars, as we shall see in Chapter 15.

7.6 THE ENERGY BALANCE OF THE OUTER ATMOSPHERE AND THE SOLAR WIND

What sort of mechanism would cause the temperature of the solar atmosphere to go through a minimum, reverse itself, and suddenly increase again? Obviously, at distances beyond that at which the temperature is minimal, some form of energy must be converted into heat, energy that has passed unhindered through the photosphere. Of the many theories that have been proposed, only one has been shown to be feasible and is generally accepted today. It states that the energy source is in the convective motion that takes place in subphotospheric layers. The up-and-down motion of convective eddies creates waves that, when moving upward into the less dense areas, become more and more violent, ultimately losing their energy by heating the gas through which they pass. Calculations make it very plausible that little if any of the wave energy is dissipated, that is, transformed into heat, in the photosphere. The major amount of dissipation occurs at densities corresponding to the chromosphere and lower corona.

There is an additional feature of this model that must be mentioned, a tiny net outflow of material through the photosphere. By the time this flow can be traced out into the corona, the flow speed is quite large—several hundred kilometers per second. It results in a constant flow of rarified, highly ionized gas away from the sun and through interplanetary space. This is the **solar wind** mentioned earlier. It is, over many years, a source of mass loss and, even more important, of loss of angular momentum. Both effects will interest us in connection with some of the current problems of stellar evolution.

A schematic view of the sun with its manifold layers and physical processes is shown in Fig. 7-9.

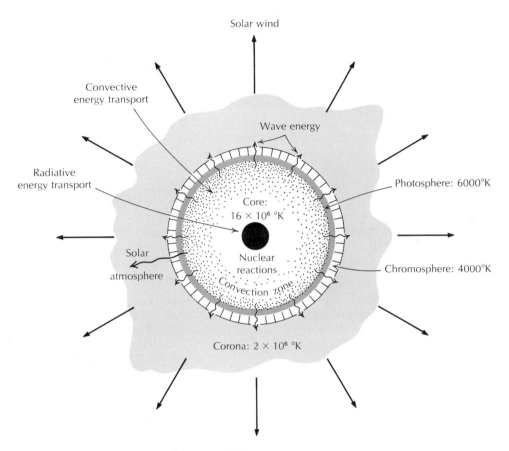

Solar wind

Convective
energy transport

Wave energy

Radiative
energy transport

Photosphere: 6000°K

Core:
16×10^6 °K

Solar
atmosphere

Nuclear
reactions

Convection zone

Chromosphere: 4000°K

Corona: 2×10^6 °K

FIGURE 7-9. Schematic view of the sun and its processes.

QUESTIONS FOR DISCUSSION

1. Why is the moon's angular diameter always about the same as the sun's, as viewed from the earth?

2. Why does the sun's apparent angular diameter change very slightly during the course of a year?

3. What would happen if the earth were to rotate differentially?

4. What happens to the energy produced in the solar core?

5. What percentage of the solar radiation falls on Mercury? On Earth? On Jupiter? What conclusion can you come to concerning these different amounts of radiation?

6. How is an ''avalanche of photons in the visible range'' created out of a γ photon originating in the solar core?

7. When a proton is converted into a neutron, the electric charge must be expelled somehow. The creation of a β^+ particle (and a neutrino) is, in principle, not the only way to achieve this end. What property of the solar core makes this process the only one possible for the sun?

8. Convective motion creates waves. What happens to the energy of these waves?

9. Why can the best photographs of solar granulation be made from balloons with relatively small telescopes, rather than from the ground with big ones?

10. Why does the sun appear to us to have a sharp edge?

11. Can you observe the chromosphere and corona with the naked eye? Explain.

12. The solar wind should have a composition of elements similar to the solar corona. Table 7-1 does not describe this composition adequately. Why?

EXERCISES

1. The limit of resolution of details on the sun is 750 km. Use that fact, the value of the astronomical unit, and the earth-moon distance to deduce the linear extent of details on the moon that can just be distinguished under the best observing conditions.

2. If the limit of resolution for solar details is 750 km, calculate the angular resolution of telescopic equipment observing the sun from the earth's surface. Compare your result with the data given in Section E.1.

3. The sun is the only star on which we can resolve surface features; all other stars appear to us as point sources. List the types of data that are therefore available only for the sun, and not for other stars.

4. What is the angular diameter of the sun in arcseconds?

5. At what time of year is the sun's apparent angular diameter largest? Smallest?

6. What is the difference between the solar luminosity and the solar constant?

7. What type of correction must be applied to the measurement of the solar constant in order to get the correct value?

8. The effective temperature of the sun is a measure of its luminosity. In what layer of the solar atmosphere is the actual temperature close to this effective temperature?

9. Check the price charged for electricity in your area, and look up last year's federal budget. Determine how long it would take the sun to spend the federal budget, assuming it had to buy its energy as electricity from your local power company.

10. Somewhere close to the center of the sun, the temperature of the solar material is about as high as the temperature of the solar corona. Why does the corona not act as a nuclear furnace?

11. What would be the weight on earth of a cubic centimeter of material taken from the solar center? How much heavier or lighter than water would that material be? Does any material on earth have a similar density?

12. Assume that there is a structure anchored on the solar surface, running from the north to the south rotational pole. Draw a picture that shows schematically the path of this structure during one solar rotation.

13. The solar luminosity and the energy released when four protons combine to form one helium nucleus are given in the text. How many proton combinations must occur per second to result in the solar luminosity?

14. Compare the average time a proton survives in the solar core (under present conditions) with the average life of a human being. How long, by comparison, is the life of the heavy-hydrogen isotope?

15. The mass difference between four protons and one helium nucleus is not totally converted into photons. Where does the missing portion go?

16. Figure C-1 gives the typical energy of a γ photon. How much more energetic is such a photon than one in the visible range of the spectrum?

17. The text gives a formula for converting a mass difference into energy. Use the formula to calculate the energy gained by converting one electron mass and positron mass (see Table H-2) into photons.

18. An electron and a positron that combine in the solar core may have kinetic energies in addition to their mass energies. Where does this kinetic energy go when the two particles are converted into γ photons?

19. Use the results of Exercise 13 to determine how many neutrinos are produced by the sun every second. How much energy is carried away by these neutrinos (which almost never interact with solar material) in 5×10^9 years, assuming 2% of the total energy of a pp chain goes into each neutrino? How many grams of matter would have to be converted completely into energy in order to result in this much energy?

20. Figure C-2 shows the energy-level scheme of the hydrogen atom. Give an example of how an ultraviolet photon with an energy of 14.5 eV can be broken up into several less energetic photons by the following chain of processes: absorption of photon and ionization of hydrogen atom → emission of photon and recombination of atom → emission of photon and transition of atom from a higher to a lower excited state → · · · → emission of photon and transition of atom from an excited state to the ground state. Calculate the pertinent energies and wavelengths.

21. Give examples of convective and radiative energy transport in the earth's atmosphere.

22. What observable feature of the solar surface indicates the existence of a convection zone?

23. What factors influence the strength of a Fraunhofer line, that is, the relative intensity drop in the line with respect to the continuum?

24. Draw a rough graph of the temperature gradient in the layers of the sun that give rise to absorption lines; of those that give rise to emission lines.

25. The hydrogen line called Lyman is observed in emission in the ultraviolet portion of the spectrum, while in the yellow region of the visible spectrum two lines due to sodium appear in absorption. Which of these lines show limb brightening? Which show limb darkening? Which lines originate higher in the solar atmosphere?

26. Compare the temperatures and densities of the solar photosphere, chromosphere, and corona.

27. There are free electrons present in the photosphere. Where do they come from?

28. What element provides most of the electrons in the solar corona?

29. There are free electrons and highly ionized atoms in the solar corona. What else is found in the corona, particularly at greater distances from the sun?

FURTHER READING

The Sun, edited by G. P. Kuiper, Chicago: The University of Chicago Press, 1953.

Abetti, G., *The Sun*, New York: The Macmillan Company, 1957.

Menzel, D. H., *Our Sun* (rev. ed.), Cambridge, Mass.: Harvard University Press, 1959.

8 solar activity

In Chapter 7 we considered the sun as a more or less static entity, in that we assumed its properties do not change in time. This, of course, gives a rather limited model. For instance, nuclear energy conversion in the solar core continuously increases the supply of helium nuclei at the expense of hydrogen; as a result, over times of the order of 10^9 or 10^{10} years, the makeup of the sun will certainly change. In addition, the sun shows an *intrinsic* variability. In comparison with events occurring in many other classes of variable stars, this is quite small. But since we are so close to the sun, we can more easily observe the details there, and use them to construct models of more violent events on other stars. Occasionally, too, we are affected directly by solar variability.

8.1 SUNSPOTS AND PLAGES

Sunspots.   We begin with a phenomenon that has been known for centuries and that can be observed easily with simple instruments, namely, **sunspots**. Figure 8-1 shows a telescopic image of the whole sun with several sunspots arranged, as is typical, in **groups**. Such a group may consist of two or three barely visible small spots of some 1,000 km diameter; it may consist of several large dark areas with hundreds of small spots surrounding them; or it may consist of one big spot and a few smaller ones. Figure 8-1 gives examples of a **young group** consisting of a few small spots (close to the center of the picture), of several large groups during **maximum development**, with the many spots arranged around two **primary spots**, and of an **old group** in which only one of the primary spots still remains (above the center of the solar disc, between the two large groups). Figure 8-2 is an enlargement of a photograph of a large group. Note the granulation pattern outside the sunspots proper.

We have implied that a sunspot group undergoes a change or development in time, and this is indeed the case. A group usually appears rather suddenly, most often with two primary spots visible at once. In the course of a few days the primary spots become much larger, while at the same time more and more small spots appear in the neighboring photosphere. Maximum development is reached after two or three weeks, depending on the maximum size the group ultimately attains, and from then on the total number of spots decreases again. After two or three months, a group usually has disappeared altogether. Since the sun rotates slowly during sunspot development, the groups seem to move from the east to the west limb of the sun.

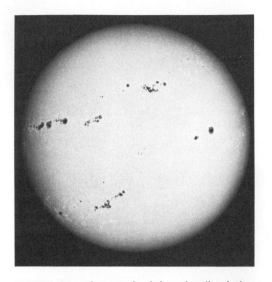

FIGURE 8-1. Photograph of the solar disc during maximum activity (December 21, 1957). The rotational axis runs approximately diagonally, from upper left to lower right. Visible are numerous spot groups arranged in two broad belts north and south of the solar equator. Also note the plage areas visible close to the limb. (*Hale Observatories.*)

Plages. Whereas sunspots are much darker than the undisturbed photosphere, the immediate neighborhood of the spots—both the areas between individual spots and the photosphere around the group—is brighter. The bright areas surrounding sunspot groups are called **plage areas**. The fact that the plage area is brighter, and the sunspots darker, than the undisturbed photosphere obviously means that plages are hotter, and sunspots cooler, than the quiescent photosphere. Indeed, the temperature in a sunspot is only about 4000°K, while the material in the plage area is usually a few hundred degrees hotter than its surroundings.

The plage area usually appears some weeks or so *before* the first spots, and may outlive the spots by several months. In some cases plage areas appear and then decay again without producing sunspots large enough to be visible from the earth. Thus, it is believed that a plage area indicates the existence of a solar **activity center** in which the spots themselves appear as the most striking manifestation. Figure 8-1 shows the plage areas surrounding sunspot groups, notably near the edge where the contrast is high. There are also several plages visible that do not appear to contain sunspots.

8.2 THE OUTER ATMOSPHERE ABOVE ACTIVITY CENTERS

We saw in Section 7.4 that the height in the solar atmosphere from which we receive photons of a given energy depends on the absorption probability for that particular energy. For example, photons whose energy level corresponds to a high

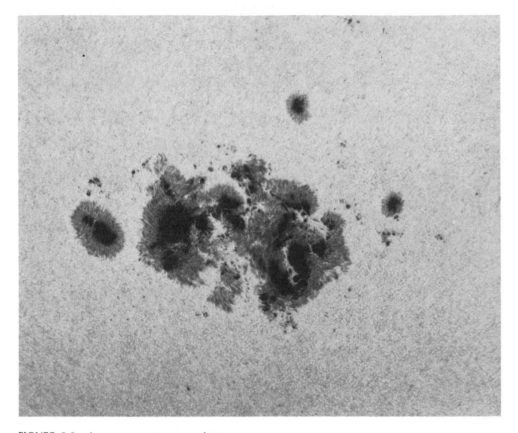

FIGURE 8-2.   Large sunspot group of May 17, 1951. Numerous
small spots are visible among the granulation elements. The complex
structure of the large spots—the dark "umbra" in the center, surrounded by the "penumbra" with its characteristic radial striations—
is obvious in this picture taken from the earth under extremely good
atmospheric conditions. (*Hale Observatories.*)

absorption probability for an *abundant* element must come to the earth from relatively high in the solar atmosphere. By receiving solar images through filters that
pass only very narrow ranges of appropriately chosen wavelengths, we are able to
get images of the solar atmosphere at different heights. Figures 8-3 to 8-5 are the
result of such an analysis; they were taken, respectively, at the wavelengths of the
continuum (photosphere), the center of a hydrogen line (lower chromosphere), and
the center of a very strong calcium-ion line (upper chromosphere).

While at continuum wavelengths the plage areas (Fig. 8-3) are barely visible
toward the solar limb, they are very distinct in both chromospheric pictures (Figs.
8-4 and 8-5). We must conclude that, relatively speaking, the signs of solar activity
are more pronounced in the outer layers of the sun.

A more detailed study of the spectrum leads to the conclusion that both density
and temperature are increased in active regions. In fact, above the activity centers,
coronal condensations exist with densities much in excess of that of the standard

 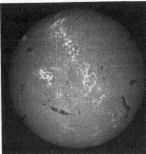 

FIGURE 8-3. Photograph (September 15, 1949) of the solar disc in the light of the continuum (photosphere). North and south poles are indicated by the small wedges at the limb (upper right and lower left). Several sunspot groups, and plage area close to the limb, are visible. By comparison with Fig. 8-1, we see that the number of sunspots and sunspot groups in December 1949 was much less than in December 1957. (*Hale Observatories.*)

FIGURE 8-4. Photograph of the solar disc in the light of the red hydrogen line (lower chromosphere); date and arrangement as in Fig. 8-3. The plages are now visible everywhere on the disc. Note their close relation to sunspot groups. The major spots are still visible inside the plage areas. There is a particularly bright plage at the limb (upper left). The dark irregular features are prominences in projection on the solar disc. The light and dark straight lines crisscrossing the disc are instrumental in origin. (*Hale Observatories.*)

FIGURE 8-5. Photograph of the solar disc in the light of the violet calcium-ion line (upper chromosphere); date and arrangement as in Fig. 8-3. Most prominent now are the plage areas whose brightness follows closely that exhibited by the hydrogen picture. The largest sunspots are just visible. The prominences have lost contrast, but are still readily distinguishable. (*Hale Observatories.*)

corona. These density increases are very long-lived and show up clearly in pictures taken during total solar eclipses. When there is no activity on the sun, the corona is roughly symmetric about the rotational axis (see Fig. 7-8). Figure 8-6 shows, for comparison, the coronal features related to activity centers: helmetlike structures at the base of **streamers** that stretch far into interplanetary space.

8.3 MAGNETIC FIELDS AND LONG-TERM VARIATIONS

Sunspot Fields. The Fraunhofer lines of sunspot spectra show the characteristic changes of a very strong **Zeeman effect,** that is, they must have been emitted in the presence of a magnetic field. Measurements indicate that *magnetic fields* typically of several thousand gauss exist in the center of a spot. This value corresponds to the field of a very large laboratory magnet. The energy per cubic centimeter stored in a magnetic field of 3,000 gauss is much greater than that associated with the heat content of the same volume in the photosphere, so it is the magnetic field that determines the physical state of the material in a sunspot.

In a typical activity center, the two primary spots have **opposite polarities**; that is, if the force direction is upward in one spot, it is downward in the other. The

FIGURE 8-6. Corona of March 7, 1970, showing fairly active sun. Several centers of activity were present, and the long coronal streamers and helmetlike structures are related to them. Prominences were found at the bases of some of them. (*High Altitude Observatory.*)

smaller spots usually follow the polarity of the nearest primary spots, so that in a typical group there is a fairly well defined separation between the "positive" and "negative" fields. Thus, we can speak of magnetically **bipolar** regions or groups.

Similar studies of the Fraunhofer lines of plage areas show that there, too, magnetic fields exist, but they are much weaker; 50 gauss is a typical value, corresponding to the field of a household magnet. Polarities in the plage parallel the spot polarities, so that the whole area of activity is usually magnetically bipolar.

Finally, still weaker magnetic fields extend all the way to the solar poles and again we find, on the average, a bipolar behavior with one polarity dominating in the northern polar regions, the other in the south. These large-area weak fields follow the time behavior of the activity fields to a varying degree, but are the ones usually referred to as the **general field of the sun**.

Origin of Solar Activity.   The fact that the sun contains highly localized, extremely strong magnetic fields is surprising for several reasons, and much research has been done in the last few years in an attempt to understand the origin and role of these fields. Most of the details are still not understood, and even some of the basic features can only be explained in a qualitative sense. Nevertheless, it is clear that the magnetic fields are the crucial factor in the appearance and maintenance of an activity center, simply because they control the physical situation through the energy

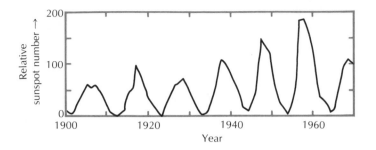

FIGURE 8-7. Relative sunspot numbers, 1900–1970. Note the activity maxima approximately every 11 years and the overall increase in activity between 1900 and 1960, followed by a drop during the last maximum (1969).

that they store. The question of the origin of solar activity in our rather simplified picture is then reduced to the question of the origin of the highly localized magnetic fields. Arguments raised in recent years would indicate that the existence of activity fields has probably to do with a combination of the differential rotation, the convective pattern, and some sort of general magnetic field. If this basic view is correct, then solar-type activity must be common to many stars in the universe.

Periodicity of Activity.   If the number of spots visible on the sun — or some measure of their area — is recorded over the years, it becomes obvious that there are distinct maxima and minima to sunspot activity. A statistical measure, the so-called **relative sunspot number** which takes into account the total number of spots and their arrangement in groups, is plotted in Fig. 8-7 for the years 1900 to 1970. On the average, a maximum occurs about every 11 years. However, such occurrences are not strictly periodic, and there is often a delay in the maximum or minimum attained in one of the hemispheres of the sun. Nevertheless, it is convenient to speak of the **11-year cycle** of solar activity. The heights of the maxima, that is, the mean numbers of sunspots at maximum activity, also vary quite significantly, as can be seen in Fig. 8-7. The appearance of plage areas and coronal condensations is related to the number of sunspot groups; therefore total plage activity, the size of the corona, and the radio emission of the sun (because of condensations above activity centers) exhibit the same 11-year cycle.

Other Regularities.   In its details, sunspot activity shows even more striking regularities. One can plot the solar latitude (defined with respect to the equator) at which the first spots of a group are sighted as a function of time. The result is a picture such as that shown in Fig. 8-8 for the years 1933 to 1947. The first spots of a new cycle appear typically around 45° latitude, north and south, while the last spots appear very close to the equator, but practically never at 0°. Thus, the main manifestations of solar activity are concentrated in two broad belts north and south of the equator. This is a clear indication of an intrinsic relation between rotational symmetry and solar activity.

Moreover, the distribution of magnetic polarities among the spots in a group in the northern hemisphere are the reverse of those in a group in the southern hemisphere; this arrangement is rigidly maintained throughout each cycle by all groups.

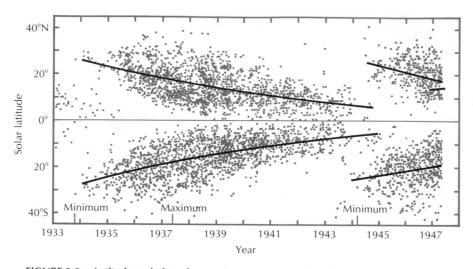

FIGURE 8-8. Latitude variation of sunspot appearance as a function of phase in the 11-year cycle. Note the simultaneous presence of spots from the old cycle (low solar latitude) and new cycle (high solar latitude) in 1934 and again in 1944. (*G. Abetti, The Sun, London: Faber & Faber, Ltd., 1963.*)

For instance, if the spots in the western and eastern portions of a group have the magnetic field polarities + and −, respectively, in the northern hemisphere, then the polarities of a similar group are − and + in the southern hemisphere. During the next 11-year cycle, the arrangement is just reversed, so that two consecutive cycles, spanning some 22 years, must represent the basic period of sunspot activity.

8.4 THE PROMINENCES

During the later phases of the development of an activity center, **prominences** appear at the outskirts of the plage region, mainly near the dividing line between magnetic polarities, on the side closest to the rotational pole. These prominences show up *dark* against the undisturbed solar atmosphere, for some rather complicated reasons. However, they are only visible in the light of the spectral lines with high transition probability, which means that the prominence material is not dense enough to absorb all the photons emitted in the underlying photosphere. Only those photons whose energy coincides with the most probable transitions of the most abundant elements are absorbed; the others cross the prominence. There are several prominences visible in Figs. 8-4 and 8-5. When seen at the solar limb, against the background of the much less luminous corona, prominences appear as bright formations, often of weird shapes, stretching thousands of kilometers across the corona. They are visible to the naked eye during *total* eclipses. A typical prominence as seen at the limb is depicted in Fig. 8-9.

A study of their light spectrum shows that their temperature (representing the kinetic energy of the free electrons) is of order of $10^{4}°$K as against the $10^{6}°$K of the corona, and that their density is approximately 100 times the density of the surround-

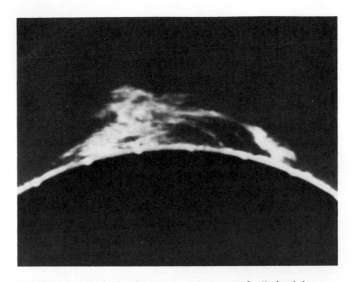

FIGURE 8-9. Typical quiescent prominence at the limb of the sun. Matter streams from the main condensation on the left along arched paths (center of photograph) back into the chromosphere. (*Hale Observatories.*)

ing coronal gas. Photographs taken under good conditions show that the prominences actually consist of large numbers of intertwined thin strands of cool gas with coronal material in between. Obviously, something must keep these cool, dense **filaments** suspended in the corona. Since there seems to be a clear relation between the positions of the prominences and the magnetic field structure of an activity center, it is commonly taken for granted that the filaments are regions in which gas is locally trapped in irregular and twisted magnetic fields.

The large prominences often outlive both spots and plage areas by months. They may, toward the end of their "lives," simply disintegrate; once in a while, though, the whole structure is lifted into space, magnetic field, trapped gas, and all. One of the more spectacular events of this kind is shown in Fig. 8-10.

8.5 THE FLARE PHENOMENON

If the phenomena discussed so far in this chapter were the sole manifestations of solar activity, they would arouse little interest outside the astronomical community. In particular, none of them has any direct, measurable influence on our planet, its atmosphere, or its magnetic field. However, we have yet to describe the most spectacular feature of solar activity, one that does have a quite direct effect on us: the **flare** phenomenon.

Solar flares were discovered when pictures of the sun could be obtained in the light of selected strong spectral lines, such as those of hydrogen and ionized calcium, as were Figs. 8-4 and 8-5. It was noted then that occasionally, and for time periods ranging from minutes to hours, the areas directly adjacent to major sunspots become

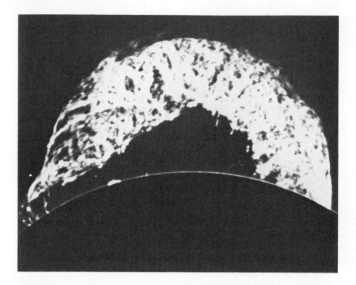

FIGURE 8-10. Early stage of a prominence disappearance, photographed on June 4, 1946. This largest prominence ever observed finally achieved a diameter of more than a million kilometers. (*High Altitude Observatory.*)

very much brighter: they "flared," showing rather chaotic structures quite reminiscent of the fine structure of prominences. In the process, the brightness on occasion increased to such an extent that the spots were no longer visible, as if they were blanketed by the luminous gases. Figures 8-11 and 8-12 show the same sunspot area before and during a flare; the pictures were taken in the light of the hydrogen line Hα at 6563 Å, which was also used to obtain Fig. 8-4.

Correlation with Sunspots. A most striking correlation exists between the flare phenomenon and sunspot activity. No flare has been observed anywhere on the sun except in the neighborhood of primary sunspots; in fact, statistical investigations make it very plausible that the initial phases of a flare occur right at the boundary between the opposite magnetic polarities of a sunspot group. Similarly, a flare is most likely to occur along with a big sunspot group at maximum development, and flare activity then is likely to appear especially violent.

Owing to its close correlation with sunspots, flare activity shows the 11-year cycle very markedly. Thus, the general level of flare activity can be readily predicted on a statistical basis. If a large sunspot group is known to exist on the sun, it is likely that some flare activity will occur, in particular at about the time of the group's maximum development. However, a prediction as to whether or not a flare will occur on a particular *date*, which, as we shall see, would be quite valuable, cannot be made on the basis of present knowledge.

Radio-frequency Effects. As it turns out, the most violent manifestations of the flare phenomenon do not occur in the visible-wavelength region. This was realized

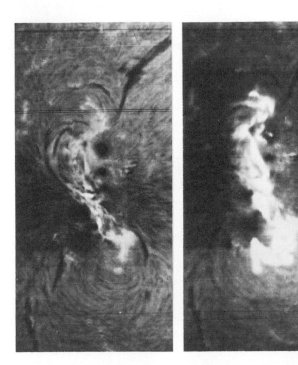

FIGURE 8-11. Area of a large sunspot group on July 25, 1946, photographed in the light of the red hydrogen line. Several of the large spots are visible, for instance, above the middle and to the right of the bright diagonal band, and to the left. Also visible are prominences, such as the one in the upper right corner. Very early stage of great flare event (see Fig. 8-12). The horizontal dark lines are of instrumental origin. *(Hale Observatories.)*

FIGURE 8-12. Same area as shown in Fig. 8-11 during maximum development of great flare. At this time all but the major sunspots have become invisible underneath the intense chromospheric emission of the flare. Brightening occurs predominantly along the line separating the two magnetic polarities. *(Hale Observatories.)*

right after World War II, when radio astronomy became an important tool, and the sun was the first object to be studied in detail. One of the immediate successes was the discovery of spectacular and very complex radio emissions during solar flares.

A really comprehensive discussion of the **radio phenomena** associated with flares would have to take into account the vast differences in their effects at different wavelengths. For our purposes it suffices to summarize two basic kinds of radio emissions due to flares. One appears as a **continuum** and may be due to the emission of of relativistic electrons in the magnetic fields of activity centers (the synchrotron radiation discussed in Section C.7). The second type of radio emission appears in the form of two broad spectral **emission lines**. There is more or less a consensus that the spectral lines occur at a frequency called the **plasma frequency** and at twice this frequency. Plasma-frequency transmission is known to arise from free electrons; the particular frequency depends on their density, decreasing with decreasing density. Frequencies at which this second type of emission has been observed fit very well with postulated electron densities in the solar corona. Nevertheless, many of the details of this particular emission mechanism are not yet understood.

Ultraviolet and X-ray Spectra of Flares.   After the discovery of the radio emissions came observations at the high-energy end of the solar spectrum, in the *ultraviolet* and *X-ray* regions. Such observations require satellites or, at least, rockets that ascend above most of our earth's atmosphere, since this portion of the spectrum is completely absorbed before reaching the ground. As had been suspected from ionospheric studies, the most drastic effects of flare activity occur in this high-energy range. The conclusion is that a significant volume of the solar corona above the chromosphere flare region must be affected by the flares, in the sense that the temperature there is increased to values between 5 and 10 times the normal value.

Effects at Highest Energies.   The explanation of flare effects in the ultraviolet and X-ray regions as being simple heating of the corona fails finally, if one studies energies of some 100 keV (500 keV is the energy equivalent of the mass of an electron). While the "quiet sun" does not radiate at such high energies, sudden and intense bursts of extremely energetic γ-rays occur in coincidence with flares. The photon energies involved are so large that it is impossible to account for them even with temperatures of 10^{7}°K. Instead we must assume that the photons are emitted in interactions among isolated electrons that in some manner have been accelerated to speeds near that of light.

The effects of such electrons have now been observed directly from satellites and spacecraft. They belong to what we loosely call the **cosmic rays**, a collection of high-energy (relativistic) particles: electrons, other elementary particles, atomic nuclei, and photons. (We shall encounter cosmic rays again in a more general context in Section 18.5.) During large flares, and sometimes unexpectedly when a relatively mild event takes place, quantities of these particles are thrown out, and their effects can be traced as far as the lower part of the earth's atmosphere. Although we cannot pinpoint exactly where the particles originate, their strict correlation with solar flares makes it obvious that they must gain their large kinetic energies somewhere in the flare region, in a manner that classifies the sun as a very efficient particle accelerator.

Other Effects.   We have seen that the physics of the upper levels of the earth's atmosphere is controlled by the influx of solar ultraviolet and X-ray photons. Thus, the increased radiation during flares must lead to changes in the behavior of these atmospheric layers. And, indeed, the ionosphere responds in a complex but characteristic manner, mostly by an increase in the degree of ionization at certain heights. The most noticeable result of this additional ionization is an increase in the absorption of radio waves (originating on the surface, for instance, at man-made radio stations) which are normally reflected back. Thus, **sudden ionospheric disturbances** are unwelcome side effects of solar flares, from the point of view of intercontinental communication. There is thus good reason why the people who operate communications networks would very much like solar physicists to be able to predict the occurrence of flares with some accuracy. Too, we would like to be able to plan manned landings on the moon, with its lack of a shielding atmosphere, at times when there is little probability of a major flare occurring.

The emission of relativistic cosmic-ray particles by our basically inert home star makes a fascinating study for the theoretician. However, more important from the energetic point of view is the emission of relatively **slow particles**, protons, helium nuclei, and the like, simply because there are so may of them. They are clearly emitted during flares. Indirect evidence of their existence had been collected for many decades; one set of data has to do with the occurrence of **auroras** a couple of days after a major flare is observed on the sun. Auroras were discussed in Section 2.4, where it was pointed out that they represent emission in the visible range by atoms colliding with solar particles in the rarefied regions of the geocorona. If we assume that the clouds of solar particles are emitted during the flare, then their transit times correspond to velocities of the order 10^3 km/sec.

Another flare effect that has been known for quite some time is the **geomagnetic storm**. If the earth's magnetic field is measured very accurately, it is seen to fluctuate continually. On occasion, the fluctuations become quite noticeable and take on rather well defined characteristics; again, these "storms" show an excellent correlation with solar flares. The straightforward explanation of the field fluctuations has them as the result of an influx of clouds of charged particles into the geocorona.

8.6   THE FLARE MECHANISM

A careful estimate of the energy expended by the sun on a large flare in all its manifestations, including the enhanced optical spectrum and the acceleration of cosmic rays and many slower particles, leads to a typical value of some 10^{30} to 10^{32} ergs. Compared to the total energy output of the sun's pp chain, about 4×10^{33} ergs/sec, the amount of energy released in flares is indeed very large. However, it is negligible in the energy balance of the sun when averaged over the years, since *large* flares occur only a few times a year. Similarly, the combined mass of all the particles emitted during a flare, some 10^{15} to 10^{16} grams, may be negligible in comparison with the total solar mass, or even the continuous mass loss of the solar wind, but it represents essentially the mass of the whole solar corona and chromosphere above the flare region.

What mechanism might be responsible for a sudden local dissipation of up to 10^{32} ergs of energy, emission of 10^{15} grams of material, and acceleration of charged particles to speeds near that of light, all in minutes or, at most, hours? Again, as in so many areas of contemporary research in astronomy, a qualitative outline of an answer is available, but nothing like a detailed explanation. Of all the various proposals put forth, the most likely appears to be one that involves *magnetic fields* in activity centers. The basic idea is that in the activity centers the magnetic fields get more and more twisted and contorted, and in the process store an ever increasing amount of energy. Finally, some trigger mechanism causes the fields to snap back

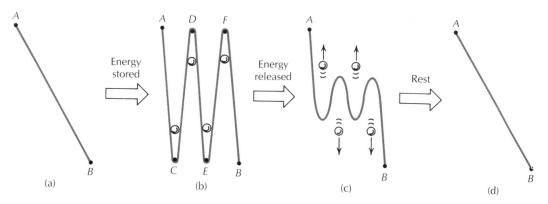

FIGURE 8-13. Magnetic energy storage and release model for solar flares. Magnetic field lines may be thought of as being distorted between (a) and (b); the energy used to distort the field is stored. If the distortion is suddenly removed, with the field lines straightening out between (b) and (d), the energy is released and available to do work (c).

into a simpler form, and the energy difference is released in the flare. Figure 8-13 gives an idea of the principle involved. In a sense, a magnetic field line can be compared to a rubber band stretched between points *A* and *B* in Fig. 8-13 (a). Work must be done to stretch the band, say, around pins *C, D, E,* and *F,* and energy is stored in the rubber band [Fig. 8-13 (b)]. Although the energy might have been stored slowly, it is released quickly when the pins are removed [Fig. 8-13 (c)]. If, for example, some metal spheres were placed as in (b), they would be given momentum when the energy was released in (c).

The flare mechanism is of interest to many scientists other than physicists and astronomers, since a convincing model may have applications beyond astronomy. The physics of hot, ionized, magnetized gases, **plasma physics**, may hold an answer to the desperate search for clean energy sources here on the earth. If we could imitate the sun's energy production in the laboratory, syphoning off the excess energy in the hydrogen-to-helium conversion, we would have a reasonably pollution-free energy source using very cheap fuel (the heavy hydrogen H^2 nuclei in seawater). However, for this purpose we must be able to *contain* the interacting gas at very high temperatures, and this in turn requires huge magnetic fields to keep the electrically charged particles from moving freely about. Progress toward feasible energy production via such a mechanism has been hampered mostly by our poor understanding of the magnetic interactions, which are extremely complex.

8.7   OTHER SOLAR-TERRESTRIAL RELATIONS

We have already seen that specific aspects of solar activity have direct effects on the earth; for instance, a flare's X-rays cause ionospheric disturbances, and the bulk of "slow" particles is responsible for auroras and geomagnetic storms. There is, in addition, a class of phenomena which appears statistically significant but for which at present no clear-cut cause-effect relation is known. Among these phenomena are variations in the quantities of crops harvested, as averaged over large areas, and variations in the water levels of large freshwater lakes. All seem to show the 11-year periodicity of solar activity.

It is clear that single sunspots do not influence terrestrial events directly; thus, the often-reported relations between sunspot activity on a specific date and, say, local weather, belong in the realm of astrology and such occult beliefs. In fact, the spots themselves—with their reduced brightness and magnetic fields—cannot really influence the earth's atmosphere or living things on its surface. It is conceivable, however, that the flares which accompany sunspot activity and which, as we have seen, influence the upper regions of the earth's atmosphere, may cause long-term variations in some properties of the atmosphere as a whole. Ultimately, then, some parameter may be affected which controls, say, the annual rainfall on a continent, or a similar large-scale climatic factor. Nevertheless, so long as no firm statistical data are available, it is speculative at best to dwell in detail on this type of solar-terrestrial relationship.

QUESTIONS FOR DISCUSSION

1. When were the first systematic sunspot observations made? Why then?

2. Why is it said that the true length of the average solar activity cycle is 22 years, rather than 11 years?

3. Why do astronomers claim that magnetic fields are needed to keep prominences suspended in the solar corona?

4. Why is it that the major aspects of flare activity seem to take place well above the photosphere?

5. How is it possible to estimate the height in the solar atmosphere at which some radio emissions connected with flares originate?

6. The nuclear-fusion reactor in the core of the sun does not require magnetic fields to keep working. Why would the man-made analog require magnetic fields?

7. It has been claimed, more or less convincingly, that the widths of the rings of very old trees show an 11-year periodicity. How might such an effect come about?

EXERCISES

1. List those quantities introduced in Chapter 7 to describe the sun as a star and which are slowly varying.

2. How large, in linear extent, is a sunspot group that appears to cover about 10% of the solar radius?

3. Compare the typical times of development of sunspot groups, plages, prominences, and flares.

4. Compare the total energy emitted by a unit area of the undisturbed photosphere and of a sunspot, making use of the temperature figures given in the text and the formulas of Section C.6.

5. Why are sunspots darker, and plages brighter, than the surrounding undisturbed photosphere?

6. What physical property of the emitting or absorbing region is measured via the Zeeman effect?

7. Determine the average length of the solar activity cycle for the years 1900 to 1965 (Fig. 8-7).

8. Compare the dates of the next few solar eclipses with the data on the 11-year cycle of solar activity in Fig. 8-7. Predict the general type of corona you expect to be seen at these eclipses.

9. Using Fig. 8-8, plot the number of sunspot groups that appeared between the solar latitudes 0° and 5°, 5° and 10°, etc., against the latitude range in which they appeared for the years 1935, 1937, and 1942. In what latitude range did most spots appear in these years?

10. During periods of minimum solar activity, sunspot groups are often found close to the equator and at high solar latitude. In what way do these groups differ as far as their magnetic polarities are concerned?

11. Does the maximum number of sunspots appear in the year halfway between the years of two successive solar activity minima? Explain.

12. The pressure of a quantity of gas is proportional to the product of its density and temperature. What do you conclude about the ratio of the pressure within a prominence to that in the corona from the data given in the text?

13. Why does the number of observed flares show the 11-year cycle?

14. Describe the evidence for flares in the γ-ray, X-ray, ultraviolet, visible, and radio ranges of the photon spectrum.

15. List the more important effects of flares on the earth's atmosphere.

16. Why are no flares observed close to the rotational poles of the sun?

17. When is there good reason to expect a major flare?

18. A solar cosmic-ray particle is observed to have a kinetic energy of 1 MeV. What would be the temperature of a gas whose mean energy is 1 MeV (see Table H-2)? Use your result to argue that the acceleration of cosmic-ray particles cannot be a thermal process.

19. What is a relativistic particle? Why is it given the name "relativistic"?

20. The particles that cause auroras in the earth's atmosphere move away from the sun with speeds of the order of 10^3 km/sec. Use this figure to check the statement in the text that auroras occur about 48 hours after a major flare.

21. Assume that the total energy expended in a flare is 10^{32} ergs, that the flare area is about 10^{18} cm², and that the flare energy is expended during 10 minutes. Compare the energy expended per square centimeter in the flare with the energy flowing through the same area as part of the normal luminosity of the sun.

22. Check the statement that the total energy expenditure of the sun in flares is negligible in terms of the sun's energy balance, by assuming that 100 flares, of 10^{32} ergs output each, occur in 10 years (an overestimate!) and comparing the flare energy loss to the energy loss of the sun as a whole.

23. About 1 out of every 10,000 hydrogen nuclei is the heavy isotope H^2. Estimate the total amount of H^2 available in the oceans of the earth.

24. Assume that human activities on our planet require 10^9 kilowatts electric power, and that the reservoir of H^2 calculated in Exercise 23 is totally available for fusion into He^4, with an energy gain of the order of 10 MeV per conversion. For how long could the H^2 reservoir sustain the electric power "needs" of humanity?

EXPERIMENTS

1. You can produce "pinhole" pictures of the sun by closing a venetian blind until the sunlight only comes through a set of tiny openings at the corner of the slats; several solar images should appear on the wall or floor opposite the blind. Large sunspot groups will show up on these pinhole pictures. How can you distinguish the images of such sunspot groups from dirt on the venetian blind or from aircraft or birds passing in front of the sun?

2. Using one of the setups suggested in Experiment 2 of Chapter 2, count the number of sunspot groups you can distinguish and the number of spots in each group. This is still the most common method of arriving at a *relative sunspot number*. Such observations, taken at many stations around the globe, are averaged daily. Each station is given a "weight" or reduction factor, that is, a number by which the observed figures are multiplied to make them compatible with the results obtained at other stations. How would you arrive at such a reduction factor? What characteristics of the station would it have to take into account?

3. (See Experiment 2.) Draw the sunspot groups you see to scale, and compare their development from day to day. Estimate their latitude and longitude on the sun. Try to find a *recurrent* sunspot group, that is, one that reappears at the east limb of the sun two weeks after it has disappeared at the west limb.

4. (See Experiment 2.) Determine the solar rotation period and the spatial alignment of the rotational axis from your observations of sunspots. Under what conditions could you use your observations to prove the differential rotation?

5. Estimate the height of the prominence in Fig. 8-10. Why is your estimate a lower limit for the actual height? Estimate the widths and lengths of some prominences visible in Fig. 8-4. Are these also lower limits for the actual dimensions?

FURTHER READING

The Sun, edited by G. P. Kuiper, Chicago: The University of Chicago Press, 1953.

Smith, H. J., and E. V. P. Smith, *Solar Flares,* New York: The Macmillan Company, 1963.

Bray, R. J., and R. E. Loughhead, *Sunspots,* New York: John Wiley & Sons, Inc., 1965.

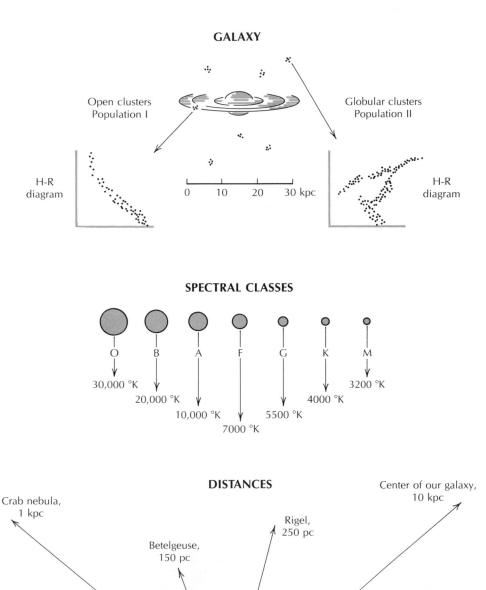

GALAXY

Open clusters
Population I

Globular clusters
Population II

H-R
diagram

H-R
diagram

0   10   20   30 kpc

SPECTRAL CLASSES

O   B   A   F   G   K   M

30,000 °K

20,000 °K

10,000 °K

7000 °K

5500 °K

4000 °K

3200 °K

DISTANCES

Crab nebula,
1 kpc

Center of our galaxy,
10 kpc

Rigel,
250 pc

Betelgeuse,
150 pc

Vega,
8 pc

Sirius,
2.7 pc

α Centauri,
1.3 pc

Earth

II the stars

In preceding chapters we have taken a close and detailed look at the one particular star we are associated with, its planets, and its other "dependents"; we know by now, to a degree, how at least one star operates.

We are ready now to turn to a discussion of stars in general, their differences and their similarities. We shall try to establish a typical sequence of evolution for solar-type stars and for stars that are hotter or cooler, and more or less massive. We will also be able, on the basis of quite recent discoveries, to fit into this overview some of the more spectacular findings from far out in space. Finally, we shall be able to predict rather accurately the future of our own star — whether the species homo sapiens will be here to witness it or not.

9 the gross properties of stars

In the chapters devoted to the sun we have seen how its average properties are found and what their actual values are. Moreover, the sun is the only star for which we are directly able to observe variations across the disc and, under special circumstances, variations in height. All other stars appear to us as *point sources*, and we must try to extract detailed information — in particular, the depth variation of the various physical parameters — from averages, or *gross properties* as we shall call them, for the star as a whole. Of course, the insight we have gained from studying the sun will be a valuable guide in this task.

9.1 THE DISTANCE SCALE

Although the distance of a celestial object from an observer on the earth is not intrinsically a property of the object, but rather an incidental quantity, it is the indispensable basis from which we derive many physical properties. We shall soon see that few meaningful results are available concerning any star if its distance is unknown. So we must have a distance scale, and it must be based on some set of *direct* observations. Then, given the original, direct observations, we can make use of theory and other observations to extend our distance scale beyond the limits of these first direct observations.

Measurement of Parallax. The original set of distance observations is based on the so-called **parallactic motion** of nearby stars, to which we have alluded on several occasions as a crucial test of the Copernican system. This parallactic motion is not performed by the star, but rather is a consequence of the revolution of the earth. The principle is outlined in Fig. 9-1. The angle θ at which a star's position appears with respect to the earth's rotational axis (to which our celestial coordinate system refers) changes slightly from December (θ_D) to June (θ_J); the quantity of interest, the angle ϕ in Fig. 9-1, can be obtained from θ_D and θ_J. The process is similar to **triangulation**, in which the exact position of an object is found from directional readings from two points. For example, knowing the astronomical unit and the angle θ_J, we can place the star somewhere on line L_1 in Fig. 9-1; knowing θ_D we can place the star on L_2. To be on both lines the star must be at their intersection. In order actually to measure θ_D and θ_J, we must define the positions of the star on the celestial sphere with respect to background objects that do not show any measurable parallactic motion, that is, to objects that are much more distant than the star in question. We must also have determined the α and δ coordinates of these distant objects beforehand.

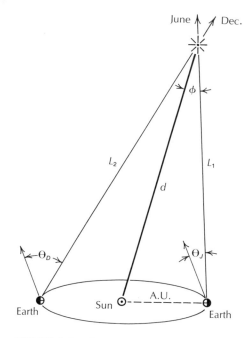

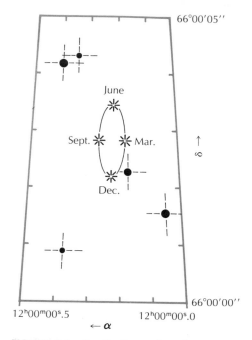

FIGURE 9-1. Geometry of parallactic motion of the earth about the sun. The star appears to be located at an angle θ_D from the direction of the rotational axis of the earth (celestial pole) in December; at an angle θ_J in June. Angles θ_D and θ_J differ by a minute amount expressed by the angle ϕ that depends on the distance d of the star from us.

FIGURE 9-2. Parallactic motion of a star on the celestial sphere. The annual apparent motion of a close-by star (*) is plotted against a hypothetical star field, represented by the dots, at much greater distance. Note the extremely fine abscissa and ordinate scales. In reality, all positional measurements are afflicted by errors, schematically represented by the dashed bars through the dots.

     Figure 9-2 explains the process schematically. The parallactic motion of the nearby star (*) is shown as an ellipse close to the center of the field of background stars surrounding our object, which, as can be seen from the α and δ scales, covers an extremely small portion of the sky. The black discs are the distant comparison objects whose coordinates are accurately known. To determine its parallactic motion, the position of the star with respect to these background objects is measured visually or photographically during the course of a year or, more realistically, of many years. (Note that the position of the star also changes in a nonperiodic fashion because of its proper motion, which has not been taken into account in Fig. 9-2.)

     A star aligned with the earth and the ecliptic pole would appear to move in a small circle that is an exact image of the earth's orbit about the sun; it would have a period that is precisely the annual orbital period of the earth. This apparent motion of the star is the parallactic motion; if the star is not positioned exactly at the ecliptic pole, the parallactic motion is elliptical in form and is the more eccentric the closer the star's position is to the plane of the ecliptic. Actually, the situation is somewhat

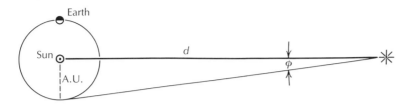

FIGURE 9-3. **Parallax angle and distance. The tangent of the angle**
ϕ **is the ratio of astronomical unit to star distance** d**. A star with a**
parallax of $\phi = 1$ **arcsec is said to be at a distance of 1 pc.**

complicated by the so-called **aberration**, which is due to the finite speed of light and
which adds an additional apparent motion to the star's image. However, the aberration
pattern is the same for stars at all distances and thus can be eliminated from
the raw observations.

Obviously, the closer a star is to the earth, the larger is the angle ϕ, which we
call the star's **parallax**. Since in Fig. 9-3 we have $\tan \phi = 1$ A.U./d, a star with a parallax
of 1 arcsec is at a distance d from the sun of 1 A.U./tan (1 arcsec) ≈ 1 A.U./
5×10^{-6}, which is 2×10^5 A.U. This works out to about 3×10^{18} cm. It is now customary
to refer to this distance as the **parsec** (pc) and use it as the unit for distances in
the universe, along with the usual multiples, the **kiloparsec** (1 kpc $= 10^3$ pc) and the
megaparsec (1 Mpc $= 10^6$ pc). It takes light about 3 years to travel a distance of 1 pc;
thus, the **light-year** is a distance of approximately $\frac{1}{3}$ pc.

Our closest star neighbors are just over 1 pc from the sun. They form the triple-
star system **α Centauri** in the southern sky, whose brightest member must be very
similar to the sun. Because of the distance involved, on the basis of present technology
manned exploration of even our nearest neighboring star system does not seem
feasible in the foreseeable future; even light signals would take about 8 years to
reach it and return to the earth.

Limitations of the Method. An angle of 1 arcsec is quite difficult to measure by
comparing star images on photographs taken half a year apart. At a parallax of 0.1
arcsec the measurement errors become quite appreciable, and measurements of
parallaxes below 0.05 arcsec are rather meaningless for single stars, although they
still provide information *on a statistical basis* for star groups. Thus, fairly reliable
direct measurements can be made for stars at between 1 pc and some 10 pc
distance, and all other distance determinations are ultimately referred to these measurements. It is therefore important to have as complete a list of nearby stars available as possible. It is relatively easy to recognize nearby stars. At present, about 50
stars are known to be within 5 pc of the sun; they are listed in Table H-10.

Extending the distance scale beyond these very restrictive limits requires the use
of other stellar properties. We shall see that such an extension is, indeed, possible,
first with the aid of luminosity-temperature relations (Section 11.2), then by consider-
ing the special case of pulsating stars (Section 15.2), and finally by means of the
redshift-distance relation for extragalactic objects (Section 20.3).

9.2 PROPER MOTIONS AND RADIAL VELOCITIES

If we compared two photographs of the same region of the sky taken some 20 or more years apart, we would find that the relative positions of some stars had changed by small amounts. Such changes have been interpreted as a relative motion of these stars with respect to the sun and the earth. This relative motion of a star with respect to the background is called its **proper motion** and is measured in angular units per time interval, say, in arcseconds per century. Note that the amount of proper motion we see is dependent on our distance from the subject star. Since it is important to measure the star's position with respect to a reference frame that does not change appreciably over the time periods in question, we must measure it with respect to very distant objects. Faraway galaxies are most suitable as reference frames.

Obviously, on the average, nearby stars will have larger proper motions than stars at greater distances, and a star with a large proper motion is an immediate candidate for a check on a possibly large parallax. Typical proper motions of stars out to 5 pc are of the order of several arcseconds per year; that is, the proper motion is in general much greater than the annual parallax. Suppose we know the distance to some star and we measured its proper motion in some *angular* unit per time interval, we could then calculate, in some *linear* unit per time interval, the component of its velocity at right angles to the line of sight, that is, the line connecting the star and the observer.

On the other hand, if we take a spectrum of the star, and if this spectrum has identifiable line features (as practically all stellar spectra have), we can measure the Doppler effect on the spectral lines. This gives us the relative velocity between star and the sun *along* the line of sight, the **radial velocity,** in absolute measure, say, in kilometers per second. We must only be careful to select stars whose line-producing atmospheres do not expand or contract, as is the case, for example, with certain classes of variable stars (Section 15.2). At any rate, the combination of proper motion and radial velocity yields, for a star of known distance, all the important information on its motion in space.

In reality, we only learn the *relative* motion of the star with respect to the sun, and it is not clear a priori that our sun is the appropriate reference point. In fact, it is not, since it revolves together with all its star neighbors about the center of our galaxy. (We can consider a galaxy as a star system for now; as we discuss galaxies further, we shall refine this "definition.") This motion of our sun with respect to objects *outside* our own galaxy can be determined from Doppler-effect measurements, and it turns out that the solar system is moving at about 250 km/sec in an orbit about the galactic center.

Hence, the proper motions and radial velocities of nearby stars are relative motions of these stars with respect to the sun. Some components of these motions are due to the *differential* galactic rotation, that is, the fact that stars closer to the galactic center than the sun move a bit faster in their orbits and thus overtake the sun, while stars further out are slower and are overtaken by the sun. The remaining stellar motions, whose velocities are typically an order of magnitude less than the rotational velocity of the sun about the galactic center, are truly random. They reflect velocities the stars achieved at birth and which were later modified in gravitational interactions with gas clouds encountered along the stellar paths.

9.3 BRIGHTNESS, LUMINOSITY, MAGNITUDE

Apparent Magnitude. If we look at the sky, we see stars of very different **brightnesses**, or **magnitudes** as astronomers usually say. Some of these differences are certainly due to intrinsic differences in the energy outputs of the stars, that is, in their *luminosities*, but others arise simply because the stars are at different distances from us. Thus, our raw observations, whether obtained with the unaided eye or with a telescope and photographic plate, or some similar recording device, are a mixture of physically meaningful quantities that describe the stars and accidental things such as their distances. In addition, some light is always absorbed on its way from the star to the earth; often this requires that quite significant corrections be made to the raw data. The uncorrected observed brightness of a star is called its **apparent magnitude.**

Magnitude Numbers. Astronomers have devised a quite unique system of expressing brightnesses in a quantitative fashion, founded in the mysteries of our science's historical development. The scale is logarithmic, but the base is neither the customary 10 nor the number $e = 2.714$; rather, it is 2.512 . . . , the fifth root of 100. In addition, the sign is "wrong" in that the **magnitude numbers** increase for decreasing brightness, so that a *third*-magnitude star gives us 2.512 . . . times as much brightness as a *fourth*-magnitude star. The *difference* between the magnitude numbers of the two stars is thus proportional to the *logarithm of the ratio* of their respective luminosities and is given by the relation

$$M_4 - M_3 = -2.50 \left(\log_{10} \frac{L_4}{L_3} \right)$$

In this text we shall avoid magnitude numbers; instead we shall use conventional logarithmic scales in plotting magnitudes, defining appropriate units wherever necessary. Nevertheless, for completeness let us look at the equation in more detail. If the brightness ratio of two stars is 100, then their magnitude numbers differ by 5. Similarly, if the two stars had a brightness ratio of 10, their magnitude numbers would differ by 2.5; we write this magnitude difference in the form 2^m5. We have already stated that a magnitude difference of 1^m0 corresponds to a brightness ratio of about 2.5. The **absolute bolometric magnitude** of the sun, that is, the brightness the sun would have if it were placed at a distance of 10 pc from us, and if *all* its light (including the invisible portion in the ultraviolet) were recorded, is given as $+4^m6$. A star at the same distance but 100 times brighter would have a magnitude of $4^m6 - 5^m0 = -0^m4$; a star 10 times brighter, a magnitude of $+2^m1$. Stars with brightnesses of only one-tenth and one-hundredth the solar value would have absolute magnitudes of $+7^m1$ and 9^m6, respectively. Finally, the faintest stars we can observe with the naked eye on a very clear night have an apparent magnitude of about $+6^m0$.

Luminosity and Absolute Magnitude. We have already noted that the distance of a star from us is not an intrinsically interesting quantity. Thus, we would like to remove distance from our considerations by reducing the actual observations to a comparison with a standard star at an arbitrary but fixed distance. In order to understand the procedure, let us go through it step by step. We first define the **luminosity** L of a star by the relation

$$L = 4\pi R^2\, l$$

where R_* is the radius of the (supposedly spherical) star, $4\pi R_*^2$ is its surface area, and l the amount of radiation passing through one square centimeter of its surface in one second. As we have done in the case of the sun, we can express l in terms of an **effective temperature** T such that

$$l = aT^4$$

where a equals 5.7×10^{-5} erg/cm²·sec·degree⁴. If l (in ergs/cm²·sec) is calculated as total energy, summed over all wavelengths, then L above is the **total luminosity** (in ergs/sec) or **bolometric magnitude** of the star. If l is measured over a certain band of energies (say, the blue portion of the visible spectrum, or the range of radio wavelengths), then L becomes a spectrally resolved quantity and is given the appropriate name (such as **blue magnitude** or **red magnitude**).

The energy of a particular star passing through a square centimeter at a distance d from the center of the star in one second is $L/4\pi d^2$, since the star's total energy output L is spread over a sphere with radius d. Thus, if we compare two otherwise identical stars and neglect all possible absorptions along the way, a star half as far away appears four times as bright to a light-measuring instrument.

Knowing the apparent magnitude and distance of a star, we can use the last formula to calculate what its magnitude would be if it were at *10 pc distance* from the sun. This figure, called the **absolute magnitude** of the star, is independent of its actual distance and so can be used to classify the star strictly in terms of observed quantitites. Again, we shall seldom have reason in this text to quote absolute magnitudes, although these numbers are as commonplace and meaningful to the professional astronomer as Fahrenheit temperatures are to the average person in the United States. Once we know to what class a certain star belongs, the difference between its apparent magnitude and the absolute magnitude assigned to its class is a measure of its distance, in units of the 10 pc standard that defines absolute magnitude.

Stellar luminosities vary by large amounts. The brightest bluish-white stars in the sky are about 10^6 times brighter than the sun, while the sun is 10^4 times as luminous as the faintest red stars. The reason for this tremendous difference in stellar luminosity is one of the most important problems of stellar astronomy and is discussed in Chapter 12.

9.4   RADII AND MASSES

Stellar Radii.   It was emphasized in Chapter 7 that the sun is the only star whose features are accessible to direct observation; no other star's surface features can be resolved, even with the largest telescopes. In fact, if the sun were removed to the distance of our nearest neighbors, its angular size would be less than 10^{-5} arcsec, which is beyond the resolving power of any optical telescope—or radio telescope, for that matter.

However, the interferometer techniques described in Section E.4 can be used to measure stellar radii, provided the stars are intrinsically bright and have radii whose angular measure is greater than the present instrumental limit of somewhat less than 10^{-3} arcsec. In this manner, the radius of Sirius was found to be 0.0030 arcsec, which at the distance of 2.7 pc corresponds to about 2 solar radii. Altogether some 20 stars have by now been measured. Although interferometer techniques only give us the angular dimension of the stellar photosphere and are applicable to just a small set of rather special stars, they are important because they yield the only really *direct* measurements of stellar radii.

All other determinations are more or less indirect and based on assumptions that are often hard to verify. We shall see in Section 10.3 that a special class of twin or binary stars, the so-called eclipsing binaries, can be used for radius determinations. The most widely applicable method employs the definition of luminosity: $L = 4\pi R_*^2\, l$. If we know l, we can compute R_* from the luminosity L which, in turn, is known for stars of known distances. Recalling our definition of l in terms of effective temperature, we see that the radius-determination problem can be reduced to the problem of finding an appropriate effective temperature from available observational and theoretical data. This task will be discussed in detail in Section 9.5.

The combined results of all these direct and indirect determinations show that there are stars whose radii are several hundred times the solar radius; even the earth's orbit about the sun would lie inside such a star. There are also some bona fide stars with radii less than one-tenth the solar value, or not much greater than Jupiter's radius. Finally, there are some very special cases of types of stars with extremely small radii, which we will discuss in Sections 13.4 and 14.3.

Stellar Masses.   In order to determine the mass of a star, we must determine and make use of the gravitational interaction of the star with some other body. Thus, direct determinations can be made only for multiple star systems; the methods involved will be detailed in Sections 10.2 and 10.3. At any rate, the masses of only 50 or so stars have been obtained directly. All other statements concerning stellar masses are essentially extrapolations from this rather narrow basis, or else they are based on theoretical considerations involving stellar evolution.

Since the stars whose masses are directly measurable are mostly rather close to us in space, we know their distances and, hence, their luminosities. A graph of mass versus luminosity (such as Fig. 9-4) for a number of stars reveals a clear correlation, known as the **mass-luminosity relation**. The mass-luminosity diagram of Fig. 9-4, in which luminosity and mass are given in *solar units*, is an important means for comparing theoretical predictions of stellar masses and luminosities with observations. We conclude that it is apparently the total mass, at least for the stars cited in Fig. 9-4, which fixes luminosity.

All data taken together, we find that there are stars considerably more massive than the sun, with an apparent upper limit in the neighborhood of 50 solar masses. On the other hand, objects with masses of only a few percent of the solar value still are stars. By way of comparison, Jupiter, which never was a star, has a mass of about $10^{-3}M_\odot$. Hence, stellar masses vary through some three, or at most four, orders of magnitude.

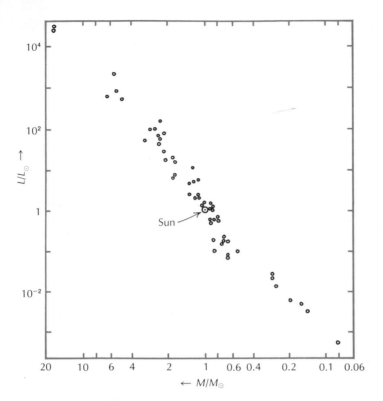

FIGURE 9-4. Mass-luminosity relation for main-sequence stars. The most luminous stars are more than 20 times as massive as the sun, the least luminous ones have a mass of less than 10% of the solar mass.

9.5 THE ANALYSIS OF STELLAR SPECTRA

In discussing the sun, we emphasized the wealth of information contained in its spectrum, even when no resolution of its surface was attempted. There is no reason to believe the situation to be different for other stars. Thus, we would expect to find, through detailed spectral analysis, all that is necessary to specify the temperature and density variations across the stellar photospheres (and, possibly, chromospheres) of most stars. In addition, we should be able to derive the chemical composition of their surface layers.

Spectral Analysis. At this point let us recapitulate the main features of the formation of the solar spectrum as we discussed them in Section 7.4. The energy extracted from nuclear sources in the interior is emitted by the sun in the radiation field which emerges from the surface, that is, the rather thin layer we called the *photosphere*. The radiative loss produces a *temperature gradient* across the photosphere, so that photons originating deeper in the star have an energy distribution characteristic of a temperature higher than that of photons emerging from upper layers. Because of varying reabsorption probabilities, photons of different energies (wavelengths) will on the average leave the sun from slightly different levels and, hence, represent slightly different temperatures. This is how we explained the existence of *absorption* or *Fraunhofer lines,* in addition to the solar *continuum.* The contours of the absorption lines (Section C.5) can be used to determine the densities of the layers from which specific photons arrive.

Finally, the existence of *chromosphere* and *corona,* with their attendant temperature reversal, adds a complication: At wavelengths for which the reabsorption probability is very large through the whole photosphere, only photons from the highest layers will be able to reach us; they thus represent the physical conditions prevailing in the high-temperature outer layers of the atmosphere. This we found to be the cause of *emission lines.* Wherever there are a chromosphere and corona, we must expect, at appropriate wavelengths, an increase in spectral intensity with respect to neighboring ("cooler") spectral areas. That is, we must expect emission lines superimposed on the continuum. In essence, then, we must be prepared to find emission spectra, absorption spectra, and a combination of both in certain classes of stars.

Hence, in principle, we will be able to derive from the observed spectrum of a star the **temperature**, **density**, and **chemical compositon** of every layer that contributes to the total radiation loss. From this information, in turn, we can predict the whole spectrum to any desired accuracy, including the ranges inaccessible to direct observation, that is, outside the visible and radio ranges. (Ultraviolet and X-ray spectra for some stars can be, and indeed have been, obtained using rockets and satellites, but the method is so expensive that actual spectra are available only for a very limited number of stars.) At that stage, we can compute an effective temperature and, if we know the radius of the star, we can find the total radiative loss. This latter quantity must be provided by internal energy sources, such as the hydrogen conversion in the interior of stars.

Obviously, there are many possible sources of error in this procedure. For instance, it may happen that the major amount of radiation energy is emitted in a frequency range not directly accessible to observation. In this case the layers from which such radiation emerges would likely be represented in the *observable* spectrum to only a very minor degree. Then most of the information needed to calculate an effective temperature would be obtained from extrapolation, which is always accompanied by a degree of uncertainty. Specifically, the absorption lines of a certain element may be expected in the unobservable wavelength range where most of the energy resides, but the abundance of this element may have been inaccurately calculated from data in the visible range.

Classification of Star Spectra. For the reason just given, stellar spectra are usually classified according to *observed* features only; extraction of the physical properties of a star from spectral data is done independently. This avoids successive and continual correction of the classification scheme as more data are extracted.

Before we describe in detail the characteristic features of each major class of stars, let us discuss the physical reasons for them. We shall compare four stars with varying photospheric temperatures.

The Behavior of Three Prominent Elements at Different Temperatures. In order to simplify the main arguments on which this comparison is based, we first discuss in detail the behavior of three elements, namely, hydrogen, helium, and iron, as a function of temperature. For our purposes, the principal difference among these three elements is the amount of energy necessary for ionization, that is, for freeing one electron from the atom. The ionization energies of the three elements, in electron volts, are 13.6, 24.6, and 7.9, respectively. Hence, of the three, helium requires the most, and iron the least, energy to free an electron.

There is, however, a second point to consider: the photons we work with in stellar spectroscopy in the visible range have energies of about 2 or 3 electron volts (eV). Now, these photons fit almost everywhere into the energy-level scheme of the iron atom (Fig. C-3); they are, in particular, upon absorption, able to remove an electron from the ground state to any of a number of excited states. The arrangement of energy levels in the case of hydrogen (Fig. C-2) and helium (which looks very much like hydrogen) is quite different: the first excited state lies about 10 eV above the ground state in the case of hydrogen, about 20 eV in the case of helium. Thus, photons of 2 or 3 eV energy can only induce electron transitions among the *excited* states of hydrogen and helium atoms, and these atoms must be subjected to very high temperatures in order that a significant number of them acquire the energy necessary to leave the ground state, before they can interact with photons in the visible range of the spectrum.

This then means that helium lines will appear in very hot stars, hydrogen lines in somewhat cooler stars, and iron lines in stars of still lower temperatures. Elements such as carbon, nitrogen, and oxygen require temperatures somewhere between the extremes of helium and iron, whereas many of the other metals behave very much like iron.

Four Typical Star Spectra.   Against this background we now turn to a more quantitative discussion of the spectra of four stars whose photospheric temperatures are 20,000°K, 10,000°K, 5000°K, and 3000°K.

At 20,000°K, the element *helium* exists mostly in the neutral atomic state; there are enough electrons and ambient photons around with energy sufficient to excite and ionize some neutral helium atoms, but not enough energy to do the same to helium ions. On the other hand, the element *hydrogen* will be mostly ionized, because of its lower ionization energy; the *metals*, with their still lower ionization energy, will be ionized twice or even three times. Thus, a star with a photosphere at 20,000°K will exhibit *strong* Fraunhofer lines of neutral helium, because the temperature is just right to excite a large number of neutral helium atoms, but not high enough to ionize most of them. It will exhibit *weak* hydrogen lines, because most of the hydrogen atoms are ionized; having lost the one electron it had, the hydrogen atom can no longer produce spectral lines. Finally, the spectrum will show the lines of several-times-ionized metals.

At 10,000°K, the mean energy of photons and material particles is below that required to excite a great number of helium atoms but just sufficient to excite the hydrogen present. The metals will be in a somewhat lower stage of ionization. We should then find, in a spectrum for this temperature, weak neutral helium lines, very strong hydrogen lines, and metal lines mostly of the once-ionized stage.

At a temperature of 5000°K, we expect all helium to be in the neutral ground state, and thus the helium lines will have vanished from the spectrum. The hydrogen lines are weaker than at 10,000°K, because only few photons and electrons have energies sufficient to excite this element. And the metals, which are now mostly neutral, will show up through neutral-state lines. In addition, some elements will form molecules of the type of C_2, or CN, the so-called free radicals. Thus, stars a little cooler than the sun will show the first distinct molecular bands (Section C.5).

This last effect is much more pronounced at still lower temperatures, such as 3000°K, where the whole spectrum is covered with molecular bands, not only of free radicals, but also of metal oxides which are stable at temperatures of the order of 3000°K. At about this temperature, we begin to get the lines of the H_2 *molecule* in noticeable quantities, while the atomic hydrogen lines almost vanish. The atomic metals, finally, are almost all in the neutral state and contribute a wealth of lines interspersed among the molecular bands.

9.6 TEMPERATURES AND SPECTRAL CLASSIFICATION

Against the background of our discussion in the last section, we can state that all that is needed to determine the *surface temperature* or, as astronomers are fond of saying, the **color** of a star is a spectrum of the object in question, with wavelength resolution sufficient to identify the spectral lines of importance. Spectra are now obtainable for objects whose apparent brightnesses are a million or more times smaller than the faintest stars visible to the naked eye. Thus, provided the energy is not absorbed in between, spectra may be obtained for any star we can observe at all.

Spectral Classification. The most widely used scheme for describing stellar temperature structure is that of **spectral classes**, based on the appearance of the Fraunhofer or absorption lines and designated by capital letters. Basically, the spectral classes represent a temperature sequence and run, from high to low temperatures, through the letters O, B, A, F, G, K, and M. Each letter is followed by a number from 0 to 9 for finer distinctions. The garbled alphabetical arrangement is due to the fact that the designations were introduced at a time—before the turn of the century—when the physics behind the temperature sequence was not yet understood.

The main characteristics of the spectral classes are summarized below.* Typical spectra are reproduced in Figs. 9-5(a) to (g), which illustrate the relative strengths of the spectral manifestations of helium, hydrogen, the metals, and the molecules. In our discussion of the physical background of stellar spectral analysis, we discussed the reasons why hydrogen, helium, and a metal such as iron behave so differently at various temperatures; for instance, we have seen why hydrogen lines are weak at very high and very low temperatures and reach a maximum strength around 10,000°K, and why neutral iron lines appear only at lower temperatures. It should be remembered, however, that the strength of an absorption or emission line also depends on the relative number of atoms of a particular element in the gas mixture

*A list of stars that are typical of their spectral classes and are easily recognizable to the naked eye is given in Section G.2.

TYPE   STAR

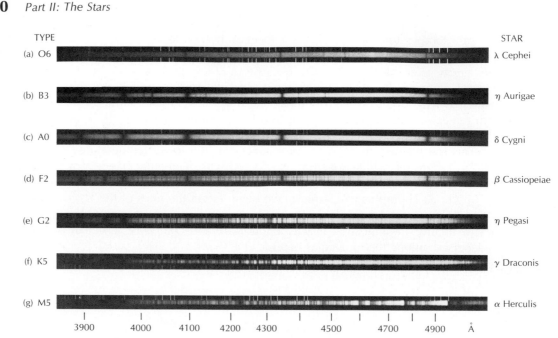

(a) O6   λ Cephei

(b) B3   η Aurigae

(c) A0   δ Cygni

(d) F2   β Cassiopeiae

(e) G2   η Pegasi

(f) K5   γ Draconis

(g) M5   α Herculis

| | | | | | | | | | | | |
3900   4000   4100 4200 4300   4500   4700   4900   Å

FIGURE 9-5. **Principal types of stellar spectra.** Reproduced are actual spectra of types (a) O6, (b) B3, (c) A0, (d) F2, (e) G2, (f) K5, and (g) M5. The spectra cover the wavelength range of about 3850 Å to 5000 Å. Compare the G2 spectrum of η Pegasi with the solar spectrum of Fig. 7-6. Among the most easily recognizable features are the lines of neutral hydrogen at 4861 Å (called "H$_\beta$"), 4340 Å (H$_\gamma$), and 4102 Å (H$_\delta$), in particular, in the B and A star spectra; the two lines of ionized calcium at 3934 Å (K) and 3968 Å (H), notably in the F and K star spectra (note, however, that the H line of Ca$^+$ coincides with a hydrogen line); the helium lines at 4387 Å and 4471 Å in the B star spectrum; and the line of neutral calcium at 4226 Å in the G, K, and M, star spectra. Finally, note the molecular bands, for instance, around 4600 Å in the M star spectrum. The white markings above and below the individual spectra are lines in comparison spectra taken in the laboratory. (*Hale Observatories.*)

comprising the photosphere from which the line originates—in other works, on its *abundance*. Assuming the approximate abundance values derived for the sun (Table 7-1), we define the spectral classes as follows:

O Stars. Photospheric temperatures of the order of 30,000°K. Spectral lines of ionized helium and triply ionized metals; very weak hydrogen lines [Fig. 9-5(a)].

B Stars. Temperatures in the neighborhood of 20,000°K. Lines of neutral helium; still rather weak hydrogen lines; lines of metals in several ionization stages [Fig. 9-5(b)].

A Stars. Temperatures near 10,000°K. Neutral helium lines still present, but very weak, at the high-temperature end of the class (A0); very strong hydrogen lines; lines of mostly once-ionized metals [Fig. 9-5(c)].

F Stars. Temperatures of about 7000°K. The hydrogen lines are now weaker, but still dominate the spectrum; lines of both once-ionized and neutral metals [Fig 9-5(d)].

G Stars.   *Solar type.* Temperatures around 5500°K. Relatively weak hydrogen lines; many metal lines, either of the once-ionized state in cases where the ionization energy is particularly small, or of the neutral stage; first strong molecular bands [Fig. 9-5(e)].

K Stars.   Temperatures of about 4000°K. Spectrum dominated by neutral metal lines; increasing number of molecular bands [Fig. 9-5(f)].

M Stars.   Temperatures typically 3200°K. Again many neutral metal lines, but TiO bands now dominate the spectrum [Fig. 9-5(g)].

The vast majority of stars can be described by this classification scheme. These stars, plus the *white dwarfs* to be discussed in Section 13.4, represent what we consider the "normal" population of the star system. (Some members are unusual in one way or another, and we shall come back to their spectral features and classifications at the end of this section.) We conclude that the normal star population contains objects whose temperatures vary roughly between some 30,000°K and 3000°K. The upper limit is probably real in the physical sense, since it corresponds to stars of very large mass, but the lower limit may be due to observational limitations; very cool stars are very faint and therefore difficult to observe. Thus, the temperatures of "normal" stars vary only by about a factor of 10, and their *surface brightnesses* by some 10^4, because surface brightness is proportional to the fourth power of *T*. The much larger range of observed luminosities is due to variations in surface area.

Luminosity Classes.   It is possible to extract data on the *density* of the atmosphere of a star from the details of the spectrum. Qualitatively speaking, we can say that, at a given temperature, a high density favors the recombination of ions and electrons to atoms, while a low density will restrict recombination. Hence, the degree of ionization varies inversely with the density.

Stars with very **extended atmospheres**, that is, very large radii, have very *low densities*, even in their photospheres. Again, in a qualitative sense, we can argue from Newton's law that larger radii result in lower gravitational forces at the surface, so that the atoms and ions of the atmosphere are not so tightly bound to the star. The atmosphere is then spread out, and has a lower density. Thus, we can estimate the radius of a star from its spectrum, going through the steps just outlined: higher degree of ionization at the same temperature means lower density which, in turn, means larger radius.

Finally, it is obvious that a star with a very extended atmosphere has a much larger surface from which photons can escape, so that ultimately we have higher degree of ionization implying lower density implying large radius implying large luminosity.

Again it is customary to classify this information in terms of a scheme that involves only *observed* features, specifically the contour or width of certain spectral lines, rather than the *computed* stellar radius. This scheme is used to define the **luminosity classes,** counted in Roman numerals from I (*supergiants*) through V (*main-sequence dwarfs*). The sun, for example, is then fully classified as a G2V star.

Color Indices. The UBV System.   Classifying a star according to its spectral class (with decimal) and its luminosity class requires not only quite a bit of theoretical background, but also the availability of rather detailed spectra. Although it is true that in principle this information could be gathered for practically any star with the 200-inch telescope, with advanced spectroscopic techniques, and with unlimited hours of observing time, in reality the procedure is too cumbersome for many purposes.

The most important scheme of a much simpler nature is the system of **color classification.** It essentially eliminates the need to take complete spectra and uses instead observations taken over selected narrow strips of the spectrum. These strips are singled out by suppressing photons of other wavelengths through **filtering**. The relative number of photons detected in a strip centered at a particular wavelength depends on the temperature of the star. Thus, counting the photons passing through the various strips gives us a measure of the temperature, although not quite as straightforwardly as would the complete spectrum. The main difficulty in this classification scheme is the problem of calibrating it with respect to the more complete spectral and luminosity classifications.

The ratio of the amounts of radiation detected in any two strips is expressed in the logarithmic magnitude system and called a **color index**. The most often used filter combinations result in the color indices of the so-called **UBV system**. The name of this classification scheme derives from the wavelength ranges in which the strips lie: U for ultraviolet, B for blue, and V for visual, the latter corresponding to the sensitivity of the human eye. Recently, additional strips have been added in the red and infrared ranges and given similar letter designations. The UBV color indices quoted in the astronomical literature then simply represent specific filter combinations. In this text, whenever we use color indices in graphs taken from the literature, we shall include spectral classes for reference.

Other Classifications.   Certain classes of stars do not fit any of the regular classification schemes. Some such stars show, in addition to absorption spectra that may well follow the patterns of the more normal spectral classes, *emission features* in spectral ranges. Typically these are cool stars with extended chromospheres and correspondingly more or less pronounced emission lines that originate high in the outer atmosphere. Other stars with emission lines may be members of very close binary systems (Section 10.4), or may rotate very fast (Section 9.7), forming envelopes about themselves. One denotes such an emission characteristic by the letter e following the spectral classification: examples are M6Ve and B1Ve.

Certain classes of stars differ from the regular spectral and luminosity classes in that the Fraunhofer lines are *systematically weaker* than those of the corresponding regular spectral and luminosity classes; the reason is that these stars contain proportionally less metals than stars such as the sun. They are called **subdwarfs**, because they are also less luminous than the stars of the corresponding regular spectral classes.

Other star classes differ from the standard only in the strengths of *certain* spectral lines, or show similar spectral peculiarities; they are usually designated by the letter p following the spectral classification. Thus, the *magnetic stars* discussed in Section 15.4 are among the **peculiar A stars** (Ap).

Finally, the letters N, R, and S as spectral classifications are reserved for the rather rare cases of cool stars that show strong absorption features in specific bands (absorption by ZrO, for instance) that are much weaker or do not appear at all in the stars of spectral classes K and M.

9.7 STELLAR ROTATION AND CHEMICAL COMPOSITION

Rotation. We saw in Section 7.1 that the sun rotates once about its axis in 24 days (at least, its equator does—recall the differential nature of solar rotation). This **rotation** period corresponds to a material velocity of about 2 km/sec at the equatorial surface. The actual figure is, of course, derived from the Doppler shift of the spectral lines at the east and west limbs. In the case of distant stars, where we cannot distinguish between "east and west limbs," information on rotation must be retrieved from spectra; this is possible provided that the rotational velocity of the material at at the star's surface is greater than some few kilometers per second.

It turns out that there is a definite relationship between rotational velocities and spectral classes. On the average, the hot stars rotate much faster than the cool ones, and few stars below about class F5 have rotation speeds of more than a few kilometers per second. In fact, this spectral type seems to represent a discontinuity in the smooth transition of stellar properties from type to type.

While the rotational velocities of most stars fall into this "normal" pattern, there are some particularly extreme cases known among the O and B stars. These stars have rotational velocities so high that they must be quite flattened, and they continuously throw off material at the equator. This material collects into a gaseous envelope and is responsible for the emission lines observed in some O and B spectra (whence they become types Oe and Be).

Chemical Composition. One of the major results of the analysis of a large number of star spectra is information on the relative frequencies of various chemical elements, in other words, the **chemical compositon** of a typical stellar atmosphere. The principle by which this information is gathered is obvious from our previous discussions: A model is constructed showing temperature and density variation with height across the layers from which photons are received; from the model, the spectrum of the star is computed. The parameters, including the abundances of the various elements that show up in the spectrum, are then varied until observed and computed spectra coincide. Obviously, there are many complications inherent in this "iterative" approach. For example, information on elements with high ionization energy can only be obtained from hot stars. Thus, the helium or neon abundance is obtained by comparing theoretical "model atmospheres" of O and B stars with observations. On the other hand, some ionized elements have only a limited number of spectral lines in easily accessible spectral ranges, and only their neutral stages can be investigated; lithium is a case in point. Then, we must turn to cool stars.

The results, however, are surprisingly uniform in that all "normal" stars in the neighborhood of the sun—and later we shall argue that these stars make up the main bulk of the observable star population—have an identical chemical composition, within the accuracy of the method. These stars are characterized by a composition that consists of about 85% hydrogen by number of particles, 14% helium, and a small admixture of the remaining elements, mostly carbon, nitrogen, oxygen, neon, magnesium, silicon, and iron (cf. Table 7-1). Later, we shall call this a typical abundance of "Population I" stars.

QUESTIONS FOR DISCUSSION

1.   How is it possible to determine the variation of temperature and density with depth for a star, if we cannot even distinguish its surface details?

2.   What would be the effect on the measurement of parallaxes if the astronomical unit were twice as large as it actually is?

3.   The annual change of a star's α and δ coordinates contains two components: one due to precession and one due to its proper motion. Why is the former more prominent for distant stars?

4.   What do we mean when we say that one star is "twice as bright" as another?

5.   Is it possible that the blue magnitudes of two stars are the same, but their red magnitudes differ? Explain.

6.   What is the relation between stellar mass and luminosity implied by Fig. 9-4? Is it true that a star with one-tenth the solar mass is one-tenth as luminous as the sun?

7.   Would you expect lines of the element technetium to be particularly prominent in stellar spectra? Justify your answer.

8.   There are distinct differences between the atomic-energy-level schemes of iron on one hand, and of helium and hydrogen on the other. What do they mean for stellar spectroscopy?

9.   Compare the main features of the spectrum of a star with a very extended atmosphere with those of the spectrum of a relatively compact star.

10.   How would you estimate the rotational speed of a star whose surface cannot be resolved?

11.   What happens to the geometrical shape of a star if it rotates *very* fast? Why?

EXERCISES

1.   Summarize the properties of the sun that indicate it is a star.

2.   Why do all stars except the sun appear as point sources, even to the largest telescopes?

3.   What is the difference between the luminosity, apparent magnitude, and absolute magnitude of a star?

4.   Convert the parallaxes given in Table H-10 into distances.

5.   Compute the time it takes light to reach us from the stars listed in Table H-10.

6.   Express the parallax of a star 2 pc from the sun as the angular diameter of a 25-cent piece at a certain distance.

7.   Figure 9-2 is used to give an approximately correct impression of the problems involved in measuring parallaxes. Several parts of the graph should be checked as to their correctness.

(a) Why is the declination chosen to be about +66°? (b) What would change if we had chosen a declination of −66°? (c) In the graph, the parallactic motion of the star is given as an ellipse. What would be (approximately) the geometric form of the parallactic motion projected on the celestial sphere? (d) Compare the scale of Fig. 9-2 with the scale on our star charts in Appendix G. Could you distinguish the stars plotted in Fig. 9-2 from each other with the naked eye? With a field glass?

8. Assume that the star in Fig. 9-2 shows, in addition to its parallactic motion, a proper motion of 1 arcsec per year in right ascension and 2 arcsec per year in declination. Draw a graph similar to Fig. 9-2, adding this proper motion to the parallactic motion shown.

9. Assume that a star at a distance of 2 pc has a proper motion of 1 arcsec per year. What is its linear velocity component at right angles to the line of sight, in kilometers per second?

10. Add to your result in Exercise 9 a radial-velocity component of 10 km/sec, perhaps found from a *redshift* in the star's spectral lines. Draw a diagram of the star's true motion through space with respect to the solar system.

11. Nearby stars typically have larger proper motions than distant stars. On the other hand, their radial velocities, as measured from the earth, do not depend on distance (within reasonable limits). Why not?

12. Would a space station orbiting the planet Mars measure significantly different proper motion and radial velocity for a particular star than the values measured from the earth?

13. Why do stars visible to the naked eye appear to have different brightnesses?

14. Assume there are two identical stars, one twice as far away from us as the other. How much brighter would the nearer star appear?

15. Assume that the nearer star of Exercise 14 has an apparent magnitude of 6^{m}5. What would be the apparent magnitude of the more distant star?

16. Assume that the *absolute* magnitude of the nearer star in Exercise 14 is 3^{m}5. What would be the absolute magnitude of the more distant star?

17. Using the results of Exercises 15 and 16, find the distances of both stars.

18. The apparent magnitude of the sun is sometimes quoted as about −27^{m}0. Verify this figure.

19. Find stars within 5 pc of the sun (see Table H-10) that are bright enough to be included in Table H-9, and compute their absolute magnitudes.

20. The absolute magnitude of the sun is +4^{m}6. What would be the apparent magnitude of the sun as seen from the star Sirius (see Table H-10)?

21. Two otherwise identical stars differ in radius. If star A has twice the radius of star B, how much larger is its luminosity?

22. Two otherwise identical stars differ in surface temperature. If star A has twice the surface temperature of star B, how much larger is its luminosity?

23. What is the range of apparent brightness between the brightest and the faintest star (about +6^{m}0) you can make out with the naked eye?

24. What are the ranges of luminosity, temperature, radius, and mass of typical stars?

25. How are stellar radii measured?

26. Jupiter has never been a star, because its mass is too low. By approximately what factor did Jupiter avoid this fate?

27. What properties of a star can be deduced from its spectrum?

28. Are Fraunhofer lines in a stellar spectrum emission or absorption lines?

29. Can you observe *all* the light that determines a star's absolute bolometric magnitude?

30. Why are some spectral lines of helium in a hot star more prominent than others?

31. Why would we not expect lines of neutral iron in the spectrum of star with a surface temperature of 30,000°K?

32. Why would we not expect lines of triply ionized iron in the spectrum of a star with a surface temperature of 3000°K?

33. List the most prominent Fraunhofer lines for spectral classes O through M.

34. For which spectral class are hydrogen lines most prominent? Why?

35. Which spectral classes show molecular bands?

36. Which star has a larger radius: one of type G8III or one of type G7V?

37. Which stars typically rotate faster: B stars or M stars?

38. Do *all* stars have the same chemical composition? Explain.

39. Which elements are most abundant in normal stars?

EXPERIMENTS

1. Visually compare the apparent magnitudes of several stars in a small area of the sky, and then take photographs of the same area with different kinds of film. Do you always get the same relative brightnesses? If not, what is the reason?

2. Make photographs of the same area of the sky with the same type of film, first using no filter, then using a red filter, and finally using a blue filter. Try to maintain the same brightness for one of the stars in all three photographs. Discuss the relative brightnesses of the other stars.

3. Obtain a red-stained piece of glass or plastic, and a blue-stained piece. Look through each "filter" at a light bulb which is painted red, and another painted blue. Comment on the brightness impressions you get. What are the astronomical analogs of this experiment?

FURTHER READING

Abetti, G., *Stars and Planets* (second ed.), New York: American Elsevier Publishing Company, Inc., 1966.

Brandt, J. C., *The Sun and Stars*, New York: McGraw-Hill Book Company, 1966.

Starlight, edited by T. Page and L. W. Page, New York: The Macmillan Company, 1967.

10 binary and multiple star systems

Before we pursue our study of the properties of the various types of stars, we pause to consider in some detail the special case of multiple star systems. The reasons are several. Most important for our purposes is the fact that some of the techniques for measuring such basic items as stellar radii and masses are applicable only to binary systems. In addition, some types of multiple systems have particularly interesting properties that are not held by single stars. Finally, as a complete listing of nearby stars reveals, close to 50% of them belong to double and even multiple systems. Thus, it appears that the occurrence of such systems is quite common.

10.1 DOUBLE STARS AND BINARIES

Two stars close to each other in the sky are said to form a **double star**. A well-known example can be found — with the naked eye or with a field glass — in the constellation Ursa Major (there the close stars are ζ Ursae Majoris, or Mizar, which itself is a multiple system, and 80 Ursae Majoris, or Alcor; the angular distance between ζ and 80 Ursae Majoris is 11 arcmin). Another example is in the constellation Orion (the system comprises λ Orionis which itself is a visual binary, and ϕ^1 Orionis; quite close is ϕ^2 Orionis which, however, does not belong physically to the λ-ϕ^1 system). Figure 10-1 shows the position of these systems in their respective constellations. Without any additional information we cannot immediately decide whether the two observed light points are close to each other because the stars themselves are actually close (i.e., physically form a system), or whether this appearance is simply a projection effect of the celestial sphere; see Fig. 10-2 for an illustration of the two cases. Only those pairs of stars that orbit about a *common center of mass*, or **barycenter**, are of interest here. We call them **binaries;** the individual stars comprising a binary are its **components.** The binary character of a system can, of course, be most directly ascertained by observing the relative orbital motions of the components; systems verified in this manner are called **visual binaries.**

Spectroscopic Binaries. In many cases the stars comprising a binary are too far away from us or too close to each other, or both, to be resolved by normal means. The multiplicity of the system can then be detected by inspection of their combined spectrum; a binary system thus verified is called a **spectroscopic binary.** Such a system may show a composite spectrum in which the Fraunhofer lines of both components appear, but very often one of the components is too weak in comparison to the other to be detectable. However, owing to their relative motions with respect to

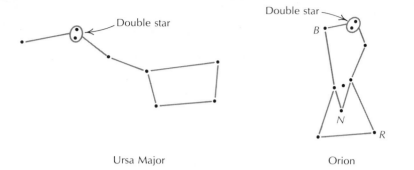

FIGURE 10-1. Two well-known double star systems in the constellations Ursa Major and Orion. The star at *B* in Orion (Betelgeuse, α Orionis) is of type M2I (red giant), whereas all the other bright stars in Orion are B stars. Betelgeuse, which does not belong physically to the rest, looks distinctly red to the naked eye in comparison with the bluish-white appearance of other stars, such as Rigel (β Orionis) at *R*. The Great Orion nebula is located at *N*.

their center of mass (and, hence, with respect to the line of sight from the earth), the spectral lines originating in the components show Doppler shifts that change in sign and absolute value during orbital motion. In other words, spectroscopic binaries are found through periodic changes in the **radial velocities** of the two components.

What happens is shown schematically in Fig. 10-3 for the highly idealized case of circular orbits. In reality, the situation is usually complicated by the ellipticity of the orbits, projection effects, and the like. Phases (a), (b), and (c) correspond to some initial time and times of a quarter-period and a half-period later, respectively. The positions marked by dashed lines are the laboratory (unshifted) wavelengths; the positions marked by solid lines are the actually observed (shifted) wavelengths.

The orbits depicted in Fig. 10-3 do not have to be in the plane of the line of sight, and in general will be inclined at an arbitrary angle to it. We then simply measure the velocity components along the line of sight to the earth by means of the

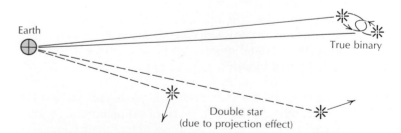

FIGURE 10-2. True binaries and double stars owing their appearance to the projection effect. The viewer is on the earth on the left. True binaries orbit about their common center of gravity, whereas stars whose closeness on the celestial sphere is due to a projection effect may have arbitrary (unrelated) motions in space, indicated by the arrows.

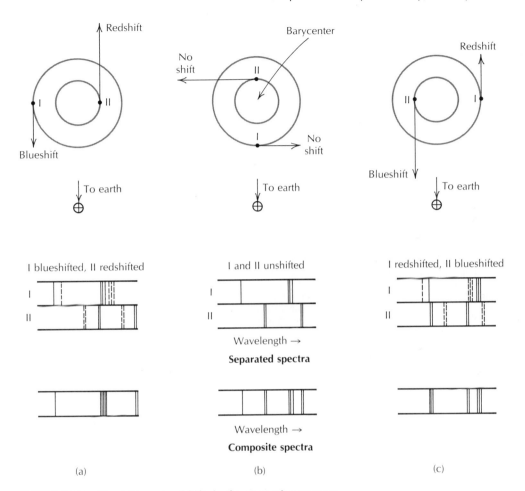

FIGURE 10-3. **Blueshifts and redshifts in the composite spectrum of a binary system. In the top drawings, the orbits of the two binary components are shown as they would appear to an observer looking down on their orbital planes; the earth's position would be in the plane of the paper. Three phases are shown: on the left, component I is moving toward us (blueshift), component II away (redshift); in the middle, both components move at right angles to the line of sight (no Doppler shift); on the right, component I moves away from us (redshift), component II toward us (blueshift). In the middle are hypothetical lines in the spectra of both components, shown separately; the dashed wavelength positions are the unshifted ones, the solid positions the observed ones, with redshifts, blueshifts, or without shifts, as the case may be for a given phase. At the bottom, finally, the spectra are combined, as would be the case in the real world, where we cannot separate the spectra of the two components.**

Doppler shifts; these, of course, would vanish if the orbits were precisely in the plane perpendicular to the line of sight.

Figure 10-4 shows actual measured radial velocities for the binary system β Aurigae with a period of 4 days and a nearly circular orbit. The velocity value at the line of symmetry (dashed in the figure) gives the radial velocity of the system as a

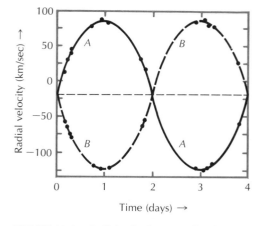

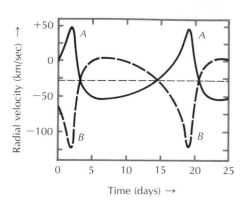

FIGURE 10-4. Radial-velocity curve for the two components of the spectroscopic binary β Aurigae. The period is about 4 days. The points show actual observations; the solid curve is a best fit. Components *A* and *B* are in nearly circular orbits. Note that the line of symmetry corresponds to a radial velocity of about 20 km/sec. This residual nonperiodic portion is due to the motion in space of the β Aurigae system with respect to the solar system. *(O. Struve and S. S. Huang, "Spectroscopic Binaries," in Handbuch der Physik, edited by F. Flügge, Berlin: Springer-Verlag, vol. 50, 1958.)*

FIGURE 10-5. Radial-velocity curve for the two components of the spectroscopic binary θ Aquilae. The period is about 17 days; the orbits of the two components *A* and *B* are highly elliptical. There is only a small center-of-mass motion of the system with respect to the solar system. *(O. Struve and S. S. Huang, "Spectroscopic Binaries," in Handbuch der Physik, edited by S. Flügge, Berlin: Springer-Verlag; vol. 50, 1958.)*

whole with respect to the earth. For comparison, we have plotted in Fig. 10-5 the radial-velocity curve of the highly elliptical system θ Aquilae, which has a period of 17 days.

Eclipsing Binaries. Of particular interest is the special case in which the line of sights is *in* the orbital plane of the binary, because then the two component stars can orbit one behind the other. Such a system is called an **eclipsing binary** system; in addition to periodic changes in radial velocity, we can observe periodic changes in the apparent brightness of the system. Thus, we can determine *light curves*, that is, measure the time variation of the apparent magnitude, for eclipsing binaries. One of the best-known examples of an eclipsing binary is the star system Algol (β Persei), one of the two prominent stellar objects in the constellation Perseus. Figure 10-6 shows the light curve for WW Aurigae, which is very similar to Algol. Eclipsing binaries are important in the determination of stellar radii.

10.2 MASS DETERMINATION FOR VISUAL BINARIES

In order to derive stellar masses with the aid of Kepler's laws, we must first collect a relevant set of observations. Such a set consists of the **orbits** of the components of a binary system, the **period of revolution**, and the **distance** of the system from the sun.

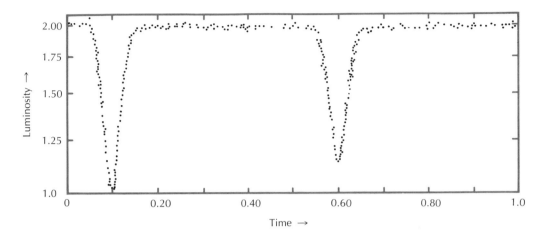

FIGURE 10-6. Light curve of the eclipsing binary WW Aurigae. The dots represent actual measurements. The two light minima correspond to the cases in which the first component moves in front of the second and in which the second moves in front of the first, respectively. (*C. M. Huffer and Z. Kopal, Astrophys. J., vol. 114, p. 297, 1951.*)

Let us assume that the distance is known somehow, say through parallax measurements. For simplicity, we first consider the **relative orbit** of one component (call it *A*) about the other (*B*). It is determined by successive observations of the **angular distance** between *A* and *B*, and the **position angle** of *A* with respect to *B*, measured from some arbitrary fixed direction. The geometry is outlined in Fig. 10-7. An actual example, the binary system ϕ Ursae Majoris, is shown in Fig. 10-8. From the unreduced observations—the open circles—which of course are afflicted with random errors because of the minute quantities being measured, a relative orbit is calculated. This orbit is obtained by standard mathematical methods which ascertain that it most probably represents the actual one.

The *observed* relative orbit is in general the projection of the *true* relative orbit onto the celestial sphere, that is, onto the plane perpendicular to the line of sight. This true relative orbit can be extracted from the observed one by an operation in which the ellipse is distorted until component *B* is at one of the foci. At this point, the semimajor axis can be found in angular measure; the period is, of course, known from the time it takes component *A* to complete the apparent or true orbit.

Now the *sum* of the masses of *A* and *B* can be obtained using a specific form of Kepler's third law.* A similar, although somewhat more complex method yields the masses of the components *A* and *B* separately; however, in this case the orbital motions of *both* components with respect to the *barycenter* must be known. Figure 10-9(a) shows the orbit of *A* relative to *B* (derived as in Fig. 10-7), while (b) gives the true orbits of the components with respect to the barycenter, for a typical combination of parameters (masses and mean distance).

*The actual formula is $m_A + m_B = d^3a^3/p^2$, where d is the distance of the binary from us in parsecs, a the semimajor axis in arcseconds, and p the period in years. In these units, the mass sum $m_A + m_B$ is obtained in terms of the solar mass.

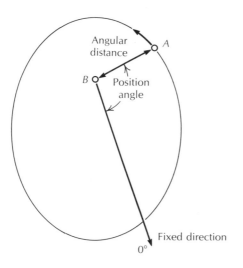

FIGURE 10-7. Geometry of the relative orbit of a binary system. The position angle of component *A* with respect to component *B* is counted from some arbitrary fixed direction (0°). At each position angle, an angular distance between *A* and *B* is measured to obtain the relative orbit.

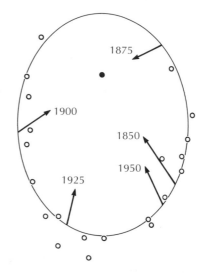

FIGURE 10-8. Relative orbit of the binary system φ Ursae Majoris. The period is about 100 years; the observations cover the years 1850 to 1950. The actual measurements, afflicted with random errors, are plotted as circles. The arrows indicate the relative positions of the components in the corresponding years. *(O. J. Eggen, Ann. Rev. Astron. Astrophys., vol. 5, p. 105, 1967.)*

The limitations of this method have to do with the fact that masses determined in this fashion depend strongly on the assumed distance of the system from us and on the semimajor axis of the ralative orbit—in other words, on a measure of the angular distance between the two components. Systematic observations have been carried out for only a hundred years or so, and thus only systems with periods of less than a few hundred years yield reasonably accurate masses. The whole scale of stellar masses has been based on this quite restricted set of direct measurements; some additional information is obtained from radial-velocity measurements of spectroscopic binaries, namely, lower limits for the masses of its components.

10.3 RADIUS DETERMINATION FOR ECLIPSING BINARIES

One of the reasons for the particular interest we have in eclipsing binaries is that they allow us to determine stellar radii directly. Depending on the geometry, that is, on the *inclination* of the orbit with respect to the line of sight, we may have **partial eclipses** [Fig 10-10(a)] or **total eclipses** [Fig. 10-10(b)]; in the latter case, we might even be able to observe **central eclipses**, in which the line of sight is *precisely* in the orbital plane [Fig. 10-10(c)].

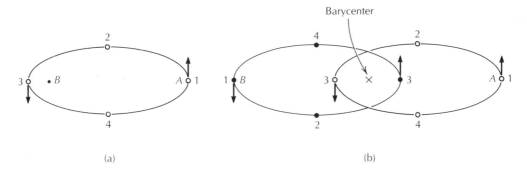

FIGURE 10-9. Relation between the relative orbit of one component of a binary system about the other, and the orbits of both components about their barycenter. Part (a) depicts a relative orbit similar to the ones shown in Figs. 10-7 and 10-8. The position of component A relative to B is given at four typical phases; the arrows indicate the directions of orbital motion. Part (b) shows the orbits of the same objects, with respect to their barycenter, for the same four phases. The arrows again denote the direction of the orbits. Note that the actual size of orbit (a) would be twice the size of the orbits (b).

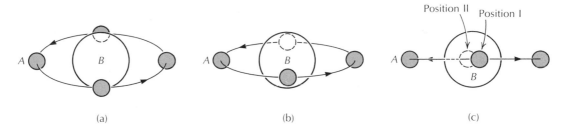

FIGURE 10-10. Eclipsing binaries: (a) partial eclipse position, (b) total eclipse position, (c) central eclipse position.

To illustrate the method of obtaining stellar radii for eclipsing binaries, consider, for simplicity, the relative circular orbit of a system in which we observe central eclipses. We construct a theoretical *light curve* for the system with the aid of the respective luminosities and radii assuming for the argument that the latter are known. The result is given in Fig. 10-11, where in position I we know that the smaller component A is in front of B, blocking out some of the light emitted by B. In position II, A is behind B, and all of A's light is blocked. To the left of point a, and between points d and e, the stars are separated, and their light is unobstructed. Between points a and b, c and d, e and f, and g and h, one of the components is partially eclipsed.

The time between points a and e in Fig. 10-11 is half the relative orbital period, while the time between points a and b, c and d, etc., is the time it takes the smaller star A to move in its orbit a distance equal to its diameter. Thus, the ratio of the time differences $t(b) - t(a)$ and $2[t(e) - t(a)]$ equals the ratio of A's diameter to the circumference of the circular relative orbit. Similarly, $t(c) - t(a)$ or $t(d) - t(b)$ yields B's diameter in terms of the size of the relative orbit.

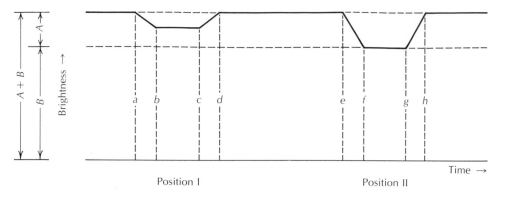

FIGURE 10-11. Brightness as a function of time for an idealized eclipsing binary system with central eclipses. In position I, the smaller component (brightness A) is in front of the larger one (brightness B), blocking out some of the light emitted by the larger component. In position II, the smaller component is behind the larger one, and all of the smaller component's light is blocked. Between the points a and b, c and d, e and f, and g and h, one of the components is partially eclipsed.

The details of Fig. 10-11 are based on several implicit assumptions, for instance, that the orbits are circular, that the stars have spherical shapes, and that there is no *limb darkening*. All these things can be taken into account in a complete theory. In principle it is even possible to extract information on the inclination of the orbit with respect to the line of sight, that is, to determine the difference between cases (b) and (c) in Fig. 10-10. In practice, one computes large numbers of theoretical light curves, including all conceivable complications, and stores them in a computer. An observed light curve is compared with the whole set of model curves, and the model curve that best fits the observed one is identified. Its parameters are then taken to be good approximations to those of the actual star system.

In order to obtain the radii in kilometers, we must know the linear size of the orbit, which we can calculate if we know the orbital velocities (with respect to the barycenter) of *both* components. The latter can be extracted from radial-velocity curves such as Figs. 10-4 and 10-5.

The stellar radii quoted in Section 9.4 were obtained in this manner, although a few very large stellar radii have been measured directly with interferometers.

10.4 ζ AURIGAE AND β LYRAE

Among the known eclipsing binaries are some systems which are of interest for individual reasons. One case is the system ζ Aurigae which consists of a huge KI star and a relatively small BV companion. During the time the B star is moving behind the K giant, and again when it emerges, it is possible to observe directly the vastly extended chromosphere of the K star. Extensive study of this and similar objects has shown that just before the B star moves behind the K star photosphere, that is, at

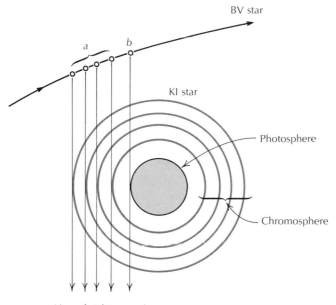

FIGURE 10-12. **Geometry of the eclipsing binary system ζ Aurigae. During the eclipse, the (smaller) BV star moves behind the KI star. Its light, in position *a*, passes through the vastly extended chromosphere of the K star, whose physical properties can be studied from the absorption features imposed on the B star spectrum. At position *b*, the B star disappears behind the photosphere of the K star.**

position *b* in Fig. 10-12 (whose radial scale is somewhat distorted), lines appear in the B star spectrum that are caused by absorption in the outer atmosphere of the K star. In fact, during phase *a* in Fig. 10-12, the depth variation of the absorbing matter in the K star chromosphere can be derived. The result is a direct verification of the theoretical prediction that the temperature in the K star chromosphere is reversed as it is in the sun.

In ζ Aurigae, the two stars are relatively far apart, in the sense that their radii (including the chromosphere of the K star) are much smaller than the distance between their centers. There are, however, systems in which this is not the case; β Lyrae is a well-known example. In fact, the components of some binaries are so close that they have developed a common **envelope** of gas ejected from either one or both members. Such envelopes often have very complex flow patterns that, in general, do not follow the orbital motions of the stars and can thus be detected through their individual Doppler shifts. The spectral lines originating in the envelopes appear as *emissions* against the background of the sky, since an envelope usually extends quite far beyond the stars proper.

A particularly intriguing possibility exists in these close systems. If one of the members, during its evolution, ejects some of its mass, and this is probably a quite common phenomenon, a close companion might capture a significant fraction of this mass. The companion could then suddenly find itself with a higher mass than its internal constitution can support. The question is, of course, "What happens next?" It has been recently suggested that this may be the mechanism responsible for the nova outbursts we shall discuss in Section 15.3

10.5 MULTIPLE SYSTEMS

If binary systems make it possible to obtain information on stellar quantities which cannot be inferred from single stars, the situation is reversed if we turn to multiple systems. One reason is the enormous complication a third component introduces into the mathematical description of the orbital motions: whereas Newton's equation of gravity can be readily solved for two bodies (leading to Kepler's laws), the corresponding three-body system and any higher system allows for usable solutions only in special cases. Similarly, the analysis of more than two superposed stellar spectra is seldom possible with sufficient accuracy. Thus, from a practical viewpoint the third component of a system is mostly a nuisance.

It then remains to point out the intricate lighting effects the inhabitants of a planet in a multiple star system (if there is any such planet) experience with the rising and setting of close-by and more distant suns, not to mention the many unusual observational opportunities such a system would give the astronomers among the hypothetical inhabitants. And it is fascinating to speculate how astronomy might have developed there by contrast to its historical development on earth.

QUESTIONS FOR DISCUSSION

1. What is the importance of binary systems in understanding the properties of stars?

2. Actual observations of most spectroscopic binaries show only one star image, and only one star spectrum. Why are astronomers then so sure that they are binaries?

3. Why don't observations of the relative position of one component of a visual binary with respect to the other give you the *true* relative orbit?

4. In Fig. 10-11 the light curve is drawn with sharp edges at points a, b, etc., and with linear increases and decreases in the apparent brightness between points a and b, c and d, etc. Discuss the reasons why an actual light curve, such as the one reproduced in Fig. 10-6, does not show these features.

5. Very close binaries such as β Lyrae have very high orbital velocities. Why? What is the consequence of this high speed for the geometrical configuration of the star? Why do such systems have gaseous envelopes?

EXERCISES

1. How are visual binaries, spectroscopic binaries, and eclipsing binaries defined?

2. Are all spectroscopic binaries eclipsing binaries? Are all eclipsing binaries spectroscopic binaries? Explain.

3. A hypothetical spectroscopic binary system consists of two stars of about the same spectral class, each having Fraunhofer lines at (laboratory) wavelengths of 4018.1 Å, 4041.4 Å,

4048.8 Å, 4055.5 Å, and 4063.5 Å. One of the stars has a maximum radial velocity of 60 km/sec, the other of 40 km/sec. Construct the actual composite spectrum corresponding to Fig. 10-3, assuming the barycenter of the binary system to have zero radial velocity with respect to the observer.

4. Revise your calculation in Exercise 3 by giving the barycenter a radial velocity of 50 km/sec away from the observer.

5. The line of symmetry of the radial-velocity curves in Figs. 10-4 and 10-5 is not at zero. Why not?

6. One of the components of ϕ Ursae Majoris completed a much greater portion of its orbit about the second component between 1875 and 1900, than it did between 1900 and 1925. Why?

7. After astronomers have had a chance to observe visual binaries for another 100 years, will they have a much larger body of observations to work with? Explain.

8. Figure 10-9 shows the orbits of the two components of a hypothetical visual binary about their barycenter. How would the orbital ellipses look if, in position 3, one of the components were twice as close to the barycenter as the other?

9. In the formula for the sum of the masses of a visual binary given on page 161, m_A and m_B are calculated in units of the solar mass. In what units is the *product d·a*?

10. In Section 5.2 a version of Kepler's third law is given that is applicable to the planets of the solar system. Compare that version with the more accurate formula on page 161, and discuss the simplifications introduced into the earlier version.

11. What specific property of an eclipsing binary system is determined by the inclination of the orbit with respect to the line of sight?

12. Compare the geometry of the eclipses of eclipsing binary systems with that of the sun-moon system.

13. Figure 10-11 shows a schematic light curve for an eclipsing binary system. Draw a similar curve for the case in which the two components are of *equal* brightness.

14. Figure 10-11 refers to the case of a *central* eclipse. Draw similar curves for the cases in in which the eclipse is *total* but not *central,* and where it is *partial*.

15. The eclipsing binary system ζ Aurigae yields direct information on the structure of the chromosphere of the K star. How is this information extracted? Compare this with the situation in which the moon moves in front of a star in a so-called *lunar occultation*; what kinds of information can be derived in such a situation?

16. (See Exercise 15.) Why can you not use a "solar occultation" of a star to obtain information on the solar chromosphere and corona? The occultation of strong radio sources by the sun are, however, useful. Why?

EXPERIMENTS

1. Find the double stars pictured in Fig. 10-1; they are visible to the naked eye. Try to estimate their angular separation using a good field glass.

2. Scan the sky with a field glass for other pairs of stars that are suspiciously close to each other, say, at an angular distance of a few arcminutes. Record their positions with respect to stars you can identify with the aid of the star charts of Figs. G-6 to G-9. Then go to your observatory, which should have a good star atlas that identifies binaries, and check your list to determine whether they are actually binaries.

3.   The eclipsing binary system of Algol (β Persei) has a period of less than 3 days, with the brightness decreasing to about half its maximum value at the primary eclipse. Make observations of such an eclipse either with the naked eye or with a field glass. Compare the apparent magnitude of Algol with the apparent magnitudes of nearby stars, and plot a light curve.

FURTHER READING

Stellar Atmospheres, edited by J. L. Greenstein, Chicago: The University of Chicago Press, 1960.

Starlight, edited by T. Page and L. W. Page, New York: The Macmillan Company, 1967.

11 the color-magnitude relations

We now return to a discussion of the basic parameters introduced in Chapter 9. We have already seen that there is a relation between the luminosity and the mass of the average star. Then, in discussing luminosity classes, it was stated without further comment that there also exist relations between the luminosity (or magnitude), radius, and surface temperature (or color) of a star under stable conditions.

This, however, is not the reason for devoting a whole chapter to color-magnitude relations. The really compelling reason is the fact that practically all modern thought on the evolution of stars and star groups is observationally based, in some way or another, on color-magnitude relations. Indeed, some of the most spectacular successes of twentieth-century astronomy were achieved on the basis of this evidence, and the theoretical interpretation of color-magnitude relations is to date among the most exciting tasks of astronomy.

11.1   THE H-R DIAGRAM FOR NEARBY STARS

Color-Magnitude Relations.   The first astronomers to investigate the relationship between temperature and luminosity, the **color-magnitude relations**, were Hertzsprung and Russell early in this century; thus, the resulting graphical representations are called **Hertzsprung-Russell diagrams**, or simply **H-R diagrams**. In such a diagram, we plot a measure of the *surface temperature* (increasing to the left) on the abscissa, and a measure of the *luminosity* (increasing upward) on the ordinate, for a number of stars. The particular measure we choose for either color or magnitude is immaterial. Commonly used as "colors" are spectral classes and color indices or, mostly in theoretical work, effective temperatures. As a measure of the star's "magnitude" we may choose its true luminosity (in units of the solar luminosity, for instance) or its absolute magnitude.

The first and most obvious thing to do, then, is to collect data on all stars with distances known from parallax measurements, and plot their absolute magnitudes, say in the visible spectral range, against their spectral classes. This actually involves several thousand stars and results in a rather crowded diagram. Thus, for a first orientation, we show in Fig. 11-1 a limited but representative selection of data. The magnitude scale is given in terms of the solar luminosity $L_\odot$.

Main Sequence, Giant Branch, White-Dwarf Sequence.   One result is immediately evident: certain combinations of surface temperature and luminosity occur with greater frequency than others, at least in our corner of the universe. A survey of

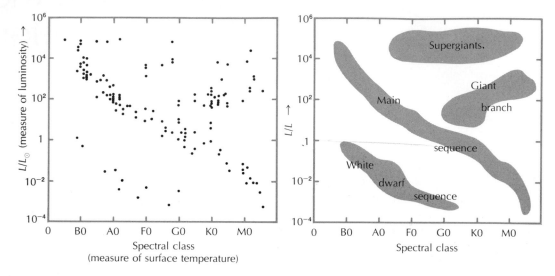

FIGURE 11-1. Composite H-R diagram for stars in the general neighborhood of the sun.

FIGURE 11-2. Main sequence, giant branch, and white-dwarf sequence in the H-R diagram of stars in the general neighborhood of the sun.

H-R diagrams of the type of Fig. 11-1 shows that the stars seem to fall into three groups, designated as **main sequence, giant branch,** and **white-dwarf sequence,** as shown in Fig. 11-2. There is a scattering of data in each group, not due solely to inaccuracies in measurement. Also, there are some stars that lie rather apart from the main bulk of positions in the diagram. This is particularly true for the very bright, rather cool stars of luminosity class I (the **supergiants**) that fall above the giant branch. Of course, we must be prepared for the possibility that concentrated in some area of the diagram there are other classes of stars that we have not yet recognized, or that may not show up among the stars close to the sun.

Information Contained in an H-R Diagram. Now, from our discussion in Section 9.3 we know that stars of the same spectral type can have different luminosities only if their radii are different. This, of course, assumes that the emission per square centimeter of stellar surface and the spectral type are directly related and, for instance, are independent of luminosity class. While this is not exactly true, it is an adequate approximation for our present purposes. At any rate, we can see by reading up in Fig. 11-2 that an M star on the giant branch is about 10^4 times as luminous as a main-sequence M star. Since luminosity is proportional to the square of the radius, the giant-branch star must have a radius 100 times larger than that of the main-sequence star. Similarly, the radii of white dwarfs of spectral type A must be about one-hundredth as big as the radii of main-sequence A stars.

If we read across in Fig. 11-2, we see that luminosity of a main-sequence M star is about 10^{-8} that of a main-sequence O star. Since, as stated in Section 9.6, their surface temperatures are in a ratio of about 10 to 1, the emission per unit of surface area of the O star is about 10^4 times that of the M star. This leaves a factor of 10^4 to be accounted for by the difference in radii, so the main-sequence O star must be 100 times as large in radius as the M star. That is, along the main sequence, from M to O,

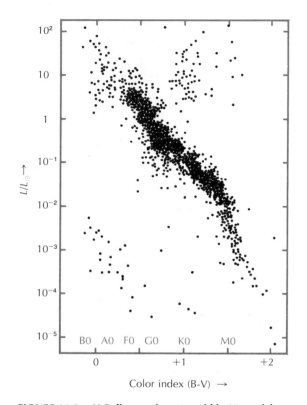

FIGURE 11-3. H-R diagram for stars within 25 pc of the sun. Note the large concentration of stars on the main sequence, and the almost complete absence of hot stars of types O and B. (*R. Woolley et al., A Catalogue of Stars Within 25 Parsecs of the Sun, Royal Greenwich Observatory, Annals no. 5, 1970.*)

both surface temperature and radius increase. We recall in passing, from Section 9.4, that the masses of main-sequence stars increase about one-hundredfold from class M to class O.

Let us now turn to a more realistic version of the H-R diagram of stars in the solar neighborhood. Figure 11-3 is one in which all the known stars within 25 pc of the sun are plotted. Again, we can identify the main sequence, giant branch, and white-dwarf sequence. Here, however, the numbers of stars in these three rather narrow areas of the diagram are different from those in Fig. 11-1; almost all the stars are on the main sequence, many fewer populate the giant branch and the white-dwarf sequence, and still fewer are scattered in the areas between.

Let us discuss, in quite general terms, the type of information that an H-R diagram *might* contain. Obviously, a multitude of interpretations are possible, if we do not restrict them by some additional principle. Thus, we first assert that an H-R diagram such as Fig. 11-3 must be typical for many, if not most, star samples; after all, there is nothing special about the position of our sun or the stars in its neighborhood. Second, we know from our discussion of the sun that it is undergoing an evolution in time, if for no other reason than that its total chemical composition is changing through the conversion of hydrogen into helium in the core. We have no a priori reason to believe that all or even most of the stars entered in Fig. 11-3 are in identical stages of evolution; in fact, it is much more likely that these stars represent many possible evolutionary stages.

On the basis of these arguments, we conclude that the H-R diagram is a snapshot showing, at any given instant in time, how a typical group of stars is distributed within the *color-magnitude plane.* As we shall see, the distribution will tell us how far stars have progressed in their evolution, in what stages they spend short periods of time, and in what stages they are almost stationary for very long periods.

To consider an analog, assume that a hypothetical satellite registers the positions of airplanes on our planet at one given time. A large majority of the airplanes will be in airports, and more airplanes will be close to airports than between airports. We know the reason: airplanes spend more time on the ground than in the air; there they are stationary (waiting at terminals or in service hangars) or in quasistationary positions (slowly moving the small distance between terminal and take-off or landing strip). Some planes, but not too many, will always be found in the air corridors, moving at great speed from one geographical location to the next. Some areas will not contain any planes, simply because they do not connect (in a reasonable manner) any two airports. And, finally, the density of airplanes in any given area is dependent upon the total number of planes serving the particular area and the time they remain there, be it due to the average delay at the terminal, or the average speed of the planes in a given corridor.

Looking at the H-R diagram in light of this analog, we can identify the main sequence with stationary or quasistationary positions, and the giant branch with an area in which the motion of our objects is much slowed down, owing, we might say, to a sort of holding pattern. We can similarly call the white-dwarf sequence a holding pattern in which the objects wait for quite a long time. The remaining areas of the diagram, not occupied by significant numbers of stars, then correspond either to traffic corridors with objects moving very fast, or else to places that are almost never visited. The transit speed of the airplanes corresponds, of course, to the speed with which an evolutionary phase is completed by the stars. Obviously, this suspiciously unquantitative "identification" is not the only one compatible with the actual data; but it happens to be the correct one.

Luminosity Function.   We can make one more observation. We have said in connection with the airplane example that the object density in any given area is determined by both the total number of planes that get there and the average time they stay there. In order to obtain an H-R diagram analog of airplane density, we could count the number of objects in our H-R diagram, say, per spectral class and luminosity class. This procedure would yield a so-called **luminosity function.** However, it would only be successful if we restricted our sample in such a manner that we could be fairly sure to include most objects present, that is, if we stayed within the rather narrow distance limits where the star count is reasonably complete.

This would not be the case if we included all stars within 25 pc of the sun. But if we restrict our sample to stars within 5 pc of the sun, where parallax measurements

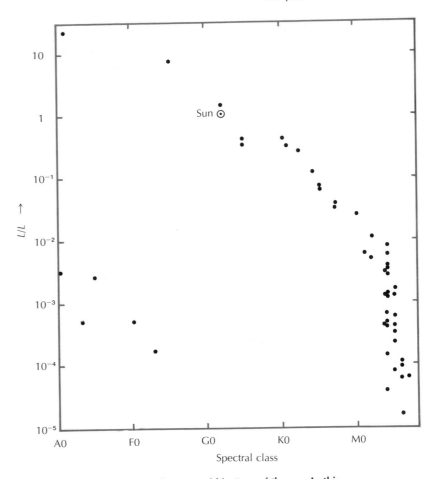

FIGURE 11-4.   H-R diagram for stars within 5 pc of the sun. In this practically complete sample, the majority are of spectral type M, with only a very few F and G stars, and no star hotter than type A. No giants are present either, but note the number of white dwarfs. (*R. Woolley et al., A Catalogue of Stars Within 25 Parsecs of the Sun, Royal Greenwich Observatory, Annals no. 5, 1970.*)

are quite accurate, we obtain the fairly definitive result presented in Fig. 11-4. The vast majority of main-sequence stars is concentrated at the low-luminosity end of the main sequence, where the small, cool, dim stars are. There are no giants in this sample, and no stars hotter than class A, but there are several white dwarfs. It is believed that the results of Fig. 11-4 are quite typical, in spite of the impression we receive when we view the sky with the unaided eye and see mostly bright O and B stars and a few red giants out to comparatively large distances.

It is the type of data presented in Figs. 11-3 and 11-4 that serves as the observational basis of all modern work on stellar evolution. H-R diagrams will, therefore, be an important part of the chapters that follow.

11.2 THE H-R DIAGRAM FOR STAR CLUSTERS

If color-magnitude diagrams could be constructed only for stars of known distance, the information derived from such analyses would be quite limited. Fortunately, we can do better. The reason is that we can construct H-R diagrams for any star cluster.

Star Clusters. A **star cluster** is defined as a group of stars which physically "belong" to each other. This grouping into a cluster does not necessarily mean that all the individual stars are gravitationally bound to each other at all times; interactions with other objects, mostly gas clouds, will give individual stars speeds above the escape speed from the cluster. Nevertheless, the notion of a cluster implies some sort of common history. In a sense, star clusters represent the continuation of a progression which leads from single stars to double and triple systems, and then to multiple systems and groups of stars. We can certainly say that the cluster members are located within a relatively limited volume of space.

The decision as to whether a star belongs to a cluster or not—a crucial one in constructing an H-R diagram for the cluster—is mostly based on the hypothesis that member stars should all share in any gross motion; that is, they should move with the same speed and in the same direction through space. Stars which have significantly different speeds or directions of motion are probably background or foreground stars, not belonging to the cluster.

The H-R Diagram. Normally, then, the relative distances of the cluster members from each other are very much smaller than their average distance from us. To a sufficient degree of accuracy we can say that they are all essentially at the *same* distance from us, but we do not know this distance beforehand. Their apparent magnitudes then differ from their absolute magnitudes by the same ratio. It is this feature which allows us to construct an H-R diagram for the cluster, because we can simply take the apparent magnitude as the measure of luminosity.

If we use logarithmic magnitude scales, the difference between the apparent and absolute magnitudes of each cluster member is some *additive* constant, common to all members.* Thus, if we plot apparent magnitude against a measure of the surface temperature, we should get an H-R diagram that differs fundamentally from Fig. 11-1 only in the sense that a common constant should be added to the numbers of the magnitude scale. This number, the so-called **distance modulus**, does not depend on the brightness of the individual stars, but only on the ratio of the distance of the cluster stars to our standard 10 pc.

We can look at this from a different viewpoint. Assume that our sun and all the stars within 25 pc of us are isolated in space, instead of being in the middle of a concentration of millions of stars, and that astronomers with powerful telescopes on a planet very far from us measure the color and the apparent magnitude of our sun and the neighboring stars. These astronomers do not know the distance to our system, but they use exactly the same units of measurement as we do. If they calibrated

---

*To see this, write the ratio of apparent to absolute magnitude as apparent magnitude = K(absolute magnitude). Then, taking logarithms gives log (apparent magnitude) = log K + log (absolute magnitude), where log K is the additive constant.

all the star magnitudes with respect to our sun, then their H-R diagram would be identical to our Fig. 11-3.

11.3 THE H-R DIAGRAM FOR OPEN CLUSTERS. CLUSTER PARALLAXES

The Pleiades. Let us now turn to H-R diagrams that have been drawn up for actual clusters. There are a few star clusters that can be identified as such even with the unaided eye. The primary example is the **Pleiades** in the constellation Taurus, whose "seven stars" (and the many more visible with a field glass) occupy so small an area in the sky that it is highly unlikely that they are not physically related to each other. They are indeed related, as one easily proves by measuring their radial velocities and proper motions. The stars that belong to the Pleiades cluster all move together through space.

Figure 11-5 is a long-exposure telescopic picture of the Pleiades, showing luminous gas surrounding the brighter stars. Altogether, some 250 members have been confirmed to date. The cluster occupies a somewhat irregular volume and shows no particular symmetry. This type of cluster is called an **open cluster**. Because of their

FIGURE 11-5. Long-exposure photograph of the central portion of the Pleiades cluster. Luminous gas is seen surrounding the brighter stars. *(Hale Observatories.)*

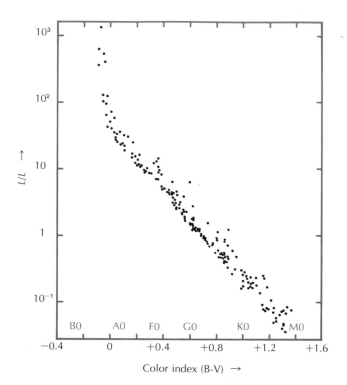

FIGURE 11-6. **H-R diagram for the Pleiades. The luminosity is plotted in terms of the solar luminosity, against the color index B-V. The approximate location of the spectral classes is added. Note the sharp lower boundary of the main sequence, and the absence of giant stars.** *(G. L. Hagen, An Atlas of Open Cluster Colour-Magnitude Diagrams, David Dunlap Observatory, University of Toronto, 1970.)*

locations in our star system, open clusters are often called **galactic clusters**. There are hundreds of them within the range of earth-based telescopes; some of the more important ones are listed in Tables H-12 to H-14.

Color-Magnitude Diagram. Figure 11-6 is a color-magnitude plot of the Pleiades similar to the H-R diagram of Fig. 11-3. The abscissa scale is again marked in color indices (with the approximate locations of spectral classes indicated). We can note several features immediately. First, the main sequence has a much better defined lower boundary, but still contains some scatter at the upper boundary. We may assume that this scatter is intrinsic and not due to inaccuracies in the determination of magnitudes; otherwise, we would find the same type of scatter at the lower boundary. Second, there are a much larger number of bright B and A stars in comparison to less luminous stars than in the diagram for solar-neighborhood stars. Finally, there is no evidence of white dwarfs or red giants, at least in any significant numbers.

Distance Determination. Another feature should be emphasized here, namely, that we can use the H-R diagram to determine the distance to the cluster. The one proviso is that we have good reason to believe that the cluster stars are of exactly the same type as the stars in the neighborhood of the sun. For instance, suppose we are convinced that the G2V stars in our neighborhood (where we know their absolute magnitude) are identical with those in a cluster. Then we can say that the absolute magnitude of our neighbors is exactly the same as that for the cluster stars. We form the difference between apparent and absolute magnitude for the G2V stars (in logarithmic units), and just that simply we have the distance modulus of the cluster. This procedure for determining distances is commonly called the method of **cluster parallaxes** and is one of the astronomer's most important tools. The only restrictions on the method are the availability of a clearly classified spectrum and knowledge of the absolute magnitudes of neighboring stars assumed to be of the same type as the subject stars.

Spectroscopic Parallaxes. In principle it is possible to use the method of cluster parallaxes to determine the distance of a single star; it then is called the method of **spectroscopic parallaxes.** Of course, when it is used for individual stars the chances of random error are greater; for example, there might be unsuspected sources of absorption located between the star in question and the solar system. This would give the observer incorrect values for both magnitude and color, resulting in an incorrect distance value.

11.4   THE H-R DIAGRAM FOR GLOBULAR CLUSTERS

Some star clusters differ in structure from the open clusters just discussed, in that they are much more regular. In fact, they seem to have a spherical symmetry; the stars are highly concentrated toward the center, and there may be quite a number of them. This type of cluster is called a **globular cluster**. A typical example is the cluster **M3**, near the visibility threshold of the naked eye, in the constellation Canes Venatici. A telescopic photograph is reproduced in Fig. 11-7.

There is no question, from radial-velocity determinations as well as from the obviously organized structure, that the stars of such a cluster all belong together physically. Thus, we can apply the arguments of the last sections and construct a color-magnitude diagram, which should show a significant amount of organization. As an example, Fig. 11-8 is the diagram for the cluster M3. Again, the abscissa scale shows color indices, with the spectral classes marked separately. The brightnesses of the member stars are given in arbitrary, not solar units. Clearly, the structure of this H-R diagram differs drastically from that of the Pleiades.

In Fig. 11-8, first note that the **main sequence** is incomplete in that most stars hotter than about 7000°K (spectral class F2) do not fall near a diagonal line corresponding to the main sequence of Fig. 11-6. Instead, these stars form a sequence of their own (a **subgiant branch**), above what would be the main sequence and leading up in a continuous manner into the **giant branch**. Second, a number of the stars

FIGURE 11-7. **Telescopic view of the globular cluster M3. Note the strong concentration of stars toward the center and the spherical symmetry of the cluster.** *(Lick Observatory.)*

form a pattern that runs almost horizontally, that is, at constant luminosity, comprising a **horizontal branch** in the diagram. Figure 11-9 outlines the main features of the diagram. Obviously, the stars of a globular cluster are either of a type different from our neighboring stars, or else we are witnessing a different phase of stellar evolution.

We probably should not assume that stars of the same spectral type in open and globular clusters have the same luminosity. It is particularly appropriate to move cautiously in this respect if we want to make use of the relative positions of, say, portions of the main sequence in H-R diagrams for different types of clusters, in order to arrive at distance figures. Such distance figures may be incorrect, if the physical properties that define the star classes are not sufficiently known.

At any rate, astronomers feel that they have learned how to avoid the major pitfalls, and that they can match diagrams correctly. On the basis of such matching, it is clear that the globular clusters, on the average, are much further away from us than the galactic clusters, simply because their magnitudes are so much less than the magnitudes of galactic clusters. It seems that globular clusters represent a quite different aspect of our galactic system.

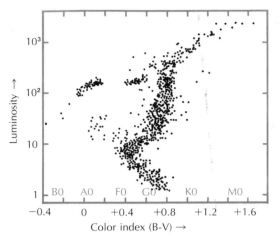

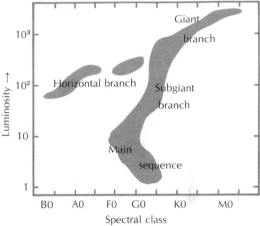

FIGURE 11-8. H-R diagram for M3. Luminosity is plotted in arbitrary units against the color index B-V. The approximate locations of spectral classes have been added. *(H. C. Arp, "The Hertzsprung-Russell Diagram," in Handbuch der Physik, edited by S. Flügge, Berlin: Springer-Verlag, vol. 51, 1958.)*

FIGURE 11-9. Main features of the H-R diagram for globular clusters: main sequence, subgiant branch, giant branch, and horizontal branch.

QUESTIONS FOR DISCUSSION

1. Discuss the differences between Figs. 11-3 and 11-4.

2. Use the traffic pattern on the roads of your state to construct your own analog of an H-R diagram.

3. Do stars that at one time belong to a cluster keep their membership forever? What might make them leave?

4. Explain how one can construct a meaningful H-R diagram for a cluster whose distance is not known.

5. How would you go about proving that stars you may have observed within the Pleiades "cluster boundaries" (see Experiment 2) actually belong to the Pleiades cluster?

6. Discuss the similarities and differences between Figs. 11-3 and 11-6.

7. Discuss the similarities and differences between Figs. 11-6 and 11-8.

EXERCISES

1. What star data are plotted in an H-R diagram? Why is it called a "color-magnitude diagram"?

2. Plot an H-R diagram by graphing the absolute-magnitude data listed in Table H-10 for all stars of classes F, G, and K, and the stars of spectral classes M0 and M1, against the spectral class (with decimal) on a linear scale. It should look like Fig. 11-4 without the very dim, cool stars.

3. (See Exercise 2.) Now plot the effective temperatures given in Section 9.6 against their spectral classes, identifying the temperatures with subclasses F5, G5, K5, and M2. Draw a smooth line through the points to obtain an approximate graph of spectral subclass versus effective temperature. Replot the H-R diagram resulting from Exercise 2, but now use absolute magnitude as ordinate, and effective temperature on a linear scale as abscissa. In what way has your H-R diagram changed? Why is it as legitimate an H-R diagram as the one you produced in Exercise 2? What are the disadvantages of the scale used in this exercise?

4. (See Exercises 2 and 3.) Finally, again with the spectral classes in a linear scale as abscissa, plot the apparent magnitudes listed in Table H-10. Why is this diagram not a legitimate H-R diagram?

5. Construct a partial luminosity function from the H-R diagram of Fig. 11-3; that is, plot the total number of stars in each spectral class, but exclude from your count stars on the giant branch and in the white-dwarf sequence. Where does the distribution have a maximum? Why?

6. (See Exercise 5.) Construct a complete luminosity function from the H-R diagram of Fig. 11-3. Where is the maximum now? What is the reason for the difference? Which luminosity function is more representative of an actual star sample? Why?

7. (See Exercises 5 and 6.) Construct one more "luminosity function," this time with the data on the 50 brightest stars in Table H-9. Where do you now find the maximum? Why is this "luminosity function" not meaningful?

8. Determine, from Fig. 11-3, the average luminosity of main-sequence stars of color index +0.5; do the same for white dwarfs of color index +0.5. From your results, derive the ratio of the average radii of these two types of stars.

9. Repeat Exercise 8 for main-sequence stars of color index +1.0 and giant stars of color index +1.0.

10. From the definition of magnitude numbers in Section 9.3, derive the formula $M - m = 5 + 5 \log \pi$, where M is the absolute magnitude of a star, m its apparent magnitude, and π the parallax in arcsecs.

11. Table H-10 lists the parallax, the absolute magnitude, and the apparent magnitude of a number of stars. Check these figures for the first 10 stars with the aid of the formula quoted in Exercise 10.

12. Use the formula quoted in Exercise 10 to show that the absolute magnitude of a star equals its apparent magnitude at a distance of 10 pc.

13. Figure 11-3 is calibrated in terms of the solar luminosity. Replace the vertical scale with absolute magnitudes, using the definitions of Section 9.3.

14. Assume that the hypothetical astronomers mentioned in Section 11.2 had constructed the H-R diagram of Fig. 11-3, using our system of magnitudes (a rather unlikely proposition!). How would their ordinate scale be calibrated, if their distance from us were 500 pc?

15. Why does the H-R diagram of Fig. 11-6 have no entries from among the M stars?

16. Outline the method of finding the distance to a cluster by means of cluster parallaxes.

17. Assume that you have obtained an H-R diagram similar to Fig. 11-6 for a cluster of unknown distance. Assume further that the G2V stars have an apparent magnitude of $+11^{m}5$. Use the method of cluster parallaxes to determine the distance of the cluster.

18. Why are cluster parallaxes more reliable than spectroscopic parallaxes?

19. What are the main observational differences between open clusters and globular clusters?

20. Of what spectral class are the most luminous stars in the Pleiades? In the globular cluster M3? Comment on the resulting visual differences for an observer.

EXPERIMENTS

1. Identify 10 or more of the stars plotted in Fig. 11-3 with the aid of Table H-10.

2. Observe the Pleiades with a field glass and try to find the approximate outline of this star cluster. How many stars do you count inside the "cluster boundaries"?

3. Use a field glass or telescope to locate the open clusters listed in Table H-12.

4. Locate the globular cluster M3 with a field glass. How does it appear to be different from the clusters observed in Experiment 3?

FURTHER READING

Bok, B. J., and P. F. Bok, *The Milky Way* (third ed.), Cambridge, Mass.: Harvard University Press, 1957.

The Evolution of Stars, edited by T. Page, New York: The Macmillan Company, 1968.

12 stellar evolution

The relation between a star's radius, surface temperature, and luminosity or total energy output presents an intriguingly complex picture. We have argued (implicitly) that these parameters change as a star evolves, and (explicitly) that groups of data concerning them must be viewed as representing a sample star population in various stages of evolution. The crowding of stars at particular combinations of radius, termperature, and luminosity must indicate that such combinations represent relatively stationary evolutionary phases. Thus, we find ourselves confronted with the task of explaining why the various branches and sequences appear where they do on H-R diagrams.

The more general problem is to understand the development of stars in time as a function of some, perhaps as yet unknown, initial parameters — in short, to reconstruct *stellar evolution*. Any of several approaches could be used to describe what astronomers claim is a fairly well-established story, but we shall try to follow a star from birth to death, on the basis of our knowledge of the physical processes involved. Whenever possible, we shall show how a particular stage of evolution gives rise to a set of observed parameters or properties.

Let us begin with the initial phases, the birth of a star.

12.1 THE INITIAL CONDENSATION

It is the basic premise of modern astronomy that stars condense out of material which is present in immense quantities in the universe, in both gaseous and solid forms. The **gases** are mixtures of typical stellar elements to which we shall refer as the **initial chemical composition.** Some of the most exciting research done in recent years is involved with this chemical composition, its distribution in the universe, and its history. The solid material consists typically of microscopic **grains** (or **dust**) of ice, some other simple molecules in frozen form, graphite, and metal crystals in various forms. We shall see later how we can find this material, and where it is concentrated. For our present purpose we have only to postulate its existence.

Initial Condensation.   When and how does the formation of a star begin? We are, at present, far from an answer, and the description to follow gives just one relatively simple train of events that is more an illustration of a possible process than a detailed answer.

The physical properties of an amorphous gas mass are not uniform. Rather, there are continued **fluctuations** in density and internal energy (temperature), simply because internal motions, ordered as well as random, once in a while will lead locally to a slightly increased or decreased density, to a **compression** or **rarefaction**. A locally compressed area will have a slightly above average pressure, and the tendency of the gas is to undo the compression and bring the material back to the initial density. Also acting within the gas are the gravitational forces through which the molecules or grains attract each other. In the slightly compressed area, the gravitational forces will be slightly greater, since on the average the separation between particles will have decreased. Thus, the gravitational force tends to counteract the pressure, maintaining the compression and increasing the density still further.

There is also an increase in internal energy resulting from the compression process; recall, as an earthly example, that the air in a bicycle tire heats up when air is pumped in, that is, when the density is increased. If it is possible to remove some of the internal energy from the condensed area, for instance by emitting more radiation than is being absorbed, then the pressure could be kept from increasing to any great extent, while the density of the gas is kept at the higher level. In this manner, a **condensation** is built up.

What we have just described is the growth of an **instability**, a process by which a small increase in density, initiated by some random fluctuation, is maintained and enlarged. Much work has recently gone into finding out under what specific physical conditions a random density increase is transformed into a continuing condensation in which the material within a certain volume falls toward one or more centers. But even if we don't know most of the details, we do have a good idea of the basic mechanism.

At any rate, after a time of condensation during which more and more of the surrounding material falls to the center or centers, one or several **protostars** will have been formed. The gas cloud then will have the basic spherical symmetry of a star, and its physical behavior will have become largely independent of its surroundings. This behavior then becomes dependent on its total mass, its mean density, and its mean energy or temperature.

Gravitational Contraction.   Once a protostar is formed, its development is much easier to follow theoretically, simply because of its self-contained nature. The dominant process is one of **gravitational contraction.** Under the action of the gravitational force that attracts each element of mass to all others, all material moves toward the **barycenter**. (We introduced the barycenter in Section 5.2 for two separate bodies, but the same concept is applicable as well to a continuous distribution of matter of the type found in a protostar. For simplicity, we can identify it with the geometrical center of the spherical protostar.) During this motion toward the center the gravitational energy of the gas mass is diminished; the energy difference is transformed into heat. Thus, during this initial **contraction phase**, the temperature at the center of the protostar increases via the conversion of gravitational energy into internal heat. The temperature of the undisturbed gas may originally have been $10°K$ but it soon advances to some $10^3°K$, while the central density increases from, say, 10^{10} to 10^{21} atoms per cubic centimeter. Note that the "initial" density is very much greater than what is considered normal for gas clouds which are not actively engaged in star formation; this corresponds to the fact that the protostar already was the product of a prolonged condensation process.

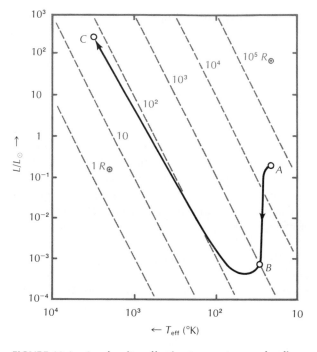

FIGURE 12-1. Luminosity, effective temperature, and radius of a star of 1 $M_\odot$ during the initial contraction phase. The evolutionary track is plotted in a color-magnitude diagram. From an arbitrary starting point *A*, the protostar's luminosity decreases, until at point *B* internal motions heat up the star. At point *C*, this internal heating mechanism reaches the surface. *(I. Iben, Ann. Rev. Astron. Astrophys., vol. 5, p. 571, 1967.)*

Arguments brought out in recent years point to a rather short duration for the initial contraction phase of a protostar, and to increasingly turbulent motions in the contracting gas ball. Figure 12-1 gives a simplified version of the results of calculations concerning this initial contraction phase, for an object of one solar mass. The data are plotted in the fashion of a color-magnitude diagram, with the effective temperature as the abscissa scale, and the luminosity (in terms of the present solar luminosity) as the ordinate. The dashed lines correspond to different protostar radii of the present solar radius. We see that, from an arbitrary starting point *A*, the luminosity of the star decreases at essentially constant temperature, until at *B* the turbulent internal motions—believed to be quite violent—heat up the protostar; the heat moves outward until, at *C*, the surface is reached. At this point, an explosive increase in brightness may occur and indeed be observable. From now on, the contraction slows down considerably.

The phase our protostar has now reached is still characterized by very large size—a radius of typically 10 or 100 times the solar value—and by a surface temperature of $10^{3°}$K to $10^{4°}$K. But it has an **internal structure,** that is, a radial variation in density and temperature, very much like that of a "finished product" such as our sun.

There is, however, still one basic difference between our protostar and a "proper" star: the energy lost through the surface in the form of radiation is replenished by continuing gravitational contraction. In other words, the protostar continues to shrink. and the energy drawn from the gravitational reservoir is what emerges through the surface. The protostar's material is now dense enough to behave as a coherent gas or fluid, so the contraction process is very much slower. In fact, we are now talking in terms of typically 10^7 or 10^8 years for the duration of the remaining contraction phase.

In most cases, the hydrogen (which comprises most of the material in the universe) is neutral at the surface, but ionized in the center. As discussed in connection with the sun, such an arrangement leads to the preeminence of *convective* over *radiative* **energy transport** from center to surface. Thus, at this stage of development, protostars are convective; in fact, calculations show that most of them go through a phase in which the whole star, from the surface to the center, transports energy by convection.

It is in this phase that a comparatively large number of stars can first be observed: their luminosity is high enough to allow detection, and the long time they remain in this stage gives us a chance to find a significant fraction of them. Among these stars are some whose brightness varies in an irregular fashion and which are known as **T Tauri stars**. They are typically associated with gas clouds actively engaged in star formation. The characteristic irregular variability of T Tauri stars is probably due to the fact that they are still in the process of settling their internal structures. They are typically above the main sequence in the H-R diagram, moving to their stable positions on the main sequence. For this reason, T Tauri stars and their like are called **pre-main-sequence stars**. The time of the contraction phase varies between some 10^5 years for what will eventually be a B star on the main sequence, to some 10^9 years for the smallest M stars; the determining factor is the total mass of the forming star.

Nuclear Reactions.   As the pre-main-sequence or contraction phase continues, the density and temperature in the core increase. Once the central temperature is of the order of 10^6°K, the first **nuclear reactions** occur, and a new energy source becomes available to our protostar. These first nuclear reactions involve the buildup of heavier nuclei from hydrogen, lithium, beryllium, and boron nuclei present in the original gas cloud, in a manner very similar to the buildup of helium from hydrogen—except that the reaction times are much shorter than that of the pp chain. Gravitational contraction continues during this phase, and central density and temperature continue to increase. Soon, densitites and temperatures are reached at which the full-scale conversion of hydrogen into helium occurs with increasing frequency. The contraction slows down, since now the energy gained in the pp-chain reaction can supply all radiation losses through the surface, without recourse to the gravitational contraction as a source of energy. Then, for all practical purposes, contraction has stopped.

The star is now in a **stable phase**; it has reached the main sequence. Just where in the main sequence it will reside is determined by its **total mass**, which fixes central temperature and density. These in turn determine the rate of production of nuclear

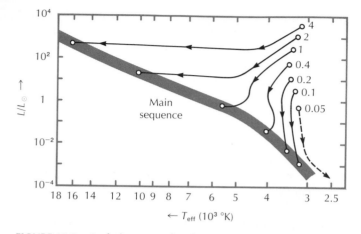

FIGURE 12-2. **Evolutionary tracks of stars of different masses onto the main sequence. The initial points on the right correspond to point** C **in Fig. 12-1. The numbers next to them indicate the masses of the stars in solar units.** *(C. Hayashi, Ann. Rev. Astron. Astrophys., vol. 4, p. 171, 1966.)*

energy and, thus, the luminosity. The balance between internal pressure and gravitational attraction keeps the star at a certain size, while size and luminosity together determine its effective temperature. A diagram can be drawn, showing the chain of effects that results in effective temperature:

core temperature and density → nuclear reaction rate → luminosity

mass

gravitational attraction → internal pressure → size

effective temperature

An **evolutionary track** is a curve superimposed on the H-R diagram that traces the development of surface temperature and luminosity in time. Recently, a number of these tracks have been computed, and examples are shown in Fig. 12-2 for stars of varying masses. The scales are, as in Fig. 12-1, the luminosity in solar units and the effective temperature. Note that the temperature scale covers roughly the spectral classes between B and M. The initial points at the right correspond to phase C in Fig. 12-1, while the numbers alongside the initial points are masses, given as multiples of the solar mass. We see that the stars all end up on the main sequence, but at different surface temperatures, depending on their initial masses.

We can see from Fig. 12-2 that there are stars in very early stages of evolution everywhere above the main sequence. However, stars remain in these portions of their evolutionary tracks for such short periods in comparison to their lifetimes that it is generally impossible to observe any of them there. Only when development slows, and they have almost reached the main sequence, do we have a realistic chance of observing them. This then is why we find no objects to the right of the giant branch in the usual H-R diagram.

Limitations on Mass. A specific comment should be made concerning the track for a star whose mass is 5% of the solar mass or smaller. Presumably, such a star never attains central temperatures high enough to initiate pp chains. What happens instead is that contraction continues, without interruption, until the central density is so high that the electrons in the star become **degenerate**.

Degenerate electrons are in the lowest energy states they can attain, although some of these states may correspond to quite large energy contents. At first glance this may seem paradoxical, but the fact is that electrons can occupy energy states only in pairs, and once a pair of electrons is in a particular state, this state is closed to all others. So, as the density increases, electrons begin to occupy energy states, beginning with the lowest available states, up to a limit which is essentially determined by the *density* of the material. Electrons in this configuration are, in a sense, frozen into a kind of crystalline pattern. Most of them find the states below their own filled, so they cannot decrease their energy content; nor can they change the volume they occupy.

Thus, once degeneracy sets in, contraction stops. No energy source is available to the protostar, and it goes directly to the white-dwarf stage (dashed line in Fig. 12-2). This argument can be interpreted as placing a lower limit on the mass of an object we can justly call a star, for such a limit must exist. The limit is at present believed to be around $0.08\ M_\odot$, between the lowest known masses of small M stars and the mass of our largest planets, which have never gone through a true stellar development.

On the other hand, we know that the heaviest stars observed so far may have masses some 50 times the solar mass. Even if our list of stars is as yet incomplete, say because stars with very large masses are quite rare, it is probable that there is some sort of upper limit on stellar masses. It is commonly believed that the core reaction of a stellar configuration with a mass above $100\ M_\odot$ would take place at such a tremendous rate that it would become unstable. Whether this instability would prevent it from being formed initially, or whether, if formed, it would break up in some way, is not clear. We should mention, however, that in recent years theoreticians have speculated about the existence of **supermassive objects** of, say, 10^6 $M_\odot$, in the centers of certain galaxies such as quasars (Section 21.4).

12.2 MAGNETIC FIELDS AND ANGULAR MOMENTUM. STELLAR ROTATION

Our story of the pre-main-sequence phase of a star is highly idealized, and in reality would be complicated by a number of details which at present are known only vaguely. Most of them have not been mentioned mainly because they are of interest solely to the specialist. However, there are two specific effects with which we should deal, since they appear on every evolutionary track.

Magnetic Fields. Most of the universe appears to be permeated by weak **magnetic fields**; in particular, they have been proven to exist in the interstellar material from which we think stars are formed. The strength of these fields is small, maybe one-millionth of the field at the earth's surface, and a small fraction of what is often observed at the surfaces of stars.

However, material even in such a weak field can move through the field on its way to the stellar core only so long as that material is completely neutral—that is, so long as it contains practically no free electrons or ions. Once there is even a small degree of ionization, however it comes about, the field is "frozen" into the ionized gas and compressed together with the contracting gas. Then the magnetic field increases its strength, and eventually exerts a force strong enough to stop further contraction, long before the gas can form a star.

We know that this is not the case, simply because stars are formed. What probably happens is that most of the material is actually neutral during most of the contraction phase, and so able to slip through the magnetic field lines. It is also possible that the magnetic field develops inhomogeneities in the contracting cloud, and that those areas in which strong fields come into being simply do not contract, but are left behind and ultimately expelled. Once the star is born, the magnetic field has little or no influence on its structure, except in cases such as the magnetic stars (Section 15.4), or in the form of localized activity such as takes place on the sun.

Rotation. A probably much more important complication is the existence of large-scale motions in the original gas cloud. They may begin because the whole condensing cloud is rotating, or because the random motions of the cloud particles do not quite average out to zero. In either case, the cloud attains a net **angular momentum** which it must either donate somehow to its surroundings, or carry into the contracted state of the star. The motion cannot simply be dissipated; in a physical system which is essentially isolated, that is, not interacting with its surroundings, the momentum residing in any rotational motion must be conserved.

Even if the rotational velocity of the original gas cloud were only of the order of a few centimeters per second, the fully contracted star would have a rotational velocity of some 100 km/sec at its surface. Speeds of this magnitude are occasionally observed in hot stars exhibiting emission lines, but are definitely absent in stars cooler than spectral class F, whose rotational speeds are mostly of the order of 1 km/sec. Hence, most stars must be able to shed almost all their angular momentum before they settle on the main sequence.

Several mechanisms have been suggested by which this may be accomplished. Aside from *mass loss* in the direction of rotation, which is probably not very efficient except at extremely high velocities, three are particularly interesting. One is related to the fact that in our solar system 97% of the total angular momentum resides in the orbital motions of Jupiter and Saturn, while the solar rotation is practically negligible in comparison. If this case is typical, then the *formation of massive planets* is one process by which the angular momentum residing in a star can be reduced. This is extremely important if it is so, since it makes the formation of planetary systems a routine byproduct of star formation.

The second type of process invokes a *stellar wind*, that is, a continuous escape of particles from a hot envelope that surrounds a star, like the solar corona that surrounds the sun. There are strong arguments for the existence of coronas around many varieties of stars. The particles that leave the star continuously reduce the angular-momentum reserve of the star's rotation.

A third mechanism by which angular momentum could be removed is the formation of a *multiple star system*. Such a system would utilize a large part of the excess angular momentum in relative orbital motion as opposed to the rotational motion of the individuals. Again, this suggestion does more than explain an intrinsic difficulty in the theory of star formation: it makes plausible the large number of multiple systems observed in the one star sample that is fairly complete, the sample made up of stars within a few parsecs of the sun.

12.3 THE ZERO-AGE MAIN SEQUENCE

We saw in Section 12.1 that toward the end of the initial contraction phase, the development of a star slows, and it settles somewhere on the main sequence. At this time, the star has essentially acquired its "final" radius, that is, the size it approximately maintains throughout the main-sequence phase. It has stopped contracting, at least noticeably, and has now attained a core temperature and density that allow the conversion of hydrogen into helium.

This stage is stable in the sense that there is a tremendous amount of "fuel" available to the star, so that it can make up for energy lost by surface radiation, for very long times. Thus, it will be almost completely stationary in the H-R diagram for such times; consequently, we find a high concentration of objects on the main sequence. We shall now take a closer look at this hydrogen-burning phase and the behavior of the stars that are in it. We take the end of the contraction phase as the starting point of our discussion; on the H-R diagram, or, specifically, on the luminosity–effective-temperature plot favored by theoreticians, such points define the **zero-age main sequence**. From a comparison of the observed mass-luminosity relation (Fig. 9-4) with the H-R diagram on one hand, and between the end points of the theoretically determined evolutionary tracks of Fig. 12-2 on the other, we see that this zero-age main sequence is a mass sequence, that is, the star's position on the sequence is determined by its total mass.

The pp Chain.   Let us first look at the nuclear processes going on in the star's core. We already know that hydrogen is being converted into helium; under the conditions prevailing in the *solar* interior (where the temperature is about 16×10^{6}°K), the route this process takes is from normal hydrogen, H^1, to H^2, a nucleus consisting of one proton and one neutron, to He^3, which consists of two protons and one neutron, to the stable helium isotope He^4. In Chapter 7 this *proton-proton chain*, or *pp chain*, was written as

$$H^1 + H^1 \rightarrow H^2 + \beta^+ + \nu$$
$$H^2 + H^1 \rightarrow He^3 + \gamma$$
$$He^3 + He^3 \rightarrow He^4 + H^1 + H^1$$

The CNO Cycle.   At higher temperatures, another chain of reactions becomes more probable. It initially involves C^{12} nuclei, consisting of six protons and six neutrons; nitrogen and oxygen nuclei are formed in intermediate steps. However, when all the reactions in the chain are completed, the original C^{12} nuclei are restored and so are free to act as "catalysts" for another of these **CNO cycles.** The details are as follows:

$$C^{12} + H^1 \rightarrow N^{13} + \gamma$$
$$N^{13} \rightarrow C^{13} + \beta^+ + \nu$$
$$C^{13} + H^1 \rightarrow N^{14} + \gamma$$
$$N^{14} + H^1 \rightarrow O^{15} + \gamma$$
$$O^{15} \rightarrow N^{15} + \beta^+ + \nu$$
$$N^{15} + H^1 \rightarrow C^{12} + He^4$$

Let us discuss this process somewhat further. First, note that the final outcome of the CNO cycle is exactly the same as that of the pp chain: four H^1 nuclei (protons) are converted into one He^4 nucleus, with the energy gain residing in two β^+ particles, two neutrinos, and emitted γ-rays. The total energy gained is, of course, the same for both sequences, although the specific distribution of energy (how much goes into γ-rays, or into the kinetic energy of positrons, or into neutrinos) may be somewhat different. For the star, the only quantity of interest is the fraction of energy carried away by the neutrinos, and this fraction is very similar in the two cases.

Now note that unstable nuclei, N^{13} and O^{15} in the CNO cycle, are created. These nuclei decay spontaneously by positron emission and hence are not observed naturally on the earth. Their lifetimes are very short (a few minutes only), so none of them remain once the particular chain is completed.

Finally, since the reaction products are essentially identical for the two sequences, the resultant energy will find its way to the star's surface through identical routes. Thus, we again have transport by means of radiation and/or convection.

Before we go any further, we should ascertain that the CNO cycle is the only serious alternative to the pp chain. This is indeed the case in the temperature range we are concerned with at present (center temperatures below $10^{8}°K$, i.e., up to six times that of the sun). Extensive study of all possible nuclear-reaction schemes has shown that no other process has a probability of occurrence anywhere nearly as high as that of either the pp chain or the CNO cycle. The main difference between the two sequences is the temperature dependence of the probabilities of the two reaction routes. In Fig. 12-3 the energy production of the pp chain and that of the CNO cycle are plotted, in arbitrary units, as functions of central terperature. The details of the graph actually depend on the relative abundance of the nuclei involved. We can see that at lower temperatures the pp chain is more efficient; at about $18 \times 10^{6}°K$, just a bit above the core temperature of the sun, the CNO cycle breaks even, and finally becomes vastly more efficient at higher temperatures.

CNO Cycle Versus pp Chain.   We are now ready to return to the zero-age main sequence. Table 12-1 is a collection of typical data for main-sequence stars. Since at a temperature of about $18 \times 10^{6}°K$, the pp chain and CNO cycle are equally efficient, stars of class F obtain about the same amount of energy from the pp chain as from the CNO cycle, whereas in stars with higher central temperatures the CNO cycle is prevalent, in those with lower temperatures the pp chain. Thus, we find again, as we did in Section 9.7 with regard to stellar rotation, that there are some basic physical differences between stars with effective temperatures above some

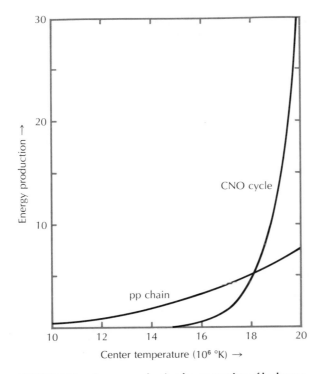

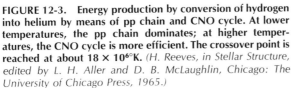

FIGURE 12-3. **Energy production by conversion of hydrogen into helium by means of pp chain and CNO cycle. At lower temperatures, the pp chain dominates; at higher temperatures, the CNO cycle is more efficient. The crossover point is reached at about 18 × 10⁶°K.** *(H. Reeves, in Stellar Structure, edited by L. H. Aller and D. B. McLaughlin, Chicago: The University of Chicago Press, 1965.)*

7000°K, and those with temperatures below that figure. Note also that the values given in Table 12-1 for a solar-type star differ from those quoted in Section 7.1 for our sun; the reason is that the sun is now no longer a zero-age star, since it has been converting hydrogen for about 5×10^9 years.

It must be emphasized that this discussion and our results depend on the initial chemical composition—in particular, on the hydrogen-to-helium ratio, and the ratio of hydrogen to the remaining elements. Table 12-1 and Fig. 12-3 refer to what

TABLE 12-1. ZERO-AGE MAIN SEQUENCE (PROPERTIES BY SPECTRAL CLASS)

Spectral class	Mass (solar masses)	Radius (solar radii)	Center temperature (10^6°K)	Center density (g/cm³)
O	15	4.2	34	6
B	6	2.7	28	15
A	1.5	1.2	19	85
F	1.1	1.1	17	90
Solar-type star	1.0	1.0	14	90
K	0.5	0.35	8.5	72

Source: I. Iben, *Ann. Rev. Astron. Astrophys.*, vol. 5, p. 571, 1967.

are known as **metal-rich** or **Population I** stars, characterized typically by compositions of about 70% hydrogen, 28% helium, and 2% "metals," including carbon, nitrogen, oxygen, neon, etc., by weight. This corresponds to about 90% hydrogen, 10% helium, and 0.1% metals by numbers of nuclei. This chemical abundance is essentially the one summarized in Table 7-1 for the sun. We shall discuss **metal-poor** or **Population II** stars in Section 18.2.

The data of Fig. 12-3, namely, the strong dependence of the energy yield on temperature, can also be interpreted as implying that the number of reactions per gram of stellar material increases drastically with increasing temperature. Thus, the core region of a more massive star with higher luminosity would produce vastly more energy than the core region of a less massive star. This has, of course, been confirmed by observation, and it was one of the great achievements of the theory of stellar evolution that predictions matched observed values so very closely.

12.4   THE HYDROGEN-CORE-BURNING PHASE

What happens to a star once it has established *hydrogen burning*, the fusion of hydrogen nuclei into helium, or, in our terminology, after it has settled on the zero-age main sequence? Obviously, it is not going to remain indefinitely in that state, because it is continuously depleting its supply of hydrogen while producing helium.

The Effect of Convection.   The main difference in behavior among stars on the main sequence lies in how the convection process is utilized. A large number of calculations concerning this process have been performed recently, and the result is briefly as follows: first, the outer portions of stars with masses below about 1.7 $M_\odot$, that is, of stars cooler than spectral class F, are convective. We usually say that these stars have **convective envelopes**, which are very shallow in stars of higher masses, but which become deeper and deeper with decreasing mass, until convection actually goes all the way to the core in stars with masses of about 0.4 $M_\odot$. Thus it is quite likely that very small stars, with masses between 0.4 $M_\odot$ and 0.1 $M_\odot$, are **completely convective**; lighter stars probably do not exist, because they never initiate hydrogen burning. Second, a **convective core** develops in stars with masses greater than 1.1 $M_\odot$, while less massive stars transport energy from the core via radiation. We can summarize the heat-transport behavior of main-sequence stars as follows:

Stars with masses greater than 1.7 $M_\odot$: radiative envelopes and convective cores.

Stars with masses between 1.7 $M_\odot$ and 1.1 $M_\odot$: convective envelopes and convective cores, separated by a layer of radiative transport.

Stars with masses between 1.1 $M_\odot$ and 0.4 $M_\odot$: convective envelopes and radiative cores.

Stars with masses smaller than 0.4 $M_\odot$: totally convective.

Note that if all solar-type stars and stars with lower surface temperatures have convective envelopes, then in all likelihood they also have *chromospheres* and *coronas* with accompanying *stellar winds*. There is ample observational evidence of this in the emission features of the spectra of most cool stars.

We emphasize that no star moves *along* the main sequence as it develops, so that this main sequence is *not* an age sequence, although an O star on the main sequence has condensed more recently from interstellar gas than a G or M star, owing to the shorter time it has spent in the contraction phase.

Stellar Lifetimes. Now, if there is core convection, that is, if the star's mass is above some 1.1 $M_\odot$, the material in the core is continuously mixed, and "fresh" hydrogen is brought into the nuclear furnace from the outer layers of the core convection zone. Stars with radiative cores, on the other hand, do not have such mixing mechanisms, and the supply of hydrogen decreases, from the edge of the hydrogen-burning core region to the center. While the hydrogen is slowly being depleted, core convection becomes less and less efficient and finally stops. Then the hydrogen in the center of the star is rapidly depleted. (The same fate is in store for the lighter stars that never had any core convection.) Without hydrogen, of course, hydrogen burning must cease, and the star's life on the main sequence is over.

Figure 12-4 shows the results of calculations of luminosity and effective temperature for stars with different masses, in the form of paths from the zero-age main sequence (points 1) to the beginning of hydrogen depletion in the core (points 2).

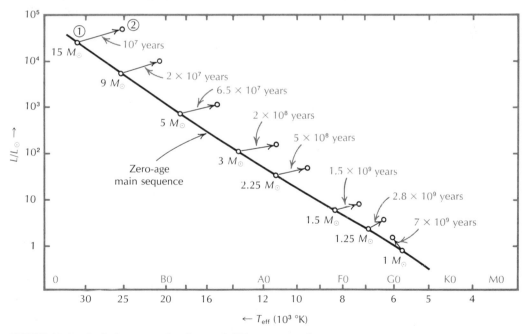

FIGURE 12-4. **Evolutionary tracks of stars of different masses from the zero-age main sequence (points 1) to the stage of hydrogen depletion in the core (points 2). The stars are identified by their masses in solar units. Also indicated are the times the stars spend on the main sequence.** *(I. Iben, Ann. Rev. Astron. Astrophys., vol. 5, p. 571, 1967.)*

Stars which initially have convective cores, and which effectively terminate convection at point 2, become a little more luminous in the process; but they also expand somewhat, so that the total effect is a reduction in effective temperature. The lighter stars essentially maintain their sizes, but their luminosities increase a bit. Thus, during the hydrogen-core-burning phase, stars of different masses and birth dates define a narrow *main-sequence band*, with the zero-age main sequence as the lower boundary.

The characteristic times spent between points 1 and 2 are also shown in Fig. 12-4. They vary from some 10^7 years for a 15 $M_\odot$ star of spectral type O to almost 10^{10} years for a solar-type star. Thus, even the oldest stars of spectral types K and M have barely moved away from the zero-age main sequence since their formation, which cannot have occurred much earlier than some 5 or 10 billion years ago.

Particularly detailed calculations have been carried out for our sun and they point to an age of about 4.5×10^9 years. Comparing this number with Fig. 12-4, we must conclude that the sun has already gone through more than half its core-burning phase. During this time it has increased its luminosity by about 25%, and its effective temperature by little more than 100°K. Most of the change must therefore have occurred in its radius, which obviously has increased too. Similar relatively minor changes will occur in the remaining part of its main-sequence phase, so for about another 10^9 years the sun should not be the cause of drastic changes in the structure of the earth. This is a very long time by any earthly standards, and an eternity in comparison with the time it has taken the human species to radically alter the face of our planet.

12.5 THE LATE PHASES

Our discussion of stellar evolution has so far followed a star from birth through the main-sequence phase to the point at which the hydrogen in the core is exhausted and, in the H-R diagram, the star has moved away from the main-sequence band. There is some justification in declaring that a new chapter in the history of a star is reached, a very brief second youth. For the vast majority of stars the initial phases discussed in Section 12.1 and the late phases to be summarized presently are but very short instants compared with the billions of years spent in and near the zero-age main sequence.

At any of the points labeled 2 in Fig. 12.4 a star has burned enough of the hydrogen fuel in its core so that a significant fraction of the hydrogen has been converted into helium—whatever the exact percentage is that defines these points. The remaining hydrogen is depleted very rapidly, until practically none is left in the core, even in stars with masses above the solar value, since the convective region comprises only a certain fraction of the star's total mass. So no further supply of fresh hydrogen is available.

Hydrogen Shell-Burning. While the star still loses energy through the surface, there is now no core source of nuclear energy. Thus, the star—to be precise, the core—has to return to its gravitational energy source, and it contracts. In the process,

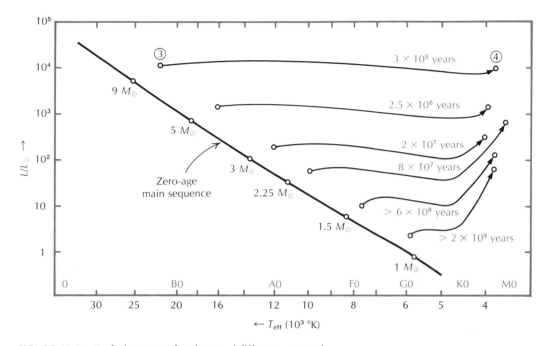

FIGURE 12-5. Evolutionary tracks of stars of different masses during the hydrogen-shell-burning phase. At the initial points 3, the hydrogen in the core is completely exhausted; at the points marked 4, helium is ignited. The stars are identified by their masses in solar units. Also shown are the times the stars spend in the hydrogen-shell-burning phase. (*I. Iben, Ann. Rev. Astron. Astrophys., vol. 5, p. 571, 1967.*)

it heats up. Soon a point is reached at which the temperature at the boundary of the hydrogen-exhausted core becomes high enough so that the hydrogen nuclei present just *beyond* this core undergo nuclear reactions, as they had previously *in* the core. At this point, a **shell source**, burning hydrogen, has been ignited.

The star again has a nuclear-energy source supplying the radiation lost through the surface. Detailed calculations indicate that in the process the radius of the star's envelope increases drastically, while at the same time the effective temperature drops, so that on balance the luminosity is almost constant; in the H-R diagram the star at first moves along an essentially horizontal line. Toward the end of this phase, the star has reached any one of various positions characteristic of the *giant branch* in the H-R diagram (Fig. 11-2). Actually, the details of the movement across the diagram appear to be rather complex; this fact, together with the presumably quite different ages and masses of observed stars, explains the diffuse character of the giant branch.

Figure 12-5 is essentially a continuation of Fig. 12-4. The starting points 3 correspond to complete hydrogen exhaustion in the core, and the lines show the H-R paths of stars of different masses during the shell-burning phase. Also shown in Fig. 12-5 are the computed durations of the passage through the shell-burning phase.

They range from some 10^5 years at masses around 10 $M_\odot$ to more than 10^9 years for solar-type stars. In comparison to the times spent burning hydrogen in the core (Fig. 12-4), these times are very short, at least for relatively massive stars.

We stated in Section 12.3 that the hydrogen-consuming pp chain and CNO cycle are the only energetically significant nuclear processes at temperatures up to $10^{8\circ}$K; some reactions, such as the transformation of N^{14} nuclei by capturing helium nuclei, occur with increasing frequency at the higher temperatures, but they do not noticeably change the energy outputs of stars.

Triple-Alpha Process. The first significant new process occurs at temperatures above $10^{8\circ}$K. Here, the chance encounters of three helium nuclei, or *alpha particles*, in the core may cause the sudden formation of a C^{12} nucleus, with the mass difference becoming available to the star's energy balance in the form of a succession of γ-photon emissions. This **triple-alpha process** is written as

$$3\,\alpha \rightarrow C^{12} + n\,\gamma \qquad (7.3\ \text{MeV})$$

with n designating the average number of γ photons emitted and the number in parentheses the energy gain. Positions 4 in Fig. 12-4 correspond to initiation of the triple-alpha process.

With the onset of *helium burning* in the core, a new relatively long-lived energy source has been tapped; nevertheless, the situation is in many respects quite different from the slow, quasistable hydrogen burning of the main sequence. First, all stars, not just the most massive ones, have by this time attained a quite considerable luminosity (the sun, for example, will be about 1,000 times as bright in the helium-burning phase as it is now); they use up their supplies of helium in much shorter times. Thus, relatively well defined positions in the H-R diagram are maintained for only short times. Second, the hydrogen shell continues, for quite a long time, to supply a significant portion of the total energy. Third, stars with masses below about 0.5 $M_\odot$ never attain the temperatures needed to initiate helium burning, and probably proceed to the white-dwarf stage directly from the main sequence.

Nevertheless, there are many similarities between the core-burning hydrogen and helium phases. For instance, core convection develops (in all cases) during helium burning, and it ceases when the helium content is essentially exhausted, leaving a core which consists mostly of C^{12}, O^{16}, and the original neon and iron. Thus, the next phase, paralleling the case of hydrogen, is the formation of a *helium shell source*, while the now-inert core contracts. For a while, then, the star may have two concentric active shell sources: an outer one burning hydrogen, and an inner one burning helium.

As mentioned, the times spent in the helium-burning phase are much shorter than the times spent burning hydrogen on the main sequence. For instance, the computed values for stars of 9 $M_\odot$, 5 $M_\odot$, and 3 $M_\odot$ are about 6×10^5, 10^7, and 4.5×10^7 years, respectively. Compare these to main-sequence lifetimes of some 2×10^7, 6.5×10^7, and 2×10^8 years, as quoted in Fig. 12-4. Thus, we should not be too surprised to find rather few stars in the solar neighborhood that—presumably—burn helium; and we would expect them to occupy positions above the giant branch in the region marked "supergiants" in Fig. 11-2.

With the establishment of a helium shell source and an inert carbon-rich core, the star has used up most of its active life. The later stages of development are not very well understood at present, although we feel rather confident that we know at least two end products: white dwarfs (Section 13.4) and neutron stars (Section 14.4). A possible third one is represented by the black holes (Section 14.8). In the remainder of this section, we summarize the processes that might lead to either white dwarfs or neutron stars.

Carbon Burning. At the time when the helium shell source eats itself outward through successive mass layers, the **carbon core** has reached a central temperature of about 2×10^8°K and a density of some 2×10^5 g/cm³ (so that a cubic centimeter of this material would weigh some 100 kg on earth!). Thus, if nothing else happened, we would expect a development which closely resembles what took place before helium core-burning set in: the carbon core would contract further until the electrons in the core became *degenerate*, that is, arranged themselves in a fixed pattern somewhat similar to a crystal structure; from then on they would resist any further contraction. The star, or at least its core, would now have reached a final stable state.

However, there are nuclear reactions possible at temperatures of some 10^8°K. The most notable is the combination of two C^{12} nuclei to form a Mg^{24} nucleus. If this stage is reached, the star has tapped a new energy source, and it can go through yet another cycle: a *carbon core source* from which, possibly, in due time, a *carbon shell source* would emerge. Other nuclear processes might be initiated thereafter, and the further development would become catastrophic; we shall come back to this alternative in Section 14.3.

In most cases, the development is probably quite different. One reason is the possible existence of a wholly new class of nuclear processes at these temperatures, processes which result in the emission of large quantities of **neutrinos**. We have seen already on several occasions that neutrinos are so unlikely to interact with existing nuclear material that, once they are formed, they are essentially free to leave the parent star unhindered. Thus, we suspect that a star with a central temperature of some 10^8°K develops an additional energy-loss mechanism by which energy is continually removed from the core in the form of neutrinos. The result is that the core never reaches temperatures beyond that attained during helium burning. *If* this mechanism actually is viable, even stars whose total mass would otherwise be quite sufficient to begin carbon burning may move toward complete degeneracy before this latter energy source can become active. There appear to be strong indications that this is indeed the case, although no definitive decision can as yet be made.

Chandrasekhar Limit. At this point, we encounter another difficulty: it has been shown beyond doubt that a completely degenerate core, in which all the electrons have been frozen into a crystalline structure, cannot support a stellar mass against gravitational forces beyond a limiting mass value somewhere in the neighborhood of 1.4 $M_\odot$. The exact limit depends on the total angular momentum of the star's rotation, the magnetic field frozen into the stellar material, and the like. However, this so-called **Chandrasekhar limit** is quite insensitive to variations in rotation or magnetic fields, say, within a few tenths of a solar mass.

We thus have to face the fact that on the basis of this theoretical knowledge a large number of stars never can reach the stable stage in which the core, containing at this point most of the stellar mass, is completely degenerate. These stars would have to go through carbon burning and the subsequent catastrophic events. Simple counting indicates that the number of candidates for such an end is orders of magnitude larger than the number of observed cases.

If stars were able to shed the mass that exceeded the Chandrasekhar limit (and in many instances this would have to be several solar masses!), then the remaining core material could simply contract into the stable degenerate state. Present observational evidence of such a process is ambiguous, although mass loss due to stellar wind might suffice; otherwise we must conclude that we are still missing one important factor which somehow might make it possible for the majority of massive stars to reach a stable phase in spite of originally excessive masses.

QUESTIONS FOR DISCUSSION

1. Why is it impossible that the sun, or any star, does not undergo changes in time?

2. Where does the energy come from which heats the air in a bicycle tire while it is being inflated? What is the analog of this situation in the early condensation stages of star formation?

3. At point C in Fig. 12-1 an explosive increase in brightness may occur, lasting a hundred days or so. If you wanted to find stars undergoing such a "flare-up," in what group or groups of stars would you look?

4. Stars observed in the pre-main-sequence phase are rather close to the main sequence in the H-R diagram. Why haven't we found many stars in much earlier stages?

5. Explain what an evolutionary track in the H-R diagram represents.

6. Most of the stars in any typical star sample are on the main sequence. Why?

7. Figure 12-3 shows the temperature dependence of the amounts of energy produced by pp chains and CNO cycles. Why does the CNO cycle depend on the chemical composition of the star (which in the figure was assumed to be the solar abundance)?

8. The sun's present position differs from the position of a star with one solar mass on the zero-age main sequence. Why?

9. How much of its life on the main sequence has the sun completed by now? What changes have occurred in this time?

10. Would you expect noticeable changes in the solar luminosity during historical periods, say periods of 1,000 years? Why?

11. Can all stars reach the state of degeneracy? Explain.

EXERCISES

1. Explain why astronomers are sure that H-R diagrams contain information on stellar evolution.

2. In what form is the material which eventually condenses to make up a star? Where does it come from?

3. What physical conditions within the cloud from which stars ultimately are formed influence the condensation process?

4. What physical process keeps an initial stellar condensation going? How?

5. What is the source of the energy that heats the core of a protostar in the initial contraction phase?

6. Compare the radius of the protostar at points *A*, *B*, and *C* in the Fig. 12-1 with distances in the solar system.

7. Find the location of the protostar at point C (Fig. 12-1) in an H-R diagram.

8. Why might one expect stars in the wholly convective phase to show strong emission lines superimposed on the Fraunhofer spectrum?

9. Summarize the main properties of T Tauri stars.

10. Give the main arguments in favor of the identification of T Tauri stars with the pre-main-sequence phase of stellar evolution.

11. What are the first nuclear-energy sources available to a star, just before it reaches the zero-age main sequence?

12. Consider the schematic diagram on p. 186. Why is the star's nuclear-reaction rate determined by its mass? By its luminosity? Why does the mass also determine the effective temperature in spite of the fact that the effective temperature depends on luminosity and the size of the star?

13. The unique relation between mass and effective temperature as indicated in the diagram on p. 146 does not hold for all stars. For what class of stars in the H-R diagram does it hold? Which link in the diagram is different for other star groups in the H-R diagram?

14. What, presumably, happens to a star of 0.05 $M_\odot$ which does not reach the zero-age main sequence?

15. Mark the approximate locations of the spectral classes on a copy of Fig. 12-2.

16. Compare the masses of small M stars (Fig. 9-4), the theoretical lower mass limit for hydrogen-burning stars, and the masses of the large planets in the solar system. What conclusion do you reach?

17. Why does a magnetic field tend to stop or delay gravitational contraction?

18. Why do astronomers feel that a star must somewhat get rid of most of the angular momentum that was contained in the original gas cloud? What happens to the angular momentum that remains in the star or star system?

19. The majority of stars on the main sequence are small, cool stars. What does this tell you about star formation? More generally, what is the importance of luminosity functions to theories of star formation?

20. Summarize the two main types of hydrogen fusion that occur in the cores of main-sequence stars.

21. Why is the C^{12} nucleus called a *catalyst* in the fusion process of the CNO cycle?

22. What happens to the β^+ particles produced in the pp chain and the CNO cycle?

23. What property of a star determines whether its energy is the result of a pp chain, a CNO cycle, or a combination of both, while it resides on the main sequence?

24. What is the gross chemical composition of a "metal-rich Population I" star? Give an example of a metal-rich star.

25. Which types of stars use on the main sequence the convective versus the radiative energy transport?

26. Which stars on the main sequence would you expect to have chromospheres and coronas? Why?

27. Why does an O star remain on the main sequence so much shorter a time than an M star?

28. What happens to the color and magnitude of a B star during hydrogen core-burning? To those of a G star?

29. Why does a star burn hydrogen in a shell surrounding the core proper?

30. What is the physical state of a star's core during the initial phases of hydrogen shell-burning?

31. Where in the H-R diagram do you find hydrogen-shell-burning stars?

32. Stars ignite the triple-alpha process at core temperatures of the order of 100 million degrees. On the main sequence, they had core temperatures of the order of 20 million degrees. From what source do they get the energy to increase their core temperatures fivefold?

33. After the core helium of a star is exhausted through the triple-alpha process, what element is likely to be the most abundant in the core?

34. Has it been established that all stars in their late stages burn carbon? Explain.

35. Many aspects of degeneracy are of interest in physics. Which aspect is the most important one in the framework of stellar evolution? Why?

FURTHER READING

Schwarzschild, M., *Structure and Evolution of the Stars,* Princeton, N.J.: Princeton University Press, 1958.

The Evolution of Stars, edited by T. Page, New York: The Macmillan Company, 1968.

13 planetary nebulae and white dwarfs

What happens to stars after they have used up all their energy sources? The evidence accumulated in recent years indicates that the last stages of activity before a star settles down to die as a white dwarf are represented by the *planetary nebulae*. The name is utterly misleading, since such an object is not simply a *nebula*, that is, a gas mass—possibly mixed with "dust"—but actually includes a *central star*. Furthermore, the system has absolutely nothing to do with planets, as we shall see presently. The reason for the name is simply that in the old telescopes of centuries ago, planetary nebulae appeared as somewhat fuzzy discs. They are among the most striking objects in the sky when seen at high resolution; this must have something to do with the fascination they have held for astronomers throughout the more than 250 years since their discovery.

The *white dwarfs*, on the other hand, are certainly not spectacular in any observational aspect. However, their importance derives from the fact that they represent the stage in which a common star slowly dies. In this chapter we shall dwell in some detail on the evidence for these identifications.

13.1   PLANETARY NEBULAE: THE OBSERVATIONS

High-resolution photographs of planetary nebulae reveal immediately that each represents a system consisting of a **central star** and the **nebula** proper that surrounds it. In some instances, the nebula is so compact, and thus so bright, that the central star is not directly observable. Altogether, about 1,000 planetary nebulae have been identified, their angular sizes varying from several arcminutes down to some 10 arcsec. Figure 13-1 is **NGC 3242** (a designation from a catalogue compiled around the turn of the century, the so-called *New General Catalogue* or *NGC*). It is a compact object whose central star is barely visible in the reproduction. The nebula in **NGC 6853**, shown in Fig. 13-2, is much less compact and reveals some complex structures. Finally, **NGC 7293**, in Fig. 13-3, is one of the prominent **smoke rings** which form a subclass of nebulae with a relatively simple geometry.

Spectrum.   The spectrum of a planetary nebula (as is to be expected from its composite nature) shows a combination of two vastly different sources. The contribution of the central star is characterized by photospheric temperatures between some $20,000°K$ and about $3 \times 10^{5}°K$. It may show either emission or absorption lines and does not fall into any of the "normal" classes of stars discussed in Section 9.6. The spectrum of the nebula proper, on the other hand, consists mostly of emission lines.

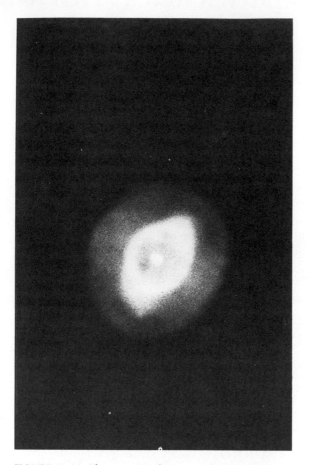

FIGURE 13-1.   The compact planetary nebula NGC 3242. The central star is barely visible in the reproduction. *(Hale Observatories.)*

The nebular spectrum is such that determinations of radial velocities can be made using Doppler shifts; if the angular diameter and the brightness are large enough, this can be done for several points in the nebula. The results of such analyses show a **radial expansion** taking place with a speed typically of some 10 km/sec, accompanied by a continuous decrease in the density of the nebular material. In addition—and this is particularly true for objects with complex structures—there are **internal motions** of about the same magnitude. The obvious explanation for this motion is an event at some earlier time during which the nebular material was ejected from the central star.

Distance.   One of the crucial parameters in most of the descriptions to follow is the distance of individual planetary nebulae, from which, for instance, we can determine the absolute magnitudes of the central stars. Few of these distances are known for sure, because direct determinations are extremely rare. The distance of NGC 7293 is known, because it is close enough to allow parallax determination. There is also a planetary nebula which is a member of a binary system, and whose distance can be inferred by matching the spectrum of the other component against typical values for its spectral class. Another is a member of a globular cluster, and its distance has been found by the method of cluster parallaxes. For a few individuals, radial expansion can be followed as changes in angular size; combined with radial-velocity measurements, this gives an indication of distance. For most other planetary nebulae, indirect methods based on theory must be applied. Whatever the method used, these distances are the basis for the determination of ages and absolute magnitudes. They are reasonably reliable for planetary nebulae as a whole, if not for each individual object.

13.2 INTERPRETATION OF THE SPECTRUM

Central-Star Spectrum. Let us now return to the observation that, in terms of photospheric temperature, many central stars are hotter than the hottest main-sequence objects, that is, O-type stars. This has been inferred through analysis of central-star

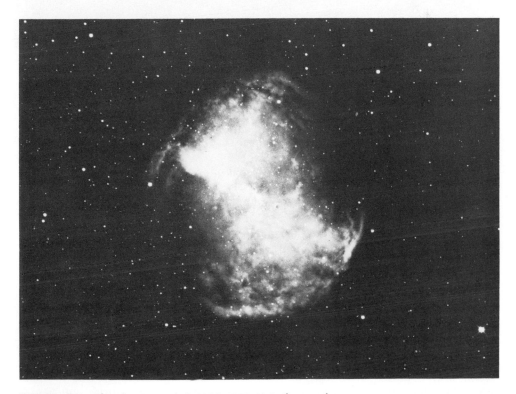

FIGURE 13-2. The planetary nebula NGC 6853. Note the complex structures. *(Lick Observatory.)*

**FIGURE 13-3. NGC 7293, one of the prominent "smoke rings."
The central star is clearly visible in the center. Photographed with
the 200-inch telescope.** *(Hale Observatories.)*

spectra, in which only very weak absorption lines, or none at all, are found. Another frequently encountered type of spectrum shows, superimposed on a continuum, extremely **broad emission lines** characteristic of the higher ionization stages of carbon, nitrogen, oxygen, etc. As an example, NGC 6751 shows strong emission lines of ionized oxygen, ionized carbon, ionized helium, and others. This type of spectrum belongs to the class of stars called *Wolf-Rayet stars*, a class we will discuss in more detail in Section 15.5

Such spectral features are manifestations of unordered, large-scale motions (**turbulence**) with speeds that may be as high as 10^3 km/sec, much larger than the mean speed of the atoms and ions due to their heat energy (thermal speed). The high-speed chaotic motions require an energy mechanism that certainly is not a part of the usual main-sequence star, and whose details at present are not understood. However, one thing is clearly suggested: stars whose atmospheres are in such a violent state of disorder are either intrinsically unstable and hence intrinsically different from main-sequence stars, or else they are in a transitory state in which their energy-production mechanisms are undergoing a rapid change from one type to another.

Nebular Spectrum. While the central star emits a continuous spectrum that corresponds to extremely high photospheric temperatures, the nebula emits a **line spectrum.** For a long time, in fact until 1928, the origin of some of the strongest lines was unclear, and, in desperation, they were ascribed by some astronomers to a hypothetical element called *nebulium*. The correct identification shows that these **nebular lines** belong to several ionization stages of carbon, nitrogen, oxygen, and neon, as well as to hydrogen and helium and other elements.

These lines of C, N, and O have one peculiarity in common with the red and green auroral lines, the spectral lines responsible for the coloration of Northern Lights in the earth's atmosphere: their emission is highly improbable. The appearance of these "**forbidden**" **lines** signals a very low gas density in the nebula. Through detailed spectral analysis the electron densities are now known rather accurately; the typical value is about 10^3 electrons per cubic centimeter, with variations of about 10 in either direction. At the same time, the fact that the atoms involved are ionized, some of them several times, means that the internal energy of the emitting gas must be relatively high; again, detailed analysis indicates temperatures typically of 10,000°K to 20,000°K.

Energy Balance of Nebula. How is the energy balance in the nebula maintained? A schematic and rather simplified description of the many complex atomic processes involved may suffice for our purposes. Basically, the energy is supplied by the central star; it emits very energetic ultraviolet photons which are absorbed in the nebular material and cause it to remain in a relatively high stage of ionization. Each time a free electron is captured by one of the nebular ions, that is, when the ion recombines, it gives off energy in the form of photons. In most cases this is a cascade of many less-energetic photons whose sum must equal the ionization energy of the original photon emitted by the central star. Thus, the energy which the nebula extracts from the central star by absorbing ultraviolet photons is lost again in its own emission spectrum.

Lifetimes. Using Doppler-shift measurements, we can compute the rate of increase in the size of the nebula, but only if the distance of the object is known. Working backward with this rate, we can find the time it has taken the nebula to expand from size zero to its present size. This has been done for objects whose expansion speed and distance are reasonably certain, and a typical result is about 10^4 years. The conclusion is then that the typical nebular shell was ejected by its central star some 10^4 years ago. The older nebulae are close to the point of final **dissipation**, that is, the point at which their motion is slowed almost to zero by the resistance of the interstellar gas they have been displacing as they have expanded. Thus, ultimately, a nebula joins the reservoir of gas and dust from which, in time, new stars will be formed.

We can at present only speculate on the reason for the initial ejection of the nebula and its subsequent expansion; most likely, it is the result of some kind of instability connected with the central star. From our discussion of stellar evolution, we would expect such an occurrence in the very early or very late stages of the development of normal stars; otherwise, we have to assume planetary nebulae to represent a stage in the development of some otherwise unknown and presumably highly unusual class of stars. This latter alternative is unlikely, simply because there are too many planetary nebulae observed. Thus, the question arises as to what particular stage in the lifetime of common stars is represented by planetary nebulae.

13.3 PLANETARY NEBULAE AND STELLAR EVOLUTION

Thus, our basic premise is that planetary nebulae comprise a short transitory stage in the evolution of otherwise *normal* stars. From the frequency of such objects in the universe, or say in the neighborhood of the sun, and their short lifetimes of the order 10^4 years, we must conclude that a very large number of stars must go through the planetary nebula stage. Indeed, the data would not even exclude the possibility that almost all stars go through this stage.

But, are the central stars of planetary nebulae at the beginning or the end of their life spans? The argument is twofold. On the one hand, we can plot absolute-magnitude and surface-temperature data on an H-R diagram as in Fig. 13-4, where the planetary nebulae are indicated by dots. For comparison, the main sequence is entered as a solid line, and some white dwarfs are shown as circles. To be sure, the data for individual planetary nebulae are afflicted with gross errors, but Fig. 13-4 should give quite an accurate picture of their position in the H-R diagram: they are to the left of the main sequence, and they are brighter than white dwarfs.

On the other hand, we can use the size of a nebula as an indication of the "aging" of the central star since ejection of the nebula. The most compact nebula typically accompanies the most luminous star, and the surface temperature of the central star continues to increase during the initial phases of nebular expansion. Then, from a certain time on, both luminosity and temperature decrease, with luminosity dropping to about the solar value for the "oldest" known objects. Thus, we can assume on the basis of their luminosities that the central stars of planetary nebulae evolve from a place near the horizontal branch (Fig. 11-9) toward the position of the brightest white dwarfs. The obvious interpretation is that planetary nebulae represent a stage in stellar evolution *just after nuclear burning and before the final death stage of white dwarfs.*

This picture fits theory very well. We have argued in Section 12.5 that, after extinction of the helium shell source, many stars are left without further nuclear processes to tap. At this stage, they would have very large envelopes (and, thus, luminosities) and very compact and highly degenerate cores. Without a source of nuclear energy, the envelope would begin to contract. Since the atmosphere accounts for relatively little mass, the gravitational energy gained by the star during the collapse of its envelope would be rather insignificant. Thus, no dramatic increase in light output is expected, and indeed none has been observed during envelope collapse. (Nevertheless, this argument should be taken as more qualitative than quantitative.) Finally, the envelope, or a part of it, is ejected by the central star and forms the nebula. But again, a relatively small mass, at most a few tenths of a solar mass, is involved.

Figure 13-5 shows schematically the path of a planetary nebula through the H-R diagram in the approximately 10^4 years between extinction of the helium shell

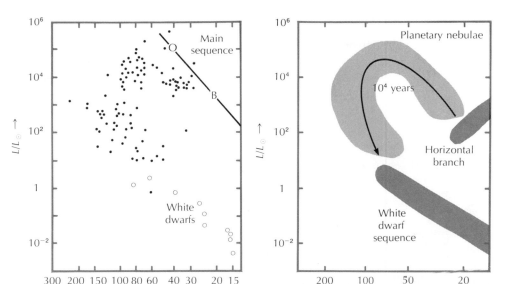

FIGURE 13-4. Observed planetary nebulae in the H-R diagram, marked by dots. The main sequence for O and B stars, and some white dwarfs observed in this temperature range (circles), are added for comparison. *(C. R. O'Dell, "Planetary Nebulae," in International Astronomical Union Symposium, no. 34, edited by D. E. Osterbrook and C. R. O'Dell, New York: Academic Press, Inc., 1968.)*

FIGURE 13-5. Suggested evolutionary track of planetary nebulae in the H-R diagram. The stars move, after expulsion of the shell, from a position in the general neighborhood of the horizontal branch (see Fig. 11-9) to the white-dwarf sequence along an arched path.

source and the dissipation of the nebula—at which point the central star enters the realm of white dwarfs.

13.4 WHITE DWARFS: THE OBSERVATIONS

Let us now turn to the group of stars we claim represent one of the final stages in stellar evolution, the **white dwarfs**; again we begin with a survey of the available observational data. White dwarfs are, as mentioned in Section 11.1, quite common in the neighborhood of the sun; in fact, among the 50 or so stars within 5 pc of the sun, 5 are white dwarfs (Fig. 11-4). This must be compared with no stars of classes O and B, one A star (Sirius), one F star, and four G stars; the vast majority are tiny M stars.

Luminosity and Radii. Since there are a number of white dwarfs close enough to allow us to measure parallaxes, we know the absolute magnitudes of these stars; and from their spectra we can find their surface temperatures. These temperatures range from about 10^5°K all the way down to 4000°K. An H-R diagram constructed from these data is shown in Fig. 13-6, which includes the position of the main sequence for comparison.

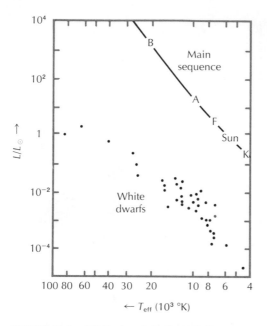

FIGURE 13-6. White dwarfs in the H-R diagram. The main sequence for stars of spectral classes B to K is added for comparison. *(C. R. O'Dell, "Planetary Nebulae," in International Astronomical Union Symposium, no. 34, edited by D. E. Osterbrook and C. R. O'Dell, New York: Academic Press, Inc., 1968.)*

A white dwarf of approximately solar surface temperature only emits one-thousandth of the sun's light. This must mean that white dwarfs have very small radii. The combination of small size and high temperature would make the brightest and earliest observed individuals appear whitish, if we could see them with the naked eye; hence their name. It must be admitted, however, that we may be prejudiced by what we can "see," and that there may be "white dwarfs" of much lower temperature and luminosity which simply have not been found yet and which, from their color, would deserve the designation red rather than white.

The white dwarf closest to us is a companion of Sirius, the brightest star in the constellation Canis Major; another well-known example is the companion of Procyon, the brightest star in the constellation Canis Minor. While Sirius is, to the eye, the brightest of all the stars in the sky, its white-dwarf companion would have to be 10 times more luminous than it is in order to be seen at all with the unaided eye. The radii of white dwarfs typically are about one-hundredth of the solar value, or close to the earth's radius. Altogether, several hundred white dwarfs are now known.

Mass. The masses of several of the white dwarfs that are members of multiple star systems have been determined by the methods outlined in Section 10.2. The three objects whose orbits are known have masses between 1 $M_\odot$ and 0.4 $M_\odot$. In other cases, mass determination is either infeasible or inaccurate, mostly because the components are too far apart to have completed a significant portion of their orbits since the beginning of photographic observation. Or, there may be a suspected third component in the system which, of course, would make a mass value arrived at on the basis of binary theory useless. Thus, we can only state that the few direct observations point to small masses.

Surface Gravity. Combining the mass estimate of about 1 $M_\odot$ with a radius of 10^{-2} $R_\odot$, we find that the gravitational force at the surface of a white dwarf is about 10^4 times the value for the sun. To see this, recall that according to Newton's law, the gravitational force is inversely proportional to the square of the distance (the radius, here), all other things being equal.

We have already noted that one can derive a surface temperature from the observed slope of the continuous spectrum. In addition, many white dwarfs show the Fraunhofer lines of elements appropriate to their respective temperatures. What interests us is the conclusion that somehow the chemical composition near the white-dwarf surface, or at least the hydrogen-to-helium-to-metal ratio, varies considerably from one object to another. This is not merely an oddity, but a very significant fact to be discussed further in the next section.

White-dwarf spectra also show an effect known as **gravitational redshift**. This phenomenon comes about because photons that move out of a gravitational field lose a certain amount of energy and, hence, appear to an observer as being *redshifted*. Thus, for instance, the hydrogen lines in the Fraunhofer spectra of white dwarfs are found at slightly greater wavelengths than comparable lines of laboratory standards. An observed redshift will, in general, be partly due to the radial-velocity component of the motion of the white dwarf relative to the sun. However, if the white dwarf is a member of a binary system, the radial-velocity contribution can be determined separately; then any excess is the gravitational redshift. This has been computed for the system 40 Eridani, and the result is compatible with the gravitational field of a star with a mass of less than 1 $M_\odot$ and a radius of 10^{-2} $R_\odot$.

13.5 THE DYING STARS

Let us now, on the basis of the data collected in the last section, attempt to understand the structure and evolution of white dwarfs from the time the nebula ejected in the planetary nebula stage is dissipated, leaving a bare central star of by now small luminosity behind. At the outset we must realize that this small luminosity is incompatible with the existence of an active nuclear-energy source. Too, a star of roughly 1 $M_\odot$ that had a nuclear source would have a radius much larger than 10^{-2} $R_\odot$.

Now, the density attributed to white dwarfs and the absence of nuclear-energy sources lead to the conclusion that the electrons in the interior are **degenerate**. As we saw in Section 12.5, such a configuration is stable against *gravitational contraction*, so not even that source of energy is available to white dwarfs. How then does a white dwarf replenish the energy lost through its radiation field? The answer is that it does not replenish it; instead, it slowly exhausts the finite reservoir of *internal heat* that had been built up earlier, when the central temperature was of the order of 10^8°K.

Reminiscent of these days, that is, the days after extinction of hydrogen and helium nuclear sources, is the observed ratio of hydrogen to helium to metals. It varies among the objects because individual stars represent their original abundancies to varying degrees in the sense that some have ejected most of their atmospheres along the evolutionary path, and now consist mostly of material that has gone through one or more nuclear fusion processes, while others have lost only portions of their atmospheres and still contain a significant admixture of unused atmosperic material.

As time passes, the internal heat reservoir shrinks, and its temperature is lowered. Eventually, the ions begin to arrange themselves into a configuration similar to that of a liquid, and still later into a crystal-like structure. Finally, they too become degenerate, as the electrons had become earlier, and the star as a whole approaches zero temperature. At this time, the star has become a **black dwarf**, a ball of dense material moving unseen through space in its final death.

How long this process takes is dependent on several things, but cooling times of the order of 10^{10} years, that is, the age of the universe, have been suggested, although the cooling rate speeds up once the crystallization of the star as a whole has begun. From the observational point of view, this slow cooling means that, in the course of time, white dwarfs decrease their energy output, that is, their absolute magnitude, and their surface temperature. In the H-R diagram, they move downwards and to the right. In other words, the **white-dwarf sequence** appears, at least in part, to be an aging sequence that stars enter at the upper left and along which they slowly move in time. This is in direct contrast to the main sequence, which is not an aging sequence, since stars enter it at any point, remain for a time, and then leave. Figure 13-7 contrasts the main sequence and the white-dwarf sequence in a schematic fashion.

QUESTIONS FOR DISCUSSION

1. Why do you think planetary nebulae are identified by NGC numbers rather than numbers in a star catalogue?

2. If the central star and nebula of a planetary nebula cannot be resolved, what are the main features of the composite spectrum?

3. What is the basis of the statement that planetary nebulae must represent an exceedingly common stage in the evolution of stars?

4. Astronomers believe their roster of planetary nebulae is rather complete, out to quite great distances from the sun. Why?

5. Astronomers hypothesize that the nebula ejected by the central star of a planetary nebula might represent the mass a heavy star must lose in order to reach the white-dwarf stage. In what ways does this hypothesis agree with observations?

6. The gravitational redshift was not mentioned in connection with stars other than white dwarfs, such as our sun. Why?

7. How would you explain the observational fact that different white dwarfs appear to have quite different hydrogen-to-helium abundance ratios?

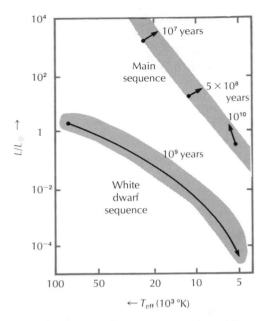

FIGURE 13-7. Main sequence versus white-dwarf sequence; the arrows show the evolution-ary tracks schematically. During its main-sequence life, a star *crosses* **the band of the main sequence, whereas as a white dwarf it moves** *along* **the sequence.**

EXERCISES

1. Why were planetary nebulae named "planetary"? Why "nebulae"?

2. How would you distinguish the emission lines of the central star of a planetary nebula from the emission lines of the nebula?

3. Under what circumstances can one obtain exact measurements of the expansion speed of the nebula of a planetary nebula?

4. The distances of very few planetary nebulae are accurately known. What properties of those mentioned in the text would make their distances measurable?

5. What is meant by the term "forbidden line"?

6. The nebula of a planetary nebula does not have an intrinsic energy source. Where does it get the energy that shows up in the form of emission lines?

7. What is the observational evidence on which is based the estimate of 10^4 years as the life of the nebula of a planetary nebula?

8. What happens to the nebula after its ejection by the central star?

9. After the extinction of the last nuclear furnaces in a star, its envelope begins to contract under the influence of gravitation. Why does this process not supply the star with energy for long periods of time as it did in the pre-main-sequence phase?

10.   It has been emphasized that white dwarfs represent a final stage in the evolution of stars. Review the arguments which make this identification very certain.

11.   In the text we mentioned the possibility that there are "white dwarfs" of still lower surface temperature and luminosity than the dimmest ones yet discovered. Assume that such a hypothetical object has a luminosity of 10^{-6} of the solar value. What would its absolute magnitude be? Its apparent magnitude, if it were 5 pc from the sun? Compare these figures with the data given in Table H-10.

12.   Identify the white dwarfs in Table H-10 and in the H-R diagram of Fig. 11-4.

13.   The distances between the components in the multiple star systems in which one member is a white dwarf are less than 1 arcmin. Is this fact compatible with our statement that the masses of these stars are fairly well known? Why?

14.   How do you find the surface temperature of a star from its continuous spectrum alone?

15.   Calculate the gravitational acceleration at the surface of a white dwarf from the data given in the text.

16.   Why can you not make an accurate determination of the gravitational redshift for a single white dwarf?

17.   Why can white dwarfs not use gravitational contraction as a continuing energy source?

18.   Where do white dwarfs get the energy they emit through the surface as radiation?

19.   What hypothetical object is called a "black dwarf"?

20.   Why does a white dwarf become less and less luminous as time goes on?

21.   List a few of the major differences between the main sequence and the white-dwarf sequence.

FURTHER READING

Abetti, G., and M. Hack, *Nebulae and Galaxies,* London: Faber and Faber, Ltd., 1964.

Galactic Structure, edited by A. Blaauw and M. Schmidt, Chicago: The University of Chicago Press, 1965.

14 supernovae, neutron stars, and pulsars

The preceding chapter was devoted to the evolution of stars from the extinction of the helium shell source through planetary nebulae to the white-dwarf stage. But it is known that under certain conditions the nuclear reactions can go beyond helium and carbon burning, and that in this case the evolution takes a vastly different form.

For more than a decade now, a phenomenon known as a *supernova event* has been identified with the sudden and catastrophic collapse of a star whose nuclear reactions have continued into the realm of heavy nuclei.* Most of the evidence concerning supernovae has been accumulated in studies of faraway star systems or *galaxies,* which are separated from our galaxy, the Milky Way, by vast reaches of space.

Until 1967, no observational evidence was available on what might remain *after* a star has gone through the supernova stage. Theoreticians argued about the existence of burned-out "neutron stars," but even staunch proponents of the theory admitted that there was a good chance these hypothetical objects would never be seen.

All this has changed almost overnight. There is nowadays a consensus that neutron stars do exist and that, moreover, they are very much alive and observable in the form of *pulsars.* Of course, so new a study is afflicted with many uncertainties about details, tends to oversimplify complex physical features, and may as yet have missed features which could turn out to be crucial. However, the basic concepts seem to be clear. And it is also clear that the observation of pulsars represents a most amazing confirmation of a theory proposed on the basis of much intuitive deduction and very little in terms of hard data.

In a sense, supernovae are related to neutron stars as planetary nebulae are to white dwarfs. Let us therefore begin by reviewing the evidence of supernova events.

14.1 OBSERVATIONAL EVIDENCE OF SUPERNOVA EVENTS

A **supernova** "explosion" is signaled by the sudden appearance of a starlike object whose luminosity, for a few days or weeks, is greater by many orders of magnitude than that of any other type of star. If a supernova explosion should occur anywhere near the sun, humanity would be treated to the most spectacular display that nature can arrange. Unfortunately, the chance of this occurring in our lifetime (or, in the lifetime of the human species) is exceedingly slim. Nevertheless, even if it happens

*The name "supernova" was introduced in the days when astronomers thought that these objects were special cases of a fairly common class of stars known as *novae* (Section 15.3).

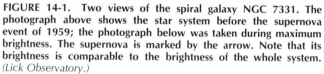

FIGURE 14-1. Two views of the spiral galaxy NGC 7331. The photograph above shows the star system before the supernova event of 1959; the photograph below was taken during maximum brightness. The supernova is marked by the arrow. Note that its brightness is comparable to the brightness of the whole system. *(Lick Observatory.)*

in the far reaches of space it is quite impressive. In the last millennium, three such events have been clearly recorded. The first one, in the year 1054, is decribed in detail in Chinese records; this particular event will occupy us considerably in later sections, for it gave rise to what is known today as the **Crab nebula**. Then, Brahe and Kepler witnessed supernova explosions in the years 1572 and 1604, respectively. At maximum brightness, the "new stars" were visible in the sky in full daylight.

From observational experience it is assumed that on the average a supernova event takes place every 30 years or so in a galaxy. Of course, since their occurrence is random, there will once in a while be several in a row; then, there might be none for several hundred years. An observer will in general miss some of these events within his own galaxy, simply because they are obscured by intervening absorbing material.

Photographic Observations.　Our main source of information on the actual supernova stage are the thousands of galaxies far away from us, but observable with large
telescopes. Figure 14-1 is a record in time of a supernova event; this one took place
in the galaxy NGC 7331. The two pictures show the galaxy in the year 1959, before
and during the maximum of the supernova. The crucial point here is the fact that the
supernova alone emits not much less visible light than the whole star system combined, something of the order of the emission strength of 10^{10} solar-type stars. It is
thus immediately clear that the supernova event must command energy sources on
a scale quite different from any we have discussed so far.

　　At present, about 200 supernovae have been directly observed or inferred from
indirect data; a much smaller number of observations, mostly the very recent ones,
are quantitative enough to be used for exploration of the physical conditions within
supernovae. The simplest data to collect are **light curves**, showing the time variation
of the light output over most or all of the visible spectrum.

　　Inspection of light curves shows that there exist at least two different types of
supernovae. The so-called **type I supernovae** are a rather homogeneous group in the
sense that their light curves are quite similar to each other. Figure 14-2 gives several
examples of type I light curves, with the designation IC 4182, etc., denoting the
parent galaxies. The observed intensity is plotted in arbitrary units against the time in

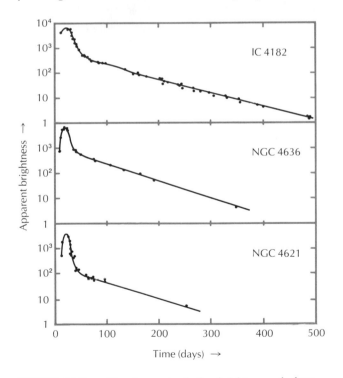

FIGURE 14-2.　Development of the brightness of three
supernovae of type I. Apparent brightness, in arbitrary units,
is plotted against time. The parent galaxy is indicated for each
event. *(R. Minkowski, Ann. Rev. Astron. Astrophys., vol. 2,
p. 247, 1964.)*

days. Note that these light curves have in common a rather well-defined maximum light output, with a subsequent rapid drop by about a factor of 10, followed by a slow decrease in intensity over years. In contrast, **type II supernovae** show neither the well-defined maximum nor the regular decrease thereafter, but rather a wide variety of more or less irregular light-intensity decreases.

Spectral Analyses.   Spectroscopic observations of supernovae require large telescopes and are consequently available for very few objects. The evidence we have indicates that type I supernovae show very similar spectra, whereas the spectra of type II supernovae are as diverse as their light curves. In all cases, the detailed structures are quite complex, and to date most have defied definitive interpretation. However, where spectral lines (either in emission or in absorption) could be identified with known features, Doppler shifts were calculated, and it turns out that the light-emitting atmosphere of a supernova expands with a speed of several thousand kilometers per second—almost a thousand times faster than the nebula of a planetary nebula. After the supernova has faded, this atmosphere remains as a nebula—still expanding—and represents what we call the **supernova remnant.**

Since, in general, the distance of the parent galaxy is known, the observed magnitude of a supernova, say at maximum, can be converted into an absolute magnitude. It is from such data that the brightness equivalent of some 10^{10} solar-type stars, quoted above, was derived. In absolute figures, a type I supernova emits, during its existence, approximately 10^{49} ergs, an amount comparable to the total energy output of the sun during its lifetime on the main sequence. Type II supernovae are less energetic by about a factor of 10. It is now believed that the type I supernovae are related to *"metal-poor"* (or Population II) stars, that is, stars with metal abundances much below the solar value.

14.2   THE CRAB NEBULA AND OTHER REMNANTS

The foremost example of a *supernova remnant* is the so-called Crab nebula; one of the most intriguing objects in the sky, it is the remnant of the supernova of 1054. Figure 14-3 shows a picture of the nebula taken in red light. While the Crab nebula has been known for centuries, astronomers only recently realized that it represents one of the few direct clues to the physics of supernovae and supernova remnants.

The crucial observation, made after World War II via radio astronomy, showed the Crab nebula to be one of the strongest *radio sources* in the sky. More detailed observations led to discovery of the *nonthermal* nature of the spectrum, which then was identified with **synchrotron radiation**, that is, the light emission by relativistic electrons in magnetic fields. It soon became clear that a significant portion of the emitted *visible light* is due to the same mechanism, so that the synchrotron mechanism is now believed to furnish the photons observed all through the spectrum, from the radio range to the visible range, and even beyond to *X-rays*. The source of this prolonged "life" of the nebula and its high total luminosity, even at present about 10^5 times the luminosity of the sun, cannot be the initial explosion witnessed in 1054. For a long time this source was a mystery, but we know now that it is the *pulsar*

FIGURE 14-3. **The Crab nebula photographed in red light. Note the complex filament structure of the nebula. The location of the pulsar is shown by the arrow.** *(Lick Observatory.)*

embedded in the nebula. We shall come back to this point in Section 14.7. Finally, among the many other features of the Crab nebula which excite astronomers is the striking **filamentary structure**. These filaments are clearly visible in Fig. 14-3.

We have already mentioned that the nebula as a whole expands; the *expansion speed* corresponds to an angular increase of a fraction of an arcsecond per year. Extrapolating this figure backward in time indicates that, except perhaps for the first few years, the expansion speed must have been fairly constant. On the other hand, the continuing expansion causes a progressive **dilution** of the nebular material; from its reasonably well-known density we must conclude that after 10^4 years or so a supernova remnant of the Crab type has essentially reached the density of the surrounding gas.

If the Crab nebula is the most important remnant of a supernova explosion visible in the sky, it may be not the most typical one. The reason for this suspicion is that none of the other remnants of known supernova explosions, such as **Tycho Brahe's** (1572) and **Kepler's** (1604), show optical features quite similar to those of the Crab nebula. Kepler's supernova has a small nebula which shows no structure and little expansion. Astronomers would certainly have been less certain about identifying this nebula with a supernova remnant if it were not for Kepler's observations, which unquestionably were of a supernova event.

On the other hand, nebulae which are not associated with known supernova events can nevertheless be identified as remnants by their peculiar properties, such as the filamentary structure, the fast expansion of a shell structure, and the synchrotron emission. Of the more prominent radio sources we should mention **Cas A**, which is clearly a supernova remnant and a young one (the explosion supposedly occurred in 1667), but for which we have no information on the actual supernova explosion. It is an essentially circular object some 2 arcmin in diameter, with an associated *jet* or *wisp*. The origin of the jet is not at all clear, but it is a source of strong radio radiation. We shall find later, in quite varied contexts, similar jetlike structures of unknown origin that give off strong radio — probably synchrotron — emissions. Nobody seems to have observed the supernova event proper associated with Cas A.

Another older supernova remnant is the nebula in the constellation Cygnus shown in Figs. 14-4 and 14-5. The various portions of the nebula have separate NGC numbers. Again, this remnant is composed of very delicate filaments and emits strong radio radiation. Its age is estimated at more than 5×10^4 years, and what is left of the original nebula has slowed down its expansion drastically, owing to the resistance of the interstellar gas into which the nebula has moved. In expanding, the nebula has swept up very large amounts of gas and at present comprises some 400 $M_\odot$, only a small fraction of which can be accounted for by the original supernova shell.

Finally, there is the **Gum nebula**, a network of faint filaments that span about 40° on the southern hemisphere. These filaments are related to the supernova remnant found in the constellation Vela, near the center of the area marked by the Gum nebula. The large angular extent indicates a supernova explosion some 10^4 years ago, and the location must be fairly close to the solar system, maybe some 400 or 500 pc.

14.3   THE PHYSICS OF A SUPERNOVA EXPLOSION

What causes the sudden huge release of energy observed during the birth of a supernova? The answer, which has emerged only in the last 10 years or so, is, in brief, the sudden **collapse** of a star's core, accompanied by a complete change in its nuclear structure.

Recall from Section 12.5 that after helium depletion, the core electrons of the less massive stars "freeze" into a degenerate state which prevents further contraction, heating, or the initiation of carbon burning. On the other hand, stars with sufficiently high initial mass are able to utilize further nuclear-energy sources. Ignition of post-helium reactions requres only a high enough core temperature (above some 10^9°K), which in the course of evolution is reached by stars of sufficiently large initial mass. Computed central densities at this stage are of the order of 10^9 to 10^{10} g/cm³.

The nuclear processes in which more massive nuclei such as Ne^{20} and Mg^{24} are formed from, say, C^{12} and O^{16}, are **exothermic**, that is, they *release* a certain amount of energy. However, as still heavier nuclei are built up, the reactions become

FIGURE 14-4. Western edge (NGC 6960) of the great nebular network in Cygnus. Note the delicate filaments. *(Lick Observatory.)*

FIGURE 14-5. **Northeastern edge (NGC 6992) of the great nebular network in Cygnus.** *(Lick Observatory.)*

endothermic; they *absorb* energy. The transition point lies in the **iron group**, consisting of iron, cobalt, and nickel, with, respectively, 26, 27, and 28 protons and corresponding numbers of neutrons — making the total number of nucleons 54 or 56. If we attempt to form nuclei heavier than these, we must add energy. If this energy is not available, the chain of nuclear reactions stops.

Thus, we obtain a picture of the star's core undergoing a sequence of exothermic nuclear-reaction chains that leads to heavier and heavier nuclei until it is producing Fe^{54} or Fe^{56} nuclei, and a few similar ones, from originally abundant C^{12} nuclei; we call this the **nucleosynthesis phase**. The reaction time is now so short that the transformation of carbon into iron takes little more than 100 seconds. Obviously, these processes have long since lost any resemblance to the stable, almost stationary energy production characteristic of the main sequence and giant branch. The sudden release of enormous amounts of energy in the core leads to the formation of explosion waves (**shock waves**) which are transmitted outward and ultimately reach the very surface of the star. The outer layers of the star are not strong enough to resist the shocks and so are simply carried along with them.

It is commonly assumed that this is the initial phase of the formation of the nebulae described in the last section. The material shed in this manner — probably equivalent to a solar mass or so — is composed mostly of nuclei heavier than hydrogen. The totality of all mass ejections during supernova explosions is probably what makes up the presently observed *chemical abundance* of these heavy nuclei in the star system, at least for nuclei not much heavier than the iron group.

The core, now consisting mainly of nuclei of the iron group, is not stable, and at a certain point it simply disintegrates. This happens when the temperature and density become high enough to break down the iron-group nuclei, into α particles and neutrons. This process is endothermic, it needs energy in large amounts, and the only source is the internal reservoir built up in preceding stages. In short, the breakdown of heavy nuclei, the **neutronization**, acts as a tremendous cooling mechanism and causes core pressure to decrease catastrophically. The core collapses under the influence of its own gravity, in a time of little more than one second.

This **gravitational collapse** does not continue indefinitely. In fact, very soon the material will have reached a density corresponding to that of *nuclear matter*, that is, the density within the core of an atom, with no intervening electron shells. The average distance between particles is only of the order of 10^{-13} cm, and the density ranges between 10^{12} and 10^{15} g/cm^3. At this density, one solar mass could be packed into a sphere of about 10 km radius. Once densities near 10^{15} g/cm^3 are reached, the neutrons become degenerate, as do white-dwarf electrons at some 10^6 g/cm^3. In other words, the stellar core contracts until the neutrons that form it become **degenerate** and halt any further contraction. What is left now is an (ultimately) inert **neutron star**, the object of some exciting new observational data to be discussed in Section 14.5.

The analogy between neutron star and white dwarf, or between neutron degeneracy and electron degeneracy, goes even farther, in that any stars with large masses cannot form neutron-degenerate cores. It is believed that the cutoff mass is about 2 $M_\odot$, although the specific number is still in dispute and may well be smaller. At any rate, the problem remains as to what becomes of massive stars if they cannot get rid of enough of their mass to reach the degenerate state. We shall speculate on this in Section 14.8.

14.4 NEUTRON STARS

The Final Stage. What next for our supernova? Its outer shell has been ejected and is expanding through space, while its core has collapsed into a ball of some 10 km in radius, filled with matter at nuclear densities. In the collapsing process the complex nuclei have disintegrated, in endothermic reactions that successively led to α particles and then further to neutrons. We should note that a gas of α particles, that is, helium nuclei, cannot stop the contraction process, since they are not subject to degeneracy, a fact that has to do with the basic physical properties of these particles.

Not all complex nuclei have to split up; this is particularly true for the very outer layers of what remains of the central star. In fact, it is commonly assumed that these layers consist of a **crust** of crystallized nuclear material, like the shell of an egg or, more appropriately, the crust of the earth surrounding the material of the interior. Underneath this crust is a sea of degenerate neutrons, held together by an enormous gravitational force and preventing further contraction through degeneracy. The properties of such a dense sea of degenerate neutrons excite physicists and astronomers alike, because they are so vastly different from anything that can be duplicated in the laboratory. For example, if a disturbance corresponding to a sound wave were introduced into the star, its propagation speed would be a significant fraction of the speed of light. In all fairness, however, it must be noted that even many of the theoretical details of such an outlandish state of matter are at present unclear.

The *final* fate of a neutron star is somewhat anticlimactic. It is, in fact, essentially the same as that of a white dwarf, namely, to move unseen through the universe, giving off ever-diminishing amounts of radiation, which slowly but inexorably cool the neutron material until, some 10^{10} (or 10^{14}?) years later, the last signs of activity have disappeared.

But note what has happened: a star was formed out of a scattered cloud consisting mostly of protons and electrons. It built up more and more complex nuclei, through more and more complex nuclear reactions, until it could no longer sustain the processes it had initiated. And it quietly ended its life as a cloud of simple particles, the neutrons. All the while it has been radiating energy, and since the energy equivalent of a proton-electron pair is not much different from that of a neutron, one might ask where all the energy came from. There was, after all, enough energy to make our star shine for 10^8 or 10^{10} or 10^{12} years, and even explode once in a while, for good measure. The answer is quite simple: it ultimately came from the *mass* of the ubiquitous gas cloud, at first scattered over a volume of a cubic parsec or so, and at the last packed into a ball of 10 km radius, that sustained the star for so long.

Rotation and Magnetic Field of Neutron Stars. Before we go on, we must mention two very important aspects of the behavior of neutron stars, since they are crucial to understanding the identification of these objects with pulsars.

The first point is the predicted fast **rotation** of a neutron star. The argument, briefly, is as follows: there is a certain total *angular momentum* stored in the rotation of a star. Since the star is essentially a closed system, as we have pointed out on several occasions, this angular momentum must be conserved. But because the neutron star has a radius so much smaller than that of the main-sequence star it was originally, it can only conserve momentum by increasing its rotation speed drastically. To see this, note first that the momentum of a rotating body is dependent on mass and surface speed, and second that surface speed is proportional to radius. If the radius is reduced drastically and the mass is unchanged, the speed of rotation must increase to conserve momentum.

The second argument concerns the existence of a very strong **magnetic surface field.** Again, we begin in the main-sequence phase, where the star had some magnetic field of average strength. *If* during the post-main-sequence phases of its development the star was unable to expel almost all of this field—and it is hard to see how such an expulsion would come about—then the field strength at the surface of the neutron star must be very large. The ratio of neutron-star to main-sequence-star field would then be approximately the inverse of the square of the ratio of their radii, or a number of the order 10^9 or 10^{10} to 1.

We now describe how the combination of fast rotation and strong magnetic field allows the neutron star a short but spectacular spasm of activity before it fades into oblivion.

14.5 THE OBSERVATION OF PULSARS

Without the discovery of pulsars our discussion of neutron stars would have been little more than an excursion into the realm of speculation. All this was changed in 1967, when sensitive radio telescopes picked up, from a point source in the sky, radiation which did not arrive in a continuous stream but in **pulses.** The difference between a "conventional" star and such a **pulsar** is comparable to the difference between the headlight of a stationary car and an emergency flasher, both seen from some distance away.

Figure 14-6 shows a typical recording of a pulsar. This one was taken at a frequency of 80 MHz (corresponding to a wavelength of 3.75 m) and emanates from the

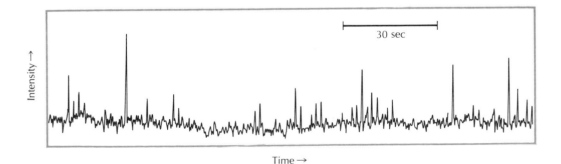

FIGURE 14-6. Recording of the pulsar CP 1133, whose period is about 1 sec. Each peak represents an individual pulse. Note the irregular variations in the pulse heights. *(O. B. Slee et al., Nature, vol. 219, p. 342, 1968.)*

object called CP 1133. The radio photons arrive about every second. The **intensity** of the pulses varies in a rather irregular fashion, so that every once in a while a pulse is missed. Nevertheless, the time lapse between two consecutive pulses, that is, the **period**, can be measured very accurately, simply by monitoring the object over sufficiently long times. In fact, if we follow the pulse pattern over, say, a few years or some 10^8 sec, and if we can fix the onset time of a pulse to within 10^{-3} sec (which is easily done), we can determine the period to an accuracy of 1 part in 10^{11}. Such accuracy in measuring a natural phenomenon is unique and seems as fantastic to the scientist as it does to the layman. As an example, we know the period of the pulsar CP 1133 to be 1.18791113 sec.

The most surprising fact, however, is that pulsar periods constantly maintain this accuracy and thus may represent the most accurate and most constant clock in the universe. Of course, there is nothing really constant in the world, and once the surprising uniformity of pulsar periods became obvious, astronomers pushed the accuracy of their measurements to the point where they finally found a slow increase of the period with time. An example is the Crab pulsar to be discussed in more detail in Section 14.7.

There are now some 50 known pulsars. Their periods range from about 30 msec (0.03 sec) in the case of the Crab pulsar to just below 4 sec. There are good reasons to believe that the lower limit, or a figure in that general neighborhood, is intrinsic (namely, it is the period of a newly collapsed neutron star). The existence of an upper limit to pulsar periods is at present an open question; we may simply not yet have detected any pulsars with longer periods. At any rate, pulsar periods have been compared to the likely ages of supernova remnants (plus neutron stars) in those cases where a relation between the two has been established. The conclusion is that the older the remnant, the longer the pulsar period. The details of such comparisons appear to fit well with the typical life span of some 10^4 years for the supernova nebulae discussed in Section 14.2. Aside from the Crab pulsar, the case in question is the pulsar **PSR 0833** with its supernova remnant in the constellation Vela. It has a period of about 0.1 sec. Its age is estimated to be about 12,000 years, and it is presumably related to the Gum nebula. The large number of pulsars with periods in the neighborhood of 1 sec are accorded typically an age of about 10^6 years, and it is not surprising that no supernova remnant has been found in these cases.

If the pulsar emission is monitored with a much higher time resolution than that used in constructing Fig. 14-6, an even more complex picture emerges. Aside from the **main pulse**, in many instances **subpulses** appear; Fig. 14-7 shows an example. The object is the pulsar in the Crab nebula, **NP 0532**, and the recordings were made in the optical spectral range. The light curve shown is a superposition of several cycles whose period is 0.033 sec. Note the main pulse on the left and the secondary pulse about 15 msec later. Other pulsars show different, but nevertheless characteristic, pulse structures. In fact, subpulse distributions can be used to identify particular pulsars, as a ship's captain can recognize a specific lighthouse from its characteristic light pattern.

Finally, we mention that the spectra of pulsars take in the whole radio range, again with minor differences, and in the case of NP 0532 includes the infrared, visual, and X-ray ranges. NP 0532 is to date the only known pulsar whose *visual*

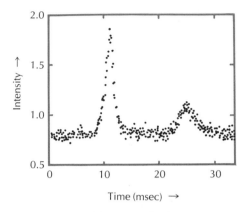

FIGURE 14-7. Light curve of pulsar NP 0532 in the Crab nebula, observed in visible light. The curve is a superposition of several cycles whose period is 0.033 sec. Note the main pulse on the left and the less prominent secondary pulse. *(R. E. Nather et al., Nature, vol. 221, p. 527, 1969.)*

light is pulsed; however, very recently two X-ray sources have been identified as pulsars with periods in the neighborhood of 1 sec; no identification in the visual or radio range could be made. They appear to be members of binary systems and therefore may represent a whole new class of pulsars.

14.6 PULSARS AND NEUTRON STARS

What are pulsars? The answer is straightforward and simple: they are neutron stars. Now that we've stated it so unequivocally, let us review the more important arguments in favor of this identification.

For one thing, pulsars are directly related to supernova explosions, and the number we observe is compatible with the expected number of fairly "young" neutron stars. The crucial point, however, is the period of the pulses, which must be related to a basic periodic phenomenon in the source; for various reasons, the only acceptable one is a **rotational motion**. Finally, a starlike object undergoing periodic phenomena with a period of some 10^{-2} sec must be even smaller than the smallest white dwarf, and the only possiblility is a neutron star.

Of course, the radiation characteristics have yet to be explained, even if we immediately propose that the pulsed nature of the radiation pattern may be due to a **searchlight effect**. If this were the case, the radiation would be transmitted into space from a small area on the pulsar, in a relatively narrow beam; the direction of this narrow beam would be at an angle to our position, and it would sweep by us periodically as the pulsar rotated. This principle is illustrated in Fig. 14-8.

In recent years, quite detailed models have been constructed to represent the main bulk of the observational data. They all involve relativistic electrons moving outward from the star along the lines of the huge magnetic field predicted for neutron

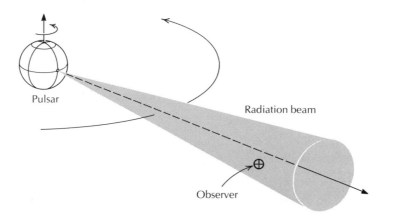

FIGURE 14-8. Searchlight model for pulsars. As the neutron star rotates, the radiation beam sweeps by the observer.

stars. One particularly intriguing aspect of such a suggestion is the fact that the electrons would be accelerated along their paths, since they would be forced by the magnetic field to take part in the rotation of the neutron star. At a certain distance from the star the rotational speed would approach the speed of light, giving rise to not yet quite understood phenomena.

At any rate, it is the combination of strong magnetic field and fast rotation that gives rise to pulsar activity. But, if electrons are emitted, energy is transferred from the neutron star to its surroundings, including the expanding nebula. Angular momentum is lost too, since the electrons leave the neutron star and, in that sense, "interact" with the outside world, making the pulsar an open rather than a closed system. The outcome of this loss of energy and momentum is that the reservoir vested in the roation is slowly depleted. Consequently, the rotation speed should decrease in time. This is indeed the case, as has been shown for the Crab pulsar to be discussed presently. We now think that a neutron star spends about 10^7 years as a pulsar; in other words, the pulsar phenomenon is a short, transitory stage entered by the star right after it has collapsed into the neutron state.

14.7 THE PULSAR IN THE CRAB NEBULA

As persuasive as the arguments may be that link the pulsar phenomenon with the initial stages of a neutron star (say, between the star's death and rigor mortis), one would like to have some direct observational evidence. Obviously the point in question is whether we can find pulsars where we would expect them—at the positions of known supernova explosions. And the justification for carrying our arguments as far as we did in the last section is the recent discovery of a pulsar right in the middle of the Crab nebula, whose origin in a supernova explosion is beyond doubt. On the other hand, though, there seem to be no pulsars associated with the supernova remnants of Brahe and Kepler, or with the radio source Cas A. In fact, there are many well-established supernova remnants not associated with any pulsar.

Whether this means simply that not all neutron stars act as pulsars, even initially, or that the beams of the pulsars are quite narrow and never fall on the earth, or, finally, that no neutron star at all was left after these supernova events, cannot be determined at this time.

The specific properties of the Crab pulsar (its very short period of 0.03 sec and the relatively significant *increase* in period, interpreted as a **spin-down** or slowing of the rotation) fit the idea that it is the youngest of all known pulsars, corresponding to the most recent supernova event linked to a pulsar. More important, we can estimate the total energy lost by the nebula: some 10^5 times the solar luminosity (mostly in the form of synchrotron radiation). The rate of decrease in the rotational speed of a neutron star corresponding to this energy loss matches almost exactly the observed changes in the pulse period of the Crab pulsar. An additional argument that links the Crab pulsar with the maintenance of the nebula is the observation that nebular filaments move in directions aligned with the pulsar.

Another exciting pulsar observation that can be understood in terms of the structure of neutron stars is that of sudden *decreases* in the pulse period. They point to rather drastic changes in the outer layers of the neutron stars and are commonly interpreted as the readjustment of internal stresses in the crystallized crust, that is, as a kind of **starquake.**

By now, the Crab pulsar has been identified through the pulsed nature of its light, at radio frequencies and in the optical and X-ray ranges. The star close to the center of the Crab nebula, indicated by the arrow in Fig. 14-3, has been observed for decades and is the pulsar. Of course, special equipment is needed to show that the light registered on a photographic plate pulses with a frequency of 30 Hz. Once this equipment was constructed, it became immediately obvious that all the optical photons arriving from the nebula are pulsed and are probably of synchrotron origin. This in turn explains the comparatively high intensity of the star image, which is orders of magnitude greater than the expected weak emission of a quiet neutron star.

14.8 THE BLACK HOLES

Let us now — briefly — expand on one remark made in Section 14.3, namely, that the mass limit for neutron degeneracy probably is not very much larger than the limit for electron degeneracy and that consequently an object with a mass above this limit cannot stop gravitational collapse once it has started. The question arises as to what happens then. It is, of course, possible that for some reason the collapse never begins in stellar masses above the limit. However, this is more a way of begging the question than of answering it.

We might, at the opposite extreme, consider the possibility that indeed the collapse never stops, but continues beyond densities of some 10^{15} g/cm³. The behavior of such dense material is not known in detail. It is clear, though, that under such conditions the normal law of gravitation does not hold, and some sort of generalization, perhaps a version of Einstein's **general theory of relativity**, is invoked.

We have already mentioned, in the case of white dwarfs, that a photon escaping from very strong gravitational fields will be *redshifted*. There comes a point at which the field is so strong that our present theories predict a redshift to infinite wavelength; a star of, say, 1 $M_\odot$ would have to collapse into a ball about 1 km in diameter before this happened. We would then say that it had collapsed into its **Schwarzschild radius**, that is, the density level from which photons can no longer escape. No photons would ever be emitted by this contracting "star": it would be a **black hole** in the universe, moving through space as did the original star, but unseen by any observer. The gravitational field would, however, still be present, and would interact with any body that came near.

This opens up the intriguing possibility to actually observe a black hole through this interaction. Particularly promising in this respect is the search among eclipsing binaries and X-ray stars. At any rate, since the number of stars that are still too massive at the end of their lives to degenerate into neutron stars or white dwarfs appears to be very large, we may speculate that black holes may be quite common in the universe and, in fact, may amount to a significant fraction of all the matter.

QUESTIONS FOR DISCUSSION

1. Describe the main features of a supernova explosion as it might be observed at a distance of about 5 pc from us.

2. Would you expect a supernova explosion within 5 pc of the sun to have much of an effect on the solar system? If so, what would happen?

3. What is the observational basis of the estimate that a supernova explosion occurs in a galaxy about every 30 years?

4. Review the similarities and differences among known supernova events and their remnants. Would you call the Crab nebula typical in this sample?

5. Review the stages of stellar evolution that immediately precede a supernova explosion.

6. Discuss the similarities and differences between planetary nebulae and supernovae on one hand, and white dwarfs and neutron stars on the other.

7. Why are astronomers still rather uncertain as to the detailed properties of the material which makes up a neutron star?

8. Review the observational evidence that links pulsars with supernovae.

9. How would you go about proving the existence of black holes?

EXERCISES

1. Where in the universe are most supernova events observed? Why? How is a supernova explosion first noticed?

2. In comparison to the sun, how bright would a supernova be if the explosion took place at a distance of 5 pc from us? Use the data in the text, the fact that the absolute magnitude of the sun is $+4\overset{m}{.}6$, and the fact that the apparent magnitude of the sun as seen from the earth corresponds to about $-27\overset{m}{.}0$.

3. Look through Table H-10. Do you think there is a chance to observe a supernova explosion within 5 pc of the sun? Explain.

4. How long after the initial explosion would the expanding nebula of the hypothetical supernova in Exercise 2 engulf the solar system?

5. What would be the apparent magnitude of a supernova 1,000 pc from us? Compare this brightness with that of Sirius, the brightest star in the sky (Table H-9).

6. What feature of a supernova gave rise to the name "new star"? What do we know observationally about a star which becomes a supernova?

7. How much brighter than the sun is a supernova at its light maximum?

8. Describe the light curve of a type I supernova. How does it differ from that of a type II supernova?

9. What structural detail is easily deduced from the spectrum of a supernova?

10. What is the mechanism by which the Crab nebula emits most of its light? What physical conditions are necessary for this process?

11. How do known supernova remnants differ?

12. The nebula in the constellation Cygnus comprises at present about 400 M . Where did this matter come from?

13. What is a typical lifetime of the nebula born in a supernova explosion?

14. What do astronomers believe causes a supernova explosion?

15. Why do supernova explosions change the chemical abundances in interstellar gas?

16. What effect stops the gravitational collapse of a neutron star?

17. Calculate the density and the mutual distance of the atomic nuclei of a neutron star of 10 km radius and 1 $M_\odot$. Compare these values with those for a white dwarf.

18. Why is the rotation period of a neutron star much shorter than the rotation period of any other stellar object known in the universe?

19. List the main properties of a pulsar.

20. Why does the rotational period of a pulsar slowly increase in time?

21. What is the source of energy of a pulsar? Is there a relation between this energy source and the nuclear sources in other stars?

22. If you could see pulsars with the naked eye, and if in all cases the visible light were pulsed, would you be able to recognize the pulsed nature? Explain.

23. Of what mechanism is the subpulse structure of a pulsar characteristic?

24. What does the "searchlight" hypothesis for the radiation emitted by a pulsar explain?

25. What is the difference between a black hole and what we called a "black dwarf" in Section 13.5?

FURTHER READING

Shklovsky, I. S., *Supernovae*, New York: John Wiley & Sons, Inc., 1968.

Pulsating Stars (reprints of articles from *Nature* magazine), New York: Plenum Publishing Corporation, 1969.

15 other classes of stars

Almost all the classes of stars discussed so far have, at any particular time, well-defined parameters that remain fairly constant, or at least do not vary to any noticeable degree over periods of observation. Only on a few occasions did we mention stellar variability, and even then it was in connection with minor properties. But there are many classes of stellar objects whose *main characteristic* is a variation in some of the observable parameters. In most such instances, we do not yet understand the causes, and we cannot say whether the specific objects are abnormal in some sense or, if so, for what reason. There is little point in listing them in great detail in a survey such as this, but one class, the *pulsating stars*, does merit detailed discussion for several reasons. For one, we think we understand the mechanism behind their pulsations, and we are pretty sure of their place in the evolutionary scheme. In addition, they provide us with one of the most important methods of measuring distance, and it is largely for this reason that we single them out.

Aside from the variable stars, there are classes of stars with well-defined but peculiar properties which, at present, cannot be integrated into our overall scheme. In some cases, to be sure, this classification will be achieved fairly soon, when we understand the implications of their basic physical features. But it is fair to expect that others will always remain special, "pathological" cases. These peculiar stars comprise quite a mixed lot, and we shall discuss only the most remarkable ones.

Finally, we shall review observations in the wavelength regions of the far infrared, where the technological means for detailed studies were acquired only recently, and of X-rays, which, because they do not penetrate the earth's atmosphere, force us to rely on satellites for systematic observation. New types of sources—some stellar, some not—have been found in these invisible spectral ranges, but our present knowledge is not nearly complete enough to allow detailed classification.

15.1 LIGHT CURVES AND SPECTRA OF PERIODIC VARIABLES

Variable Stars.   If the total light reaching the earth's surface from a **variable star** is plotted as a *light curve*, the result might show quite a number of irregular variations. But more important, we would find light curves in which the intensity varied in time with a definite **period**. It is on variable stars with such periodic light curves that we focus our attention first. The difference between maximum and minimum brightness (the relative **amplitude** of the variation) may also vary periodically, but we shall not, for the moment, concern ourselves with it. Figure 15-1 shows one cycle of a typical light curve (brightness is given in terms of the minimum brightness); the star in ques-

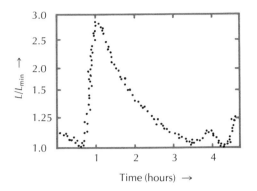

FIGURE 15-1. **Light curve for the periodic variable RR Lyrae. Brightness is plotted in units of the minimum brightness during one cycle, which spans about 4 hours.** *(P. Ledoux and T. Walraven "Variable Stars," in Handbuch der Physik, edited by S. Flügge, Berlin: Springer-Verlag, vol. 51, 1958.)*

tion is **RR Lyrae**. Although the curve in Fig. 15-1 is rather smooth, some do contain small bumps, valleys, and other irregularities which are of interest primarily to the specialist. Literally thousands of **periodic variables** have been classified. Periods range, with a few exceptions, from just over 1 hour to several years, and relative light amplitudes vary from barely noticeable (Polaris is such a case!) to impressive ratios of 100 or more.

There are three important classes of periodic variables. The first class is comprised of the so-called **long-period variables**, with periods above some 100 days and, in general, large brightness variations. The best-known example is a star called Mira in the constellation Cetus in the southern hemisphere, visible in North America near the southern horizon in winter. Normally, its brightness is below the sensitivity threshold of the human eye, but during light maximum, which occurs somewhat irregularly about every year, it becomes easily visible. Long-period variables are the least regular periodic variables, and they are all giants, typically of spectral class M.

The second class, the **cepheids**, named after the star δ Cephei, consists of variables with very regular light changes. Their periods range from about 1 day to 50 days, with much smaller relative amplitudes than the long-period variables. Their spectra are typically of the F, G, or K variety. One part of this class belongs to the metal-rich stars of Population I; these are the so-called **classical cepheids** which will occupy us more in the next section. Others are found in globular clusters with their metal-poor Population II stars. All cepheids are characterized by large intrinsic luminosity: they are all supergiants.

Finally, there are the short-period variables, with periods of up to 1 day, which are called **RR Lyrae stars** after their prototype. They, too, are present in globular clusters and belong to the metal-poor Population II. They are intrinsically much less luminous than other periodic variables; their spectra mark them as members of the A and F spectral classes.

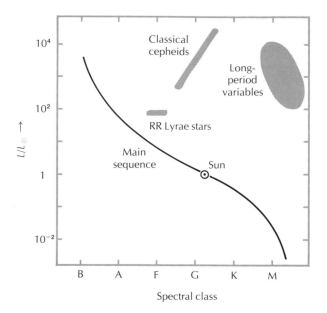

FIGURE 15-2. **Positions of long-period variables, classical cepheids, and RR Lyrae stars in the H-R diagram. The approximate location of the main sequence and the position of the sun are added for comparison.** *(J. S. Cox, "Pulsational Instability," in International Astronomical Union Symposium, no. 28, edited by R. N. Thomas, New York: Academic Press, Inc., 1967.)*

The location of these groups in an H-R diagram is shown in Fig. 15-2. Cepheids and RR Lyrae stars occupy quite narrow strips above the main sequence. In particular, the position of the RR Lyrae stars is highly localized. This is obviously no coincidence, and explanations must be sought in terms of stellar evolution and stability.

The Pulsation Mechanism.　Careful study of Doppler shifts in the spectra of these variable stars has shown that their **radial velocities** change in exactly the same fashion as their light intensities. In fact, the radial-velocity curves of these stars are basically mirror images of their light curves, as is shown schematically in Fig. 15-3, based on measurements for η Aquilae. In reality, of course, many of these objects exhibit more complex variations, in which, say, the light and radial-velocity curves may be shifted slightly with respect to one another.

At any rate, we can conclude that the material responsible for the absorption lines in the spectrum, that is, the whole outer atmosphere of the variable star, performs a periodic motion. The cycle begins, say, with some increasing velocity toward us, that is, away from the star's center. This velocity is maximal roughly at the time of maximum light. Then the atmosphere slows and becomes stationary for a very short time. It then reverses to move away from us and toward the center, reaching a maximum inward velocity at about the time of minimum light. Finally, it slows and stops again, and then starts a new cycle. Note that we have identified the stationary phases

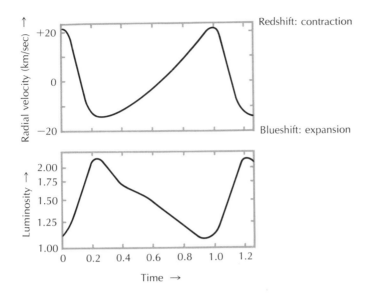

FIGURE 15-3. Radial velocity and brightness variation of a typical cepheid; time is given in periods. During the contraction phase, redshifts are observed in the spectrum; during the expansion phase, blueshifts. Maximum luminosity occurs near maximum expansion. The minimum and maximum radii are reached when the Doppler shifts are zero.

with the points of zero radial velocity in Fig. 15-3, by subtracting out the motion of the star with respect to the sun-earth system.

The only consistent explanation of this behavior is that these are pulsating stars whose atmospheres undergo periodic **radial oscillations**. The maximum radius is reached when the motion changes from outward to inward, at which point there is a slight "pause"; the minimum radius is achieved at the opposite point. In a very real sense the atmosphere expands and contracts periodically. The star is brightest at about the time of maximum expansion speed (maximum blueshift), and dimmest at maximum contraction speed (maximum redshift).

Two major questions are raised by these hypotheses. For one, how does a stellar atmosphere get into a state of sustained periodic oscillations? Progress has been made toward a credible answer to this question, although many of the details are still to be explained. In principle, the explanation involves all the quantities that interact to build a stable star such as the sun, with its radial temperature and density profiles, and its energy flow from the production region in the core to the loss region at the surface. Suppose such a star had to expand a bit to maintain stability. If in expanding, it overshot its goal – expanded too far – the internal forces would tend to contract it again, to reinstate stability. But, in contracting it might overshoot its goal again, so that the cycle would start anew. Normally, such cycling would not last very long, and the star would soon settle into a stable configuration; the oscillations would be **damped out**. But there may be some specific combination of density, temperature, mass, energy transport, etc., that results in continuous oscillation, and does not allow the star to settle into stability. Under these conditions the star would continue to pulsate.

Theoretical work has verified that certain combinations of parameters will make stellar atmospheres **pulsationally unstable** and will support the contraction-expansion cycle more or less indefinitely. The range of parameters that allows for this instability is quite limited, which may be why all the known pulsating stars are located in rather narrow strips of the luminosity-surface-temperature diagram. Indeed, a plausible theory of pulsation must ensure that the vast majority of stars is unable to sustain pulsations.

The second question which arises is concerned with whether these very special conditions can occur only in very special types of stars, say with particular initial chemical compositons and total masses, or whether they represent a short phase in the development of most stars. Present evidence strongly suggests the latter, at least for a rather wide variety of objects. Thus, we anticipate that most stars more massive than the sun will cross—perhaps several times—the **cepheid instability strip** in Fig. 15-2 and for a short time become pulsating variables. Then, after thousands or millions of years of pulsation, the internal structure of the stars will have changed to the point where they cannot sustain the pulsations any longer; they then will have ended the cepheid phase of their lives.

15.2   THE PERIOD-LUMINOSITY RELATION OF PULSATING STARS AND THE DISTANCE MEASUREMENTS

We now come back to the determination of the distances (or absolute magnitudes) used in constructing Fig. 15-2. At this point we must recall once again that all the stars we see with the naked eye, and many more, belong to a huge star system which we call our *galaxy*, and that other similar systems or galaxies exist, separated by vast stretches of space. The two *Magellanic systems* are examples, as is the even more distant *Andromeda system*. The discussion to follow is mostly concerned with the distances to these star systems.

The Period-Luminosity Relation.   Even though we do not know the actual luminosities of a number of pulsating stars in a group, but only their apparent magnitudes, we can study the relation between luminosity and period. For we do know their relative luminosities, which are proportional to the actual luminosities; the "constant of proportionality" is unknown but it is immaterial, since it applies to all the luminosity values. The first such studies were made for cepheids in the two nearby galaxies known as the Magellanic systems. Similar work was conducted for globular clusters which belong to our own galaxy and whose stars all are essentially the same distance from us. The result is a clear one-to-one relationship between period length and brightness, the famous **period-luminosity relation** for cepheids. Figure 15-4 is a graph of brightness, in arbitrary units, versus period for a sample of cepheids in the Small Magellanic system.

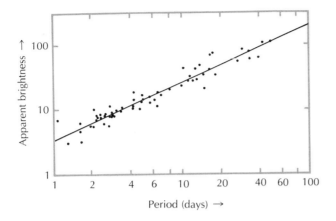

**FIGURE 15-4. Observed period-luminosity relation for ce-
pheids in the Small Magellanic Cloud. Apparent brightness is
plotted in arbitrary units versus period.** *(R. P. Kraft, in Basic
Astronomical Data, edited by K. A. Strand, Chicago: The University of Chicago Press, 1963.)*

The Distance Problem.   In principle, it is relatively east to determine the distance
of cepheids in globular clusters or in the Magellanic systems, because we can always find normal stars in the same groupings, say, in the main-sequence phase,
whose luminosity is predictable on the basis of a vast amount of evidence. Observationally, however, this task is rendered difficult by the extreme faintness of the stars.
But the problem of determining distance is much more difficult for cepheids which
do not belong to any grouping and do not happen to be members of binary systems.
What one has available in this case are only very indirect indications which carry
a significant possibility of error, in particular, that due to interstellar absorption.

Instead of taking this chance, in the past astronomers calculated distances for
lone cepheids by assuming that their physical behavior is the same as the behavior
of cepheids in globular clusters, and that consequently the absolute magnitudes of
any two cepheids are equal if they have the same period. This led to one of the few
spectacular errors in astronomy, an error that was not corrected until 1952. The
cause of the "disaster" is the difference in chemical composition between the cepheids in globular clusters (Population II) and the "classical" cepheids (Population
I), which gives rise to a difference in the physical parameters that govern pulsational
instability. In short, these two types of variables have different absolute magnitudes
for the same pulsation period, but astronomers had been calculating absolute magnitudes and distances as if the two types of cepheids were alike.

Since individual cepheids are known in several nearby galaxies, their (errone-
ous) absolute-to-apparent-magnitude ratios had been used to establish the distances
to all these galaxies, including the Andromeda system. But once the mistake was
discovered, we had to realize that all objects outside our own galaxy were twice as
far away as had been thought before.

The mistake came to light in the following manner: it was known from studies
in our own galaxy that RR Lyrae stars are about four times fainter than globular-

cluster cepheids with a period of 7 days or so. Of course, cepheids of longer periods are still more luminous—as we can see in Fig. 15-4—and many of these, but no RR Lyrae stars, were found on photographs of the Andromeda system taken with the 100-inch telescope on Mount Wilson. The 200-inch telescope on Mount Palomar, which became operational around 1950, should have detected the fainter RR Lyrae stars in that system. It did not, and astronomers wanted to know why not.

The Revised Relation. At this point one could have argued that the Andromeda system's RR Lyrae stars in reality were fainter than any we know, or else that the known cepheids in the Andromeda system were brighter than the globular-cluster cepheids we knew. As was made clear before, the absolute magnitudes of lone cepheids relatively near to us had never been well established because of the difficulty of obtaining reasonably accurate data on their distances. By now it is beyond doubt that the second argument is the correct one, and that the cluster-type cepheids are about four times fainter than the individual variety of Population I, for stars with the same period. Our present understanding of the two sets of period-luminosity relations is summarized schematically in Fig. 15-5. The observed data from Fig. 15-4 would fall into the shaded area identified as belonging to Population I cepheids.

The period-luminosity relation for cepheids is the basis of one of the most important techniques used in estimating distances to extremely far objects. All one has to do is measure the period of the light variation and the apparent magnitude of the pulsating star. The period-luminosity relation then immediately yields the distance. The method is particularly useful because the cepheids are among the brightest stars known (see Fig. 15-2), and thus can be monitored at very great distances—in fact, as far as we can resolve single stars at all. In addition, the method requires no spectral information whatsoever.

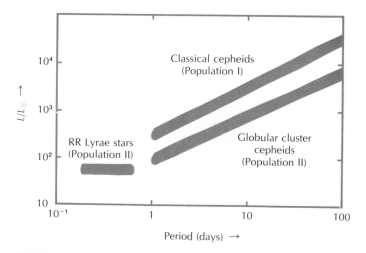

FIGURE 15-5. Schematic period-luminosity relations of RR Lyrae stars and cepheids of Population I and Population II. Luminosity is in solar units.

15.3 NOVAE AND OTHER VARIABLE STARS

Novae. The regular pulsations of cepheids comprise one possible manifestation of stellar variability, but it may take other forms. We shall discuss several of these, beginning with the **novae** which once in a while, suddenly, and in rather drastic fashion, change their stellar characteristics.

When a nova flares up, it suddenly increases its light output by a factor of 10^3 to 10^4, and then returns more or less rapidly to the approximate brightness level of the **prenova stage**, that is, of the stage before the outburst. Thus, it is not a "new" star, but a star that for one reason or another undergoes a sudden change in its energy-conversion mechanism. Most of the novae observed in our own galaxy are found near its plane of symmetry; others have been found in nearby galaxies such as the Andromeda system and the Magellanic systems.

Figure 15-6 shows the light curve of the nova DQ Herculis during the first 200 days after the outburst in 1934, with the short-term (daily) fluctuations averaged out; "zero time" in the figure is very soon after the increase. The luminosity is calibrated in multiples of the star's brightness before the event. Note that the behavior during the period immediately following the outburst is very complex; this complexity will turn up again in the spectral observations to be mentioned presently. The "deep minimum" is not a common feature of all novae. Instead, there may be semiregular variations which look suspiciously like pulsations or, at least, some kind of more or less regular oscillation. An example, the light curve of V603 Aquilae is shown in Fig. 15-7, where the luminosity is calibrated as in Fig. 15-6. The irregularities that show up right after the outburst are typically followed by a slow decline which, in the case of DQ Herculis, for instance, continues to this day.

From these examples and many more, we know that the durations of typical outbursts, as well as the light curves themselves, vary a great deal; so do the periods

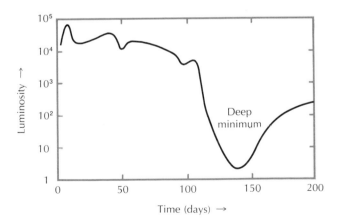

FIGURE 15-6. Light curve of DQ Herculis during the first 200 days after the nova outburst in 1934. Note the slow decrease in luminosity in the first 100 days, and the deep minimum after about 130 days, followed by a slow increase. *(C. Payne-Gaposchkin, The Galactic Novae, Amsterdam: North-Holland Publishing Company, 1957.)*

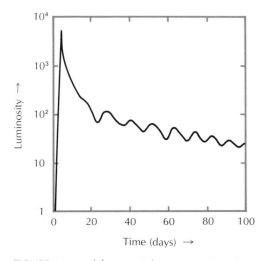

FIGURE 15-7. **Light curve of V603 Aquilae in the first 100 days after the outburst. After an initial fast decrease, fairly regular variations reminiscent of oscillations set in.** *(C. Payne-Gaposchkin, "The Novae," in Handbuch der Physik, edited by S. Flügge, Berlin: Springer-Verlag, vol. 51, 1958.)*

of initial decay from the maximum and the subsequent slower decays toward "quiescent" conditions. In many cases a second outburst, similar to the first, has been observed. Since the behavior patterns of novae are so vastly different, it would be of little use to review the classification schemes proposed by astronomers. Instead we conclude that nova outbursts are probably due to a variety of causes or, at least, represent the responses of rather different stars to some physical mechanism.

Mass Ejection.   The prenova stage, that is, the conditions before the outburst, typically shows the spectrum of a blue star—a continuum corresponding roughly to class B or A—whose absolute magnitude is smaller than that of a main-sequence star (**subdwarf**). Right after the outburst, the spectrum of a nova shows emission lines originating in a very hot **shell**, or **envelope**, surrounding the main body of the star. Such a nova shell typically has an expansion velocity of several hundred kilometers per second. The shell is actually ejected as a consequence of the outburst; this was observed directly in some cases in which **nebulae** appeared surrounding the stars proper. One is shown in the photograph reproduced in Fig. 15-8. It is GK Persei, photographed in 1949, 48 years after the original outburst.

Many investigators have tried to determine the physical conditions prevailing— or possibly prevailing—in the radiating layers of a nova at and after the outburst, but little is known as to the cause. It is clear from observation that the star sheds a significant portion of its outer layers, at least most of its photosphere, in an outburst. The expansion speed is much higher than that of a planetary nebula, and the star that remains after shedding is not very similar to the central star of a planetary nebula. We therefore cannot assume that novae are simply stars moving toward the white-dwarf stage. Another piece of evidence counter to this view is the existence of

FIGURE 15-8. **Expanding nebula about Nova Persei (1901). Photographed with the 200-inch telescope in 1949.** *(Hale Observatories.)*

recurrent novae, that is, stars that have undergone more than one outburst in the 100 years or so during which we have observed them.

Many, and possibly all, novae are members of close binary systems, and one might argue that the nova phenomenon is due to this specific property. We have already seen in Section 10.4 that there occurs a transfer of mass among close binary stars. In a certain stage of stellar evolution, one of the components may become unstable and erupt—become a nova—because it has accumulated too much of the hydrogen-rich material given off by its close neighbor.

An Intermediate Class of Variables. There is a small class of variable stars named after their prototypes, U Geminorum and Z Camelopardalis, which are afflicted with quite frequent novalike flare-ups. Figure 15-9 shows the light curve of SS Cygni which, on the average, has an outburst every 50 days, but which is not really periodic. Note that the total light intensity changes by a factor of from 10 to 100. As in the case of novae, the decay-phase spectra show outward motions, although there is no clear evidence of mass ejection; even more significantly, the character of a close binary system has been established for most of the stars in this class.

Other Variables. If there are stars that frequently increase their light output by a large factor, there are also some which decrease it in similar fashion. One example

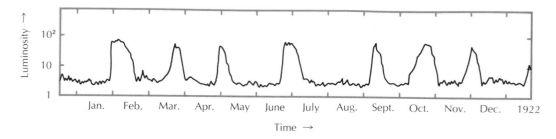

FIGURE 15-9. **Light curve of SS Cygni. The star undergoes a nova-like outburst every 50 days, on the average. Its luminosity increases by a factor of about 50 for a week or two.** *(P. Ledoux and T. Walraven, "Variable Stars," in Handbuch der Physik, edited by S. Flügge, Berlin: Springer-Verlag, vol. 51, 1958.)*

is R Coronae Borealis, whose light curve is shown in Fig. 15-10. Apparently, the high luminosity is the norm here, and one can argue that the decreases have to do with absorption phenomena around the star. But if this is indeed the case, then the gas motions about the star must be quite complicated.

Another group of stars with completely irregular light changes are the T Tauri stars discussed in Section 12.1. We stated there that they are in the last phases of gravitational contraction on their way to the zero-age main sequence, a conclusion based on their positions above the main sequence in the H-R diagram and their close spatial relation to interstellar gas clouds active in star formation.

We pointed out in Secion 9.6 that many cool stars—of types K and M—show emission lines that originate high up in their atmospheres. In other words, they show evidence of extended *chromospheres* with an accompanying increase in temperature at the very outer layers. In the case of the sun, this behavior was related to the existence of a convection zone and the conversion of mechanical energy into heat in the layers above the photosphere proper. It is then not farfetched to expect that if a star shows a highly extended version of the solar chromosphere, it will also produce something like solar flares, on a grand scale. Only very strong *stellar flares* can be seen from afar in the light output of such a **flare star**, but in some cases this is possible. UV Ceti, a star of spectral type Me, shows sudden extremely sharp outbursts of radiation, the maximum being reached in minutes or even seconds, with normal brightness returning after only tens of minutes, that is, in times typical of solar flares. The similarity here is made more suggestive by spectral observations which show clearly that the outer atmosphere of the star is most affected by the outbursts, and by the fact that radio emissions which are typical of the solar phenomenon have been picked up from UV Ceti.

15.4 MAGNETIC STARS

A property of the solar atmosphere which we have claimed is of great importance to the behavior of the sun, and especially to the development of solar activity, is its magnetic field. This field is generally weak, but is quite strong in centers of activity.

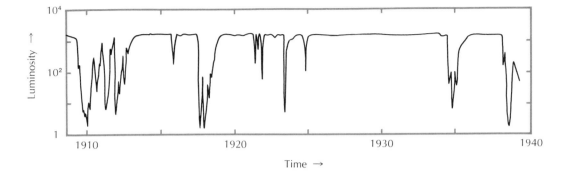

FIGURE 15-10. Light curve of R Coronae Borealis between 1910 and 1940. The star undergoes irregular and sudden decreases in luminosity, which have reached as much as a factor of 1,000. *(P. Ledoux and T. Walraven, "Variable Stars," in Handbuch der Physik, edited by S. Flügge, Berlin: Springer-Verlag, vol. 51, 1958.)*

Recall that neither the general field nor the strong spot fields could be found from an analysis of the spectrum of the whole sun: the general field is too weak, and the spot fields too localized. Thus, to be observable, a stellar magnetic field must be very strong and, in addition, must prevail over a much larger fraction of the stellar surface than is the case on the sun; it must represent something "peculiar" about the star.

Magnetic fields with typical overall strengths of several thousand gauss have been observed in dozens of objects, and values of more than 30,000 gauss have been reported. Also typical is a variability, to the extent that the field may even change its polarity. Variations with the same period as the variation in luminosity or some other spectral feature have been observed. It can be taken as established that all **magnetic stars** are variable.

Magnetic stars are scattered through the spectral classes, but the vast majority correspond to A stars. In practically all cases, the spectra show characteristic peculiarities and define a class of **peculiar A stars** (**Ap**). In particular, the absorption lines of certain elements are vastly enhanced, in comparison with standard spectra. Typically these elements include silicon, chromium, manganese, and some rare earths. If the line intensity is simply interpreted as due to an abnormally high abundance of the element, one finds, for instance in the case of the star α^2 Canum Venaticorum, that *europium* is 2,000 times as abundant there as in a standard star. If this is indeed so, one might explain these abundance anomalies by nuclear reactions taking place *close to the surface*. However, we have at this time no real idea of how a star could support this.

15.5 WOLF-RAYET STARS

In concluding this survey of star classes which in some way or another appear abnormal or, at least, difficult to classify in the general evolutionary framework, we should mention the **Wolf-Rayet stars**. They were first noted about 100 years ago by the astronomers whose names they bear, and they are characterized by broad, strong *emission* lines in the yellow and green portions of the visual spectrum. Aside from hydrogen and helium transitions, these lines belong typically to several-times-ionized carbon, nitrogen, and oxygen. Usually, either the carbon and oxygen lines are predominant, or else the nitrogen lines are strongest; in the former case we give the stars the class name **WC**, in the latter case **WN**.

We pointed out in Section 13.2 that many central stars of planetary nebulae have such spectral characteristics, and thus a good number of the central stars of planetary nebulae are classified as WC or WN stars. This group, then, consists of old objects. On the other hand, many Wolf-Rayet stars are known (because of their very characteristic spectra) to belong to star groups that include young O and B stars. They must have been formed somewhere near their present locations and, consequently, are also comparably young (10^8 years or less). There appears to be a clear distinction between these two extremes of age, corroborated by mass determinations which place typical masses for young Wolf-Rayet stars in the neighborhood of 10 $M_\odot$, and those of central stars of planetary nebulae below 1 $M_\odot$.

As to the reasons for the unusual spectral behavior of Wolf-Rayet stars, we can only point once again to the fact that some of the (presumably) young objects are members of close binaries and may have undergone atypical evolution, perhaps because of a significant mass exchange between the two components.

15.6 X-RAY AND INFRARED OBJECTS

In the last few years, observation of celestial objects in wavelength regions outside the main "windows" of the earth's atmosphere, namely, the visible range between about 3500 Å and 7000 Å, and the radio range from about 1 mm up, has become technically feasible and has led to exciting new data whose interpretation is by no means clear at present.

The first region of interest is in the **X-ray** portion of the spectrum (Section C.1), at wavelengths of the order of 1 Å up to some 100 Å. As we know from our discussion of the earth's atmosphere, observations in this spectral range must be made from satellites or rockets which rise above the ionosphere. Another region of interest is the **far infrared**, between the near infrared and the short-wavelength end of the radio window, that is, between 1 micron and 1 mm. Here, there are sporadic small windows where observations can be made from the ground (at 2 microns, for instance). More important, at heights in the terrestrial atmosphere that can be reached by high-flying aircraft or balloons, the water vapor responsible for most atmospheric absorption at these wavelengths is depleted, so that the atmosphere is in fact transparent. Much of our discussion of infrared objects is based on observations made at, say, 10 to 50 microns, in this manner.

X-ray Objects. Aside from a more or less uniform **background** of X-ray photons, a number of discrete sources have been found. Among them is a group of stars, the best known of which is the object Sco X-1 in the constellation Scorpius, identified as a star on photographic survey plates that go back to the 1880s. Another example,

Cyg X-2, is located in the constellation Cygnus. Its optical spectrum reveals several peculiarities, such as the parallel presence of emission and absorption lines, mostly of ionized elements, and in this respect resembles the spectra of novae. The surprisingly high X-ray intensity in such stars is thought to originate in circumstellar clouds which are heated to temperatures of the order of $10^{7\circ}$K and in which photons are emitted during chance encounters between electrons and ions. It is at present impossible to say with any degree of certainty what specifically makes a star an X-ray object. One of the more exciting prospects is the possibility that some of the X-ray stars are black holes interacting with surrounding material.

One specific property of X-ray stars is their *variable output*, with quite significant fluctuations taking place in times as short as minutes. Very recent observations suggest rather complicated periodicities in some cases. At one time the source Cen X-4 in the constellation Centaurus was brighter than Sco X-1, but a few months later it could not even be seen. Optical identifications of X-ray stars are, at best, rather uncertain, and the origin of the fluctuations is simply unknown.

Also "visible" in the X-ray region of the spectrum is the Crab nebula (Section 14.2). Both the nebula and the pulsar emit X-ray photons, those of the latter being pulsed with the same frequency as its optical and radio sources. We must assume that the mechanism by which this pulsar gives off light in the typical pulsed fashion operates across the spectrum, from the radio range all the way to the high-energy X-ray range. (Note, however, the X-ray observation of pulsars for which neither optical nor radio emissions were found.) The emission of the nebula proper, on the other hand, is an extension of the synchrotron emission postulated for it in a large portion of the visible and radio spectra.

Other X-ray sources identified with reasonable certainty are the supernova remnants Cas A and the remnant of Tycho Brahe's supernova. The Large Magellanic system and several other galaxies also emit X-rays.

Infrared Objects. Recent work in the far-infrared region of the spectrum has turned up a colorful variety of source types, intensities, and spectra. For example, it is possible to determine, via infrared analysis, the average surface temperatures of the *planets*, which range from about $-40°C$ in the case of Mars, to below $-175°C$ on Saturn. This method was used to verify the values obtained at radio frequencies and quoted in Sections 5.3 and 5.4. Interesting also is the observation that localized areas of Jupiter appear to radiate photons in the far-infrared spectrum, well in excess of the amount expected on the basis of the average surface temperature.

Galactic infrared sources have been identified with both stars and nonstellar objects. In many instances the emission mechanism is reasonably well known: the objects are surrounded by dense clouds of very cold material, circumstellar shells whose grains and dust particles absorb photons of higher energy and reradiate the energy as very large numbers of low-energy infrared photons. This channels a major portion of the total thermonuclear energy production into the infrared spectrum. The reason for the existence of these circumstellar shells is, however, still quite open to discussion. It appears that both very young objects and older ones are involved, the latter possibly as a consequence of violent ejections of stellar material. Particularly relevant in this respect is the observation that several novae emit large amounts of energy in the infrared region some time after their flare-ups. Right now the search is on for extremely cool stars whose brightness in the visible range is too low to detect with relatively small telescopes and short observation times.

At least some of the more spectacular interstellar infrared sources — for instance, Ori IR A and Ori IR B inside the gas nebula NGC 1976, the great Orion nebula — may be related to star formation in that the collapse of a protostar or even a group of protostars may take place behind a very thick curtain of cold interstellar material.

Finally, a variety of *galaxies* (among them our own) emit infrared radiation. The origin of these infrared sources, and their emission mechanisms, must be tied in with the structure of active centers in galaxies. An explanation of this wider problem will have to precede an understanding of the details of infrared observations.

QUESTIONS FOR DISCUSSION

1. In what respect is the sun a variable star? If you observed the sun from the distance of α Centauri, would you notice any variability?

2. What are the arguments for interpreting cepheids as pulsating stars?

3. Only a very small percentage of stars pulsate. Why?

4. Why are cepheids among the most important indicators of distance?

5. What is current thought as to the reason for nova outbursts?

6. Close binary stars appear to be abnormal in many respects. Describe some star classes whose properties are probably due to the close binary character of the members.

7. Why were systematic observations in the far-infrared region of the spectrum only obtained in the last few years?

8. Does the far-infrared emission of stars typically come from their photospheres? Explain.

EXERCISES

1. What kind of data are most easily obtained for variable stars? Explain.

2. Describe the characteristics of the main classes of periodic variables.

3. Do you need very accurate measurements of the amplitude of a periodic variable in order to determine the period? Explain.

4. What is the color impression of a long-period variable? Can you tell from Fig. 15-2?

5. The star δ Cephei is not listed in Table H-11. Find the minimum value of its distance from the data given in the text.

6. Improve your estimate in Exercise 5 by using the additional information that the period of δ Cephei is about 5 days.

7. What are the differences among classical cepheids, globular-cluster cepheids, and RR Lyrae stars?

8. Why are so many cepheids known, some even at great distances?

9. Which periodic variables belong to the metal-rich Population I? Which to the metal-poor Population II?

10. In what phase of the contraction-expansion cycle of a pulsating star is its brightness greatest? Least? When is its radial velocity greatest?

11. Change the radial-velocity scale in Fig. 15-3, assuming that the cepheid is moving away from us with a speed of 20 km/sec.

12. What is the reason for the fact that not all cepheids with a given period have the same luminosity?

13. Describe the period-luminosity relations of the various types of pulsating stars discussed in the text.

14. The Andromeda system is a star system similar to our own galaxy. Why were RR Lyrae stars not found in the Andromeda system a long time ago?

15. What led to the name "new stars" for novae?

16. A certain nova had an apparent magnitude of 13^m0 in the prenova stage. Would you have a chance to see it with the naked eye at maximum? Explain.

17. What does the spectrum of a nova reveal shortly after maximum?

18. A nova shell expands at a rate of 100 km/sec. It has also been determined that its angular size increases by 1 arcsec per year. How distant is the nova?

19. Why are T Tauri stars identified with very young stars?

20. What types of observations make astronomers think that flare stars and solar activity are related?

21. List some properties of peculiar A stars.

22. Why is it believed that Wolf-Rayet spectra describe at least two distinct types of stars?

23. Why should one not attempt to make far-infrared observations of stars in Maine or Florida?

24. List the classes of X-ray objects.

25. What type of object is known under the name Sco X-1? What kind of mechanism do astronomers currently believe is responsible for its X-ray emission?

26. The Crab nebula is a highly structured X-ray source. Describe the main components of its radiation.

27. List the classes of far-infrared objects.

EXPERIMENTS

1. Try to locate the star Mira (o Ceti) with the aid of the star charts (Fig. G-8). If you are lucky, you may see it with the naked eye. Why is it most probable that you won't see it?

2. Make soap bubbles by dipping a straw in soapy water, or use a commercial kit from a toy store. Try to induce the bubbles to oscillate by moving the straw back and forth while blowing bubbles. You will find that a bubble usually will stop oscillating before it blows up; that is, the oscillation is heavily *damped*. What causes this damping? The oscillations are not predominantly radial pulsations, as is the case with cepheid stars. Try to describe the motion of the surface of the bubble with respect to its center. Do you find different types of motions (oscillation *modes*)? Do they depend on the size of the bubble, or on how you got it to oscillate in the first place? What would this dependence correspond to in the case of a star?

3. An example of a system able to oscillate, if not pulsate, is a dish of gelatin. Make a few in pots of different sizes and shapes, and get them to oscillate by pushing them. Do you observe any relation between size and period?

FURTHER READING

Stellar Atmospheres, edited by J. L. Greenstein, Chicago: The University of Chicago Press, 1960.

Stellar Structure, edited by L. H. Aller and D. B. McLaughlin, Chicago: The University of Chicago Press, 1965.

Payne-Gaposchkin, C., *The Galactic Novae,* New York: Dover Publications, Inc., 1964.

Frontiers of Astronomy: Readings from Scientific American, edited by O. Gingerich, San Francisco: W. H. Freeman and Company, 1970.

THE LOCAL CLUSTER OF GALAXIES

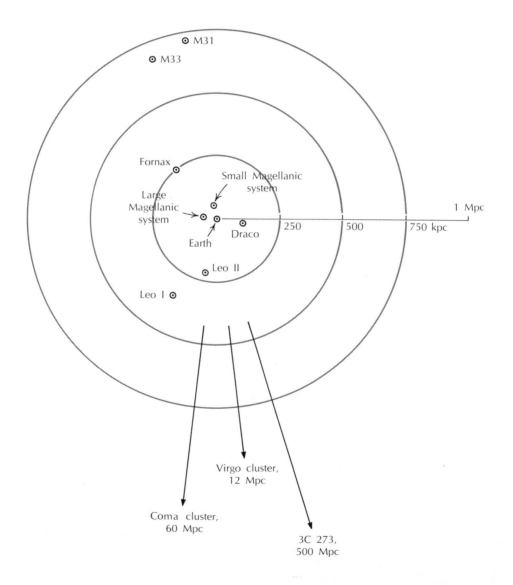

III the star systems

We have by now a fairly complete idea of the many, very diverse types of stars around us, the features that characterize each type, and at least some of the reasons for their specific properties. We also have an idea of how stars are born, live, and die.

We have seen that there are groupings of stars, from simple systems of three, four, or five individuals to great clusters. We distinguished these clusters according to their chemical compositions, and introduced the notion of metal-rich Population I stars and metal-poor Population II stars. Prototypes of the former are the open clusters and the classical cepheids; of the latter, the globular clusters, and the cluster-type cepheids and RR Lyrae stars. Finally, we saw that stars and star groupings of all these types are arranged in a sort of supercluster we call our galaxy; beyond this supercluster there are others, and beyond them still others.

In the remainder of the text, we examine the structure of these galaxies, taking our system as the obvious starting point, and attempt to understand their distribution in space. Do they stretch to infinity, or to some sort of an "edge" of the universe? How did they evolve? In brief, we shall review what astronomers think are the state and the history of the universe as a whole.

16 interstellar material

Up to this point, we have dealt largely with highly condensed material in the universe, with planets and stars. On occasion we saw that the universe contains material in much less condensed form, for instance, the gases streaming from the sun, or the material from which stars presumably are formed. To understand the arrangement of stars in space — the structure of our galaxy and others — one obviously must know something about the material which eventually becomes a star. Thus, we ought to take a detailed look at the *interstellar material* present in the vast expanses between stars. In the last few years, especially with the advent of radio astronomy, it has become clear that this interstellar material holds the answers to many quite fundamental questions concerning the beginnings of our universe. The great spaces between stars seem to be as important as the stars themselves.

16.1 THE OPTICAL OBSERVATIONS

As the quality of telescopes improved during the eighteenth century, and more and more objects could be studied in detail, some were found which — in contrast to stars proper — had measurable angular extent. By the beginning of the nineteenth century quite a few of these *nebulae* were known and catalogued. To be sure, many of these entries have now been identified as unresolved clusters of stars or even whole galaxies, but there are true **emission nebulae**, that is, clouds of luminous diffuse material. Two of the better known examples, a portion of the **Great Orion nebula** and the nebula with the call number **M20** in the constellation Sagittarius, are shown in Figs. 16-1 and 16-2. Note that the Orion nebula is just barely visible to the naked eye (see its location as marked in Fig. 10-1).

At the other extreme are clouds of absorbing interstellar material, the **dark nebulae**, which obscure starlight issuing from behind them. The best-known examples are visible to the naked eye as structures in our galaxy, the **Milky Way**, a luminous band which stretches across the sky and which has been known since the early days of telescopic observations to consist of myriads of faraway stars. Some of these structures are shown in Fig. 16-3, a photograph of the Milky Way taken in the direction of the constellation Cygnus, where there seems to be a bifurcation (the so-called **dark rift**). We shall show presently that in these areas the light is diminished by some absorbing material, and that the number of stars per unit volume is not smaller than usual. We almost always find, adjacent to emission nebulae or embedded in them, localized areas which are dark and are therefore of the absorbing variety. A well-known example is the so-called **Horsehead nebula**, IC 434, in the constellation Orion (see Fig. 16-4).

FIGURE 16-1.   The Great Orion nebula. Dark absorbing material and gas illuminated by nearby stars are mixed in a chaotic form. The bright features that look like picture-book stars are actually over-exposed star images. *(Lick Observatory.)*

FIGURE 16-2. The gas nebula M20 in the constellation Sagittarius, known as the Trifid nebula. Note the sharp bright edges of absorbing material jetting into the main portion of the nebula at the lower edge. The ringlike feature at the top is an overexposed star image. *(Hale Observatories.)*

The Emission Mechanism. These facts bring to mind two questions: first, why is some of this diffuse material luminous, while other portions are dark, and second, what are the chemical composition and physical state of the nebula? The answer to the first question, in a qualitative sense, is relatively simple. Whenever an energy source such as a star is positioned near interstellar material, the material is heated up by absorbing some of the star's emission, in particular the ultraviolet portion. What we see as the cloud's luminosity is simply the energy that it reemits at wavelengths characteristic of its constituents. In addition, some starlight is reflected in a manner similar to the reflection of solar photospheric light by the outer corona, causing the *zodiacal light*; we then speak of a **reflection nebula**. In a sense, then, the normal state of interstellar cloud matter is one of cold absorbing material; only in the immediate neighborhood of sources such as hot stars is it seen in emission.

The second question warrants a much more complex answer. Basically, the material consists of a blend of atomic and molecular **gases**, with small solid particles of mostly unknown chemical composition, perhaps metallic particles, ice crystals, or graphite, which we loosely subsume under the term **dust**.

FIGURE 16-3. **Milky Way in the constellation Cygnus. In the apparently dark areas in the center of the picture, starlight is absorbed by material in front.** *(Lick Observatory.)*

FIGURE 16-4. High-resolution photograph of dark absorbing material in front of luminous gas: the so-called Horsehead nebula in the constellation Orion, 200-inch telescope photograph. *(Hale Observatories.)*

Gases. The gases are relatively easy to identify. All we have to do is look for the characteristic absorption spectra of the interstellar constituents in the light that shines through the clouds—making sure that we do not confuse absorption by interstellar material with Fraunhofer lines in the spectrum of the star whose light we are using. This, again, is easy to achieve by selecting stars whose Fraunhofer spectra do not show the lines we expect from the interstellar material. Too, the stars usually move with a speed and direction different from that of the interstellar material, so that the stars' Fraunhofer lines and the interstellar absorption show different Doppler shifts. Figure 16-5 shows **interstellar absorption lines** (of neutral sodium) superimposed on the Fraunhofer lines of several O and B stars.

A variety of elements in atomic form have been identified as constituents of interstellar clouds, as have some simple molecules such as CN. Summarizing all these investigations, we find that the element composition of interstellar gas does not differ significantly from the chemical composition of stars. An interesting anomaly is the apparently much greater abundance of the elements lithium, beryllium, and boron in interstellar matter, elements which are destroyed early in the life of a star by the first set of nuclear reactions.

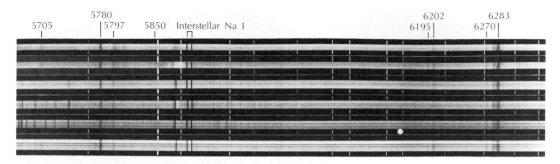

FIGURE 16-5. Various interstellar absorption lines, identified by their wavelengths in angstrom units, in the spectra of O and B stars. Most prominent are two lines of neutral sodium. The spectra are aligned in such a fashion that the interstellar lines appear at the same wavelength positions; the wavelength positions of the stellar lines then show Doppler shifts according to the individual motions of the stars. The white markings above and below the individual star spectra are lines of comparison spectra taken in the laboratory. *(Lick Observatory.)*

Solid Particles. Identification of the solid particles is more difficult, since they do not show up through spectral lines as atoms do, or even as a set of absorption (or emission) bands characteristic of molecules. Thus, we are still largely restricted to speculation when it comes to the chemical compositon of the solid components: graphite, metal crystals, ice. The presence of solid components, however, is well established in both bright and dark nebulae. In the former the solid particles contribute to the light we receive from the nebula in that they **scatter** starlight, that is, they act for all practical purposes as diffuse *reflectors*. In addition, very recent observations in the far infrared have found evidence of emission by interstellar grains that is characteristic of solid constituents, such as SiO; in the visible range this emission is completely obscured by radiation originating in other mechanisms.

On the other hand, the solid components reduce the amount of light passing through dark nebulae. The ratio of reduction depends somewhat on chemical composition and, of course, on the extent and density of the cloud—but only in a very minor way on wavelength in the visible range. Thus, for instance, blue photons are somewhat more likely to be absorbed than red ones and, consequently, starlight that has gone through a dust cloud appears to be redder than it is. This **interstellar reddening** is a very important facet of light transmission through interstellar space. For our purposes it is important to realize that almost all the absorption we notice, say in the structures of the Milky Way, is due to the solid constituents and not the gases comprising the interstellar material. With graphite being one of the possible solid constituents, the name Coalsack for the dark areas in the Milky Way close to the celestial south pole turns out to be much more accurate than the sailors of old, who named them, could have imagined.

16.2 THE RADIO OBSERVATIONS

Radio-range photons with wavelengths between about 1 mm and several tens of meters pass more or less unaffected through our atmosphere and through interstellar clouds, consequently, we are able to look much farther into the galaxy in the radio range than at optical wavelengths. Since both atoms and molecules have spectral lines at radio wavelengths, the methods of spectral analysis, employed with so much success in the visible portion of the spectrum, are equally useful at radio frequencies.

H II Regions.   The first objects to be investigated in the radio range were emission nebulae, that is, material that is heated by nearby stars. Study of their radio emissions showed both continuous emission due to the **bremsstrahlung** mechanism, that is, to encounters between free electrons and positive ions (see Section C.7), and emission *lines*. The latter have been identified as originating in atoms such as hydrogen in which the electron has a very high internal energy relative to the nucleus—in fact, so high that it is almost free to leave the atom. Thus, we see that the interstellar material surrounding a star is usually heated up to such a degree that hydrogen is mostly ionized; temperatures must be of the order of 8000°K to 12,000°K. In line with a terminology that distinguishes between (singly) ionized (II) and neutral atoms (I), we label the areas where hydrogen is ionized as **H II regions**. Note that at the temperatures given most solid particles evaporate, and atoms and ions are the most abundant components of an H II region.

H II regions and their well-defined physical properties have fascinated astronomers and physicists in recent years, for several reasons quite aside from their direct importance in stellar evolution. For one, the energy balance of an H II region, given its input of high-energy (ultraviolet) photons from the star and its output of low-energy visible, infrared, and radio photons, is quite subtle and involved. In addition, the mechanism comprises a variety of unusual features, quite different from those exhibited by a laboratory gas. The reason is mostly the low density of about 10^2 to 10^4 particles per cubic centimeter, which allows radiation processes to take place that are highly unlikely under more normal conditions, such as those in stellar atmospheres (with densities of 10^{12} particles per cubic centimeter) or in laboratory gases (10^{16}, for instance); these processes may result in the emission of *forbidden* spectral lines of the type observed in the upper atmosphere of our earth.

Also, observations show violent and often chaotic patterns of motion inside H II regions; velocities are sometimes above the local velocity of sound. The aerodynamics of these crisscrossing **shock waves**, that is, explosion fronts with supersonic speeds, are not well understood, but may be of crucial importance to the structure of H II regions.

The 21-Centimeter Line.   Areas of interstellar space where the material is not ionized by nearby stars must obviously be much colder; they contain *neutral* hydrogen and are called **H I regions**. At optical wavelengths there are no measurable emission lines, and the main characteristic is the more or less featureless absorption of starlight. At radio frequencies, the situation is fundamentally different in that the solids do not absorb significantly, whereas the hydrogen atoms that abound may emit a spectral line even at very low temperatures (say, about 10°K or 100°K). This spectral line occurs at a wavelength of 21 cm. It is the famous **21-cm line**. It comes about because the electron and proton of the hydrogen nucleus both **spin** and can do so either in the same direction (**parallel spin**) or in opposite directions (**antiparallel spin**); no intermediate spin directions are possible. The two spin combinations result in slightly different electron energies, and an electron that "flips" its spin changes its energy by an amount that just corresponds to the energy of a 21-cm photon. In other words, such a photon is either emitted or absorbed in every spin flip of the electron in the lowest-energy (ground) state of the neutral hydrogen atom.

H I Regions. Twenty-one centimeter emission has been observed from everywhere in our galaxy and, in fact, much of what we know of the structure of our galactic system is due to radio studies. In every accumulation of interstellar material, we find 21-cm photons emanating from those areas where the hydrogen is neutral and mostly in the ground state. These areas are the H I regions of neutral hydrogen, and they surround the H II regions in the neighborhood of hot stars.

Some H I regions are known to contain within them a significant amount of material in which the *hydrogen* is in the *molecular* state, that is, where two hydrogen atoms are bound together in a stable configuration. This has a strong bearing on the accuracy of estimates of the total mass of our galaxy, since these estimates would have to be much greater if a significant fraction of the interstellar gas were in molecular form and, thus, invisible at 21 cm. On the other hand, there are indications that outside the clouds proper the gas is much less dense and, at the same time, maintains a rather high internal energy (temperatures of several thousand degrees) by interaction with low-energy cosmic rays.

The Laser Effect. More recently, other equally interesting lines have been identified. The first ones to be found—in 1963—come from a molecule consisting of one oxygen and one hydrogen atom; this **OH molecule**, a *free radical* in the language of the chemist, is not stable under density and temperature conditions that can be produced in a laboratory. It has a large number of transitions in the radio range which can be detected fairly easily, and it may show either absorption or emission lines. Its most interesting feature, though, is the fantastically high intensity of its emission lines. In fact, the only known mechanism capable of producing the observed intensity is the **laser** (or **maser**, if the term is specifically applied to radio photons).

In a laser device, whether natural or man-made, photons of a specific wavelength are used to "stimulate" electrons in an equally well-defined energy state to drop to a lower state by emitting other photons of identical wavelength. If enough electrons are excited, an avalanche of photons is created leading to the emission of huge quantities of energy in just that one wavelength. The problem in sustaining laser emission is to bring the electrons back into the excited state as fast as they drop to the lower state. Strenuous attempts have been made by theoreticians in the last few years to understand the details of the laser process, specifically for the case of the OH molecule. We have come quite a way toward explaining the observed features, but to date there still are at least as many unsolved as solved problems.

Source Size. Owing to the intrinsic properties of light, the angular resolution of a radio telescope is not nearly as good as that of an optical telescope of comparable size, a fact discussed in some detail in Section E.1. Thus, our biggest radio telescopes can just about relate the positions of extended H I and H II regions to the corresponding optically observed nebulae. When the same correspondence was attempted for OH emissions, it became immediately clear that the size of these sources is far below the resolving power of normal radio telescopes, and that the *intercontinental interferometer* (discussed in Section E.4) must be used.

It has now been established that OH emission originates in extremely small areas, with angular diameters of the order of 10^{-3} arcsec, somewhere in or near H II regions. At this time, we are essentially at a loss to comprehend why OH molecules emitting tremendous amounts of radiation in the radio range should be found in extremely small regions—fractions of a parsec in diameter, sometimes as small as the solar system—in the neighborhood of gas clouds. What we are witnessing may be the formation of a protostar or a proto-solar system.

The phenomenon has been further complicated by the detection of other molecules since 1968, first of **ammonia** (chemical formula NH_3) and **water vapor** (H_2O), and then of **formaldehyde** (HCHO), **hydrocyanic acid** (HCN), **formic acid** (HCO_2H), **cyanoacetylene** (HC_3N), **methyl alcohol** (CH_3OH). The list, rapidly expanding, already contains some of the major building blocks of basic organic material. In all cases, the sources are extremely small and positioned somewhere in or near nebulae. At any rate, the developments of the last few years have convinced astronomers that one of the dominant factors in the behavior of interstellar material is its complex *chemical* structure.

The mere existence of these comparatively complex molecules shows that interstellar gas clouds must contain areas in which conditions are physically quite different from their surroundings. Another manifestation is the existence of so-called **globules** of extremely low temperature, maintained over quite significant periods of time. We shall come back to these, in the framework of star formation, presently.

16.3 INTERSTELLAR GAS AND STAR FORMATION

We emphasized in Section 16.2 that the ionization of hydrogen and other elements in certain areas of interstellar clouds, leading to H II regions embedded in the cold material of the H I region, is due to the absorption of radiation emitted by hot stars. The question now arises as to whether or not these stars are close to interstellar gas masses by chance. Of course, we would suspect not, and indeed this is the case. The evidence points to the stars being the progeny of the nearby clouds.

First note that many of the stars physically related to interstellar clouds are of types O and B, which are quite young; they reached the zero-age main sequence typically only some 10^7 or 10^8 years ago. From radial-velocity measurements we know that they are not particularly fast-moving. So, we observe the O and B stars essentially at the places where they were formed.

There is a strong correlation between the positions of young O and B stars and the positions of interstellar clouds. Where we find an accumulation of interstellar gas with its density of about ten thousand times the density of its surroundings (0.1 particles per cubic centimeter), we also find exceptionally many young stars; these groupings of young stars are the so-called **O-and-B associations**. Equally significant is the fact that O-and-B associations usually contain a number of T Tauri stars, identified as being in the early stages of stellar evolution. Finally, infrared sources, highly localized in interstellar clouds, seem to be related to the processes involved in star formation. Again, the evidence points to interstellar clouds as the birthplace of stars.

What is the lifetime of an interstellar cloud and the star group that originates from it? If we take 100 pc as the average size of a cloud, and 10 km/sec as a star's random velocity, then it would take a star about 10^7 years to pass through a gas cloud. Thus, we expect star associations to hold together some 10^7 to 10^8 years. Obviously, as time goes on, more and more of the cloud material condenses into stars, slowly depleting the reservoir of gas and dust. While this is taking place, the cloud tends to stay together under the influence of its own gravity, that is, the mutual attraction of the atoms, molecules, and grains. But then, there is the mutual gravitational interaction of gas clouds, and of gas clouds and stars in neighboring associations, which tends to disrupt the clouds. One of the most interesting problems of celestial mechanics is the prediction of **dissolution times** for gas clouds and star associations.

It would be natural at this point to ask where the interstellar material comes from, how it is distributed in the sky, and why it forms clouds. In order to understand the answers, we must know more about the general distribution of matter—condensed as well as diffuse—in space. We discuss this in the chapters that follow.

QUESTIONS FOR DISCUSSION

1. How would you prove that the apparently less populous areas of the Milky Way contain as many stars as the obviously more congested areas?

2. Why is the abundance of the elements lithium, beryllium, and boron in interstellar clouds of particular interest?

3. Why do the spectral lines observed in H I regions differ from the spectral lines observed in H II regions?

4. What are the physical characteristics of interstellar sources of far-infrared emission?

5. List the processes involved in the formation of stars from interstellar gas clouds (see Section 12.1).

6. Why are O and B stars of particular importance in determining the physical state of interstellar clouds? Why T Tauri stars?

EXERCISES

1. What is the energy source of emission nebulae?

2. Describe the main features of the spectrum of an emission nebula.

3. How do we obtain spectral information on dark nebulae?

4. What is the chemical composition of interstellar material?

5. What are the differences in physical characteristics between dark nebulae and emission nebulae?

6. How do we distinguish interstellar absorption lines from stellar Fraunhofer lines?

7. What is meant by "interstellar reddening"?

8. What are the main differences between H I and H II regions?

9. Spectral lines are emitted and absorbed in the radio region as well as in the visible region of the spectrum. List the most prominent types of spectral lines in the radio range.

10. Which radio lines are observed in H I regions? In H II regions?

11. How does the 21-cm line come about?

12. Where do H II regions obtain the energy to keep hydrogen ionized?

13. What is the reason for the interest astronomers have in the amount of molecular hydrogen present in interstellar space?

14. How does the bremsstrahlung mechanism work?

15. Under what physical conditions do we observe the so-called forbidden lines?

16. If gas moves with supersonic speed, it produces shock waves. Give at least three examples of shock waves, astronomical or otherwise, and the influence they have on their surroundings.

17. What is the peculiarity of the observed OH-molecule spectral lines?

18. List a few of the molecules detected in interstellar space. Which molecules not yet detected might be among the next ones to be detected in space?

19. Describe some of the characteristics of regions that emit OH lines.

20. What is some of the evidence of a physical relation between interstellar clouds and the stars embedded in them.

21. What is an O-and-B association?

22. Describe some of the mechanisms that affect the lifetimes of gas clouds and the corresponding star associations.

23. Assume that there are 10 atoms per cubic centimeter in a gas cloud of diameter 100 pc. How many solar-type stars could be formed from all the cloud material?

EXPERIMENTS

1. Find the Orion nebula with a field glass. Describe the difference in visual impression between the nebula and faint stars.

2. Locate some dark nebulae in the Milky Way, for instance the "dark rift" in the constellation Cygnus. Try to estimate the drop in apparent star density in comparison to neighboring areas of the Milky Way.

3. Making use of the star charts in Section G, draw the outline of the Milky Way; you will need a clear night in a pollution-free area (if you can find one). To what are the irregularities in the outline due?

FURTHER READING

Stars and Clouds of the Milky Way, edited by T. Page and L. W. Page, New York: The Macmillan Company, 1968.

Nebulae and Interstellar Matter, edited by B. M. Middlehurst and L. H. Aller, Chicago: The University of Chicago Press, 1968.

17 the galactic disc

In the last chapter we discussed the physical properties of interstellar gas, but left open the question of why it forms clouds, and where these clouds can be found. The answers to these questions will lead, in this chapter, to the fact that all matter—gaseous as well as stellar—is distributed in a highly organized fashion.

The existence of such nonuniform distribution of matter is quite obvious from naked-eye observation of the *Milky Way*. In this luminous band the star density is much greater than elsewhere; even Galileo's simple telescope was capable of resolving some of the particularly bright areas of the Milky Way into individual stars. By the eighteenth century astronomers realized that the sun, the earth, and the other planets belong to a larger system in which stars are arranged in a sort of flattened, saucerlike configuration, and that in viewing the Milky Way we are actually looking along the "saucer," the principal plane of this distribution. Nowadays, we call this the *galactic plane* and say that the stars are concentrated in the *galactic disc*.

17.1 THE SPATIAL DISTRIBUTION OF INTERSTELLAR GAS

We stated in Section 16.2 that most of the interstellar clouds not closely surrounding stars have temperatures and densities at which the element hydrogen is in the neutral state and so able to emit (or absorb) a spectral line at a wavelength of 21 cm. We have also seen that at this radio wavelength solid particles do not appreciably absorb or emit, so that they are unable to obscure our "view," as they do in the visible range. As it turns out, using the 21-cm line, we are able to see across whole star systems with only minor obstruction. Thus, we would expect to get a good idea of the distribution of matter in our portion of the universe by simply plotting the intensity of the 21-cm line on a representation of the celestial sphere.

Galactic Coordinates.   For this representation, one uses a *galactic coordinate system* as shown in Fig. 17-1. In essence, the central plane (latitude 0⁰) corresponds to the great circle marked in the sky by the luminous band of the Milky Way. In Fig. 17-1 this is opened and flattened out, so that the left and right ends refer to the same position in the Milky Way (longitude 180°). Analogously to our procedure in Section 3.1, we can use this plane of symmetry, the **galactic plane**, to define the **galactic equator**, with the **galactic poles** at right angles to it, and in this manner define the coordinate system represented in Fig. 17-1. We then count **galactic latitudes** from 0° at the equator to +90° at the north pole, and to −90° at the south pole. Along the equator we measure off **galactic longitudes**, starting from some arbitrary zero point, for

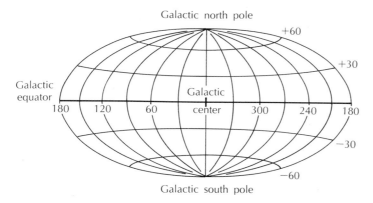

FIGURE 17-1. Galactic coordinates. The galactic plane closely follows the plane of symmetry of the Milky Way. Latitudes are counted from 0° at the equator to +90° at the galactic north pole, and to −90° at the south pole. Longitudes are counted from 0° to 360°, starting at the galactic center in the constellation Sagittarius.

instance, by defining 0° longitude at the **galactic center**. This point is located in the Milky Way, in the constellation *Sagittarius*, close to its boundary with the constellations Scorpius and Ophiochus in the southern sky ($\alpha = 17^h42^m$, $\delta = -28°55'$); the galactic north pole, in the constellation Coma Berenices, has the coordinates $\alpha = 12^h47^m$ and $\delta = 27°40'$.

The Galactic Disc. If we plot the distribution of H I regions, or of H II regions in the sky, we find immediately that they are concentrated in the plane defined by the Milky Way. Figure 17-2 shows such a plot (H II regions). On the other hand, we would have found an identical result if we had marked the location of star clusters in the sky. Even if we had simply counted the stars within each area of the sky (**star gauging**), a method which goes back to the eighteenth century, we would have found a similar concentration towards the Milky Way.

The interstellar gas and the stars concentrated in the Milky Way comprise the **galactic disc**. Again, it must be emphasized that the sun and the solar system are situated inside this disc, almost in the plane of symmetry. A particularly large number of interstellar clouds lie in the direction of the *galactic center* (longitude 0° in galactic coordinates), and they also extend farther than usual in galactic latitude; this indicates that the galactic center is indeed a center in the *physical* sense.

17.2 GALACTIC ROTATION AND THE SPIRAL STRUCTURE

Galactic Rotation. One of the first studies performed after the discovery of the existence of a neutral hydrogen line at a wavelength of about 21 cm was concerned with possible Doppler shifts due to galactic motions. Immediately, a rather complex picture emerged. Its main features are shown schematically in Fig. 17-3. H I regions in the direction of the galactic center and the anticenter (the opposite direction in

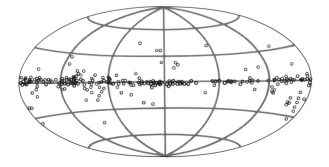

FIGURE 17-2. Positions of H II regions in galactic coordinates. The strong concentration toward the galactic equator is immediately obvious. *(S. Sharpless, in Galactic Structure, edited by A. Blaauw and M. Schmidt, Chicago: The University of Chicago Press, 1965.)*

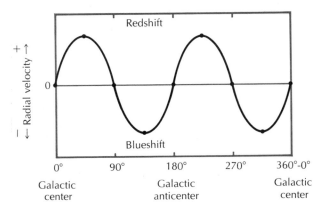

FIGURE 17-3. Double wave of radial velocities of radio sources in the galactic plane. Redshifts are observed from 0° to 90° and 180° to 270° galactic longitude, blueshifts from 90° to 180° and 270° to 360°. The sources thus must move at right angles to us in the directions of the galactic center and anticenter, and halfway between them.

the sky at 180° longitude) and halfway between have close to zero Doppler shifts and, thus, zero radial-velocity components in the direction of the sun. This same phenomenon had been found in the motions of stars, and is called the **double wave** *in radial velocities* in the galactic plane. Material in other directions has the velocity shown, depending on galactic longitude.

The simplest and most straightforward explanation of this feature is a general **rotation** of all material in the galactic disc about the point we called the galactic center. Measurements show that the whole galaxy does not have the same angular speed; roughly speaking, the further out the material, the smaller its angular speed.

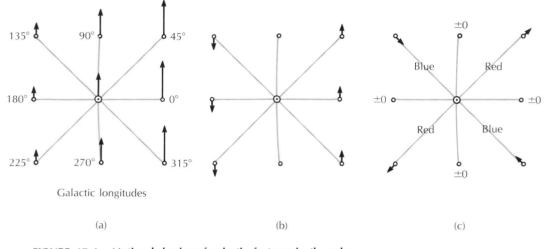

Galactic longitudes

(a)   (b)   (c)

FIGURE 17-4. Motion behavior of galactic features in the solar neighborhood. (a) Velocities as measured by an observer outside our galaxy. The lengths of the arrows indicate the absolute values of the velocities. (b) Relative velocity with respect to the sun. (c) Radial-velocity components with respect to the sun. Coordinates are galactic longitude: 0° points to the galactic center, 180° to the anticenter. Note the increase in rotational velocity toward the center.

Thus, the sun overtakes material farther away from the center, while being overtaken by material nearer to the center.

How this results in the observations plotted in Fig. 17-3 is outlined in the sequence of Fig. 17-4(a) to (c). Figure 17-4(a) shows the sun in the middle with some galactic features, say H I regions, in front of it (at 90° galactic longitude), behind it (at 270° longitude), closer to the galactic center (at 315°, 0°, and 45° longitude), and farther away (at 135°, 180°, and 225° longitude). We are, essentially, looking down on these objects from, say, the galactic north pole. The arrows indicate velocities with respect to the center of our galaxy. Note that velocities increase to the right, closer to the galactic center. Relative to the sun, the velocities appear as in Fig. 17-4(b): objects closer to the center overtake us; those farther out appear to move in the opposite direction. The radial components of these motions are, finally, plotted in Fig. 17-4(c), where red- and blueshifts are indicated; they are obtained from the relative velocities of Fig. 17-4(b) in the manner outlined in Section B.2. The data of Fig. 17-4(c) are shown by dots in Fig. 17-3.

The data of Figs. 17-3 and 17-4 refer to relatively nearby objects that are located mostly in what we shall presently call our own spiral arm of our galaxy. The rotational behavior of the galaxy as a whole is quite complicated and by no means completely understood. The central portion apparently rotates as a **rigid body**; that is, close to the center, rotational velocity is simply proportional to distance from the center. Then, however, velocity increases more slowly, reaching a maximum at about 8 kiloparsecs (kpc) from the galactic center, as shown in Fig. 17-5. From there outward, velocity decreases; in the solar neighborhood, that is, at about 10 kpc from the galactic center, the situation is as depicted in Figure 17-4(a). The furthest

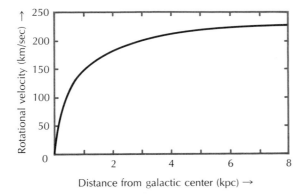

FIGURE 17-5. Schematic plot of the rotational velocity of our galaxy as a function of radial distance from the center; region inside the solar orbit. The velocity at first increases proportionally to the distance from the center (rigid-body rotation), but then becomes differential, increasing slowly to a maximum of about 230 km/sec inside the solar orbit.

portions of our galaxy probably follow **Keplerian orbits** which result in decreasing speed with increasing distance from the center.

It is worth remembering that most of these studies are rather recent; they were made and interpreted after it became clear in the 1920s that galaxies such as the Andromeda system are star systems very similar to our own. Thus, often we could simply study the gross features of these *extragalactic* systems to obtain an idea of what to look for in our own neighborhood. This is, for instance, the case with general rotation, which is well documented in the Andromeda system.

The importance of rotation curves like Fig. 17-5 lies in the fact that they permit a determination of the **matter distribution** of the galaxy. The computations are quite complex, but basically they follow from Newton's law, which states in the present context that the motion of a mass in the galaxy is determined by all other masses—stars as well as diffuse matter—and that therefore the rotation and the distribution of matter must be mutually consistent. As a result we find the total mass of our galaxy to be about 10^{11} $M_\odot$.

Spiral Arms. So far, we have mentioned only half (and, to a degree, the less important half) of the story of Doppler shifts in the 21-cm line. If we take a detailed look at the 21-cm line in any particular direction along the galactic plane, we see that typically two or three distinct Doppler shifts occur. In addition, the amount of shift changes in a very characteristic manner as a function of galactic longitude. An example is shown in Fig. 17-6, where the observed intensity of the 21-cm line is plotted for three directions, toward galactic longitudes of 120°, 180°, and 240°. Notice that several sources, with different radial velocities, show up; the most prominent ones are marked with arrows. Obviously, we have detected several H I regions that are at quite specific distances from us, with essentially nothing between those sources.

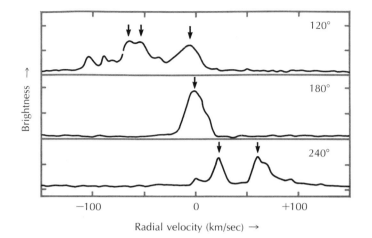

FIGURE 17-6. **Observed Doppler-shift patterns in the 21-cm line of neutral hydrogen at the galactic longitudes 120°, 180°, and 240°. Note the predominance of blueshifts at 120°, of unshifted lines at 180°, and of redshifts at 240°.** *(L. Velden, Beiträge zur Radioastronomie, Bonn: Dümmler-Verlag, vol. 1, p. 172, 1970.)*

Again, what we know about extragalactic objects with structures similar to the suspected structure of our own system provides the blueprint for the explanation of Fig. 17-6: our galaxy has **spiral arms**. This means that the material in the galactic disc is not distributed uniformly, or even with a simple continuous gradient towards the center. Rather it is made up of streaks that originate somewhere in the central region and then wind around in a manner observed in other galaxies, such as M31 (Fig. 19-1) and M33 (Fig. 19-6). It is worthwhile to note that it is much harder to find conclusive optical evidence of this effect in our own galaxy, simply because interstellar matter makes it impossible for us to obtain more than an occasional glimpse of the next spiral arm from our position. It is fascinating to speculate on how our sky would look if we were situated at the very edge of a spiral arm, with an unobstructed view of the neighboring arm.

In recent years, efforts at mapping the spiral structure of our galaxy have been quite successful, and the results for the solar neighborhood are summarized in Fig. 17-7. We are situated in a spiral arm called the **Orion arm**; it can be traced for quite some distance about our galaxy. Further in, toward the galactic center, is the **Sagittarius arm**, and there is probably one more arm still further in. Outside our position is the **Perseus arm**. Although their shapes are not fully known, we can identify the major features of Fig. 17-6 either with portions of the Orion arm (240° and 180°), or with a combination of the Orion and Perseus arms (120°).

While the existence of spiral arms and even their distribution about the galaxy are fairly well established from observation, we have at present only qualitative ideas as to their evolution. The differential rotation of the galaxy should have resulted in the spiral arms being tightly wound about the galactic center, which is obviously not the case. More recent theory has departed drastically from this simple picture, and the spiral-arm structure is considered more or less as the result of an equilibrium

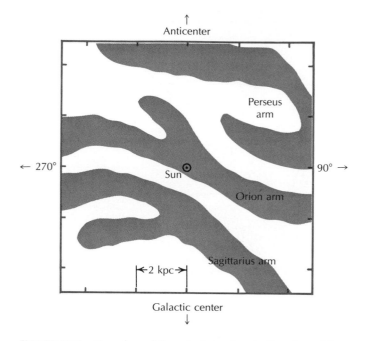

FIGURE 17-7. **Overview of the spiral structure in the solar neighborhood. Outlined are the three major spiral arms, the Perseus arm toward the galactic anticenter, the Orion arm to which we belong, and the Sagittarius arm closer to the center. The outlines of the arms in their details are still fairly uncertain.**

between continual formation of new clumps of matter and dissolution of old ones in which the spiral arms represent a sort of wave pattern.

Dimensions of Our Galaxy. In summary, it is fairly well established that we are about two-thirds of the way from the center of our galaxy, whose "edge" is defined by a rather sudden drop in matter density. We are situated in one of the spiral arms, rather close to the galactic plane. The system as a whole, aside from the spiral arms, is dominated by a very large accumulation of matter in the galactic plane, with a greater concentration towards the center. The whole system—stars, planets, interstellar matter, and all—rotates about the galactic center; but the radial variation of rotational speed is rather complicated. The speed of the sun (about 250 km/sec) is such that it completes a revolution in about 200 million years. As pointed out on several occasions, our sun is about 5×10^9 years old, while our galaxy was formed maybe 10^{10} years ago, so that the sun has completed about 25 revolutions since its birth.

Finally, we should mention the overall dimensions of our galaxy as they emerge from the various data: the linear extent of the galactic disc from edge to edge is about 30 kpc, with the sun about 10 kpc from the center. The Sagittarius and Perseus arms are each about 2 kpc away from us, with our own Orion arm being about 1 kpc in width, and the sun displaced a few hundred parsecs from the center

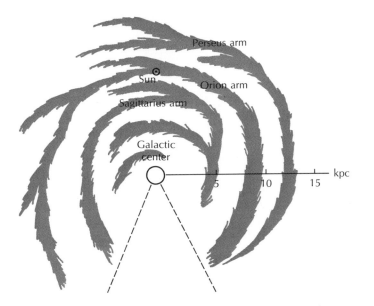

FIGURE 17-8. Schematic overview of the galactic disc as seen by a fictitious observer above the disc. Note again the Perseus arm, Orion arm, and Sagittarius arm in the solar neighborhood. The details of the arms are still fairly uncertain. No observations are available in the area limited by the dashed lines.

of the arm. A highly idealized overview of the galactic disc is presented in Fig. 17-8. No observations are available for the areas that have been left blank.

In concluding this section we must point out an omission: when we discussed the galactic center, we referred to it essentially as being a geometrically defined marker with no particular structure. In reality, the innermost portions of our galaxy are very intricately structured. We shall review the features of this galactic nucleus later, in Section 18.4, against the background of the galaxy as a whole.

17.3 INTERSTELLAR CLOUDS AND OPEN CLUSTERS

Ages of Open Clusters. Let us return to the star population in the area of our galaxy that we are able to survey optically. We saw in Section 11.2 that there are large associations of stars, localized, with the stars physically related to each other, which we called galactic or **open clusters** at that time (the Pleiades and the Hyades are typical examples). We noted that an explanation of their characteristic H-R diagrams is found in an application of the principles of stellar evolution. We now are at the point where we are able to combine our understanding of stellar evolution with the observed features of cluster diagrams to determine the *ages of clusters*.

Let us first emphasize that only physically related stars should be plotted in any H-R diagram; several criteria can be applied to assure this, mostly concerning proper motion and radial velocity. The first stars to condense must be about as old as the interstellar cloud itself, and star formation most probably continued until the cloud was depleted or otherwise dissolved. We suspect that the time interval between the first and last star condensation is small in comparison with the age of the galaxy and, in that sense, the stars of a cluster are essentially of identical "age."

Next, recall from our discussion of contraction and later phases in the evolution of stars (Chapter 12) that the time it takes for a star to evolve varies by orders of magnitude, depending on the mass of the star. After 10^8 years of evolution, for example, stars less massive than the sun would not even have reached the zero-age main sequence, while stars with masses two or three times the solar mass would be burning hydrogen in a stable phase. Stars with still higher masses might already have evolved away from the main sequence toward the giant branch of the diagram. Precisely these features are evident on the H-R diagrams of open clusters.

In the Pleiades, whose H-R diagram is given in Fig. 11-6, the brightest stars are of spectral types B6 and B8; the Hyades do not contain stars hotter than spectral type A5. There are other clusters that contain still hotter (younger) stars than the Pleiades and, similarly, clusters whose hottest stars are of type F or G, cooler than the hottest stars in the Hyades. The obvious interpretation of these differences in the temperatures of the hottest main-sequence stars observed is in terms of age: once star formation has stopped, the most massive stars quickly move away from the main sequence. Thus, by determining the temperature of the brightest star of a cluster remaining on the main sequence, and comparing this with the duration of evolutionary periods, we can establish the ages of open clusters. Independent age information can be extracted from young clusters in which many of the small cool stars have not yet reached the main sequence, and in which we can find T Tauri stars. Figure 17-9 shows the deduced ages of the double cluster η and χ Persei,

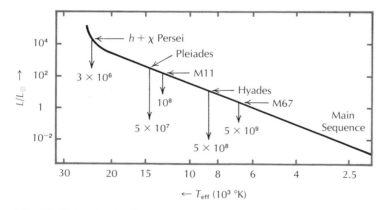

FIGURE 17-9. **Break-off point from the main sequence of the brightest stars, and estimated ages in years of some typical open clusters.** *(G. R. Burbidge and E. M. Burbidge, "Stellar Evolution," in Handbuch der Physik, edited by S. Flügge, Berlin:Springer-Verlag, vol. 51, 1958.)*

the Pleiades, M11 in the constellation Scutum, the Hyades, and M67 in the constellation Cancer. The last cluster is particularly interesting because of its great age.

The Field Stars in the Galactic Disc. Suppose now that we want to make a similar analysis of the general field stars in the galactic disc, that is, stars that do not belong to any cluster, in order to interpret the H-R diagram for solar-neighborhood stars. We immediately run into difficulty: we cannot expect the times of formation of these stars to be the same. To be sure, whatever O and B stars we find must be young, and, if they do not have exceptionally great proper motions, are still quite close to their places of origin. Our sun and the smaller and cooler K and M stars, on the other hand, were formed much earlier; otherwise, they would not yet be in the main-sequence area of the H-R diagram. Indeed, the solar-neighborhood stars must be a mixture of older and younger stars, since there are both massive stars still close to the zero-age main sequence (young) and stars already off it (old). Of the latter, many may have moved from their birthplaces, through random motion, into the general population of the disc; some may even be in the spaces between the spiral arms. Thus, we find that the star associations and their ages are direct indicators of the time scales that govern the development of the physical features in the galactic disc.

Gas Clouds and Star Clusters. How do the structures of the galactic disc come about? Very few of these really basic problems have as yet been solved satisfactorily. For instance, we do not know for certain why our system has spiral arms, although we suspect that their existence is due to the properties of the primordial gas mass from which our galaxy was formed, a long time ago. We are fairly sure that the spiral structure is an intrinsic (and thus old) feature of our galaxy that has survived a significant number of galactic revolutions. Similarly, we have no reason to believe that these structures will dissolve in the "foreseeable" future (some 10^9 years or so).

The mass reservoir from which new stars are continually formed is located in the spiral arms. Here are the accumulations of interstellar material which produce not only the brilliant and thus very obvious O and B stars, but also myriads of faint small stars like the sun and its even smaller relatives. Again, we do not know enough of the workings of stellar formation at present to predict unambiguously, say, the ratio of stars with a mass of 10 $M_\odot$ to those with a mass of 1 $M_\odot$, or the ratio of multiple systems to single stars. All we can say is that over a period of maybe 10^8 years a goodly fraction of the material in a cloud will condense into stars. After a time of the order of 10^9 years they will have left the realm of the cloud from which they were formed. Over a period of some 5×10^9 years, interstellar clouds will form and disperse in the spiral arms; they will condense partially into stars, and these stars will more and more populate the galactic disc.

Why does the gas and dust of the spiral arms accumulate into clouds? Again, we do not know the details, but we suspect that a mechanism similar to the one which causes the initial condensation of a protostar from cloud material is at work. What we do know, directly from observation, is that interstellar clouds of all sizes exist, from very dense miniature blobs totaling a few solar masses to huge accumulations totaling thousands of solar masses. Given the wide range of cloud masses, it is not surprising that star clusters vary greatly in membership, so that we can list star clusters with a total of tens or at most hundreds of stars (if we acknowledge that we probably missed a few!), and clusters whose populations may be in the tens of thousands.

17.4   CHEMICAL ABUNDANCES IN THE DISC; POPULATION I

Population I.   The stars in open clusters have approximately the same chemical composition: they represent the metal-rich **Population I** which includes the sun, and whose major chemical abundances are listed in Table 7-1. The chemical abundance of a specific element can be obtained from its Fraunhofer lines only within certain limits; very fine differences in composition between stars in younger and older clusters may be masked by the errors inherent to the detection method, or they may be due to a certain amount of randomness in the abundances. Nevertheless, there appear to be some systematic differences: the younger the cluster, the greater the ratio of metals to hydrogen.

What might be the cause of this difference in abundance as a function of age? During the lifetime of a star, it returns matter to the "parent" interstellar gas at various stages and through various mechanisms, from slow evaporations of the solar-wind type, through the shedding of the outer atmosphere in the planetary-nebula stage, to the violent explosions of supernovae. Most of this material has undergone some measure of alteration owing to nuclear reactions; its chemical composition differs from the original in the sense that it contains a greater percentage of heavy nuclei. Hence, with the years, the "metal" content of the interstellar gas and, by implication, of the stars formed from it, should increase. The youngest clusters currently active in star formation thus define the **extreme Population I**, whereas the stars in the oldest open clusters are referred to as the **older Population I**.

Disc Population.   Among individual stars in the disc that do not belong to clusters are some with more noticeable metal deficiencies, involving a factor of as much as 5 in certain cases. These are particularly prevalent among planetary nebulae, novae, and RR Lyrae stars, all relatively old. They make up the so-called **disc population**. Thus, we find an increase in metal abundance from the disc population to the older Population I to the extreme Population I, but within rather narrow limits. So *all* stars in the galactic disc must have been formed of material with a quite noticeable metal content.

The metal-poor Population II stars will be discussed in Section 18.3.

QUESTIONS FOR DISCUSSION

1.   Why is it that we can map our galaxy at radio wavelengths much more efficiently than at optical wavelengths?

2. Why would you expect plots in galactic coordinates of the distribution of H I regions and of H II regions to be very similar?

3. The observations reported in Fig. 17-4 do not cover a significant fraction of the rotation curve of the galaxy. Why not?

4. Why were astronomers able to distinguish many of our galaxy's complex features long before detailed data concerning their spatial distribution were available?

5. Do you expect to obtain essentially the same information from studies of the 21-cm line and studies of OH emissions? Why?

6. Describe the visual impression of the sky that might be obtained by an observer on a planet at the edge of our spiral arm.

7. How is the range of masses observed in interstellar clouds related to the range of numbers of stars in clusters?

8. How do astronomers decide that an open cluster is very old?

9. Why is it much more difficult to determine the mean age of a sample of single stars in a spiral arm than it is to determine the age of an open cluster?

10. Why do younger stars in general have greater metal abundances? How do older stars influence the metal abundances of younger stars?

EXERCISES

1. What spectral line has so far been used most extensively to explore the structure of our galaxy? How does the line come about?

2. How are galactic coordinates defined?

3. What feature of the sky, visible to the naked eye, approximately defines galactic latitude 0°?

4. Locate the galactic equator on the star charts of Appendix G.

5. Locate the galactic north pole, the galactic center, and the galactic anticenter on the star charts in Appendix G.

6. What are the right ascension and declination of the galactic south pole?

7. What spectral features are used to identify H I regions? H II regions?

8. What is the method of "star gauging" used for?

9. What features—visible to the naked eye or to radio telescopes—define the galactic disc?

10. Were the first indications of the galactic rotation obtained from studies in the visible or the radio portion of the spectrum? Why?

11. Describe the double wave of radial velocities. How does it come about?

12. At what galactic longitudes do you observe maximum radial velocities?

13. Complete Fig. 17-4(a) to (c) by adding velocities at the galactic longitudes 22.5°, 67.5°, 112.5°, 157.5°, 202.5°, 247.5°, 292.5°, and 335.5°.

14. Extrapolate Fig. 17-5 to the "edge" of our galaxy. How approximate is your extrapolation?

15. How does rotational velocity depend on radial distance according to the rigid-body law?

16. How does rotational velocity depend on radial distance in the case of Keplerian orbits?

17. What are the principal steps in estimating the mass of a galaxy, once you know its mode of rotation as a function of distance from the center?

18. Only the more obvious sources are indicated in Fig. 17-6. Identify a few more and try to correlate them to galactic features. Why are their emissions less prominent?

19. Use Fig. 17-8 to identify the parts of the galaxy detailed in Fig. 17-6.

20. Assume Fig. 17-8 to be an accurate view of the galactic disc. Construct theoretical radial-velocity curves similar to Fig. 17-6 for the galactic longitudes 45° and 315°, assuming we are able to receive radiation from all spiral arms. Why could you not expect to observe all the features on your curves?

21. Which objects visible to the naked eye do not belong to the spiral arm in which our sun is located?

22. Assume that the spiral structure we observe at present could only be altered by differential rotation of our galaxy. In what fashion would the structure depicted in Fig. 17-8 change during the next 10^9 years?

23. What time period would you call a "galactic year"?

24. Over what time period would you have to observe the Milky Way in order to see changes due to a rotation of 1°?

25. You observe a certain very bright star in one of the neighboring spiral arms. If its absolute magnitude is -5^m0, approximately what would its apparent magnitude be? Comment on the possibility of observing stars in neighboring spiral arms with the naked eye.

26. What are the two main pieces of evidence for an open cluster being very young?

27. From the data in Chapter 12, find the break-off point from the main sequence for a star cluster in which star formation stopped 10^9 years ago.

28. What do astronomers presently think is the cause of spiral-arm structures?

29. List the principal steps in the method of estimating the masses of interstellar clouds.

30. The name "Population I" is applied to somewhat different subclasses of stars. Describe these subclasses and their differences.

FURTHER READING

Bok, B. J., and P. F. Bok, *The Milky Way* (third ed.), Cambridge, Mass.: Harvard University Press, 1957.

Stars and Clouds of the Milky Way, edited by T. Page and L. W. Page, New York: The Macmillan Company, 1968.

Western United States photographed from Apollo 9 spacecraft. Parts of Nevada, California, Arizona, and Utah are visible. Note the Colorado River and Lake Mead (NASA).

Earth photographed from Apollo 13 spacecraft during its journey home. Most landmasses are covered by clouds. The visible landmass includes the southwestern United States and northwestern Mexico. Note the Peninsula of Baja California (NASA).

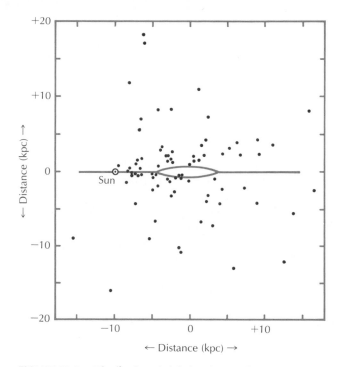

FIGURE 18-1.   Distribution of globular clusters about our galaxy. Distances are in kiloparsecs. The solid lines outline schematically the galactic disc and the central condensation. The positions of the clusters are projected onto a plane at right angles to the galactic plane. *(J. H. Oort, in Galactic Structure, edited by A. Blaauw and M. Schmidt, Chicago: The University of Chicago Press, 1965.)*

galactic halo. Since globular clusters are relatively bright and large (a typical cluster diameter is 10 arcmin), we should have a fairly complete list of those not obscured by the dust of the galactic disc. Current estimates of the grand total in existence in the galaxy run in the neighborhood of 150. The number of individual stars in a cluster varies from some 10^3 to over 10^6. Figure 18-1 shows the spatial distribution of globular clusters projected onto a "vertical" plane through the sun and the galactic center, perpendicular to the galactic plane.

Cluster Motions.   Estimates of the three-dimensional motion of individual clusters about the galactic center have been made, using the method by which the orbits of stars and interstellar clouds in the disc, and the existence and location of spiral arms, were determined. It was found that globular clusters move in elliptical orbits about the galactic center.

When we discussed radial-velocity measurements for stars in the solar neighborhood, we pointed out that these values are relatively small, typically of the order of 5 or 10 km/sec, since they give only relative velocity of the stars *with respect to the sun*. On the other hand, the rotation speed of the sun with respect to the galactic center is of the order of 250 km/sec. Being outside the disc, globular clusters do not take part in its rotation, although globular clusters execute their own rotational motions. When we measure the radial velocity of a globular cluster, then, we are actually measuring a component of the revolution of both the sun and the cluster *with respect to the galactic center*. Typical values are of the order of 100 km/sec.

There is no significant amount of interstellar gas or dust within globular clusters. This may be either a consequence of the process by which they were originally formed, or the result of successive losses of interstellar material as the cluster moved in its orbit through the galactic plane. At any rate, the material from which stars are formed is no longer available to globular clusters, and we conclude that they must have stopped star production at some time in the past.

Halo Stars.   It should come as no surprise that, when careful investigations were made of single stars in our galaxy with exceptionally high radial velocities of up to several hundred kilometers per second, these objects were found to move outside the disc. They have their own individual orbits about the galactic center and define yet another group of stars, the **halo stars**. Aside from their distribution outside the galactic disc, we know that halo stars are typically metal-poor, a fact which relates them to the stars in globular clusters.

Our galaxy is thus made up of two basic structures: the *disc* with its old and young stars and open clusters, including a large reservoir of gas and dust, and the *halo* with its globular clusters and individual halo stars, moving in splendid isolation through the void.

18.2   THE H-R DIAGRAM FOR STARS IN THE HALO

When we reviewed the properties of the inhabitants of the galactic disc and, in particular, their ages in Section 17.3, the fundamental results were obtained by combining the observed structure of their H-R diagrams with our theoretical knowledge of stellar evolution. The same method will help us to understand the history of the halo and its population.

The H-R Diagram of Globular Clusters (Revisited).   Since the distance between stars in globular clusters is so much smaller than the distance of the cluster from us, we do not need the former to construct an H-R diagram. In Section 11.4 and Fig. 11-8 (see page 177) we saw that the low-mass stars in globular clusters define a *main sequence*; they all must be in the stable phase of hydrogen core-burning. This main sequence is terminated at a usually reasonably well-defined *turn-off point*; that is, the great majority of stars with temperatures greater than the temperature at this turn-off point have left the main sequence and now form a continuous transition through the *subgiant branch* to the tip of the rather narrow *giant branch*. Here are found the most luminous stars in the clusters, some reaching 10^4 times the solar brightness. From the tip of the giant branch, downward and to the left, stretches the *horizontal branch* with its blue stars, clearly absent from the open-cluster H-R diagrams. Finally, there are a few blue stars whose position in the H-R diagram is approximately on the extension of the main sequence to higher temperatures beyond the turn-off point. The origin of these cluster members, the *blue stragglers*, is at present not completely clear.

There is no question as to the qualitative explanation of these features: globular clusters are very *old* structures in which star formation has long since terminated. The stars at the turn-off point of the main sequence are the most massive stars in the globular cluster still engaged in hydrogen core-burning, and all more massive stars have already completed this phase of hydrogen burning. The time spent on the main sequence by stars that are now at the turn-off point must then be approximately equal to the age of the globular cluster. From such an analysis we find that typical globular clusters have ages in excess of several billion years. Comparison with the ages quoted in Fig. 17-9 for open clusters shows that globular clusters are older than practically all open clusters.

It now follows immediately that *all* stars with masses above a certain limit must be beyond the main-sequence phase of their development; that is, they have started to burn helium or, at least, are burning hydrogen outside the core proper. We expect many more stars in the giant region of the globular-cluster diagram than was the case with open clusters.

Their core hydrogen depleted, the globular-cluster stars move up on the red-giant branch, burning hydrogen in the shell, until they reach the tip of this branch and, at the same time, maximum luminosity. Here, the triple-alpha processes are suddenly ignited in a helium flash, probably in a rather catastrophic fashion. Afterward, the stars burn helium in the core and find themselves on the horizontal branch, to the left if they are less massive, to the right if they are more massive. In a sense, the stars in this phase define another zero-age line, the **zero-age horizontal branch**, in principle very similar to the zero-age main sequence of the hydrogen-core-burning phase. As core helium slowly is depleted, the stars move upward (with higher luminosity) in the H-R diagram, presumably undergoing all the instabilities and other complications mentioned in Section 12.5. When the core helium is finally exhausted, contraction toward the white-dwarf stage begins, at least for stars of small mass.

The late stages of the evolution of globular-cluster stars are very similar to those of open-cluster stars. The H-R diagrams for the two types of stars look so different because of the uniformly great age of globular-cluster stars. In most open clusters there are simply not enough low-mass individuals old enough to have reached the helium-burning stage; consequently, they do not form anything like a "horizontal branch."

In trying to establish H-R diagrams for the general star population of the halo, we run into the same difficulty we had with the disc population: in most cases we cannot tell the distance of a star for certain. Nevertheless, indications are that the general star population follows a pattern comparable to that of the globular clusters. The inference is that the individual halo stars must be about the same age as cluster stars.

18.3 POPULATION II STARS AND THE HISTORY OF THE GALAXY

Population II Stars. Generally speaking, the stars comprising globular clusters are *metal-deficient* by comparison with the sun and the other stars of the galactic disc, and hence are part of what we have called **Population II**. In extreme cases, the metal deficiency is quite significant; there we find less than 1% of the solar value for the total fraction of metal atoms (itself less than 1% of the total mass). This type of star makes up the **extreme Population II**. In other globular clusters the metal abundance is somewhat higher, reaching about 10% of the solar value. At the same time the helium abundance is close to 30% in weight or 10% in number of atoms, the rest being hydrogen.

The **ages** of all globular clusters, as determined by the method explained above, are between 8×10^9 and 15×10^9 years. Of course, the individual figures are uncertain since, for instance, the turn-off point on the main sequence is never quite well defined. This may lead to ages that are incorrect by as much as a factor of 1.5. Thus, at present we really have only a slight hint that the older globular clusters are the ones with the lowest metal abundances.

Birth of Our Galaxy.   We are now faced with two interesting facts concerning the population of our galaxy: first, metal abundances vary through an almost continuous range from very low in extreme Population II clusters through intermediate values in both the halo and disc populations to their extreme high in very young galactic clusters. Second, there are in the disc open clusters that are not much younger than some of the globular clusters and have high metal abundances.

Halo Collapse.   These data form the basis for an explanation—probably more speculation than theory—of the evolution of our galaxy. It appears that some 12 to 15 billion years ago a gas ball containing all the material in and about our galaxy separated itself from the rest of the universe. It probably reacted to gravitational contraction in the same way a protostar does in emerging from its surrounding cloud. But on the scale of a whole galaxy, with its 10^{11} or so solar masses, something seems to have happened that does not occur when the mass involved is only about one solar mass: the gas ball collapsed into a disc, and only a fraction of the material remained in the space taken up by the original ball. This **halo collapse** signaled the birth of our galaxy. Out of the material left in what now is the halo, the globular clusters and single halo stars were formed: at almost the same time, the oldest galactic clusters and disc stars emerged. The halo was rapidly depleted of any material that could serve for further star formation, whereas this formation process continues in the disc and, in particular, in the spiral arms.

We should not hide the fact that even this rather general explanation is not accepted universally. For instance, it has been argued that the original collapse into the disc had to be much more violent than proposed above, and that in the process the material which today makes up the globular clusters was *ejected* from the center of the gas ball. The most serious complication concerns element abundances: the original galactic material must have been pretty much free of heavy elements, as is corroborated by the metal deficiencies of the extreme Population II stars. But heavy nuclei were formed almost immediately, so that when the galactic ball collapsed into the disc, most of the abundances we find now were established. The problem is in explaining how they were established. We can at present only speculate that some very powerful nuclear furnaces were present at the time of collapse, most likely in the center of the galaxy.

A summary of the presently available data, in terms of solar metal content, is given in Fig. 18-2 in schematic form. We see that globular clusters such as M2 and

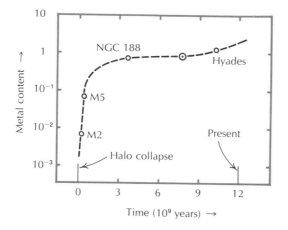

FIGURE 18-2.   Metal content in solar units for some selected globular and open clusters, as a function of age. Note the significant difference in metal content between globular clusters (M2, M5), on one hand, and open clusters (NGC 188, Hyades), on the other. It is assumed that the halo collapse occurred about 12 billion years ago. *(A. Sandage, in Galaxies and the Universe, edited by L. Woltjer, New York: Columbia University Press, 1968.)*

M5 date back to the time of collapse of the halo into the disc; note that the observed metal contents of such globular clusters vary approximately by a factor of 10. Then, only a few billion years later, galactic clusters such as NGC 188 and M67 were formed; their metal contents differ little from that of the sun and the even younger stars in the Hyades.

In Fig. 18-3 we have drawn a sequence of schematic pictures that summarize the various steps that may have led to the formation of our galaxy; the details suffer from many oversimplifications. In addition we must admit that some of the depicted steps may have occurred in different succession and that they are based more on speculation than on undisputed facts.

18.4   THE GALACTIC NUCLEUS

The innermost portion of our galaxy, measuring some 1 to 1.5 kpc in diameter and called the **galactic nucleus**, comprises a variety of structures, some of which have been mapped only in the last few years. It has also become increasingly clear that these structures are crucial to an understanding of the galaxy as a whole. Hard data are at present still rather sketchy and in some areas simply missing, but what has emerged and been interpreted in analogy to other systems is the following: in the nucleus is a huge accumulation of stars with a somewhat flattened distribution in space, paralleling the geometry of the galactic disc, with an additional **central condensation**, that is, a small area of still greater star density. The chemical composition of these latter stars presumably corresponds to that of Population II stars.

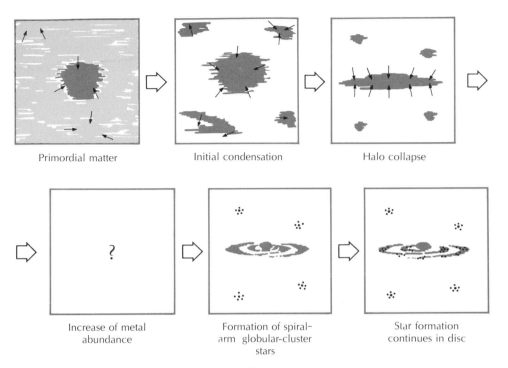

Primordial matter   Initial condensation   Halo collapse

Increase of metal abundance   Formation of spiral-arm globular-cluster stars   Star formation continues in disc

FIGURE 18-3.   Schematic view of the formation of the galaxy.

Then, the central condensation must date from the initial collapse of the galactic material into the disc. The nucleus contains little gas or dust of the type found in the spiral arms, so that star formation in the usual sense probably does not take place there.

The material in these very central parts of the galaxy rotates in the manner of a rigid body, with speed proportional to distance from the center. In addition there seem to be a general **expansion** and an organized *circulation of gas* centered in the nucleus. It also appears that the spiral arms of the galaxy extend to the very boundary of the nucleus. Finally, in the very center of our galaxy, sources that emit X-rays and even γ-rays, as well as sources responsible for the emission of large quantities of far-infrared radiation, have recently been observed. Their relation to the galactic nucleus is at present unknown, but violent activity and occasional explosions are rather common phenomena within galactic nuclei.

18.5   THE MAGNETIC FIELD OF THE GALAXY AND THE COSMIC-RAY FLUX

One of the ways in which halo and disc parts of our galaxy interact is in maintaining an overall gravitational field. There is, though, another structure that they hold in common, the galactic **magnetic field**.

Magnetic fields are quite difficult to observe; this is especially true for the galactic variety, which is usually very weak, of the order of 300,000 times weaker than the solar field. Such a field is observable only because interstellar dust grains have a tendency to align themselves in the field, thus altering the arrival pattern of photons moving through the dust clouds. The photons are *polarized*, that is, given a directional coherence; process and effect are much like those exhibited by polarized sunglasses.

The Magnetic Field in the Disc.   At any rate, we know there is a magnetic field present in our own spiral arm, and it appears to follow closely the contour of the arm. We must then conclude that the spiral distribution of matter in the disc is accompanied by a parallel spiral distribution of magnetic-field lines. Which came first, the matter or the field? We suspect that the magnetic field somehow helps to establish and maintain the spiral structure. Its strength at present is about 10^{-5} gauss or less.

The Field in the Halo.   There is evidence of the existence of **cosmic rays** throughout our galaxy. These are particles of extremely high energy, both electrons and nuclei, from protons up to nuclei of the heaviest known elements. Some cosmic rays undoubtedly are produced right now by means available even to the sun during times of increased activity. Others originate in supernova explosions, and possibly in pulsars. At any rate, theoretical studies imply a spatial density that could hardly be maintained if cosmic rays were free to leave the galaxy at any time. In some way or another, they appear to be stored in and about the galaxy, and the obvious means for such **storage** is a magnetic field. As we have pointed out on several occasions, charged particles cannot move freely in a magnetic field; in fact, their motion is mostly restricted to directions along the magnetic-field lines. If the field lines are closed about the galaxy, they are essentially trapped, and can only occasionally escape into intergalactic space. If it is a galactic magnetic field that traps the cosmic rays, then it must have an overall structure embracing the galaxy as a whole, halo as well as disc. The same arguments apply to the *electron* component of the cosmic rays, which is present both in the disc and the halo.

   The relation between the magnetic field observed in the disc and that in the halo is not known in detail. However, it is clear that these fields are not separate entities, if only for the reason that the material in which the field lines of both fields are anchored is concentrated in the disc. Thus, it is generally concluded that the magnetic-field structure of the galaxy is a property of that system as a whole.

QUESTIONS FOR DISCUSSION

1.   Review the differences between the visual impressions of open clusters and globular clusters.

2.   Describe the motion characteristics, such as orbits, of globular clusters.

3.   What may be the reason for the absence of interstellar gas in globular clusters? Is it likely that some as yet unobserved globular clusters contain interstellar gas? Why?

4.   Describe the visual impression of the sky an observer would have from a planet bound to an individual halo star.

5. Describe the visual impression of the sky an observer would have from a planet bound to a star at the edge of a globular cluster. From close to the center of a globular cluster.

6. Why does the existence of the "blue stragglers" in globular clusters present a puzzling problem? Try to suggest a solution.

7. Where on the horizontal branch are the more massive stars? The less massive stars? Contrast your answer to the situation on the main sequence during hydrogen core-burning.

8. What are the arguments for the existence of a magnetic field in the halo region?

EXERCISES

1. Look up the globular clusters in Tables H-13 and H-14 and position them on the star charts in Appendix G.

2. How is the distance of a globular cluster determined?

3. What is the average distance of globular clusters? How does this compare with the distance of known open clusters? What influences the two figures?

4. What is the galactic halo?

5. What is the linear diameter of a globular cluster if its angular diameter is 10 arcmin and its distance 10 kpc?

6. Contrast the radial velocities of globular clusters and open clusters. What is the reason for the difference?

7. Estimate the distances of the closest and most distant globular clusters from Fig. 18-1. Why are your estimates lower limits?

8. What is the main consequence of the absence of interstellar gas in globular clusters?

9. How much fainter than the faintest star visible to the naked eye would the sun be at the distance of a "typical" globular cluster (10 kpc)?

10. The galactic halo is populated by single stars as well as clusters. How does one pick out the halo stars from among the myriads of faint stars?

11. Somebody claimed to have found a halo star with the coordinates $\alpha = 18^h30^m$, $\delta = 30°02'$. What is your comment? Why?

12. Contrast the age-determination procedures for open clusters (Chapter 17) and for globular clusters.

13. Do you have to know the distance of a globular cluster in order to estimate its age? Why?

14. Compare the luminosities of the brightest stars in the Pleiades and the brightest stars in M3. How do these stars differ otherwise?

15. Determine the turn-off point for stars on the main sequence of M3 (Fig. 11-8), and check the quoted age of this cluster with the aid of the stellar-evolution times given in Chapter 12.

16. Why are no K or M stars entered on the main sequence in Fig. 11-8?

17. What kind of nuclear-energy source do stars on the subgiant branch of the H-R diagram of globular clusters have?

18. Figure 18-2 includes the old open cluster NGC 188. Draw an H-R diagram for this cluster from the age information given, and contrast it to the diagrams for M3 and the Pleiades.

19. Why do the H-R diagrams of globular clusters show so many stars in the giant branch?

20. What is the nuclear-energy source of stars on the horizontal branch of the H-R diagram for globular clusters?

21. Why did we enter the approximate location of the horizontal branch in the schematic diagram for planetary nebulae (Fig. 13-5)?

22. How different are the positions of a star in the H-R diagram immediately before and immediately after the helium flash?

23. What are the chemical-abundance characteristics of Population II stars?

24. Which star types belong to Population II?

25. What are the differences in chemical composition among globular-cluster stars?

26. What are typical ages for globular clusters? Contrast these with open-cluster ages.

27. Does the chemical composition of a globular cluster depend on its age? Explain.

28. What do astronomers usually consider the "moment" of birth of our galaxy? How long ago was it born?

29. How was the material distributed which later made up our galaxy?

30. What is the main difference between the oldest stars formed in the galactic disc and the stars in globular clusters? What does this imply as to the origin of the elements?

31. To what general population do stars in the nucleus of the galaxy belong?

32. You are located on a planet bound to a star close to the galactic nucleus. What is the color of most of the stars you can see with the naked eye? Why?

33. How do we know that there is a magnetic field aligned with the galactic disc structures?

34. What are cosmic rays?

35. Why are more cosmic rays observed in our galaxy than one would expect on the basis of production estimates of their sources?

FURTHER READING

Galactic Structure, edited by A. Blaauw and M. Schmidt, Chicago: The University of Chicago Press, 1965.

Rossi, B., *Cosmic Rays,* New York: McGraw-Hill Book Company, 1964.

19 the local group of galaxies

One of the greatest discoveries of our times was the realization that the "nebula" M31 in the constellation Andromeda is an immense collection of stars, very similar to our own galaxy. This discovery was made possible to a significant degree by the construction of the first really large telescope—the 100-inch telescope on Mount Wilson in California—which allowed the resolution of systems we now recognize as extragalactic, that is, outside our own galaxy, into single stars.

If there are other systems as large as our own galaxy, which stretches such vast distances that it takes light tens of thousands of years to cross from one end to the other, then the whole universe must be many times larger. Man becomes still smaller, even more of an accidental by-product on one insignificant planet in the household of one very common star out of the billions that make up our galaxy. And even this galaxy is only one of a seemingly innumerable multitude.

This universe of ours is, for one reason or another, constructed in such a way that the overwhelming emotional response it evokes in the human being is one of complete isolation. That this response is indeed justified will be clear when in this chapter we enumerate our closest "neighbors," all millions of light-years away.

19.1 THE ANDROMEDA SYSTEM

The **Andromeda system**, dimly visible to the naked eye in the northern hemisphere, is alternatively labeled **M31**, that is, entry No. 31 in Messier's catalogue of "nebulae," or NGC 224, entry 224 in the *New General Catalogue*. It is a galaxy like our own, and the nearest one of this basic type to us. Indeed, all the features we discussed in connection with our own galaxy show up in M31. In fact, M31 served as a guide in the development of data concerning our galaxy, data that were hidden from us as the observers within.

Spiral Structure. Figure 19-1 is an overall view of the Andromeda system. Immediately obvious is the *spiral structure*, the arms that wind all the way around the central portions. The inner structure of these arms is precisely as we visualize our own spiral arm, portions of which we see in the Milky Way: irregular accumulations of stars, interspersed with clouds of absorbing matter, and (from a distance) a preponderance of young, hot stars. The sharp dark edge just below the center portion of M31 is due to a cloud of cold interstellar material in a spiral arm between us and the galactic center. A detailed view of one of the spiral arms is shown in Fig. 19-2. The similarity to Fig. 16-3, showing a portion of the Milky Way, is obvious. An H-R diagram for the

FIGURE 19-1. Overview of the Andromeda system photographed with the 48-inch Schmidt telescope. Note the spiral arms, outlined by open clusters and dark interstellar material, and the bright central condensation. The two dwarf-elliptical galaxies NGC 205 and NGC 221 are satellites of the Andromeda system. *(Hale Observatories.)*

FIGURE 19-2. **High-resolution photograph of the outer spiral arm of M31 (upper left in Fig. 19-1), showing resolution into stars.** *(Hale Observatories.)*

stars in the spiral arms shows the typical features of the extreme Population I, with the high metal abundances we are familiar with in our own system.

The Disc. The center portion, like our own, has a much greater star density than the outlying spiral arms. And, like those in our own nucleus, these central stars show the characteristics of Population II; that is, they are old stars with no newcomers, and have low metal content. Not visible in the photograph is a strong **condensation** in the very center, just within the resolving power of the largest telescopes. There are indications of a disc population of stars that we cannot resolve individually, but whose integrated light corresponds very closely to what we would expect from a comparison with our own system: a large number of solar-type and cooler stars.

In the photograph, the shape of the disc seems to be elliptic. However, we do not know the inclination of the galactic plane of M31 with respect to our own position, so the disc of the Andromeda system may in reality be circular. If it were, then we would be observing it almost edge-on; it would be inclined about 15° to the line of sight.

Rotation. This angle is of importance in the interpretation of the **rotation curve** shown in Fig. 19-3, which gives the rotational velocities of objects in M31 as a function of distance from the galactic center. The dashed portion of the curve replaces a rather complex and not well-understood behavior in the very center. The velocities given are relative to the center, which itself has a velocity of about 300 km/sec toward us. We conclude that M31 and our system are approaching each other at this speed. This does not mean that our two systems are on a collison course, since radial-velocity measurements give only the line-of-sight component of an actual three-dimensional velocity. Instead, this radial velocity is an indication of the internal motions of the so-called **local group**, comprising our nearest neighboring galaxies.

The velocities given in Fig. 19-3 are very similar to those deduced for our own galaxy. Based on these velocities, we can estimate the **mass** of the Andromeda system. The calculation is afflicted with some uncertainty, mostly because we can make only an educated guess as to the inclination of the disc, and so as to the rotational orbits. The outcome is some 10^{11} $M_\odot$, again practically the same as deduced for our own system.

Halo. In the regions of M31 that correspond to our **halo**, we find **globular clusters.** The two brightest objects near M31 are small galaxies in their own right. The globular-cluster stars in M31 are similar to our Population II stars and presumably the system has much the same halo structure as our own, complete with high-energy electrons and a general magnetic field.

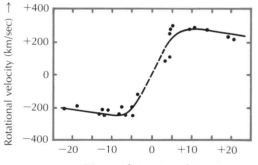

FIGURE 19-3. Rotational velocity as a function of distance from the center in M31. The circles represent individual measurements. The rotational behavior of the center portion is fairly complex in its details and left out of the diagram. The velocity values are relative to the center. The galaxy as a whole has a velocity of about 300 km/sec toward us. (V. C. Rubin and W. K. Ford, "The Spiral Structure of Our Galaxy," in *International Astronomical Union Symposium, no. 38,* edited by W. Becker and G. Contopoulos, Dordrecht: D. Reidel Publishing Company, 1970.)

Overall Dimension. The central portion of the Andromeda system has an angular size of some 30 arcmin, about the size of the solar disc or the full moon. To translate this into a linear size, we need to determine its distance. This has been accomplished by comparing presumably identical types of stars in M31 and our system, primarily cepheids, with due recognition given the dependence of internal properties (period versus luminosity) on chemical composition (Population I versus Population II). The most reliable data give a distance of 600 kpc or about 2 million light-years. The size of the disc is then some 20 kpc, depending on what one considers as the "edge"; the quoted value refers to the perimeter defined by the brighter spiral arms.

All these data taken together indicate that M31 and our own system are strikingly alike in all significant properties, such as structure, chemical composition of primary parts, and age. This is hardly a coincidence; as we shall see in Section 20.1, our system and M31 are examples of one of the most common forms of star systems in the universe: spiral galaxies.

19.2 THE MAGELLANIC CLOUDS

In the southern hemisphere, the naked eye can easily make out two more extra-galactic systems, the **Large Magellanic Cloud**, with an apparent angular diameter about four times that of the Andromeda system, and the **Small Magellanic Cloud**, about twice the size of the Andromeda system. Since they are not clouds by any stretch of the imagination, we prefer to call them **Large** and **Small Magellanic systems**, although this contradicts common astronomical practice. The telescopic photograph of the Large Magellanic system, Fig. 19-4, reveals it to be an isolated extragalactic star system, although its internal structure is quite different from that of M31 or our own galaxy.

The two Magellanic systems are indeed galaxies in their own right, and not somewhat misplaced portions of our own system, such as the remains of an otherwise dissolved spiral arm. This is verified simply by a distance determination, which shows the two systems to be about 60 kpc away from us. Their angular sizes then translate into linear diameters of 9 and 2.5 kpc for the large and small systems, respectively.

Internal Structure. Figure 19-4 shows no structure comparable to the spiral arms of our galaxy, not even the rotational symmetry of our disc. The same is true for the Small Magellanic system. Instead, they give the impression of more or less randomly joined masses of stars and gas. They are therefore called galaxies of **irregular type** (to be precise, of type I or **IrrI**). In reality, though, the Magellanic systems are much more regular than the figures suggest. There is, for example, a rather regular rotational structure to the main bulk of the objects. And indeed, if photographs are taken with red-sensitive plates, which emphasize the many cooler stars rather than the O-and-B associations most prominent in Fig. 19-4, the Magellanic systems appear to occupy flattened, elliptical, and thus rather regularly shaped spaces. Note, however, that there is no noticeable central condensation in either system.

FIGURE 19-4. The Large Magellanic Cloud. Compare its irregular outline with the spiral structure of M31 as seen in Fig. 19-1. *(Lick Observatory.)*

From the existence of so many O-and-B associations in both Magellanic systems, we conclude that a significant portion of their material is still in the form of gas and dust, and that the formation of new stars is proceeding vigorously at this time. This is borne out by H-R diagrams for the systems, which correspond closely to Population I diagrams for our own galaxy, with a suspected strong admixture of stars of the type present in our disc. The chemical composition of these stars, as expected, corresponds to the metal-rich and presumably young variety. The Large Magellanic system appears to be surrounded by a cloud of neutral hydrogen gas.

Relative Motions. Whereas M31 moved toward us with a line-of-sight velocity of about 300 km/sec, the Large and the Small Magellanic systems move away with radial velocities of about 300 and 170 km/sec, respectively. These motions, if they could be translated into three dimensions, would probably define a rather complex system of orbits about some common center, the relative orbits of a multiple system. Because the Magellanic systems are so much smaller than our galaxy and so very close (in comparison with M31), we suspect that they are **satellites** of our own galaxy, that is, gravitationally bound to its center.

FIGURE 19-5. High-resolution photograph (200-inch telescope) of the companion NGC 205 of the Andromeda galaxy. Note the resolution into individual stars, the symmetrical outline of this dwarf elliptical galaxy, and the strong concentration of stars toward the center. *(Hale Observatories.)*

19.3 THE REMAINING MEMBERS OF THE LOCAL GROUP

Figure 19-1, which gives an overview of the Andromeda system, shows two extragalactic systems which are neither globular clusters (they clearly have the wrong symmetry and are too large and too far away from M31) nor nebulae proper, that is, gas masses (they can be resolved into individual stars). They are essentially at the same distance as M31, as has been shown by the standard methods. We conclude that they are satellites of M31; their designations are M32 or NGC 221 for the one closer to Andromeda's center, and NGC 205 for the one farther out. Figure 19-5 is an enlarged view of NGC 205.

NGC 205 and NGC 221 are examples of an exceedingly common type of galaxy, the **elliptical** or, in their case, **dwarf elliptical** galaxy. Their linear diameters are about 1 kpc and their combined mass is much less than the mass of either our system or M31. Elliptical galaxies are highly symmetric. From spectroscopic studies we infer that their stars are of Population II, and that either they have little or no interstellar gas left, or the remaining gas is highly concentrated toward the center.

One of the most important observations in this context is that the Population II stars of *all* members of our local group point to a fairly uniform age of about 12×10^9 years for the parent clusters.

What other galaxies are "nearby"? For one, there is another spiral galaxy, called **M33** or NGC 598, shown in Fig. 19-6. Although it is quite similar to M31 or our own system, with the well-developed spiral arms, a disc, globular clusters in the halo, and the like, there are also subtle differences. One, quite obvious from the photograph, is the much less developed central condensation. What corresponds to our own galactic nucleus is, in M33, almost starlike, unresolvable with our largest telescopes and indeed very small. In addition, the transition from Population I stars plus disc population in the outlying regions, to Population II stars in the center, is much less drastic, for reasons we do not quite understand at present.

M33 is in the constellation Triangulum at about the same distance as the Andromeda system, but is only about one-third its size. The total mass is probably smaller too, perhaps by a factor of 10, and so would be about the same as the mass of the Large Magellanic system.

Evidence is even now accumulating that our local group has two other massive members, called Maffei 1 and Maffei 2. Both galaxies are in the constellation Perseus in an area of the sky that is heavily obscured by dust in the plane of our galaxy, and the two objects are therefore difficult to identify as full-fledged galaxies.

This completes the list of our relatively large galactic neighbors. However, there are a number of small systems nearby, both of the dwarf elliptical type and of type Irrl. Among the former are the small galaxies in the constellations Sculptor and Fornax, with distances of the order of 100 to 300 kpc. Also of the dwarf elliptical type are the two systems in Leo, about 500 kpc from us, with diameters of about 1 kpc, comparable to the two satellites of M31. Their total masses are about 1% of the mass of our system or of M31, and their radial velocities vary both in magnitude and in direction (in some cases the motion is toward us; in others away from us).

Among the irregular systems are NGC 6822 in the constellation Sagittarius and IC 1613 in the constellation Cetus. They are both some 500 kpc away, and are of a linear extent of 1 or 2 kpc. All told, there are about 20 extragalactic systems within about 1 megaparsec (Mpc) of us. Aside from a few systems that may be hidden behind the Milky Way, we have a fairly complete roster of this local group. A break in the density of systems seems to occur at a distance of about 1 Mpc; the number of galaxies per unit volume of space decreases rather suddenly there. We thus come to the conclusion that our galaxy, M31, M33, and the smaller systems form a **cluster of galaxies**, tied together, at least at present, by their mutual gravitational attraction, and moving along complicated orbits dictated by the simultaneous interaction of all members. We shall see in the next chapter that such associations, and much larger ones, are common in the distribution of galaxies through space.

QUESTIONS FOR DISCUSSION

1. The existence of spiral arms in M31 is obvious upon inspection of a photograph; its rotation is easily measured, at least, in principle. Discuss the difficulties involved in identifying similar features in our galaxy.

FIGURE 19-6. The spiral galaxy M33 in the constellation Triangulum. Note the well-defined spiral arms, complete with star clusters and interstellar material, and the central condensation, which is quite small compared to that of the Andromeda system of Fig. 19-1. *(Hale Observatories.)*

2. We have quoted only radial velocities for the members of the local group. Why are we unable to determine three-dimensional velocities?

3. What are some of the structural differences between the Magellanic systems and our own?

4. Why are we certain that star formation is occurring at present in the Magellanic systems?

5. Why is it unlikely that elliptical galaxies such as NGC 205 are active in star formation?

6. Why is the status of Maffei 1 and Maffei 2 as member galaxies of the local group difficult to ascertain?

EXERCISES

1. How was the Andromeda system identified as a galaxy? Approximately in what year did this take place?

2. Assume that the scale of the universe is such that the Andromeda system has the apparent size of a quarter. At what distance from it would our own galaxy be?

3. Review the main structural features of M31 and their counterparts in our galaxy.

4. What type of star is mostly responsible for the visual impression of M31 in Fig. 19-1?

5. In Fig. 19-3 the central portion of the rotation curve of M31 is replaced by the dashed line; in reality, complex irregularities are observed. Which region of the system does this portion cover (see Fig. 19-1)? Identify a corresponding region in our own galaxy (Fig. 17-8).

6. Give and justify an approximate date when astronomers will be able to determine three-dimensional velocities for the members of the local group, assuming present technology.

7. Locate the members of the local group (Table H-17) in the star charts in Appendix G.

8. M31 approaches our galaxy with a speed of about 300 km/sec. What would the physical conditions have to be for a collision or a near-collision? When would it happen?

9. Assume that the stars of a galaxy such as M31 or our own system were all visible to the naked eye, and were distributed uniformly over the celestial sphere. How many would there be in an area corresponding to the apparent size of the full moon?

10. Check the figures given in the text for the linear size of M31 and the two Magellanic systems with the aid of their angular sizes and their distances.

11. What name do astronomers usually use for the two Magellanic systems? How do you think this name came about?

12. Compare the sizes of the Magellanic systems and the size of our own system. Find their distance and make a drawing of the three systems, approximately to scale.

13. What principal structural detail is missing in galaxies of the type Irr1 as compared with our galaxy and the Andromeda system?

14. How long does light emitted in the Andromeda system and in the Magellanic systems travel before it reaches us? What was the state of our earth when the light we see now was emitted?

15. How do the satellite galaxies of the Andromeda system differ from our own satellite galaxies?

16. What are the major differences between M31 and M33?

17. If the roster of galaxies in the local group (Table H-17) is typical of the universe, which types of galaxies appear to be most abundant?

EXPERIMENTS

1. Locate the Andromeda system with the naked eye or with a field glass. On an exceptionally clear night, you might even find M33. Contrast their apparent brightnesses.

2. Try to trace the more prominent spiral arms in M31 with the aid of Fig. 19-1.

3. Check the statement made in the text that the inclination of the disc of M31 to the line of sight is 15°, provided its outline is circular, by measuring Fig. 19-1 and comparing the result with the shadow cast by a circular disc held at the appropriate angle. What would be the inclination angle if the outline of M31 were really elliptical, and the lengths of the semimajor and semiminor were in the ratio 1.2 to 1? In the ratio 2 to 1?

FURTHER READING

Baade, W., *Evolution of Stars and Galaxies*, Cambridge, Mass.: Harvard University Press, 1963.

Shapley, H., *Galaxies* (rev. ed.), Cambridge, Mass.: Harvard University Press, 1961.

20 the general field of galaxies and its expansion

There are galaxies everywhere. We count some 20 in our immediate neighborhood, and every high-resolution photograph of unobscured areas of the sky, such as the sheets of the "Sky Atlas" prepared at the Hale Observatories reveals myriads of them, fading into the background brightness of the sky. Undoubtedly, photographs taken with still larger telescopes or from positions outside our atmosphere would show more of them.

Are there any standard types? Is our Milky Way with its spiral structure a typical galaxy? These are the questions we try to answer now. Then we shall discuss how these star systems are distributed and how they move in space. This will lead us to the phenomenon of universal expansion. And gradually we shall build up the knowledge needed to attack the most comprehensive problem in astronomy, the one that concerns our universe as a whole, in the last chapter of this text.

20.1 THE BASIC TYPES OF GALAXIES

We have seen in our own neighborhood, in our local group, two basic types of galaxies, aside from the irregulars: one is the very flat type with disc and spiral arms, of which both our system and M31 and M33 are examples; the other has no such detailed structures, but is rather uniformly elliptical in shape. If we now turn away from the local group and collect samples at greater distances, we find that our local experience serves us well.

Spiral Galaxies.   Innumerable spiral galaxies are visible to the large telescopes, each, of course, from a different angle with respect to its plane of symmetry. Figures 20-1 to 20-3 give three examples we view from a direction close to the axis of rotation. They are NGC 488, NGC 3031 or M81, and NGC 5457 or M101, respectively. In all cases, the main structures are the same: a central condensation surrounded by a disc with spiral arms in which an ample supply of interstellar material is located. Spectral analysis shows that the age distribution of the stars, too, is quite similar to that of our own system, in that the spiral arms contain a large number of young O-and-B associations, whereas the central condensation is mostly composed of old Population II giants. In addition, in the case of not-too-distant objects, globular clusters can be seen surrounding the disc, and other observations make persuasive arguments in favor of a halo structure similar to our own.

The differences among these systems concern mostly the size of the central condensation and how tightly the arms are wound around the nucleus. They are commonly classified as **(regular) spirals** of type a, b, or c (written **Sa**, **Sb**, or **Sc**).

FIGURE 20-1. The spiral galaxy NGC 488 (type Sa) seen along the rotational axis. Note the tightly wound spiral arms and the massive center condensation. *(Hale Observatories.)*

FIGURE 20-2. The great galaxy M81 (type Sb) in the constellation Ursa Major, seen along the rotational axis. Note the well-developed spiral arms and center condensation, similar to M31 (Fig. 19-1). *(Hale Observatories.)*

FIGURE 20-3. **Spiral galaxy M101 (type Sc) seen along the rotational axis. The appearance is similar to that of M33 (Fig. 19-6): long, trailing spiral arms and small center condensation.** *(Hale Observatories.)*

An Sa system would be one like NGC 488 in which the spirals are tightly wound around the central condensation; Sc would denote a small central condensation and an extended large system of spiral arms, like NGC 5457. Sb systems such as NGC 3031 are somewhere in between. Our own system and M31 qualify as Sb systems, while M33 is of type Sc.

If a spiral galaxy is seen edge-on, the spiral arms are, of course, not distinct. Nevertheless, their main feature, the clouds of interstellar absorbing material, is still clearly visible in the central plane of symmetry, as is evident from Figs. 20-4 and 20-5 which show, respectively, NGC 4594 or M104 and NGC 4565. The former, in the constellation Virgo, is one of the most often photographed galaxies. Both are presumably of type Sa or Sb, but the distinction is impossible to make in an edge-on view.

We should note at this point that there are certain differences in the sizes of spiral systems, indicating differences in the present—and possibly initial—amounts of material encompassed by the systems. The largest known spiral galaxies may be about 10 times the size of the smallest. This is not an impressive range; we shall compare this figure with one derived for elliptical systems presently.

FIGURE 20-4. M104 seen edge-on. Large center condensation, probably type Sa or Sb. The galactic disc is clearly marked by the dark absorption band. The ringlike feature in the lower right is an overexposed star image. *(Hale Observatories.)*

Not all spiral galaxies fit into the three subgroups: in fact, some have quite a different structure. They are somewhat less abundant, and it is at present not altogether clear how basic the difference really is. They are called **barred spirals**, and typical examples are shown in Figs. 20-6 (NGC 1398) and 20-7 (NGC 1300). Their main characteristic is the presence of only two spiral arms that extend from the nucleus at two diametrically opposite points. This clearly contrasts with the regular spirals, such as M31, in which several arms extend from various points around the perimeter of the nucleus. Again, in the barred spirals, we find that the arms are developed to different degrees. The classification of these systems includes a B for "barred," so we have the subgroup **SBa** in which the two spiral arms are very smooth, the intermediate subgroup **SBa,** and the subgroup **SBc** whose members show a small nucleus with wide, trailing spiral arms.

Elliptic Galaxies. The second major type of galaxy we encountered in the local group is the **elliptical galaxy**. In the local group (which we know more completely than any other) there is a significant number of them, mostly rather small objects. We suspect that most low-mass galaxies are elliptical, and that there may be a

FIGURE 20-5. NGC 4565 seen edge-on. This spiral galaxy has a somewhat smaller center condensation. The disc with the spiral arms is clearly visible. *(Lick Observatory.)*

FIGURE 20-6. The barred spiral NGC 1398 seen along the rotational axis. Note the tightly wound inner arms concentrated toward two points on opposite sides of the large center condensation. *(Hale Observatories.)*

FIGURE 20-7. The barred spiral NGC 1300 seen along the rotational axis. In this case, the spiral arms are much less tightly wound, the central condensation smaller. *(Hale Observatories.)*

smooth transition from these galaxies to the globular clusters; after all, NGC 205 and NGC 221 are not very different in size and mass from the largest globular clusters of M31 or our own Milky Way. Many more such dwarf elliptical galaxies are found farther out, although they soon become too dim to be made out against the background of the sky.

There are also **giant elliptical galaxies**; in fact, the largest and brightest galaxies known are ellipticals. Figure 20-8 shows M87 in the constellation Virgo. Note the many globular clusters visible near the galaxy. The mass of M87 is estimated to be about four times the mass of our own system. The range of masses of elliptical systems then stretches from several times our galactic mass at the high end to a few percent of it at the lower limit, close to the range of globular-cluster masses.

Elliptical galaxies are classified according to their ellipticity, that is, the ratio of their principal axes. This may vary from practically unity (the spherical case) to about 3 and it defines the numbers 0 through 7 placed after the class letter E: **E0**, **E1**, etc. Of couse, depending on the angle from which we view the galaxy, we may see a foreshortened image, and the observed ellipticities must be corrected by some statistical means to yield the true ones.

FIGURE 20-8. **The giant elliptical galaxy M87. Long-exposure photograph showing the symmetrical outline of the system. Also note the numerous globular clusters. The jet (see Fig. 21-1) is barely visible in this picture close to the lower edge at the center.** *(Lick Observatory.)*

Irregular Galaxies.   The last class of galaxies we know from our local group, the **IrrI galaxies**, is also well represented in the universe, although again they are generally small and thus of low brightness. This makes it difficult to determine their real abundance in space.

There are other galaxies which show rather chaotic internal organization and are therefore also called *irregular*, but of *type II*, or **IrrII**. The prototype is M82, shown in Fig. 20-9. The chaotic structure is probably due to some gigantic "explosion" in the nucleus; we shall discuss this type of galaxy later, in Section 21.1, in a more proper context.

20.2 THE TIME DEVELOPMENT OF GALAXIES

The question now arises as to a possible explanation for the existence of such a varied set of galactic forms. We have already commented on the fact that we can do

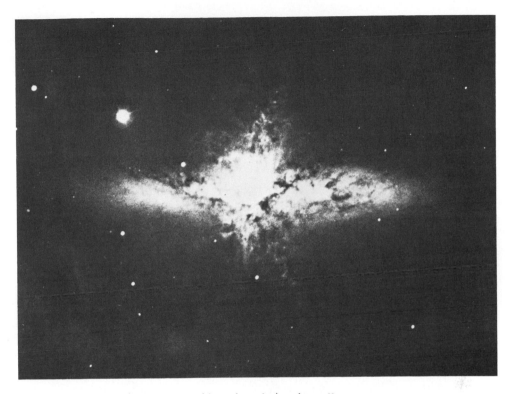

**FIGURE 20-9.   M82, the prototype of irregular galaxies of type II.
A gigantic ''explosion'' in the nucleus may have destroyed any regular, organized structures that had been there.** *(Hale Observatories.)*

little more than speculate at present as to why some spiral galaxies are barred and
others are ''regular.'' The suspicion is that the differentiation is tied to some basic
property of spiral galaxies—for instance, the angular momentum whose obvious
manifestation is the galactic rotation, or the general magnetic field, or both.

Similarly, there is as yet no consensus on the reason for the difference between
the properties of elliptical systems and those of the spiral classes, or on the differences among a, b, and c spirals. It is clear that the c-type spirals (together with the
IrrI-type galaxies) contain the largest percentage of interstellar material and young O
and B stars. In passing from subclass c to b to a, we observe a progressive depletion
of uncondensed material and an increasing percentage of old stars. At the same
time, the systems lose the wide spreading of the spiral arms, until in the a-type
spirals they are tightly wound about the nucleus. It is tempting to interpret the sequence a to b to c as an ''age'' sequence, with a referring to the oldest and c to the
youngest systems. However, there are very old stars in the centers of all these systems, even if their relative frequencies are not the same. In that sense, the ''oldest''
systems may simply have developed fastest, with the time at which formation began
being the same in all cases.

The elliptical systems, on the other hand, normally show no traces of interstellar material and should therefore have terminated any significant star-formation
activity. Indeed, elliptical systems show none of the characteristics of young star

FIGURE 20-10. The lenticular galaxy NGC 5866, a transitional form between spiral and elliptical galaxies (type S0). The spherical nucleus is surrounded by a flattened outer envelope. Note the uncondensed material that forms a ring around the nucleus. View is almost edge-on. *(Hale Observatories.)*

populations, and we therefore tentatively interpret them as an end product in the development of galaxies.

An Intermediate Group of Galaxies. It is now well established that the elliptical systems are more or less flattened, but in none of them is the ratio of the disc diameter to the thickness of the disc nearly as large as it is in the spirals, even if the most outlying spiral arms are not included. So if we propose that the spirals may some day lose their arms, we should be able to find some transitional group of galaxies which have already lost their spiral structure, but still retain the very flat discs, and some interstellar material.

Such a transitional group indeed exists and is called **lenticular (S0).** An example, the galaxy NGC 5866, is shown in Fig. 20-10. It has an extensive outer envelope, still quite flattened in outline, surrounding a spherical nucleus. Typical S0 galaxies contain some uncondensed material, often arranged in the form of a photon-absorbing ring between nucleus and outer envelope. It is clearly seen in Fig. 20-10.

20.3 DISTANCE DETERMINATIONS AND UNIVERSAL EXPANSION

The Distance Scale.   Before we can continue our discussion of galaxies in the universe, we must recapitulate the data on which we base our estimates of distances. We said in Section 9.1 that ultimately all distance determinations are based on direct measurements of parallax. This quantity makes it possible to calibrate H-R diagrams or, in the present context, to find the absolute magnitude of a given spectral type. In particular, we calibrated the cepheids and their period-luminosity relation (after one unfortunate error) and at that point were able to reach out of our own system to determine the distances of the local group of galaxies, and some even beyond.

In the same manner, we can measure distances that are quite a bit larger, out to the point where our telescopes are no longer able to resolve single stars or clearly identifiable features such as open or globular clusters. There are a sufficient number of galaxies of various types in the space encompassed by this limitation so that we can amass statistics, in the sense that allows us to make statements about "average" properties of galaxies. Of particular importance is the luminosity of the brightest galaxy in a cluster of galaxies similar to our own local group. By comparing the apparent brightness of such a galaxy with the true luminosity derived for members of its subclass on the basis of known distances, we can obtain a measure of its distance, precisely as we arrived at distances for single stars. At present we have distance estimates for objects up to about 10^3 Mpc from the sun. The limitation is strictly technological; beyond that distance even the brightest galaxies of the types discussed so far fade into the background of a photograph taken with the largest telescope and with the longest feasible exposure time.

Two items of importance should be recorded at this point: one is that apparently no significant changes are occurring in the distribution and structure of galaxies in that part of the universe available to at least a partial survey by our present telescopes. This result is of some interest, since the photons that reach us now from an object 300 Mpc away were emitted about 1 billion years ago; it takes the light that long to travel the distance from the galaxy to us. The second is that we have absolutely no indication of a change in the distribution or internal structure of galaxies at the boundary where our largest telescopes can detect them. However, there is evidence of such a change farther out, as we shall discuss in Section 21.4.

The Universal Redshift.   If surveys of internal parameters of galaxies via standard techniques do not bring any surprises, studies of wavelength-shift behavior as a function of distance do. In fact, the single most important discovery from the cosmological viewpoint is just this wavelength-shift–distance relation for extragalactic objects. It is the celebrated **expansion of the universe** phenomenon. Let us look at it carefully, a step at a time.

We first emphasize that there is an overlap among the regions of applicability of the various methods of determining distance. We stress this point in order to make it clear that there is now little doubt as to the accuracy of the established distance scale; accuracy means here, as usually, that our errors are within certain tolerable limits.

The wavelength shift refers to the displacement of some identifiable spectral feature, characteristic of an object, with respect to the position of the same feature in the laboratory. It is usually defined as a ratio

$$z = \frac{\lambda - \lambda_0}{\lambda_0}$$

where z is the *relative* shift, λ_0 is the wavelength of the spectral feature in the laboratory (rest system), and λ is the observed wavelength from the extragalactic source.

If the observed wavelength shift z is plotted as a function of a source parameter related to the distance, such as the apparent brightness of a well-defined type of galaxy, the result is the relationship shown in Fig. 20-11. The observational data (circles) are for the brightest members of clusters, out to a distance of approximately 10^3 Mpc, close to the current limit. There is no indication whatsoever that different types of galaxies behave according to different relationships. Note that all objects, except for relatively few nearby galaxies have redshifts ($\lambda > \lambda_0$); no blueshifts were recorded anywhere else, and no indication was ever found that the values depend on direction in space. We have at this point established the existence of a **universal redshift** for all extragalactic objects, with the amount of redshift being simply proportional to the distance.

The Redshift as Doppler Shift.   The next step must be the identification of a physical cause for the redshift. By now, some 40 years have elapsed since the universal redshift was firmly established, and in these years every conceivable explanation — including some wild ones — has been advanced, discussed back and forth, and discarded, with the exception of one: the redshifts are **Doppler shifts.**

Recall that in Section 5.3 we discussed the relation between the line-of-sight component of the velocity of an object relative to the earth, and the difference in wavelength of photons emitted by the object (λ) and recorded on earth (λ_0):

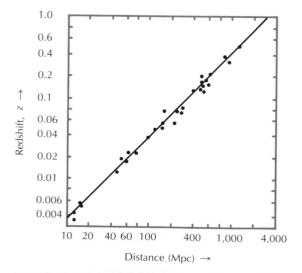

FIGURE 20-11.   Redshift of galaxies as a function of distance. *(A. Sandage, in Galaxies and the Universe, edited by L. Woltjer, New York: Columbia University Press, 1968.)*

$$z = \frac{\lambda - \lambda_0}{\lambda_0} = \frac{v}{c}$$

We noted there that a redshift (in which $\lambda > \lambda_0$) means the two bodies are moving apart, a blueshift (in which $\lambda < \lambda_0$) means source and observer are moving toward each other. The simplified relation given above holds for relative speeds that are much smaller than the speed of light. For the present discussion, this simplification is permissible.

Let us return to the universal redshift, now identified with a universal Doppler shift. In mathematical terms, the observed relationship can be rewritten as

$$z = \frac{Hd}{c}$$

where d is the distance of the extragalactic object from us, z and c are the relative wavelength shift and the speed of light, respectively, and H is the so-called **Hubble constant,** which is somewhere between 50 and 100 km/sec · Mpc, but probably closer to the value of 50 than 100 km/sec · Mpc. In other words, extragalactic objects move away from us with a speed that increases with increasing distance; the recession speed of an object at a distance of 10 Mpc is about 500 km/sec, at 100 Mpc about 5,000 km/sec, if we take for the Hubble constant the value of 50 km/sec · Mpc, and so on. Note that recession speeds in our local group are of the order of 100 km/sec or less, that is, below what one would expect as the orbital speeds of gravitationally interacting galaxies in close proximity. Indeed, the radial velocities of the members of the local group are typically a few hundred kilometers per second; some are directed toward us, some away from us; thus, some members of our local show blueshifts.

There is only one interpretation of this phenomenon: the universe, so far as we can see it, is undergoing a *universal expansion*, with the expansion speed proportional to the distance from us here in our solar system. At first glance, this statement seems contrary to all our hypotheses and appears to make a mockery of the bitter fight of Galileo and his disciples. In fact, this argument demands that astronomers find an explanation for the expansion such that *everybody* in the universe would see himself in the center of the expansion; this task is one of the crucial problems of cosmology. For the present, we return to the *observed* properties of our universe.

20.4 THE LARGE-SCALE DISTRIBUTION OF GALAXIES

Clusters of Galaxies. The local group of galaxies is more or less defined by the fact that its members are within a distance of approximately 1 Mpc from us. Beyond that distance there seems to be an abrupt decrease in the number of galaxies until, quite a bit further out, the "density of galaxies" increases again. Of these more distant galaxies, a large percentage are arranged in space in clusters similar to our own local group, bound together by mutual gravitational interaction. Many such **clusters of galaxies** are known and are immediately obvious in high-resolution surveys of the sky. This is particularly true for the giant clusters with hundreds of major members.

FIGURE 20-12.   The large cluster of galaxies in the constellation Coma Berenices at a distance of about 100 Mpc from us. Many galaxies of various types can be distinguished. *(Hale Observatories.)*

Among them are the clusters in the constellation Virgo (about 12 Mpc away) and Coma (100 Mpc from us). Figure 20-12 shows a portion of the Coma cluster. Many faint galaxies of all types can be distinguished. Figure 20-13 is an enlargement of the central portion of this cluster.

FIGURE 20-13. Portion of the Coma cluster, centered about the giant elliptical galaxy just right of and below the center of Fig. 20-12. Note, in particular, the double galaxy to the left of and below the giant elliptical in the center. Almost all images in the picture are of distant galaxies. *(Hale Observatories.)*

Coma Cluster.   The Coma cluster is one of the best studied and has provided us with an exciting puzzle: In the same manner as star clusters, clusters of galaxies require a certain minimum mass in order to stay together by means of their mutual gravitational interaction. From observation, it is now clear that the Coma cluster is in this sense "bound." On the other hand, our best estimates yield a total mass which is too small by a factor of about 10 to hold the cluster together, and it is at present simply not clear where a large "missing mass" could be hidden. Interstellar or intergalactic gas in such quantities should probably be observable, and it has been argued recently that maybe the cluster galaxies contain large numbers of black holes.

Among the many smaller groups is the so-called *Stephan's Quintet* consisting of five large galaxies: two ellipticals, two regular spirals, and one barred spiral, of which at least four are physically related (see Fig. 20-14). Of course, we may well be missing some smaller members. Often there are *bridges* detectable between some pairs of members; these consist either of many unresolved stars, or of luminous gas, or, probably, of both. Examples are the twin systems NGC 5432 and NGC 5435 (Fig. 20-15), and the group NGC 6027 of five galaxies (Fig. 20-16). In fact, gaseous envelopes around individual members, and around relatively close multiple systems,

FIGURE 20-14. Stephan's Quintet, a small cluster of galaxies, of which at least four are physically related. Some are joined by luminous bridges. *(Lick Observatory.)*

seem to be rather common. Recall, for instance, the observation in Section 19.2 that there seem to be significant amounts of hydrogen surrounding the Large Magellanic system. The bridges may then simply be localized condensations.

There does not seem to be any large-scale structuring of the galactic matter in the universe, aside from the "clumpiness" due to clustering and the **superclusters**, or groups of clusters, occasionally encountered. This is true throughout the parts of the universe we can reach with our largest telescopes and is one of the features that must also be accounted for by a successful theory of cosmology.

20.5 THE OTHER LARGE-SCALE COMPONENTS OF THE UNIVERSE

Intergalactic Gas. So far we have seen that the material of the immediately accessible portion of the universe is concentrated in clusters of galaxies and that each

FIGURE 20-15. **The twin system NGC 5432 and NGC 5435. Note the luminous connections between the spiral arms from one system to the other.** *(Lick Observatory.)*

galaxy in turn has a complex structure of stars and interstellar matter. What else is there in the universe? If we have interstellar gas, we may also have **intergalactic gas**. It would seem reasonable to assume that such gas consists mostly of hydrogen, either in the neutral or the ionized state. The subject is under intensive investigation, for even the existence of a minute amount would add an avalanche of matter to the universe as a whole, and would have crucial consequences in the framework of cosmology.

If the gas is neutral, it should show up as an absorption feature superimposed on spectra from very distant radio sources in the area of the 21-cm line. The evidence in this respect is inconclusive, but the most probable interpretation at present does not allow for densities which are even much less than one neutral hydrogen atom per cubic centimeter. Thus, either there is very little gaseous material in the universe at large, or else it is ionized. We feel unable to express a preference for either of the two alternatives.

Particles. Then, we would expect cosmic rays, that is, highly energetic particles, both positive nuclei and negatively charged free electrons, in intergalactic space. Again, their actual density is unknown, since observations only give us indications of the cosmic-ray density inside our own galaxy, and theoretical work is so complicated and subject to so many uncertainties that definitive statements are almost

FIGURE 20-16. Group of five interconnected galaxies in the constellation Serpens. *(Hale Observatories.)*

impossible to make. This is also true for the *neutrino density* in the universe. As we saw in Sections 7.2 and 12.3, some 5% or so of the total energy output of a star during its active life as a nuclear furnace escapes in the form of neutrinos, which then move freely about in the universe not interacting with anything.

The 3°K Radiation.   Finally, there are the *photons*. In a sense, they are like the neutrinos: they are continuously produced by stars and let loose everywhere in the universe, but they interact much more often than do neutrinos. There is, everywhere in the universe, a certain photon density due to **diluted starlight**, that is, the combined light emitted by stars in the universe. Since most photons are emitted by stellar gases whose temperatures are in the range between some 10^{4}°K and 10^{3}°K, their energies correspond mostly to wavelengths centered on the visible range. Since we have a good idea of the number of photon-emitting stars, we can calculate fairly accurately the expected photon density in the universe due to diluted starlight.

A few years ago, measurements were made of the background brightness of the sky, in areas where no known discrete sources are located. The level of brightness was found to be far in excess of what would be expected from our galactic halo or scattered starlight More detailed investigations showed that the spectrum is described by a Planck curve (Section C.6) for a temperature of about 3°K.

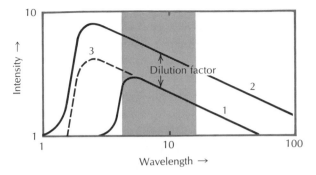

FIGURE 20-17. Black-body and diluted radiation. Wavelength in arbitrary units. The maximum of curve (1) for a temperature of 3°K would occur at about 1 cm wavelength.

In order to understand this crucial point, we must discuss **black-body radiation**, that is, radiation that can be fully described by Planck's law. A somewhat loose definition, but one that is sufficient for our purposes, is the following: a source emits black-body radiation if we can ascribe to the source an unambiguous temperature according to Planck's law. Curve (1) in Fig. 20-17 shows, in arbitrary units and in schematic form, the amount of radiation emitted by a black body at some temperature T as a function of wavelength. Curve (2) shows the black-body spectrum for a source at twice as high a temperature. The two curves describe the spectrum an observer would measure right at the surface of a black body emitting radiation, with the temperature of the radiation spectrum being equal to the temperature of the radiating body. Now, if the observer were a certain distance away from the source, the photons would have dispersed in all directions, that is, the radiation would be *diluted* by a certain factor dependent on the distance, and at a certain distance the observer might detect spectrum (3) instead of (2).

On the longer-wavelength side of the intensity maximum, the "surface" and "distance" spectra would not differ. However, they are readily distinguishable if the observed wavelength region includes the intensity maximum. **3°K radiation** has its maximum near 1 mm wavelength, which is just detectable through the radio window of the earth's atmosphere. Thus, the available observations cover the shaded area in Fig. 20-17 and make the identification of the observed spectrum with black-body radiation virtually certain.

The temperature of 3°K may appear to be minute compared to those of many thousands of degrees we have been dealing with, but it must be considered in its proper context, namely, the level of radiation expected and its particular spectral range. The situation is such that this 3°K radiation is dominant in only a very narrow strip of the radio spectrum, whereas at all other wavelengths (say, in the visible range or at longer radio wavelengths) other sources, such as starlight or the radio emission of our own galaxy, are more intense.

The full impact of this discovery will become clear when we discuss cosmological problems and, in particular, the early phases of our universe in Section 22.5. For this purpose it is important to remember three crucial observational facts: first, the 3°K radiation is isotropic, that is, its intensity is independent of direction, so that a galactic origin is excluded (it would otherwise have to show some intensification, say, in the direction of the galactic center). Second, its level is about 3°K (and not 5° or 0.5°). Finally, its spectral characteristics are indeed those of a black body.

QUESTIONS FOR DISCUSSION

1. If the positions of extragalactic systems in the sky are mapped, a so-called *zone of avoidance* is found, that is, a band in which practically no extragalactic objects are observed. With what feature in the sky does this zone of avoidance coincide? What is the reason for our inability to find galaxies there?

2. Review the steps by which the techniques of distance determination proceed from parallax measurements in the solar neighborhood to distance determinations for extragalactic systems.

3. How would you reconcile the hypothesis of a universal expansion with the belief that our galaxy is not in the center of the universe?

4. Why should gas, if it is present between galaxies in significant quantities, be "hot"?

5. Why couldn't the astronomers of the 1920s observe the 3°K radiation?

EXERCISES

1. Name the spiral galaxies in our local group.

2. Contrast the appearance of a spiral galaxy seen edge-on with one seen along the axis of rotation.

3. Describe the main differences between the subclasses a, b, and c of regular spirals.

4. What are the main differences between regular spirals and barred spirals?

5. In what features are the subclasses a, b, and c of regular and barred spirals similar?

6. There are several dwarf elliptical galaxies in the local group. Does the local group contain any giant ellipticals? What do you know about them?

7. In what properties do elliptical galaxies differ among themselves?

8. Why is it unlikely that the spiral and elliptical forms of galaxies are simply earlier and later stages in their evolution, so that the elliptical galaxies were formed long before the spiral galaxies?

9. Lenticular galaxies have some properties in common with ellipticals, some with spiral galaxies. Which properties are these?

10. Contrast spiral and elliptical galaxies in terms of star populations.

11. Does a redshift in the spectrum of a star or galaxy imply a Doppler shift in all cases? Give examples to justify your answer.

12. For which galaxies were blueshifts observed? Why does this observation not contradict the hypothesis of a universal redshift?

13. What is the velocity of a galaxy with a relative redshift $z = 0.1$ with respect to us? How far away is the galaxy? How long ago did the photons we observe now leave their source?

14. Name a few clusters of galaxies.

15. What is the redshift of the Virgo cluster? The Coma cluster?

16. What is a typical wavelength for photons in diluted starlight? Does diluted starlight follow a Planck curve?

17. Review the basic properties of 3°K radiation. Why is the 3°K radiation of so much interest to astronomers?

18. Curves (1) and (3) in Fig. 20-17 coincide at wavelengths above the wavelength of maximum intensity. Sketch the curve for black-body radiation with a temperature of three times the value T assumed for curve (1). Then, draw the corresponding curve for diluted radiation such that it, too, coincides with the new "surface" curve (1) at wavelengths above the maximum. What do you know about the *dilution factor* of this radiation field?

19. Suppose the earth's atmosphere were not transparent to photons between 1 mm and, say, 5 cm. What effect would this have on our knowledge of the 3°K radiation?

FURTHER READING

Schatzman, E. L., *The Structure of the Universe*, New York: McGraw-Hill Book Company, 1968.

Baade, W., *Evolution of Stars and Galaxies*, Cambridge, Mass.: Harvard University Press, 1963.

21 radio galaxies and quasistellar objects

In the preceding chapters we have presented a survey of the population of our universe as it appeared until very recently on the basis of telescopic observations in the visible spectral range. Our interpretations were little more than a straightforward application of our knowledge of stellar evolution and the statistics of large assemblies of stellar material. Admittedly, we were unable to state exactly why a "typical" galaxy has the complex structure we observe, or in what way many of the fine details come about; nevertheless, such questions appeared accessible to solutions in the framework of well-known physical theories. Of course, we still have to incorporate the general expansion into our view of the universe.

We also saw that some extragalactic objects (for instance, the IrrII galaxies) do not quite fit into the smooth scheme of spiral, intermediate, and elliptical galaxies, and again one might have the impression that these objects are pathological—cosmic accidents—and of no particular consequence to our understanding of the millions of "normal" galaxies.

But, how normal are normal galaxies? Or perhaps we should ask, "How abnormal are the others?" That this question is more than an idle dallying with words is one of the most important astronomical discoveries of the last decade. It began with the identification of "radio galaxies" as a large class of objects with quite specific and unexpected characteristics; today it centers on the interpretation of objects that have become known as "quasars." In the process, we begin to speculate that in some form or another the "pathological" events may be part of the norm. Or are they? We have come to think that the answer to this question may help us understand the structure of the universe at large.

21.1 WEAK RADIO SOURCES

Angular Resolution. The acceleration of extragalactic research in the last decade or so was made possible by vast improvements in radio-astronomy instrumentation, to the extent that whole new frontiers were opened. Let us therefore briefly review the peculiarities of astronomical work at radio frequencies.

The *angular resolution* of a telescope, that is, the degree to which it is capable of differentiating between two neighboring objects such as stars, depends primarily on its size or, in the case of a reflecting telescope, on the diameter of its mirror (see Section E.1). The larger this diameter, the better the angular resolution, and the smaller the details that can be distinguished. This resolving power also is directly dependent on the energy of the photons picked up from the source, so that it is inversely proportional to the wavelength. Thus, an optical telescope can resolve details less than one ten-thousandth the size of those that can just be made out by a radio reflector of the same diameter. As an example, our biggest conventional radio telescopes barely are able to make out gross features of the solar surface.

However, as is pointed out in Section E.4, modern radio-frequency techniques involving so-called *interferometers* placed halfway across the earth, can (within certain limitations) distinguish details as small as 10^{-4} arcsec, or more than 1,000 times smaller than the best we have done with optical telescopes. The price paid for the fine resolution is a very elaborate setup and a long data-collection process; thus, to date, we have made observations of only a handful of objects. Note that, in contrast to what happens in the optical spectral range, "radio scintillations" due to the ionosphere do not limit the resolving power of radio telescopes.

Weak Radio Sources. With these remarks in mind, we can now try to establish at least a morphological classification of extragalactic radio sources. The first group is quite obvious, and some members have already been mentioned: M31, the Magellanic systems, and many other galaxies outside the local group but still close by. They all emit radio photons, and it is commonly assumed that the photons originate throughout these galaxies, as they do in our own galaxy. Their apparent radio brightness decreases with the square of the distance, as does the brightness of the galaxy as a whole in the visible range, and in general there appears to be little of specific interest in the radio spectra of this group.

Then, there are certain peculiar galaxies that emit radio photons in varying degrees of intensity. Among them are the IrrII galaxies already mentioned in Section 20.1; the prototype is M82, shown in Fig. 20-9. The hypothesis is commonly accepted that some time ago a huge explosion of unknown origin occurred in the center of M82 which, incidentally, harbors an extended infrared source; the explosion must have completely altered the structure of the galaxy. The same is postulated for the other known galaxies of its type. The radio emissions of M82 are not particularly strong, and the number of IrrII galaxies is not very large, so that it is generally assumed that these objects are really uncommon and, in that sense, of interest mostly to the specialist. All these radio sources are relatively weak.

Peculiar Objects. The situation is somewhat different with objects that show **jets** and other peculiar protrusions; M87 (Fig. 20-8), a giant elliptical galaxy, has one close to the center. It can be seen in Fig. 21-1, which was taken with a much shorter exposure time than Fig. 20-8, so that only the center portion of the galaxy is resolved. The spectrum of this jet shows that the emission mechanism is synchrotron radiation; that is, the jet must contain a large number of relativistic electrons and the appropriate magnetic field. This, in turn, requires an energy source which we usually identify with an "explosion" in the center of a galaxy—although this term is used to cover our ignorance of the basic physical mechanism that is at the root of it all. M87 has recently been identified as an X-ray source.

The list of such "peculiar" objects could be continued at some length. Jets are rather common, and, even more so, *bridges*. The latter designation, as we have seen, includes all sorts of luminous connections between multiple galaxies. Some of

FIGURE 21-1. Short-exposure photograph of the giant elliptical galaxy M87; compare with Fig. 20-8. We now see the center portion with its large concentration of stars and a very bright starlike nucleus from which the jet, a source of strong radio emission, appears to emanate. *(Lick Observatory.)*

them are clearly composed of stars (as is seen from their unmistakably stellar spectra), and may well be the result of a relatively close encounter among the parent objects, others must include at least a large proportion of gas, and still others appear to emit mostly synchrotron photons, even in the optical range. In many cases these features are radio sources as well. But in summary, we have to admit to the lack of a satisfactory explanation for the consistent presence, let alone the origin, of these peculiarities.

21.2 RADIO GALAXIES PROPER

In the 1950s it became possible to determine accurately the positions of discrete radio sources (the first comprehensive collection of such data is the *Third Cambridge Catalogue*, listing sources by number with the prefix 3C). Astronomers then began to search sky maps based on the visible spectral range for objects that could be identified with the radio sources. In a number of instances, the identification was immediately obvious. What came out of these endeavors was the realization that there

FIGURE 21-2. **The peculiar galaxy NGC 5128, otherwise known as the radio source Centaurus A, photographed with the 200-inch telescope. An unusual amount of uncondensed material is present in this elliptical galaxy.** *(Hale Observatories.)*

is a group of **radio galaxies**, or *strong* extragalactic radio sources, quite apart from the isolated examples mentioned in the last section. It is doubtful that these radio galaxies comprise a specific class of galaxies in the physical sense, because they seem to be widely different objects in presumably different stages of development. It is more likely that "radio galaxies" represent a specific stage in the development of several classes of galaxies.

What then are radio galaxies? Some of the strong radio emitters are classical elliptical galaxies. In some cases, peculiar features such as the jet in M87 could be made out; in others, no distinguishing property is discernible in the optical range. Ellipticals are among the strongest radio emitters. Their radio luminosity might possibly be connected with the large amounts of gas present in some ellipticals but normally absent from galaxies of this class. One such elliptical is NGC 5128 (the radio source Centaurus A), shown in Fig. 21-2.

There are also **double galaxies** of the type exemplified by 3C 405 (shown in the center of Fig. 21-3), better known as the radio source Cygnus A, one of the strongest in our sky. These double galaxies are not chance occurrences; the components are in some way physically related, and of common origin. "First cousins" to these

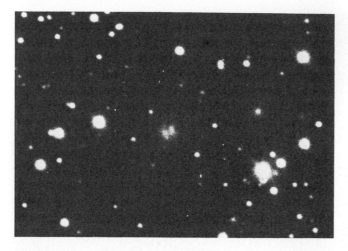

FIGURE 21-3. Double galaxy, known as radio source 3C 405 or Cygnus A. The two nuclei visible in the center are surrounded by a common envelope. *(Lick Observatory.)*

objects are the **dumbbell galaxies**, which optically present the image of two well-defined nuclei in a common, probably stellar, envelope. The structural peculiarity of one or more bright nuclei in a large envelope characterizes **D-type galaxies**, of which the dumbbells can be taken as a special case. Often, a giant D-type galaxy is the largest member of a cluster.

Finally, among the strong radio sources, there are the so-called **N-type galaxies**. They are characterized by an unresolved bright starlike nucleus in an envelope that is usually rather faint. Not so very different in photographic appearance from N-type galaxies are the **Seyfert galaxies** which are obviously *spiral galaxies* with extremely bright, starlike nuclei. These, of late, are being recognized in increasing numbers.

The most significant optical property of Seyfert galaxies is the spectrum of the starlike nucleus, which shows a number of bright emission lines, typically of several-times-ionized elements. This means that the light is emitted by high-temperature gases which, for some reason, are concentrated in the very centers of the galaxies. In addition, there are time variations in both overall intensity and spectral characteristics. There is no question that catastrophic processes have occurred in the nuclei of these galaxies; there are many unanswered questions about the physical nature of these processes, in particular because some Seyfert galaxies have been identified as X-ray sources (NGC 4151), and (in the case of NGC 1068) as containing extremely small infrared sources. NGC 4151 is shown in Fig. 21-4.

In summary, a great variety of galaxies seem to be able to emit extraordinary amounts of radio radiation. Among the sources are ellipticals in which apparently nothing is "abnormal," others with an unusual admixture of gas or dust, and still others with quite specific, peculiar properties. One might conclude that radio emission is tied to a phenomenon (probably in the nucleus) that is independent of many of the details of galactic structure.

FIGURE 21-4.   NGC 4151, a Seyfert galaxy. Typical of these spiral galaxies are extremely bright starlike nuclei and often an array of very localized radio sources. NGC 4151 has recently been identified as an X-ray emitter. *(Hale Observatories.)*

21.3   THE RADIO STRUCTURE

Configurations.   Our survey has so far dealt mostly with the optical images of identified extragalactic radio sources. We now take a closer look at the spatial structure of the sources. Typical is the case of the radio source 3C 405 (Cygnus A), identified with the giant D-type galaxy of Fig. 21-3. The radio contour shows two regions well separated from the parent galaxy, but symmetric about it. The optical source is shown in the center of Fig. 21-5, with the nuclei and surrounding envelope shaded. The elliptical contours mark the areas where most of the radio emission originates; to be precise, each boundary is placed where the radio intensity is one-half the maximum value. The dashed contours outline the optical images of other objects, mostly distant galaxies, in the field of view; compare with Fig. 21-3.

Another example, 3C 338, identified with the double galaxy NGC 6166, shows basically the same structure—two symmetric radio sources, one on each side of the parent galaxy. In this case the sources are much closer together, and almost touch the envelope surrounding the nuclei. We should point out, however, that there are some other sources in which no double structure has been found so far.

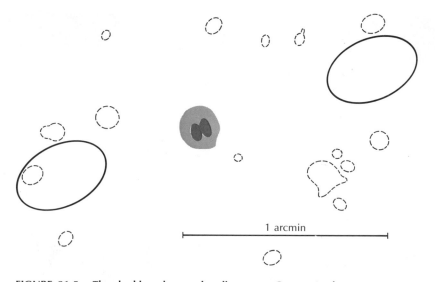

FIGURE 21-5. The double galaxy and radio source Cygnus A of Fig. 21-3. The field of view is approximately the same. The galaxy is in the center of the picture, with other identified stellar features indicated by dashed outlines. The positions of the two radio sources are shown by the two solid ellipses. *(T. A. Matthews et al., Astrophys. J., vol. 140, p. 35, 1964.)*

The presence of two main radio sources, separated from the optical galaxy and located along one of the main axes of the galaxy, is quite common among radio galaxies, in particular those of type D. An analysis of the physical properties of the radio sources indicates that the emission mechanism is synchrotron radiation. The most obvious way to explain this structure is to postulate some sort of explosion some time ago (maybe 10^6 or 10^8 years) which threw out large quantities of relativistic electrons, presumably together with other material, along an axis probably defined by the general magnetic field of the parent galaxy. In the process, they carried the magnetic field along, and they now are in the two positions defined by the radio contours "above" and "below" the plane of the parent galaxy. At some time in the future, they will have expended their energy (through expansion and radiation losses of synchrotron photons) and become lost in intergalactic space.

Complex Structures. Very often, if not always, in addition to the main extended sources, there are very small and compact but very bright radio-emitting regions. For instance, in the case of the Seyfert galaxy 3C 120 a whole hierarchy of subsources of essentially equal brightness has been found; their diameters range from some 10 arcmin down to the present resolving power of the intercontinental interferometers, or less than 10^{-3} arcsec. Since in the case of 3C 120, a spiral galaxy, there is no question that the observed redshift is a distance indicator, we can translate the angular diameter into linear size and obtain for the smallest source the tiny diameter of about 0.1 pc.

Source Size. This directly observed diameter is of interest because it is corroborated by a rather theoretical but nevertheless powerful argument. 3C 120 is variable, with a fluctuation time of the order of months, say 3×10^6 sec. Now let us assume that a source of linear dimension R cm changes its light output with a characteristic period of 3×10^6 sec. If we look at this source, the photons from the part of the source closest to us will arrive earlier than the photons from a more distant portion. If r_1 is the distance to the nearest part, and r_2 to the furthest, it will take the photons from the furthest part $(r_2 - r_1)/c$ sec longer to reach us, where c is the speed of light. This is true because a photon from the furthest part has to travel the extra distance $r_2 - r_1$, at the speed c, to reach us. The difference $r_2 - r_1$ will depend somewhat on the geometry of the source but will be close to R, the linear dimension.

The fluctuation period we observe at our distance must be at most equal to the time it takes light to travel from the furthest point of the fluctuating source to the closest point; that is, $(r_2 - r_1)/c \leqq R/c$. Otherwise the fluctuations would be washed out by the difference in arrival times of photons from the closest and the furthest points. [This situation would be somewhat similar to the case of a person listening to a choir whose members are all singing the same song (with "fluctuation times" of, say, 1 sec), but who are spread over a huge arena, that is, over a distance much greater than the distance that sound traverses in 1 sec. The poor listener would not hear a song, but a constant cacophony of sound.] Thus, the fluctuation time t must be at most equal to R/c. With $c = 3 \times 10^{10}$ cm/sec and $t = 3 \times 10^6$ sec, we find a diameter of $R = 10^{17}$ cm, or less than 0.1 pc.

There is yet another important aspect to the complexity of source structures. The fact that we are dealing with multiple sources of varying diameters is most simply explained by assuming repeated events in the galactic nucleus, each expelling a cloud of relativistic electrons with magnetic field attached. Thus, we come to the conclusion that whatever type of explosion occurs in the center of a radio galaxy, it is one that is usually repeated and therefore involves a mechanism that cannot be very unusual.

21.4 QUASISTELLAR OBJECTS

Soon after the strong radio sources were accurately located, it became obvious that the *Third Cambridge Catalogue* contained yet another group of sources. These radio sources had *starlike optical images* and did not show any of the attributes of bona fide galaxies, such as the spiral arms of the Seyfert galaxies, or the stellar envelopes of D- and N-type galaxies. They were called **quasistellar objects**, or **quasars** for short.

The brightest of them, 3C 273, is shown in Fig. 21-6; it is a peculiar object in that it has a well-resolved protrusion or jet which by itself is a strong source of synchrotron radiation. Intercontinental interferometers have ascertained the existence of additional very compact subsources of exactly the type of those found in the Seyfert galaxy 3C 120. The quasar 3C 273 is an X-ray source; in addition, it is variable, with a characteristic fluctuation time of the order of weeks. Most other quasars are much fainter and only as bright as the most distant galaxies. As an example we show in Fig.

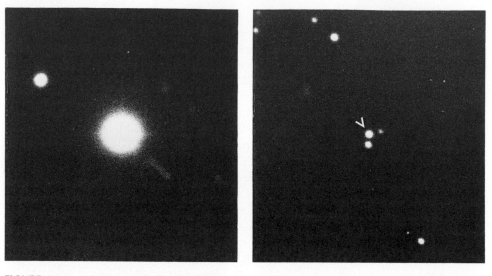

FIGURE 21-6. 3C 273, optically the brightest quasistellar source in the sky. The quasar proper is not resolved (the finite size of the "stellar" image is instrumental). However, the jet, which in the reproduction is just visible and points to the lower right, is resolved. *(Hale Observatories.)*

FIGURE 21-7. 3C 147, a quasistellar source identified on this 200-inch-telescope photograph as one of innumerable starlike images. *(Hale Observatories.)*

21-7 the field surrounding 3C 147. By now, hundreds of these quasars have been optically identified, right down to the limiting brightness of the 200-inch telescope. Obviously, they are quite common in the universe.

Optical Spectra. The uniqueness of quasars revealed itself the very moment the optical spectrum of 3C 273 — and of many fainter quasars — was taken. They all share, with certain inconsequential variations, the following characteristics: the continuous spectrum is not of a type we associate with either stars or hot interstellar gas; it is, by comparison, too bright in the blue region of the visible spectrum and has a very intense infrared component. The suspicion is that at least a significant portion is due to synchrotron radiation. Superimposed on the continuum are exceedingly wide *emission lines* and, often at the same time, sets of *absorption lines*, most originating in several-times-ionized elements such as carbon, nitrogen, oxygen, and iron. While it is not clear precisely how the emission lines come about, the absorption lines correspond roughly to shells of cooler, rather dilute gas. Due to their characteristic optical spectra, quasars can be recognized without recourse to radio observations, and indeed a large number of *radio-quiet* quasars are known.

Redshifts. In identifying the spectral lines above, we very nonchalantly left out the central argument involving quasars to this date: these lines show redshifts (z values) that range from values similar to those of not-too-distant galaxies to values of 2.8. Now the highest z values from galaxies in the most distant clusters are in the neighborhood of 0.5, implying a relative recession speed of half the speed of light (Fig.

20-11): for *z* values close to or above 1.0, our simple Doppler formula, $z = v/c$ (from Section 20.3) is obviously meaningless, since values of *z* above 1.0 imply speeds exceeding that of light, and such speeds are impossible in the universe. In this case, a more complex version of the formula must be employed to translate *z* values into actual speeds; however, we need not be concerned with its details. As an example of the redshift phenomenon, though, suppose that in the laboratory we could give photons a "middle" *z* value of 1.6. Then a line emitted at a wavelength of 1800 Å, far below the high-energy limit of the window in the earth's atmosphere, would be detected at about 4700 Å, or right in the blue-green region of the visible spectrum!

Cosmological Versus Local Hypothesis.   If we accept the redshifts of quasars as Doppler shifts indicating huge relative velocities—and there appears to be no other explanation—two alternative hypotheses become possible. Are these velocities due to the process which causes *all* distant galaxies to recede from us (the **cosmological hypothesis**)? Or do they indicate that an explosion took place somewhere in our local group of galaxies some time ago, and that we are seeing the fragments fly away (the **local hypothesis**)? We are sure that quasars are not nearby galactic objects, because of the absence of proper motions; 3C 273 has been found on photographic plates dating back to the last century. Both hypotheses affect the very foundation of our understanding of the physics of galaxies. With all due respect to the dissenting section of the astronomical community, the author feels that the cosmological hypothesis is correct.

A concentrated effort is now under way to find evidence for the cosmological hypothesis by observational means, namely, by identifying quasars in clusters of bona fide galaxies. Cluster membership is, at least statistically, ascertained by coincidence of location on the celestial sphere and equality of redshifts for the quasar and the cluster galaxies. The method is standard, as we recall from Section 17.3, in deciding whether or not a star belongs to an open cluster. Thus, the argument is simply this: if we find a quasar which, according to these criteria, belongs to a cluster of galaxies, then we have proven the cosmological hypothesis for this one quasar and, by implication, may assume that all quasars are at cosmological distances. In addition, not one single quasar with a blueshift (motion toward us) has been found so far; under the local hypothesis, this would mean that the original explosion took place in our own galaxy or in another member of the local group, and that the fragments have already traveled a significant distance from us. This latter consequence would require an original explosion of almost as much energy as that required by the cosmological hypothesis. In either case, the energy expenditure is beyond the values known for any object. This becomes particularly disturbing if one identifies most of the optical continuum with synchrotron radiation, which would require huge magnetic fields whose energy, again, has to come from somewhere.

The redshifts of the emission and absorption lines often differ, and there are even different absorption redshifts for different sets of lines. The interpretation of this phenomenon is another unsolved problem, but there are indications that the multiplicity of redshifts is one of the basic features of quasars. It appears likely that in many cases the bewildering array of spectral lines consists mainly of a few strong lines seen with several different redshifts.

Most quasars show a degree of *variability* with characteristic times that require exceedingly compact sources. These in turn indicate radiation-field densities so high that otherwise unlikely energy-exchange processes between electrons and photons become predominant. At least in some cases (such as 3C 273) intercontinental interferometers have directly shown the extremely small sizes of radio sources associated with the quasar.

In summary, we must admit that a description of the physics of quasars at this time is a catalogue of unsolved problems: the mechanism responsible for the enormous energy expenditure in the quasar nucleus, the structure and dynamics of the gas clouds we register as radio sources, their internal processes, the difference between radio-active and radio-quiet quasars, etc. It appears that we are still missing one of the fundamental processes that occur or occurred in a large number of galaxies.

Once we accept the **cosmological distance** of quasars, that is, the distance determined by their redshift together with the universal expansion, we note their obvious similarity to at least some of the radio galaxies on one hand, and to Seyfert galaxies on the other. In all fairness, however, we admit that there are also some systematic differences whose significance at present is not quite clear. If we take the redshift as a distance indicator, we see that most quasars are much farther away than any of the "normal" galaxies known at present. We have seen in Section 20.3 that the furthest known normal galaxy, with a redshift of $z = 0.45$, is at a distance of about 10^3 Mpc. The largest redshift known at present for a quasar ($z = 2.8$, for 4C 05.34) would correspond to six times this distance, if we simply extrapolate the distance-redshift relation of Fig. 20-11 in a linear fashion, of itself a highly dangerous procedure. At any rate, at such distances it is not surprising that we are unable to observe any spiral structure or envelope, but only the superluminous nucleus with its mysterious energy source.

Similarly, one can argue that the actual luminosity of the nucleus will change drastically during and after an explosion, so that a quasar will be much brighter at one time than at another. We must also recognize that the travel time of light from a quasar with $z = 0.8$ and from another with $z = 0.2$ differs by about 4×10^9 years, and so in effect we are comparing two objects at vastly different times. If we take all these caveats seriously, we cannot expect the apparent magnitude of a quasar (either in the visible or in the radio range) to be more than loosely related to its distance as expressed by its redshift. This, unfortunately, is exactly the result of observation. Whereas a plot of apparent magnitude versus redshift for, say, the brightest elliptical galaxy in a cluster, yields the rather well defined linear relation of Fig. 20-11, a corresponding plot for quasars is, at least at first glance, almost meaningless.

Another curiosity is the fact that quite a large number of quasars are known with redshifts of the order of 2, but very few with a z value of 2.3 or above. Whether this is an effect of observational selection or an intrinsic cosmological feature has not been decided.

Thus, we are left with the tantalizing fact that quasars may represent the most distant objects visible to man. Because of the time it takes their light to reach us, they show us portions of the universe at a much earlier stage than do any other objects. However, we are simply not yet qualified to structure the wealth of data into a history of these early days of the universe.

QUESTIONS FOR DISCUSSION

1. The first object studied through radio astronomy was the sun, not the radio galaxies. Why?

2. In the text, the sizes of some infrared sources were specified, but not those of any X-ray sources. Why?

3. Review the arguments that led theorists to believe that fluctuation periods of weeks or months are compatible only with extremely small source sizes.

4. What are the main arguments for and against the cosmological hypothesis?

5. A hypothetical radar operator finds a group of four fast-moving aircraft on his screen. How could he determine their speed? Then he sees a fifth aircraft very close to the other four. What arguments would convince him that the fifth aircraft belongs to the same formation as the first four?

6. Modify your answer to Question 5 to make it a proof of the cosmological hypothesis for quasars. You can now use only half the information the operator had in Question 5. Why?

7. Why are quasars so interesting to cosmologists?

EXERCISES

1. What differentiates radio galaxies from "normal" galaxies?

2. What is commonly believed to be the reason for the peculiar behavior of galaxies of type IrrII?

3. If the jet of M87 emits synchrotron radiation, what type of particles must it contain?

4. Bridges are believed to appear between galaxies that came close to each other on gravity-determined orbits. What would be the corresponding phenomenon in the realm of stars?

5. What are the special features of dumbbell galaxies, D-type galaxies, and N-type galaxies?

6. Describe the main features of Seyfert galaxies and contrast them to those of N-type galaxies; to those of quasars.

7. Many extragalactic radio sources show the characteristic double-source structure of Fig. 21-5. What is the current explanation of this feature?

8. What is supposedly the reason for the dissipation of radio sources after perhaps 10^7 years?

9. What new information was obtained with intercontinental interferometers concerning the radio-source structure of some Seyfert galaxies and quasars?

10. Calculate the distance of 3C 120 from the data given in the text.

11. What are the main characteristics of quasars?

12. Compute the recession speed of a quasar with $z = 1.6$ with the aid of our simple formula and argue that your result is physically meaningless. What has gone wrong?

13. Where is the Lyman-alpha line of neutral hydrogen (laboratory wavelength 1216 Å) found in the spectrum of a quasar with $z = 2.8$?

14. You observe certain levels of radio, infrared, and optical emission from a quasar. Why does the assumption that the quasar is at a cosmological distance result in a much greater energy requirement than the assumption that it is somewhere in the local group?

15. (See Exercise 14.) Suppose the quasar is 10^3 Mpc from us. How much greater is the energy required by the cosmological hypothesis than that required by the local hypothesis?

16. The discussion in the text implies that quasars have widely varying absolute magnitudes. Why?

FURTHER READING

Burbidge, G., and M. Burbidge, *Quasi-Stellar Objects,* San Francisco: W. H. Freeman and Company, 1967.

Kahn, F. D., and H. P. Palmer, *Quasars,* Cambridge, Mass.: Harvard University Press, 1967.

Frontiers in Astronomy: Readings from Scientific American, San Francisco: W. H. Freeman and Company, 1970.

22 cosmology and the history of the universe

We have almost reached the end of our journey through the astronomer's universe. Along the way we have looked at all the building blocks, from the smallest to the largest, from the nearest to the most distant. We have summarized the development of the stars and their associations in time and have speculated on the history of galaxies. So, in principle, we have seen almost everything.

But not quite yet. There are still two fundamental issues to tackle: for one, how do all the manifold parts fit into the whole, the all-embracing universe? And then, assuming we find a reasonably satisfactory answer to this question, how did it develop in time to its present stage—and how, possibly, is it going to continue in the next 10^9, 10^{10}, or 10^{11} years?

These questions are in the realm of *cosmology*, started thousands of years ago in the myths of ancient religions and crystallized today in the cool interpretation of the most recent data and theoretical models. This is still mostly the astronomer's thought world, but it is enclosed within the boundaries imposed by the physical facts, those "simple" facts which for centuries appeared as self-evident to the scientist and layman alike.

22.1 THE FUNDAMENTAL PHYSICS OF THE UNIVERSE

The discussion to follow would have little meaning if it were not based on a principle that has guided all scientists always, namely, that the results of *identical* experiments should be *identical*. In other words, science is based on the premise that what is true in laboratory A at time t_1 must be true (under *identical* conditions) in laboratory B at time t_2. If this principle is not followed, then anything we come up with has only the ephemeral value of an accidental result obtained for some unknown and, in principle, unperceivable reason; the universe becomes unphysical and unpredictable, and science becomes irrelevant to reality.

Now, of course, we know that identical experiments do give identical results, and that these results can be predicted correctly. However, if we restrict ourselves to actual experiments, even with the inclusion of astronomical "experiments," that is, the interpretation of data received from quite distant objects, we only know that physics is the same everywhere within a certain portion of space—say as far as the 200-inch telescope reaches, and over times that span the few billions of years light travels from the most distant galaxy to us. We should emphasize that every conceivable test has been applied to our assumption that physics is the same everywhere within these space and time limits, and that no departure from uniform behavior according to fundamental laws of physics has ever been detected.

The Cosmological Principle.   Nevertheless, our present task of describing the whole universe requires a more sweeping approach. It requires the generalization of this principle of "equal physics everywhere we can observe" into what is known as the **cosmological principle**: the universe looks the same to any observer anywhere. Of course, due notice must be made of the fact that we may have to average over suitable volumes of space, that is, smooth out local fluctuations in whatever quantity is under consideration. We stated in Section 20.3 our firm belief in such a principle, when we said that the first task in assessing the consequences of universal expansion must be to construct a theory that would require every observer in the universe to see the same phenomenon.

We have purposely left out the time element so far, because it is by no means obvious that we must postulate temporal as well as spatial homogeneity for our universe. But if we accept this further postulate, we introduce a so-called **perfect cosmological principle** and claim that the universe looks the same to any observer anywhere at any time. In a sense, this much more restrictive view is more pleasing to scientists, because it removes a point of asymmetry, namely between space and time. On this basis, the so-called *steady-state theory* of the universe has been developed; it requires not only that the universe be the same, on the average, to all observers everywhere, but that there be, on the average, no change in its makeup over time.

The Physical Laws.   What, now, are the physical laws that we would like to apply so uniformly everywhere? First of all, that space and time are measured in the same fashion everywhere. Thus, at any place in the universe (and, preferably, at any time) the relations of **special relativity** (Section B.2) should hold locally, and with them the value of 300,000 km/sec for the *speed of light*. Thus, we have introduced into our universe the first apparently completely arbitrary number, and we make no claim to understanding why this number is 300,000 km/sec and not 100,000 or 3,000,000.

Another of these arbitrary numbers is **Planck's constant**, which shows up in physics in many more instances than the one we are familiar with, namely, as the conversion factor from frequency to the energy of a photon (Section C.1). Again, most people will agree that the figure of 6.62×10^{-27} erg/sec is just what it is, a folly of the gods.

We are not so sure about the universality of some of the properties of the *elementary particles*, say the mass of the electron or the proton. At present, there is a bewildering "zoology" of particles and properties, and although quite some progress has been made in the attempts to bring order to the chaos, we have not yet formulated a consistent theory from which these mass values and the other particular properties would follow. Of course, once such a theory is found, we can then claim that its main features are somehow built into the universe for no further detectable reason.

It is worthwhile mentioning at this point that some other basic properties of matter are much more open to speculation. We are all made up of atoms whose building blocks are *electrically charged*, but the atoms are so constructed that under most conditions they are electrically neutral. It is a common belief that this holds true as well for the universe at large. However, the nucleus of an atom is positively charged and contains almost all the mass of the atom, whereas the electron cloud is negative and contains very little of the total mass; but this need not be true everywhere. On several occasions astronomers have speculated that there may be regions in the universe—as large as galaxies—in which the atomic nuclei are massive but negative (built from the **antiprotons** and **antineutrons** of Section D.2) with the "electron cloud" made up of **positrons**. Obviously, so long as there is little direct interaction between a galaxy and such **antigalaxies**, nothing drastic would happen in such a matter-antimatter universe.

Of much more direct importance in cosmology is another number, namely the ratio of gravitational to electric forces between electron and proton. It turns out to be of the order of 10^{-40}, and for decades scientists have looked for some hidden meaning in such an unusually small constant. Another problem concerns the **gravitational constant,** in numbers 6.67×10^{-8} dyn $\cdot$ cm²/g². The question centers on whether it is of the same unchanging quality as is presumably the speed of light, or whether, for instance, it could change in time, preferably being much larger at an earlier epoch. Attention has been focused on this particular problem because the theory of gravitation is the obvious and first step in any grand cosmological scheme, as we shall see presently.

Before we conclude this very sketchy and incomplete list, we must mention at least two more fundamental restrictions on any kind of universal physics: one is the fact that certain entities, such as energies, are **quantized**; that is, they cannot be divided into arbitrarily small fractions. The other restriction is expressed by the **uncertainty principle**, which states that certain pairs of quantities—energy and time, for instance—always act in such a fashion that their actual values are uncertain to some calculable degree. It is commonly accepted nowadays that this basic uncertainty is built into the universe, although admittedly there is still the possibility that the uncertainty principle and the laws of quantum mechanics which are intimately connected with it are only approximations, however accurate, to what really would be the fundamental law of interactions.

Our list, and more complete ones, are outlines of a "dream program" for cosmology, requests for a complete theory of everything that exists in the universe, perhaps a sort of ultimate demon. We are far, very far, from such a scheme. What theorists are contemplating at present (often with violent disagreement as to proper procedures) is the formulation of a universal theory which would include at least one phenomenon on an a priori basis, namely, gravitation. This choice is a simple one to make, because gravity is present everywhere in the universe, in contrast to, say, electrical forces, which we believe appear only if the internal structure of atoms is perturbed, and then only in rather localized areas.

Before we can report on the success or failure of this endeavor, we must review the modern interpretation of space and time, quantities we have so far simply taken for granted as a part of the everyday experiences of the unconcerned observer.

22.2 THE GEOMETRY OF THE UNIVERSE

It is a rather simple chore to draw a straight line. We start it somewhere on a sheet of paper, run our pencil along a straightedge, and stop after some distance. The result is a rather unique construction, with two highly individual, **singular points** at the ends. Why did we start and end it where we did, and not a bit farther, or a bit nearer; in fact, why did we end it at all? Of course, we know all the answers to these simple questions. Maybe the pencil broke, or we were interrupted by something, or we just wanted to draw the line exactly as we did. But if the graphite crystals of the pencil stroke had a life of their own, they would not know (and it would be highly unlikely that they ever found out) how they got where they are; they would find themselves arranged in a completely incomprehensible pattern.

This example is, of course, a poor model for our universe; it requires the pencil-line universe to be caused by the whims of a capricious nature (us), with no relation between subject and object. Most objectionable of all, it is not a "simple" universe: it has two highly singular points.

The last-mentioned difficulty can be eliminated. In a *gedankenexperiment*—a thought experiment—we can go on drawing the line forever and ever (to continue the analogy), in this manner building an infinite universe. We can also be more modest and draw a square, which is finite, but then we have built into our universe four singular points, that is, points at which everything suddenly and drastically changes. But we wanted to avoid singular points. Maybe we should not have drawn a straight line in the first place, but a circle. This universe is not infinite, yet it has no singular points. Of course, instead of a circle we could have drawn an ellipse or any of a number of more complex figures.

We can demonstrate something else with this example: suppose we used quite a large piece of paper and made a really big circle, and then cut a small piece out of the circle. If we gave the small piece to someone, could he determine, from it alone, what the construction had been? This would depend on how accurately he could follow the course of the line, always assuming that it was an absolutely perfect circle. In the real world, all measurements are subject to errors, and the chances are that he could not distinguish between a small piece of a large circle, or an ellipse, or an oval, or any number of similar constructions on the one hand, and a straight line on the other. Our graphite crystals would be in precisely this situation if they could communicate only with other crystals nearby, and were subject to a finite measuring error. They would not be able to figure out whether their universe was part of a circle, or a straight line, or what.

Let us at this point introduce some simple terminology. First, our example concerned a **one-dimensional manifold**, a line (straight or curved), and not a surface or a volume. One number suffices to define any one point on this figure. If we draw a circle, however, then the drawing encloses a certain portion of the paper and so determines the surface of a **two-dimensional manifold**, while the circle itself is a one-dimensional manifold. Second, we say that the straight line has **zero curvature**, whereas the circle, etc., have finite curvatures: they are simply not straight. Zero-curvature manifolds are called **Euclidean**, those with other curvatures **non-Euclidean**. Third, points enclosed within a one-dimensional universe are not part of that universe; the center of the circle does not belong to the universe which consists of the circular line only, but is situated somewhere outside, in the two-dimensional manifold of our sheet of paper. Also note that we can construct **finite** universes such as the circle, or **infinite** ones such as the straight line with no beginning and no end. Among the finite cases there were **bounded** ones (the line that went from one finite point to another) and unbounded ones, such as the circle, on which we can go round and round, never coming to a boundary.

What we just discussed in the framework of one-dimensional manifolds can be extended by one more dimension, that is, to surfaces. We can start with a sheet of paper, say $8\frac{1}{2} \times 11$ inches, but we reject it as a model because of the singularity encountered at the edges. Again in a gedankenexperiment we can extend the paper into an infinite Euclidean plane or—to keep our model finite but still eliminate the singularity—to a curved surface without edges, such as the surface of a balloon. Obviously, the surface of a spherical balloon is the simplest one, but we can also look at fancy ones with odd shapes. All these balloons have curved (non-Euclidean) surfaces, they are finite, and they are unbounded. Each has a two-dimensional surface that exists in **three-dimensional space**; we need two numbers to define a point on such a two-dimensional manifold.

At this point, we have reached the limit of the ability of the human brain to picture spaces: it can register all sorts of one-dimensional and two-dimensional spaces, and it can register three-dimensional spaces, but the latter must be Euclidean. This is quite an unfortunate restriction from the point of view of modern cosmology. For to add another dimension to our manifold we either have to return continually to analogies in the realm of one- and two-dimensional spaces, or we must become highly mathematical.

Thus, we can ask only on a purely formal basis whether our real world, our three-dimensional space, is Euclidean or not, and in the latter case what its curvature is, whether it is bounded or unbounded, finite or infinite. Clearly, from our day-to-day experience, we conclude that our "neighborhood" behaves as a "flat," Euclidean space, and this conclusion holds throughout the portion of our universe within reach of present technology. However, we also know that this statement simply means that whatever curvature there may be to our universe at large does not (not yet?) show up in this limited space, and with our present means of detection.

Thus, our universe may be Euclidean. But it may also be non-Euclidean, and really a three-dimensional "surface" existing in **four-dimensional space** (corresponding to the three-dimensional skin of a four-dimensional balloon). In that case the curvature over distances of the order of 10^3 Mpc is simply too small for us to detect with our present means of observation.

22.3   A GEOMETRICAL MODEL FOR UNIVERSAL EXPANSION

Against this background, recall the observation that all extragalactic objects recede from us with speeds proportional to their distances from us; recall, too, that in the spirit of the cosmological principle the universe ought to be of such a form that every observer everywhere would come to the same conclusion about its physical properties. What does this mean in terms of our ideas of the universe at large?

The Universal Expansion.   Let us immediately point out that from the expansion argument alone nothing can be said about the geometry of the universe. Assume that an explosion occurred on a plane surface, and the fragments scattered in all

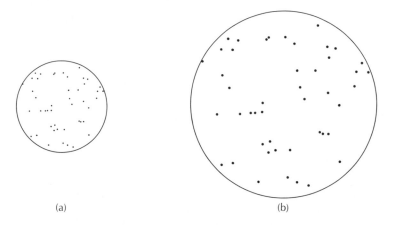

(a)   (b)

FIGURE 22-1.   Expanding spherical balloon with surface markings, seen from the outside: (a) time t_1, (b) some time t_2 later. The relative positions have not changed.

directions. They would fly away along the surface with their distances from the point of explosion proportional to their speeds; that is, barring any acceleration or deceleration along the way, the fastest fragments would have gone the furthest. This universal recession would be observed by everybody attached to one of the fragments, but there is one point on the surface singled out as the origin of the expansion, and this type of model is at variance with the cosmological principle and cannot satisfy us.

Next, consider a spherical balloon upon which dots are painted in some pattern. Now, inflate the balloon at a constant rate. An observer on any dot would see all the other dots recede from him, each with a speed proportional to his distance from that dot. At a given time t_1 the balloon would look to a (fictitious) observer *outside* this two-dimensional surface as Fig. 22-1(a); at some later time t_2, after some expansion, the balloon and its dots would look like Fig. 22-1(b). If we could cut into the fabric of the balloon (in the real world, this means a cut through the three-dimensional surface in four-dimensional space), we would find the geometrical relations depicted in Fig. 22-2, provided that the expansion was uniform in time: at time t_1, an observer *on* the balloon surface would find two objects A and B at distances of, say, 1 and 2 units, respectively, while at time $t_2 = 2t_1$ he would find them at distances of 2 and 4 units. The change in distance per time unit $(t_2 - t_1)$, which is the recession speed in the case of uniform expansion, would be 1 for A and 2 for B, exactly proportional to their distances.

Note that the center of the balloon "explosion" does not belong to the dotted surface on which all areas are now indeed treated alike. Thus, the two-dimensional surface of the balloon is a possible model for our three-dimensional expanding universe.

At this point we have at least *one* model which can explain the main feature of universal expansion. It is, of course, not the only one. For instance, we were not required to specify the curvature of our world (as determined by the radius of the "balloon") at any of the times referred to; the balloon could be so huge that over

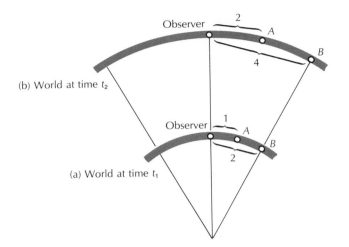

FIGURE 22-2.   Geometry of uniformly expanding sphere. Between t_1 and $t_2 = 2t_1$ the distances of the objects A and B from the observer would have changed from 1 and 2 units to 2 and 4 units, respectively. The change in distance per unit time — the recession speed — would be exactly proportional to distance.

the distances we are able to measure, the balloon surface would be indistinguishable from a plane Euclidean surface. Similarly, we could start with an elliptical balloon, or one of some other shape, and we would still arrive at the same conclusion concerning the recession-speed–distance relation.

In addition, we imagined the balloon as being inflated at a truly constant rate, whereas in reality the expansion may be accelerating or decelerating at a pace undetectable with present equipment. That is, in the real world, the range of distances and times covered by the observations quoted in Section 20.3 is too small to allow unambiguous detection of any departure from a linear expansion.

The three-dimensional volume enclosed by the surface of the balloon in our model does not belong to the balloon's universe. By the same token, anything that is enclosed by our curved three-dimensional universe, being in four-dimensional space, does *not* belong to it. It is as much outside the universe as is the four-dimensional region "beyond" the universe. Our universe consists wholly and only of the three-dimensional "balloon surface." In contemplating a three-dimensional universe curved in such a fashion that it occupies a finite space in a four-dimensional manifold — similar to the two-dimensional surface of a balloon floating in a three-dimensional room — one is tempted to ask whether there may be many universes, each unaffected by the others, in fact, each being in principle unable to detect the others. The answer is simple (and quite satisfactory): since, in principle, we cannot communicate with them, their existence or nonexistence is irrelevant.

22.4   SOME PHYSICAL MODELS

The discussion of the last section was based on rather simple geometrical ideas, with little regard for the physical facts surveyed in Section 22.1. Let us now try to make our model somewhat more concrete.

Olbers' Paradox.   The first phenomenon of interest here comprises **Olbers' Paradox**. About 150 years ago, it occurred to Heinrich Olbers that, if the universe were infinite in extent, and if this universe were populated at random by stars, then the sky could not be dark.

Olbers' main argument is extremely simple: consider a spherical shell of space surrounding an observer, say at a distance r from him, and with a thickness Δr. The volume of this shell is then $4\pi r^2 \Delta r$; it is *proportional* to the square of the distance from the observer to the shell. Let the shell be filled with a number of stars or galaxies, so that it has a certain average luminosity. Of this luminosity, however, only a fraction which is *inversely proportional* to r^2 reaches the observer, because the starlight is diluted by a factor proportional to $1/r^2$. Since the light emitted is proportional to the volume of the shell, and thus to r^2, but the light reaching the observer is proportional to $1/r^2$, the two factors cancel, and the amount of light received by the observer in the center of the shell does not depend on its radius. Now add another shell of the same thickness outside the first, then another, and so on; in an infinite universe we can add as many concentric shells as we wish, each contributing the same luminosity at the observer's position, assuming that there is about the same density of stars or galaxies in each shell. As the number of shells becomes infinite, the radiation density becomes infinite at the observer's position and, hence, everywhere in the universe.

This is obviously nonsense. One can argue that we have left out an important effect, namely the absorption of photons originating far out by matter in between, for instance, by stars that are closer to the observer. As a result of this effect, the radiation density at any point of observation would be about equal to the mean surface brightness of the average star—a result which is still nonsense. Obviously, one of the assumptions must be utterly wrong and, from our modern viewpoint, we conclude that the assumption that led us astray was that of a *static* universe: in reality it is expanding, and the contribution of shells farther out is continuously decreasing. It is irrelevant at this point whether or not the universe is infinite.

A Steady-State Universe.   The next point we should emphasize is the significant difference between a finite world and an infinite world in terms of the physical parameters. If we think in terms of a spatially *infinite* world, we might assume at the same time that this world has existed forever and will exist in eternity. It is reasonable to postulate the prefect cosmological principle of Section 22.1 and to construct a type of model known as a **steady-state** world. Here, any observer, anywhere and at any time, would see the same kind of universe.

Unfortunately, as soon as we try to integrate universal expansion into this scheme, we run into a difficulty: if the world is expanding, and if this expansion has been going on for an infinite amount of time, the matter in the universe should have long since thinned out to the point where no galaxies would be left for us to observe, unless additional ones were constantly being formed. Thus, in a steady-state universe, matter would have to be supplied at a high enough rate so that something close to a constant density of matter was maintained: such a universe requires the continuous **creation of matter** (and, hence, energy). There is nothing particularly obnoxious, or even inconceivable, about this suggestion, provided the required rate of addition of matter does not contradict observational evidence. All the proposed variations of the steady-state theory require that matter be added to the universe at a rate which is undetectable with present instrumentation.

An observer in a steady-state universe would see, everywhere and at all times, a statistical average of galaxies, young and old; on the basis of detailed mathematical models we can make predictions as to the percentage of ensembles that would be seen in the various stages of development—if we could survey a large enough volume of this universe.

An Evolutionary Universe.   The obvious alternative is to postulate a *finite* universe. But if this finite universe is expanding at present, it must have been much smaller at some point in the past. All the material of the universe would have been stuffed into a nutshell of incredible energy density, with physical conditions so different from today's world that we are barely able to guess what they were like. What we are constructing now is the model of an **evolutionary universe**.

That such an evolutionary universe has a real "beginning," that is, that there is a truly singular point in time, say some 10^{10} years ago (a thought that makes most astronomers and physicists decidedly uncomfortable), does not follow. In fact, it is equally acceptable on the basis of our present knowledge that our universe is **expanding** now but will some day in the future (maybe billions of years from now) slow down, reverse itself, and start **contracting** until it reaches a highly compact stage and starts a new cycle. Such an **oscillatory** or **pulsating universe** would, in a sense, bring us back to the main premise of a steady-state world, namely, that the time scale should not have a singular role in the universe, and that, on the average, the universe should always stay the same. "On the average," of course, now encompasses a very long time by earthly standards. The observer's position in time (say in an early or late contraction or expansion phase) would be as accidental as his spatial position (say inside or outside a young or old galaxy). The ability of the universe to change its motion from expansion to contraction depends on its matter content: if the density of matter per unit volume is below a certain limit, most cosmological theories (but not all) do not allow for reversal of motion. Obviously, whether the total mass of the universe is above or below this limit can in principle be decided by observation. This was part of the reason for the great interest we took in the total mass of our galaxy and the possible existence of significant amounts of intergalactic material. At present our best estimates of the *known* masses in the universe lead to a total mass that is, by at least a factor of 10, smaller than the limit. However, it is generally suspected that we simply have not yet been able to identify all matter, for instance, if it were hidden in black holes, or if some of our mass estimates were significantly in error.

Physical Models.   To arrive at a detailed model of the universe some version of that universal physical theory we dreamed about in Section 22.1 must be introduced. Of all the physical properties and relations known to man, the most universally observed, in spite of its relative weakness, is gravitational interaction. Thus, in very general terms, it is postulated that this gravitational interaction, or the underlying matter distribution, determines the shape and geometry of our universe. It is possible to write this premise and others that follow from it as a set of mathematical equations. One can then solve the equations to determine what the theory predicts for the universe at large, in particular for spaces the size of, or just greater than, the portion open to observation.

It is clear that any solution must include the local properties of space, time, and matter as detailed in both the laws of special relativity and Newton's law of gravitation. Unfortunately, this condition is rather weak and allows a wide variety of formulations. Some of them, for instance, allow for a secular change in the value for the gravitational constant; others fix this number forever. In any case, whatever variations there may be cannot contradict properties or phenomena that can be checked by observation or experiment. Since the early days of Einstein's general relativity theory (which corresponds to one specific set of plausible mathematical models) other theories have been produced, guided mostly by the principle that any mathematical theory of the universe as a whole should be as simple as possible.

The models differ in their predictions of what is to be found beyond the furthest limits of our present observational capabilities. Assuming that quasars are at cosmological distances, we may soon be able to use them for mapping much larger volumes of the universe than we can now; this may make it possible to check some of the predictions. The only conclusion possible at this time is that a steady-state theory would have to be much more complex (and then presumably less likely) than an evolutionary theory if it were to explain some of the crucial observations, notably the existence of the 3°K radiation field.

We shall try, in the next section, to describe the history of our universe qualitatively, on the basis of an evolutionary model.

22.5   THE HISTORY OF THE UNIVERSE

The Present.   According to the evolutionary viewpoint, we are now at some point in an expansion phase of a closed, finite universe with a finite and approximately known matter density. Uncertainties in the determination of this matter density make it infeasible at present to predict when the expansion will be reversed into a contraction. So far as we can tell, the expansion has not accelerated or decelerated markedly over the last few billion years, so we must be in a relatively stable phase.

The Past.   If we now go back in time, we see the universe as smaller and smaller in extent, until we approach the epoch (some 10^{10} years or so ago) when galaxies were formed out of primordial matter. Whatever the mechanism was, it must have proceeded very rapidly. Just before the galaxies condensed, matter was spread everywhere, although we cannot tell how uniformly the material was spread, whether there were localized inhomogeneities or, if so, in what still earlier phase they came about.

Together with the uncondensed matter, there must have been a radiation field whose remnants we now observe at the 3°K level. The strongest point in favor of an evolutionary universe is its present black-body character, because universal expansion would leave that *intact*. Thus, if the radiation is now of the black-body type, it must always have been of this type; moreover, at one time there must have been an equilibrium between the radiation field and the matter, through much more frequent interactions. This stage of the evolution of the universe is usually referred to as the **primordial fireball**. The energy density in the universe at that time—owing to both matter and radiation—could be described by a single temperature value, again because of its black-body character. This was, of course, much higher than 3°K, since all the energy "trapped" in the universe was concentrated in a much smaller volume. What has changed since then is the black-body radiation *temperature*, which in the course of expansion has decreased to the level we observe today; the matter has separated from, and is no longer linked to, the radiation field.

If we go still further back in time, we come to a situation in which the energy density in the now extremely small universe is so high that *nuclear reactions* occur freely everywhere. The chemical composition of the material in the universe is exactly the chemical composition of the material from which the first-generation stars were formed. Hence, one of the crucial observables is the chemical composition, in particular the hydrogen-to-helium ratio, of objects in parts of the universe where it has been least affected by subsequent nuclear reactions in the interiors of stars or, possibly, galactic nuclei.

Still further back in time we reach a point where extrapolation from knowledge gained in laboratory experiments (on the physics of elementary particles, for instance) becomes so uncertain that little more than unconfirmed speculation is possible. In addition, we no longer can assume uniform expansion, but must consider a change in expansion speed; it is quite possible that the **big bang** (as astronomers usually call the moment of the beginning of the expansion) was preceded by a cycle of contraction.

The Future.   And what about the future? Obviously, the expansion of the universe is not soon to come to a halt. It will spread the galaxies farther and farther apart, while in each of them more and more stars will develop toward their ultimate fates: white dwarfs, or neutron stars, or even black holes. Perhaps whole galaxies will become black holes.

And maybe the expansion of the universe is only a phase in an unending cyclical motion, and at some future time it will stop and then reverse into contraction. The world would then change quite drastically, in ways no one has bothered to conjure up in detail; after all, this appears to be as moot a question as any the human mind may ask. But if this is the kind of world we live in, then at some still more remote time the universe will contract back into yet another fireball, and start anew with another big bang, and all memory of what there was will be gone forever.

QUESTIONS FOR DISCUSSION

1. The basic premise of the physical sciences is that the universe is rational, that is, that repetitions of experiments will give the same results if the experimental conditions are the same. Discuss the importance of this statement and the data on which it is based. Was this principle always at the base of human thoughts concerning nature? Can you imagine alternatives?

2. What are the spatial and temporal restrictions imposed by today's technology on our knowledge of the universe?

3. How does antimatter come about? Why would a collision between a normal galaxy and a galaxy made up of antimatter be catastrophic? (Recall the discussion of nuclear processes in Chapters 7 and 12.)

4. Review the properties of finite and infinite spaces, and bounded and unbounded spaces, as cosmological models.

5. Why is the assumption of a simple explosion somewhere in a Euclidean universe not a desirable explanation for the origin of galaxies? Contrast this explosion model of the universe with that of an expanding spherical surface.

6. Describe one hypothesis other than those discussed in the text that circumvents Olbers' paradox.

7. Why would the existence of other finite closed universes besides ours be irrelevant for us?

8. Discuss the possible future of the universe. What may happen to the galaxies? The 3°K radiation? Assume in your answer that the expansion reverses into contraction; also consider Olbers' paradox. Do you think you will witness any of this? Will any of your progeny?

EXERCISES

1. What types of problems belong in the realm of cosmology?

2. What is the difference between the cosmological principle and the perfect cosmological principle?

3. What is a fundamental constant? What fundamental constants have you encountered in the text?

4. The gravitational constant affects the densities of stars through Newton's law. Discuss the effect this constant would have on nuclear-energy processes if it changed in time.

5. Why is gravitation probably the most important physical interaction to be accounted for in a cosmological theory?

6. What type of two-dimensional surface within a three-dimensional space corresponds to the one-dimensional circumference of a two-dimensional circle?

7. Why are singular points upsetting to cosmologists?

8. Why may it be impossible to determine the curvature of space on the basis of a specific set of observations? Use one- or two-dimensional analogs.

9. (a) Does the surface curvature of a perfectly spherical ball change along the surface? (b) Give examples of two-dimensional surfaces within three-dimensional spaces with variable curvature.

10. What is meant by Euclidean space?

11. You cannot paint a dot on the center of the balloon. Why is this fact relevant to comprehension of the geometry of the universe?

12.   A spherical shell is static and more or less uniformly filled with light sources. Why is its contribution to the luminosity measured by an observer at its center independent of the radius of the shell? What changes if the shell is expanding?

13.   Which cosmological theory is based on the perfect cosmological principle? Explain.

14.   What happens to the energy content of a volume in the steady-state theory? Why is the continuous creation of matter necessary?

15.   Contrast a simple evolutionary universe with an oscillatory one. Would you argue for or against the statement that, in a sense, an oscillatory universe fulfills the perfect cosmological principle? Why?

16.   What physical property of the universe is responsible for reversal of the universal expansion to a universal contraction?

17.   How would you go about checking, observationally, whether the expansion rate of the universe is presently increasing or decreasing?

18.   Discuss the importance of 3°K radiation to our understanding of the evolution of the universe.

19.   What is meant by the term "primordial fireball"?

20.   What was the relation between matter and radiation during the fireball phase?

21.   What happened to the matter after the fireball phase? To the radiation?

22.   Does the energy content of the universe as a whole (understood as a closed system) change during expansion?

23.   Repeat Exercise 22, but this time for the energy content of a unit volume. What does the difference between your answers mean in terms of what is now observed as the 3°K radiation?

24.   Why were nuclear reactions possible among free particles at a very early stage of the universe? What did they determine? Is it possible to obtain observational evidence concerning this stage of the universe?

EXPERIMENTS

1.   Buy a few balloons of different shapes and blow them up slightly. Paint dots on them, and then blow them up further. Compare the relative motions of the dots on a spherical balloon and on odd-shaped balloons. Discuss the observations that might be made by two-dimensional people living on the balloons' surfaces.

2.   (See Experiment 1.) Mount your balloons in such a fashion that you can control the flow of air. If you increase the rate of inflow (or outflow), the expansion (or contraction) of the surface accelerates; if you decrease the rate, it decelerates. Plot the distances between your dots as a function of time during acceleration and deceleration and describe what happens.

FURTHER READING

Hoyle, F., *Frontiers of Astronomy,* New York: Harper & Row, Publishers, Incorporated, 1964.

Bondi, H., *The Universe at Large,* New York: Doubleday, Anchor Science Study Series, 1960.

Gamow, G., *The Creation of the Universe* (rev. ed.), New York: The Viking Press, Inc., 1961.

Alfvén, H., *Worlds—Antiworlds*, San Francisco: W. H. Freeman and Company, 1966.

Sciama, D. W., *Modern Cosmology*, Cambridge: Cambridge University Press, 1971.

appendices

A some everyday
mathematics

A.1 THE POWER NOTATION

We all know that 2 times 2 is 4, and 2 times 2 times 2 is 8, and so on. Rather than write the number 64 as $2 \times 2 \times 2 \times 2 \times 2 \times 2$, one commonly uses the **power notation** to write it as 2^6. Hence, T^4 in Section 9.3 is shorthand for the product of any number we want to substitute for the name T, multiplied by itself four times.

Scientific Notation. We really make the best use of power notation for very large and very small numbers: 10^4 equals 10,000, 10^6 equals 1,000,000, etc. Then 1.56×10^4 is shorthand for $1.56 \times 10,000$ or 15,600. So, we can write the approximate grand total of individual federal income taxes withheld in 1968 (namely, 57,300,000,000 dollars) as 5.73×10^{10} dollars.

Each time we increase a number by a factor of 10, we say that we increase it by **one order of magnitude**. And if we do not know, or if it doesn't make much difference, whether a number is, say, 5,000 or 15,000 (but not 1,000 or 100,000!) we say that it is **of the order of** 10^4.

To express very small numbers in this shorthand notation, we first remember that $\frac{1}{2}$ can be written as 2^{-1}. Then $\frac{1}{2} \times \frac{1}{2} = (\frac{1}{2})^2 = 2^{-2}$, which we can also write as $(2^2)^{-1}$ or as $(2^{-1})^2$. So we have $\frac{1}{8} = 2^{-3}$, $0.01 = \frac{1}{100} = 10^{-2}$, and so on. Thus, $2 \text{ Å} = 2 \times 10^{-8}$ cm is decidedly shorter (and easier to write) than $2 \text{ Å} = 0.00000002$ cm. A large or small number written as a number between 1 and 10, multiplied by a power of 10, is said to be in **scientific notation**.

Absolute Value. While discussing numbers we should mention that occasionally we employ the **absolute value**, for instance, in Section 5.3, in connection with the Doppler effect. In some of our applications we are interested only in the magnitude of a number and not whether it is positive or negative. The absolute value of the number A, written $|A|$, gives us its magnitude only. So, for example, we may write $|A| = |-A|$ and $|5 - 3| = |3 - 5|$.

A.2 EQUATIONS AND PROPORTIONALITIES

Equations. In the definitions above, we implicitly used **equations**. "Two times two is four," or $2 \times 2 = 4$, is an equation. It essentially shows two different ways of writing the same thing, separated by an "equality sign." Let us, for illustrative purposes, express a simple everyday situation as such an equation. Say, we go to the supermarket and find that apples are 5 pounds for a dollar. We know that the price paid is proportional to the amount bought, and we express that relationship as

$$p = kw$$

defining p as the price we have to pay being equal to the value of w pounds of apples. The **constant of proportionality** or **conversion factor** k in our example is found by substituting known quantities, in this case $p = 1$ and $w = 5$, into the equation. This gives us $k = 0.2$ dollar per pound, if we measure p in dollars and w in pounds. Of course, we could measure p in cents and w in ounces; then, k would equal $0.2 \times 100/16 \times 1.25$ cents per ounce. The constant k has, in the two cases, the dimensions dollars per pound and cents per ounce, which we could write as (dollar)(pound)$^{-1}$ or (cent)(ounce)$^{-1}$. An example from Section 9.3 is the equation $I = aT^4$, where the amount of radiative energy I passing through 1 cm² of the star's surface in 1 sec is related to the temperature T, with the dimension of a being ergs/cm² · sec · degree⁴ or (ergs) (cm)$^{-2}$(sec)$^{-1}$(degree)$^{-4}$.

Proportionalities.   If we are not so much interested in the actual price of apples, but rather in the fact that 10 pounds simply cost 10 times as much as 1 pound, we can replace our equation by an expression of **proportionality** and write

$$p \propto w$$

This is read "p is proportional to w"; we can also say that the price of the apples **depends linearly** on the weight. Note, though, that in this case we have no idea of the value of the constant of proportionality.

Linear relations are particularly simple, but there are many laws of nature which are anything but linear. An example of a nonlinear relation is that between the total radiation emitted by a hot body and temperature, namely the relation $I \propto T^4$ mentioned earlier. We would say that I depends more strongly on T than did p on w in the preceding example.

In the text proper we develop and apply several relations of a more complex nature, but do not express them in mathematical form. Instead, we usually use a graphical representation.

A.3   GRAPHICAL REPRESENTATION

Linear Scales.   Let us begin with a **graphical representation** with which at least some people are familiar, namely the daily average stock prices. Figure A-1 shows the behavior of "50 combined stocks" as published by *The New York Times* in the fall of 1970. The vertical scale, the **ordinate**, gives values for these selected stocks in some units, running from 400 to 450; the horizontal scale, the **abscissa**, gives the days. The vertical bars give the price ranges during the daily sessions, with the closing prices marked by the small horizontal bars. Let us redraw this graph in the manner of the text, discarding the "highs" and "lows" and indicating only closing values. The result, Fig. A-2, looks very much like one of our representations of astronomical data. We have also renamed our ordinate and abscissa scales, by defining

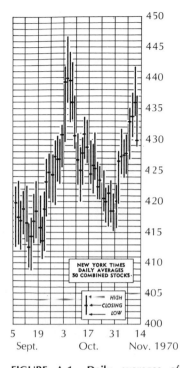

450
445
440
435
430
425
420
415
410

NEW YORK TIMES
DAILY AVERAGES
50 COMBINED STOCKS·

405

HIGH
CLOSING
LOW

400

5   19   3   17   31   14
Sept.   Oct.   Nov. 1970

FIGURE A-1. Daily averages of stock prices from *The New York Times* **November 12, 1970. (©** **1970 by the New York Times Company. Reprinted by permission.)**

our own value unit (called *v*) as 100 *New York Times* units, and by numbering the weeks in order, starting with the week of 5 September 1970 as zero. In other words, we have plotted value *v* against time *t*, with weeks as time units.

Now, if Fig. A-2 represented astronomical data, we would probably think that some of the short-term irregularities were due to measuring errors, and we would try to remove them from our representation; in other words, we would want to average them out. There are various methods for doing this, but in any case the result would look similar to Fig. A-3. The line is the result of the "averaging"; note that the "experimental points" are shown.

Let us return for a moment to our example concerning apples and the equation $p = kw$. We can transform that equation into a graph which gives the price *p* in dollars (ordinate) of any amount *w* in pounds (abscissa). It is given in Fig. A-4. All we needed to know was one price for one weight (in our case, 5 pounds for a dollar) and the fact that zero pounds cost zero dollars. Then, because the relationship is *linear,* we drew the graph as a *straight line* between the two known points.

We can complicate our graph by plotting on it the price as a function of weight for different kinds of apples, namely, a kind which costs only 10 cents per pound, another at 20 cents per pound and, finally, a deluxe quality at 50 cents per pound. The quality of the apples would be called the **parameter** of the problem, and we

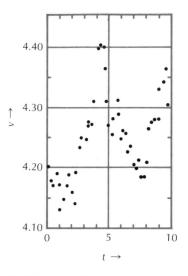

FIGURE A-2. **Closing prices from Fig. A-1.**

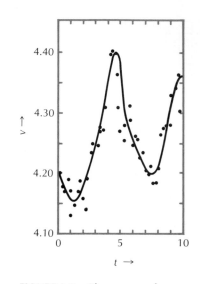

FIGURE A-3. **Time-averaged curve based on Fig. A-2.**

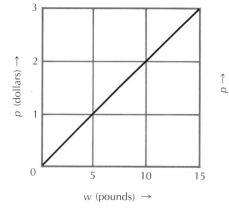

FIGURE A-4. **Price of apples as a function of weight.**

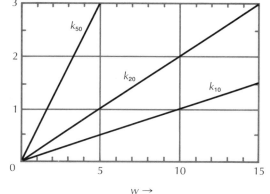

FIGURE A-5. **Price versus weight for three classes of apples identified by the parameter** k.

might identify the three price classes with the parameter names k_{10}, k_{20}, and k_{50}. The result is shown in Fig. A-5.

The weight w of a round table top is proportional to the square of the diameter d; that is, $w \propto d^2$. It would produce the graph in Fig. A-6. We might not be interested in the actual weight in pounds, so we would simply plot the weight and the diameter in **arbitrary units** realizing, of course, that no table top (diameter $d = 0$) results in no weight ($w = 0$).

Logarithmic Scales.   Now there is really no reason to make the steps on the ordinate and abscissa scales equal, provided we label them properly. For instance, in Fig.

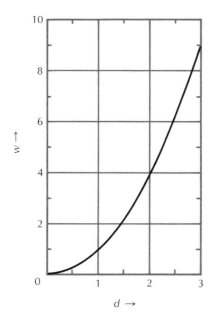

FIGURE A-6. Weight of round table top versus radius in arbitrary units. Abscissas and ordinates in linear scales.

A-6 the diameter scale is twice the weight scale. Further, if it is of help in presenting data, we could make either or both scales **nonlinear**, that is, of unequal steps. Figure A-7 shows the data of Fig. A-6 plotted in such a nonlinear manner. The advantage of the choice of ordinate in Fig. A-7 is obvious: the curve now is a straight line. But there is also a grave disadvantage: if the diameter is 2.5 arbitrary units, we are not immediately able to read out the weight w, except in that the graph tells us w is somewhere between 4 and 9 units.

In order to overcome this kind of uncertainty, scientists use a specific nonlinear scale, the so-called **logarithmic scale**. On a logarithmic axis, the values increase by a *factor of 10* in each *full step*, and the values in between are placed according to a progression of numbers known in mathematics as the "logarithm to the base 10." We have plotted the weights of our table tops once again in Fig. A-8, where now the ordinates (the weights) are on a logarithmic scale, the abscissas (diameters) on a linear scale. To make the correspondence between the scales of Fig. A-8 and those of, say, Fig. 14-2, clearer, we have this time plotted a much larger range of weights and diameters.

A.4 SOME GEOMETRY

Throughout the text we deal with certain basic geometric forms: straight lines, circles, spheres, and the like. In this section we summarize the facts and relations on which many of our arguments are built.

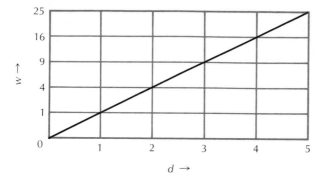

FIGURE A-7. Weight of round table top versus radius in arbitrary units. Abscissas linear, ordinates nonlinear.

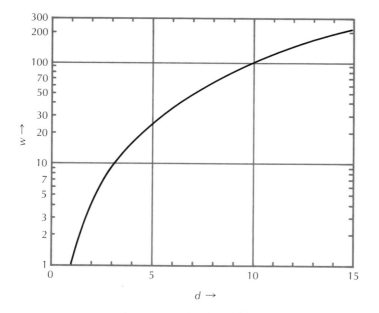

FIGURE A-8. Weight of round table top versus radius in arbitrary units. Abscissas linear, ordinates logarithmic.

Circles and Angles. A **circle** is defined by the property that every point on its **circumference** is at the same distance from its **center**; this distance is the **radius**. Mathematicians say that the circle is the **locus** of all points equidistant from the center. If the radius is 1 unit, say, 1 cm, the circle is a unit circle; its circumference is then 2π cm, where π is short for the number 3.14159 . . . (the three dots stand for infinitely many more decimals). In general, the circumference of a circle is 2π times its radius.

An application of the unit circle is in measuring **angles**. The angular units we employ are based on the **degree**, and a full circle corresponds to 360°; two lines

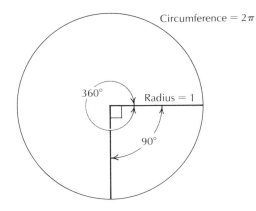

FIGURE A-9. Angles in the unit circle.

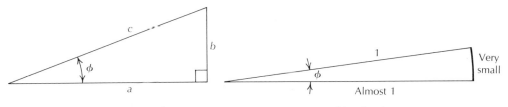

FIGURE A-10. Right triangle.   **FIGURE A-11.** A very thin triangle.

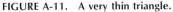

that are **perpendicular** to each other (at **right angles**) include an angle of 90° (see Fig. A-9). For smaller angles we use **arcminutes** (60 arcmin = 1°) and **arcseconds** (60 arcsec = 1 arcmin). For still smaller angles we go to scientific notation.

The **area** within a circle is πr^2, where r is the radius of the circle. A circle of radius 1 cm has a circumference of about 6.3 cm and an area of a bit more than 3 cm².

On a few occasions, we need the basic relations of **trigonometry**, namely, the **sine**, the **cosine**, and the **tangent** of an angle in a right triangle (a right triangle includes a right angle). The definitions are found from Fig. A-10, where the right angle is included between the sides a and b. The longest side, the one opposite the right angle, is the **hypotenuse** c. For the angle ϕ we define $\sin \phi = b/c$, $\cos \phi = a/c$, and $\tan \phi = b/a$.

We can use **radians** as units of angular measure, instead of degrees. Then, a full circle contains 2π radians, so that $360° = 2\pi$ radians or $57.3° = 1$ radian. In radian measure, for very small angles, we have ϕ, $\sin \phi$, and $\tan \phi$ approximately equal to each other (Fig. A-11).

Spheres.   A **sphere** is defined as a three-dimensional figure, every point on whose surface is the same distance (the radius r) from the center. The area of the surface of a sphere is $4\pi r^2$, and the volume within the sphere is $\frac{4}{3} \pi r^3$.

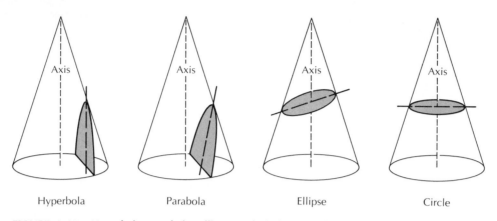

Hyperbola   Parabola   Ellipse   Circle

FIGURE A-12. Hyperbola, parabola, ellipse, and circle as conic sections. The shape of the section depends on the configuration of the cutting plane.

The geometry of spherical surfaces accompanies us throughout the text, in particular concerning astronomical coordinate systems. A cut through the sphere that includes the center produces a **great circle**, that is, the circle on the spherical surface with the greatest radius, namely, the radius r of the sphere. Cuts not including the center produce **small circles**.

Suppose that, in the center of a sphere of radius R, 10^6 photons are emitted uniformly in all directions. If none of them is absorbed, there will be $10^6/4\pi R^2$ photons passing through one unit of surface area. If the radius is twice as large, then $10^6/4\pi(2R)^2$ photons pass through a unit of surface area. Thus, the density of photons *varies inversely as the square of the distance*. On the other hand, if we know the number N of photons passing through a unit area at a radial distance R from the

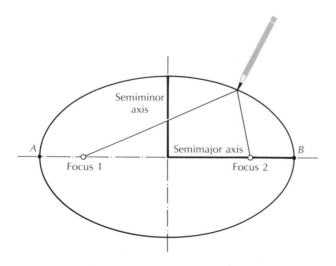

FIGURE A-13. Construction and geometry of the ellipse.

source, we can calculate the number passing through a unit surface at a radial distance R'. It is simply $N(R/R')^2$. This is the basis, for instance, of our statement in Section 9.3 that we can calculate the luminosity of a star if we know its apparent magnitude and its distance.

Conic Sections. **Ellipses, parabolas,** and **hyperbolas** are **conic sections**. One way of generating them is by cutting through a right circular cone at various angles (Fig. A-12). If the cut is close to perpendicular to the cone's axis, we get an ellipse; if it is nearly parallel to the axis, we obtain a hyperbola. The circle is the result of cutting *exactly* at right angles to the axis; the parabola, of cutting *exactly* parallel to the surface of the cone.

An ellipse can be constructed on paper by tying a string around two pins (the **foci**), stretching the string with the point of a pencil, and then tracing a curve on the paper, always keeping the string taut. This defines the ellipse as the locus of all points whose combined distance from two points is a constant, namely, the length of the string (Fig. A-13). If the ratio of the **semimajor axis** to the **semiminor axis** is large, we call the ellipse highly **eccentric.** The ellipse becomes a circle when these axes are equal. In terms of orbits, if we place the sun at focus 1, then position *A* in Fig. A-13 would be the perihelion, position *B* the aphelion.

B basic physics

B.1 SPACE AND TIME

Physical and astronomical phenomena occur in **space** and **time**, so our first task is to agree on a manner in which to measure **lengths** and **time intervals**: we need some universal **units**. Quite obviously, their definition is arbitrary and dictated by convenience. The sciences use the **centimeter** (cm) or the **meter** (1 m = 100 cm) as a length unit. Most people grow up using this **metric system**, but English-speaking countries retain the antiquated inch-foot-yard-mile system which is carefully avoided in this text.

There are about 2.5 cm to the inch, whereas the yard is about 90 cm, or 10% smaller than the meter. A **kilometer** (km) equals 1,000 meters — the *kilo*, as always, stands for "10^3 times the basic unit." Also used are the **millimeter** (1 mm = 10^{-3} m = 10^{-1} cm) and the **micron** (1 μ = 10^{-3} mm = 10^{-6} m). We mention in passing that a "statute mile" equals about 1,610 m.

Areas are measured in **square centimeters** (cm²) or the corresponding units of square meters (m²), square kilometers (km²), etc., while **volumes** are measured in **cubic centimeters** (cm³), etc.

For the very large distances encountered in the universe, we can, of course, always use powers of 10 together with our basic units. We also use a more convenient unit, the **parsec** (pc) and the **kiloparsec** (1 kpc = 10^3 pc), whose definitions are given in Section 9.1. It suffices to note here that 1 pc = 3.08×10^{18} cm. Also used are the **astronomical unit** (A.U.) defined in terms of the earth's orbit about the sun (1 A.U. = 149.6×10^6 km), and the **light-year** which is the distance light travels in an earth year; 1 pc equals about 3 light-years.

The very small distances encountered in atomic and nuclear physics are again measured with reference to the basic centimeter unit. The most common small unit is the **Angstrom** (Å), with 1 Å = 10^{-8} cm.

We should record at this point some rather self-evident facts, namely, that it takes just one number to define the position of an object on a line (*one dimension*), it takes two to define a position on a surface (*two dimensions*), and it takes three in space *(three dimensions)*. These sets of one, two, or three numbers are called **co-ordinates**, and they form the **reference frame** in which we express the positions of things or events.

Time is measured in **seconds** (sec), **minutes** (min), **hours** (h), **days** (d), and **years** (y). Numerically, this is a rather confusing system based on the specifics of the earth's celestial motion (Section 3.3); it goes back to the days of Babylonian astronomy. We often need the fact that the year has 3.1×10^7 sec.

B.2 VELOCITY AND RELATIVITY

Space and time together allow us to define **velocity** as the change of position with time, which we then measure in centimeters per second or kilometers per second. All this is straightforward, since we have a feeling for velocities from day-to-day experience, except that this experience is restricted to velocities of at most some 10^3 km/h.

We now must realize that velocities are **vectors**, that is, they are completely determined only when we know both the numerical **absolute value** (say, in kilometers per second) and the **direction** of the motion; admittedly, in our context the absolute values (**speeds**) are often sufficient. In other cases, however, the complete three-dimensional velocity is required. Then, three separate numbers, the velocity **components**, must be given.

Let us, for illustrative purposes, consider the two-dimensional analog, for which we need only two numbers to describe a velocity completely (see Fig. B-1). A body B moves along the line CD with a speed v whose absolute value may be indicated by the length of the arrow. This velocity can be specified by recording the components v_r along the **line of sight**, that is, the line that connects body B with the observer at point A, and the component v_p at right angles to the line of sight. In astronomy, the component v_r is usually called the **radial velocity**. It is v_r and not v itself which is usually measured; for example, the radar instruments used by traffic patrols register v_r only. So, if CD were a highway, B a car moving at 100 km/h, and A the position of the radar set, the car's speed would be clocked at about 87 km/h (compare the relative lengths of the arrows for v and v_r). Note that a velocity such as v can be resolved into components simply by completing the rectangle Bv_rvv_p in Fig. B-1.

Phenomena that take place at extremely high speeds must be described by the so-called **special theory of relativity**. Although the implications of relativity reach much further, we can summarize them by stating that no velocity in our universe can exceed the value $c = 299{,}776$ km/sec. This is the **speed of light**. If a material body moves with a speed "close" to the speed of light, we call its velocity **relativistic**.

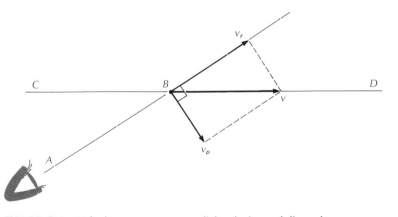

FIGURE B-1. Velocity components: radial velocity and line of sight.

This definition is obviously rather vague, but the term is used only as a shorthand notation, indicating the presence of certain effects which occur only if the body moves with a speed close to c.

There is also a **general theory of relativity** whose primary application to astronomy is in describing the universe at large. It is much more than a generalization of the special theory of relativity.

B.3 ACCELERATION AND MASS; FORCES; GRAVITY

Acceleration.   If velocity changes in time, we call the motion **accelerated** or **decelerated**; the latter case is usually subsumed under the former, since a negative acceleration is a deceleration. Since we are concerned with the change per time interval (in seconds) in a quantity measured in centimeters per second, the unit of acceleration is centimeters per second per second or cm/sec².

Mass.   Before we discuss just what might change a velocity, let us introduce the concept of **mass**. We all have a feeling for the masses of material bodies through their weight. However, the mass and weight of a body are not the same; weight, while it is proportional to mass, depends on things other than the body itself, such as its position, say on the surface of our earth or on another planet. But weightless astronauts still retain their masses. The mass of a body is an absolute property of the body; its weight depends on gravity.

We measure masses in **grams** (g), **kilograms** (kg), etc. One gram is the mass of one cubic centimeter of water. At atomic dimensions, the gram unit is often replaced by the **mass of the proton**, which is 1.67×10^{-24} g. Matter of astronomical dimensions is usually measured in **solar masses** of about 2×10^{33} g.

Density.   We often use the term **density** in the text, either as a notation for the **number of particles**, atoms, molecules, or free electrons per cubic centimeter ("electron density"), or in its more proper meaning as **matter density**. In the latter case, it is simply the amount of mass per unit volume. Note that, by definition, water has a density of 1 g/cm³; the corresponding values for air, rocky material, and a typical metal (iron) are 10^{-3} g/cm³, about 3 g/cm³, and 8 g/cm³, respectively.

Gravity.   Let us now return to acceleration. A system in motion is accelerated by a **force** acting on the system. If *no* force acts on the system, it moves with *constant velocity*, including the zero velocity (in which case the system is **at rest**). This is a statement of *Newton's first law:* force f, acceleration a, and mass m are related by the equation

$$f = ma$$

which holds if the velocities are well below the speed of light. If we measure a in centimeters per second squared, and m in grams, the unit force is measured in gram-centimeters per second squared; 1 g · cm/sec² = 1 **dyne**.

We deal with several kinds of forces in the text. One is the **gravitational** force between any systems that have masses. It is always *attractive*, acting to pull the systems together. Experiment shows that the gravitational force f_{gr} acting between two systems of masses m_1 and m_2 depends on these masses and the distance between them in the following manner:

$$f_{gr} = G \, \frac{m_1 m_2}{r^2}$$

This is **Newton's law of gravitation**. We introduce the constant of proportionality G in order to have a proper equation, and not just a relation of proportionality. If we measure f_{gr} in dynes, the masses in grams, and the distance in centimeters, then the numerical value of the **gravitational constant** is $G = 6.67 \times 10^{-8}$. Presumably, G is the same everywhere in the universe and, maybe, even at all times. It is one of the few really basic numbers that structure our world.

We can combine the last two equations to determine the acceleration a body of mass m_1 gives a body of mass m_2 through the mutual gravitational attraction. If a_{gr} is the **gravitational acceleration**, we have

$$f_{gr} = m_2 a_{gr} = G \, \frac{m_1 m_2}{r^2}$$

or

$$a_{gr} = G \, \frac{m_1}{r^2}$$

If we let m_1 be the mass of the earth (6×10^{27} g), and r the distance between the surface and center of the earth (some 6,500 km), we find $a_{earth} = 981$ cm/sec². In similar fashion we can obtain gravitational-acceleration values for other celestial bodies.

B.4   FORCES AND FIELDS

An **electric force**, or **Coulomb force**, in contrast to the gravitational force, may be either *attractive* or *repulsive*. Basically, all matter consists of two types of building blocks, which we characterize by saying that they are of either (electrically) **positive** or **negative charge**. Any material system consists of both types; if they are present in precisely equal numbers, the system is electrically **neutral** and does not exert any electric force. Often, however, there is a slight excess of one charge over the other. If two systems have an excess of the same type of charged particles, they repel each other. Similarly, if the excess charges are of opposite sign, the systems attract each other.

Related to electric forces are **magnetic forces**, whose strengths are usually given in **gauss**, a unit named after the eminent mathematician, physicist, and astronomer. A magnetic force can be detected through its effect on the properties of light emitted or absorbed in its presence (**Zeeman effect**).

Another basic force type is the **nuclear force**, acting between the constituents of atomic nuclei; we discuss this force in our summary of nuclear physics in Section D.1.

Finally, we mention one aspect of the force concept about which much has been written: forces can act over large, even unlimited distances, and we can think of space as permeated by a variety of forces from many sources. In technical language we say that there are **force fields** present, be they gravitational, magnetic, or otherwise. In the same somewhat loose manner we speak of the presence of a **radiation field** in a volume permeated by radiation.

B.5 WORK AND ENERGY. CONSERVATION OF ENERGY AND MOMENTUM

Work and Energy.   We must exert a force in order to do **work** on a body in motion. The work done by a force is the product of the force and the distance traversed by the object on which it acts. Thus, the greater the force or the distance, the greater the work done. In physics and astronomy we are usually not so much interested in the work that a system actually has done as in the *capability of a system to do work*. This is called **energy**.

Energy and work have the dimension **erg**; 1 erg $= 1$ dyne $\cdot$ cm $= 1$ g $\cdot$ cm^2 $\cdot$ sec^2. The erg is small, too small for most technical uses. Thus, the wattsecond or **joule** has been introduced, so that 1 joule $= 10^7$ ergs. We are all familiar with the *kilowatt-hour* (3.6×10^6 joules), the basic unit that power companies use in billing for energy. Another measure of energy we encounter in the context of atomic and nuclear physics is the **electron volt**: 1 eV $= 1.6 \times 10^{-12}$ erg. Multiples are the **kilo electron volt** (1 keV $= 10^3$ eV) and the **mega electron volt** (1 MeV $= 10^6$ eV), derived in the familiar fashion of the metric system.

Kinds of Energy.   The energy of a system at a given time is one of the most important of the parameters that characterize its physical behavior. As there are many types of forces, so there are many types of energy. A material body can do work through gravitational interaction: a falling weight can crush stone. The higher up the body initially is, the more work it can do; the greater is its gravitational energy. Similarly, an electrically charged body can do work while it is being attracted or repelled. Or, it can do work against a magnetic force. Thus, we have the concepts of electrical and magnetic energy. The **total energy** we ascribe to a system is made up of many contributions; some depend on its mass (such as the gravitational energy); others are not directly related to its mass (such as electrical energy). Thus, we would expect to find systems to which we must ascribe finite amounts of energy but zero mass.

Another form of energy is the so-called **kinetic energy** of a body in motion. If the body's mass is m, and the absolute value of its velocity is v (when v is small in comparison with the speed of light), then its kinetic energy is

$$E_{kin} = \tfrac{1}{2}mv^2$$

Note that if we measure m in grams and v in centimeters per second, we find E_{kin} in ergs. We have said that energy is the capacity to do work. Thus, the kinetic energy of a moving body can be transformed into work.

Conservation of Energy.   Implicit in our discussion is the notion that the several energy forms we ascribe to a system at a given time may be *transformed into each other* by physical processes. As an example, consider the transformation of gravitational into kinetic energy: a stone initially at rest is dropped. It loses a certain amount of gravitational energy, but gains kinetic energy. Conversely, a stone thrown vertically into the air (that is, given a certain kinetic energy) comes to a momentary stop at the highest point of its path, where its gravitational energy is greatest and is equal its original gravitational energy plus its original kinetic energy. Almost immediately, the stone begins to drop again, converting gravitational to kinetic energy. The sum of the two energy forms stays constant throughout the process (if we neglect extraneous complications, such as air drag). We extract from this example, and from all experiments ever conducted by physicists, the concept that the energy of a system (in our case, the stone and the earth) is **conserved**; it does not change so long as there is no loss or gain of energy through interaction with anything *outside* the systems (that is, provided it is a **closed system**). The fact that the energy of a closed system is always conserved is one of the most basic properties of our universe.

The *motion characteristics* of a closed system are also conserved. To clarify this statement, we introduce the **momentum** of a body, which equals the product of its mass and its velocity. Note that this definition includes not only the absolute value of the velocity (as does kinetic energy), but also its direction. We now state that *the momentum of a closed system is conserved*. This means that a body moving along a straight line with constant speed will continue to do so provided it does not interact with anything else. Similarly, a body which is rotating and not interacting goes on rotating; its rotational momentum, or **angular momentum**, is conserved. In many astronomical problems the conservation of energy and momentum, in particular the angular portion, is crucial to theoretical arguments.

B.6   TEMPERATURE

Temperature as a Measure of Energy.   Any material body can be described as a large assembly of atoms or molecules; the solid, liquid, and gaseous states differ in the amount of freedom the basic constituents have to move about. Now, if these constituents move about, they must have a certain *average speed* with respect to an arbitrary fixed point, and this in turn means that they have an *average kinetic energy*. This kinetic energy, inherent in the motion of all the atoms or molecules of a material body, is described by its **temperature**. At higher temperatures, the mean speed (kinetic energy) of the atoms is higher, and vice versa. Obviously, there must be a situation in which the atoms or molecules do not move at all; this is described by a temperature of *absolute zero*.

Temperature Measurement. Temperatures are measured in **degrees**, and there are several scales in use. Most of the world uses **degrees Celsius** (or centigrade), defined by the melting or freezing point of water (0°C) and its boiling point (100°C). Absolute zero then is about −273°C. Science has based its scale (**degrees Kelvin**) on the size of the centigrade unit but starting with 0°K at the absolute-zero point. Thus, water freezes at about 273°K and boils at 373°K.

Equilibrium. It must be emphasized that this concept of heat as **internal-energy content** makes sense only for large assemblages of atoms or molecules. Single atoms freely convert their individual kinetic energies into other forms (such as excitation and ionization energies). Suppose we could keep a material body from interacting with the outside world, making it a perfectly closed system, and we waited until a steady or stationary state was reached, in which on the average no statistical changes occurred in any physical quantities. We would then have an **equilibrium** among the various forms of energy residing within the atoms. In the equilibrium state, *one* parameter (the temperature) would suffice to describe the energy distribution of the system completely. Although no natural system is strictly in equilibrium in this sense, the concept is sufficiently valid for the majority of astronomical applications.

Pressure. We conclude this discussion of the *statistical properties* of matter by pointing out that it is the kinetic energy of the random motion of the atoms and molecules of a gas that results in its **pressure**. Ultimately, the pressure is due to the constant pushing of the gas atoms and molecules against whatever contains them. The greater their speed (temperature), the greater the pressure. It is the pressure corresponding to a particular temperature that maintains the structure of a star against its own gravity.

C light and matter

To this day, astronomy more than any other science is dependent on information gathered through the medium of light. Even though some additional means of "communication" with distant sources have been discovered in the last few years, practically everything we know about the universe has been derived by careful analysis of what we usually refer to as "*light.*"

Almost every astronomical problem involves the interpretation of some particular feature of the light emission of a celestial body in terms of physical parameters, such as temperature, density, and chemical composition. It is in this area that astronomers use the concepts of *atomic physics*. Although we do not have to worry over many of the details, it is important to understand at least the most basic facts concerning atoms, molecules, and ions.

C.1 PHOTONS AND THEIR SPECTRUM

Light. **Light** is *energy,* radiated in the form of very small "packages" we call **photons**, which move through the universe at the *speed of light* c, introduced in Section B.2. Photons have zero mass. If they impinge on our eyes, they activate sensors which signal the sensation of light to the brain. If there are many photons arriving from a source, the source appears *bright* to us. To each photon we ascribe a specific energy which we can measure in any of the energy units discussed in Section B.5. The amount of energy in a photon determines the **color** impression our eyes give us, in the sense that blue photons are more energetic than red ones. Normally, a light source emits photons of a variety of energies; it is the relative numbers of blue, red, and intermediate photons that determines the color of the source.

The distribution of the number of photons of each energy or color arriving from a source is what we call its **spectrum**. Actually, the situation is complicated in that the eye reacts differently to different energies, that is, it needs to detect more photons of some colors than of others to convey the impression of equal brightnesses (**intensities**); the same is true for any other sensor, such as a photographic plate. Statements about brightnesses in the text all concern "adjusted" brightnesses in which the peculiarities of the sensor have been eliminated. In some cases, photons of only one well-defined color or energy arrive from a source; this is **monochromatic** light. By means of instruments such as spectrographs we can artificially eliminate all arriving photons but those of a specific energy, and in this manner produce a monochromatic image of our source.

Wavelength. Instead of specifying the photon type by its energy, measured for instance in ergs, we usually divide the energy by **Planck's constant**, $h = 6.62 \times 10^{-27}$ erg · sec, which gives us **frequency,** measured in sec^{-1}. One sec^{-1} is called one **hertz**, abbreviated Hz, with the usual multiples: the **kilohertz** (1 kHz = 10^3 Hz), the **megahertz** (1 MHz = 10^6 Hz), and the **gigahertz** (1 GHz = 10^9 Hz). Thus, the frequency we attribute to a photon is proportional to its energy: The frequency of blue light is greater than that of red light. In order to avoid confusion, frequencies are usually not quoted in the text. The scale used in the text is based on the **wavelength** λ that can be ascribed to photons. It is found by dividing the speed of light c (centimeters per second by the frequency ν (in hertz or sec^{-1}). Or, we can calculate λ by dividing the product of Planck's constant and the speed of light by the photon energy ϵ:

$$\lambda = \frac{c}{\nu} = \frac{hc}{\epsilon}$$

Either formula gives us the wavelength in centimeters. Since the photons to which our eyes respond have rather small wavelengths, we usually employ the angstrom unit. Note that the energy of a photon is inversely proportional to the wavelength, so that the longer wavelengths imply smaller energies.

Frequency and wavelength are normally introduced by describing light as a wave motion rather than through the photon concept. However, for most astronomical applications the latter is more convenient. We have tried to avoid confusion by omitting any reference to the wave nature of light, defining frequency and wavelength simply as units related to the photon energy.

Light of "dark" red color consists predominantly of photons of a wavelength around 6000 Å (or 6×10^{-5} cm), corresponding to a frequency of 5×10^{14} Hz or an energy of 3.3×10^{-12} erg (or about 2 eV). The figures for blue light are wavelength, about 4500 Å; frequency, 6.7×10^{14} Hz; and energy, 4.4×10^{-12} erg or 2.8 eV. Between 6000 Å and 4500 Å we find orange, yellow, and green in descending order of wavelength.

Nonvisible Range. The question now arises as to whether there are photons with wavelengths below 4000 Å or above 7000 Å, that is, below or above the response range of the human eye. There is no reason to believe that the laws of the universe prohibit their existence. And they do exist, even if our eyes do not notice them. Energies just above the high-energy limit of the human eye correspond to the **ultraviolet** photons that tan our skin. They can easily be detected by photographic film. This ultraviolet region extends to higher and higher energies, merging with the region in which we find **X-rays** of 10 Å to 100 Å wavelength. Here, the photon energy is some 100 times greater than the energy of visible-light photons. At still higher energies we find the **γ-rays** of nuclear origin. There is no upper energy limit to this continuum, although the physical processes that produce superenergetic photons become less likely to take place as the energy increases.

Similarly, there are photons of *less energy* than those in the visible region of the spectrum. Those near the lower limit of the sensitivity of the eye, the **near-infrared** photons, are detected by our skin as a sensation of heat. With decreasing energy or increasing wavelength, we lose even this sensory detection and have to rely solely on technical means, such as specific photographic emulsions. Here we have the **far-infrared** photons of wavelength about 5 to 50 microns. Then, photons whose wavelength is about 10^4 times that of the visible range comprise the upper limit of the **radio range**. At **centimeter wavelengths**, or frequencies of the order of 10 GHz (10^{10} Hz), we find the radar and television bands, the ultrahigh frequencies, and the very high frequencies; at wavelengths above a few **meters**, or frequencies below 100 MHz (10^8 Hz), are the shortwave bands and the AM frequencies (the latter around 1 MHz). So "890 on your dial" means that the radio station emits photons with a frequency of 890 kHz. Thus, radio waves are really streams of photons with comparatively small energies. Again, there is no low-energy limit to the spectrum, but its usefulness disappears as the wavelengths reach dimensions comparable to the size of our earth.

A γ-ray with wavelength $\lambda = 0.1 \ \text{Å} = 10^{11} \ \text{m}$ has 10^{13} times the energy of a radio photon with $\lambda = 100 \ \text{m}$. In this tremendously wide spectrum visible light occupies a range whose maximum and minimum energies differ by just a factor of 2, yet all the astronomical information we had up to the year 1940 came from this narrow band. The atmosphere of the earth does not pass all photons unhindered. In fact, most astronomical work is based on a band only slightly wider than the visible spectrum, along with the "radio range" between wavelengths of several millimeters and some 100 m. The equally important high-energy band, comprised of ultraviolet, X, and γ photons, is only accessible from satellites and spacecraft.

Figure C-1 shows the photon spectrum in its entirety. The shaded areas show the approximate positions of the two principal "windows" in the earth's atmosphere.

C.2 THE DOPPLER EFFECT

The photon energy (and thus wavelength, color, and frequency) detected by an observer changes if there is a motion of the source with respect to the observer. This is the **Doppler effect**. Suppose three observers watch the same source, the first being at rest with respect to the source, the second moving toward the source, and the third moving away from the source. The energy of the impinging photons appears greater to the second observer (he sees a **blueshift**) and lower to the third observer (**redshift**), than to the man at rest.

To describe this change in energy (or frequency, or wavelength) in quantitative terms, we must first note that only the component of velocity along the line of sight between observer and source, that is, the *radial velocity* v_r, is of moment. Second, write E_0 (or ν_0, or λ_0) for the energy (or frequency, or wavelength) of the photons as measured with source and observer at rest, and E (or ν, or λ) for the corresponding quantities observed by a moving observer. Then we have $E_0 > E$ (or $\nu_0 > \nu_1$, or $\lambda_0 < \lambda$), that is, a redshift, if the motion of source and observer is away from each other; but $E_0 < E$ (or $\nu_0 < \nu_1$, or $\lambda_0 > \lambda$), that is, a blueshift if the motion is toward each other. The absolute value of each difference is related to the absolute value of v_r by the formula

$$\frac{|E - E_0|}{E} = \frac{|\nu - \nu_0|}{\nu_0} = \frac{|\lambda - \lambda_0|}{\lambda_0} = \frac{|v_r|}{C}$$

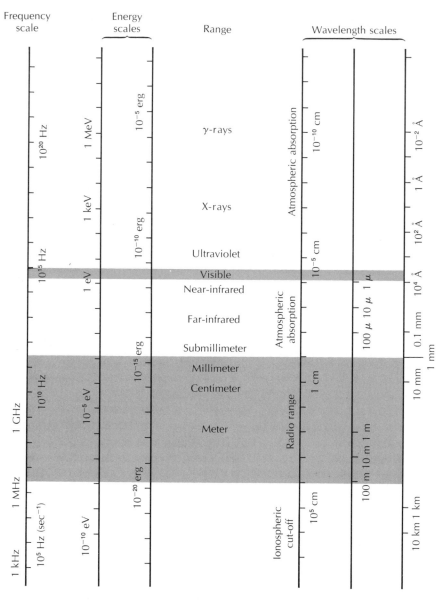

FIGURE C-1. Photon spectrum.

where c is the speed of light. This relation holds for values of v_r much smaller than c and is sufficient for our purposes, except in one case (Section 21.4).

We are, of course, all familiar with the Doppler effect, since it also affects sound waves; in this case, our ears sense the frequency as pitch (higher pitch = higher frequency = shorter wavelength). An oncoming car using its horn appears to the observer to emit a frequency above the one the driver of the car hears; the frequency decreases as the car passes and moves away. Hence, a stationary observer hears the horn of the passing car suddenly change from higher to lower pitch.

C.3 ATOMS AND MOLECULES

Matter. Before we can describe where photons come from and where they go—in brief, how they interact with matter—we must discuss the structure of matter.

Every piece of matter is made up of a finite number of **atoms**, or groups of atoms called **molecules**. They are very small (of the order of angstroms) and can be arranged in innumerable patterns, each resulting in one specific material. If the atoms or molecules that make up the material are very rigidly bound to each other, the material is a **solid**, such as a piece of iron (in iron, the basic entities are single iron atoms). If the atoms or molecules have a certain freedom to move about, they comprise a **liquid** (such as water, whose basic entity is a molecule consisting of two hydrogen atoms and one oxygen atom bound strongly together). And if they are completely free to move with respect to each other, they form a **gas**; air is a mixture, mostly of two types of molecules, one consisting of two nitrogen atoms, one of two oxygen atoms.

Physicists and chemists have compiled a list of all the types of atoms, or **elements** as they are called; in this list, the *periodic table*, the elements are arranged by increasing mass or weight. It is reproduced in Table H-3, which also gives the **chemical symbols**, a shorthand notation for the elements.

If we increase the temperature of a gas consisting of molecules, there is a temperature at which the molecules **dissociate**, and the atoms go their separate ways. Again, the temperature at which specific molecules break up into single atoms depends on the constituents.

Atomic Structure. The atoms themselves are highly structured systems. The mass of an atom is almost totally concentrated in its center, in a volume that is a minute fraction of the volume of the atom itself. This central region is called the **nucleus**. It is surrounded by a **cloud of electrons** of much smaller mass. Whereas the atom normally appears electrically neutral to the observer, its two subsystems are electrically charged; the nucleus is *positive*, and the electron cloud *negative*. Since electrical charges come in integer multiples of a basic unit, the **elementary charge**, there must be an equal number of positively charged heavy particles (**protons**) in the nucleus, and negatively charged **electrons** outside it. In addition to the protons, the nucleus contains electrically *neutral* particles, **neutrons**, each of almost the same mass as a proton. Table H-3 lists the number of protons in the nucleus of each element as well as the number of protons plus neutrons.

Each element can exist in several variations, called **isotopes**. They differ in the number of neutrons contained in the nucleus and, hence, in the weight of the nucleus; otherwise, the isotopes of a given element behave pretty much alike. To distinguish among isotopes, we sometimes write the number of protons and neutrons as a superscript to the chemical symbol; thus, the most common isotope of oxygen would be O^{16}. All elements found in the universe, including our planet, are mixtures of isotopes, some of them more abundant than others, some stable, others not. The most abundant isotope of the element iron, Fe^{56}, has 26 protons and 30 neutrons in its nucleus. Table H-3 lists the most abundant isotopes of each element; in the case where all isotopes are unstable, the longest-lived isotopes are listed.

The number of protons (and the equal number of electrons) determines the position of an element in the periodic table and is responsible for the chemical

TABLE C-1. ASTRONOMICALLY IMPORTANT MOLECULES

Compound	Chemical symbol	Occurrence in the universe (text reference)
Hydrogen molecule	H_2	Stellar atmospheres (9.5); interstellar material (16.2)
Oxygen molecule	O_2	Earth atmosphere (2.2); planetary atmospheres (5.3)
Ozone	O_3	Earth atmosphere (2.5)
Nitrogen molecule	N_2	Earth atmosphere (2.2)
Free radicals	OH, CH, CN, C_2, NH_2	Cometary matter (6.3); stellar atmospheres (9.5); interstellar material (16.2)
Carbon dioxide	CO_2	Earth atmosphere (2.2); planetary atmospheres (5.3)
Water	H_2O	Earth atmosphere (2.5); planetary atmospheres (5.3); interstellar material (16.1, 16.2)
Ammonia	NH_3	Planetary atmospheres (5.3); interstellar material (16.2)
Methane	CH_4	Planetary atmospheres (5.3)
Hydrocyanic acid	HCN	Interstellar material (16.2)
Formic acid	CHO_2H	Interstellar material (16.2)
Formaldehyde	H_2CO	Interstellar material (16.2)
Cyanoacetylene	HC_3N	Interstellar material (16.2)
Methyl alcohol	CH_3OH	Interstellar material (16.2)
Silicon monoxide	SiO	Interstellar material (16.1)
Titanium oxide	TiO	Stellar atmospheres (9.5)
Zirconium oxide	ZrO	Stellar atmospheres (9.5)

behavior of the element, its ability or inability to form molecules, etc. Note that no elements are "missing" from Table H-3, in the sense that the number of protons runs from 1 to 103; of course there may be some beyond the latter figure.

The chemical symbols are also used in describing the composition of molecules. For instance, oxygen and nitrogen in our earth's atmosphere combine pairwise to form O_2 and N_2. Water, a compound of two hydrogen atoms and one of oxygen, has the composition H_2O; formaldehyde is H_2CO (Section 16.2). Table C-1 lists the molecules encountered in this text; some of them, such as O_2 and N_2, exist under the conditions of our earth's atmosphere but not, for instance, in stars; others are not stable in our atmosphere but exist elsewhere in the universe. An example is the so-called *free radical* OH. For each molecule, typical occurrences in cosmic sources are listed along with references to the text proper.

C.4 THE ELECTRON CLOUD

Let us now take a closer look at the electrons surrounding the atomic nucleus. We have already seen that in their neutral states the various elements differ in the total number of electrons they contain. The atom is often represented as simulating a microsolar system in which the smaller electrons orbit about the larger nucleus on well-prescribed paths. This picture, in spite of its beauty, is neither correct nor adequate. In fact, we cannot really locate any one specific electron in a given atomic system; instead, we visualize the electrons as somehow surrounding the nucleus in an electron cloud, and we ignore spatial arrangement.

We characterize the behavior of electrons in the following somewhat abstract manner: we first note how many electrons there are altogether in the cloud. In one of the possible arrangements of the electrons, their *internal-energy content* (with respect to the nucleus) will be minimal. We call this the **ground state** and arbitrarily assign it an energy value of zero. In any other of the very large number of possible electron arrangements, the internal-energy content will be greater. These **excited states** are **discrete**; that is, they occur at specific energies, rather than continuously, and a change from one state to another usually involves only one electron at a time. The particular excited states that are possible are determined by the total number of electrons present, and the complete energy-level scheme is thus characteristic of a given element.

Figures C-2 and C-3 show as examples the energy diagram of the simplest atom, hydrogen, and a portion of the energy diagram of a complex atom, iron. The only thing we must remember here is the very well defined values by which the various excited states differ from the ground state. The other parts of the figures will be discussed in the next section.

Note in Fig. C-2 that the excited states tend to converge toward a finite value. At this value (13.6 eV for hydrogen), the energy of the electron is great enough so that it can leave the atom for good and become a **free electron**, not associated with (or *bound to*) a specific atom. If an electron escapes from an atom, we say the atom is **ionized**; the remaining nucleus plus the electrons (whose number is now reduced by one) is called the **ion**. In the case of hydrogen, the ion is simply a proton. Note, too, that because a negative electron leaves the neutral atom in forming an ion, the ion becomes positively charged. Occasionally an additional electron becomes attached to a neutral atom to form a **negative ion**, such as the H^- ion consisting of one proton and two electrons.

The electrons of a positive ion again define a ground state and discrete excited bound states; if additional energy is given them, they reach a point where one more electron is freed, and what is left is a **doubly ionized** atom. Obviously, the electrons of an element like iron, which has 26, can be removed one by one. But the ionization energy, that is, the energy a specific electron must acquire in order to leave the atomic system, increases rapidly as the atom proceeds from the neutral state to multiple ionizations. Of the more frequently mentioned elements, helium has the highest ionization energy; that of hydrogen is about half this amount; those of metals such as iron, about one-third.

C.5 ELECTRON TRANSITIONS. EMISSION AND ABSORPTION OF PHOTONS

Transitions. Energy cannot be manufactured or destroyed, so an electron that moves to a higher-energy bound state must receive an amount of energy equal to the difference between the energy of the original state and that of the new state. Under astronomical conditions, the most important process that provides atomic electrons with this energy requires photons of precisely the right energy. Such a photon is **absorbed** by the atom, and the energy is transmitted to the atomic elec-

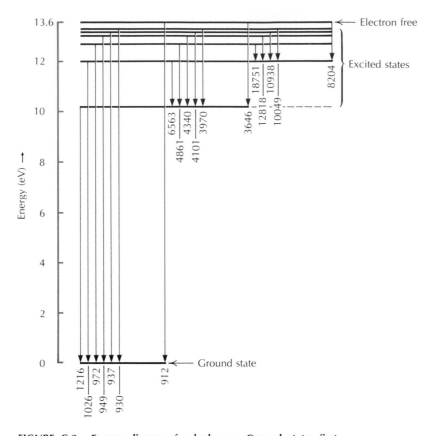

FIGURE C-2. Energy diagram for hydrogen. Ground state, first six excited states, and continuum state (where the atom is ionized) are indicated by the horizontal lines at their specific energy levels. The wavelengths of the photons emitted in the principal electron transitions (spectral lines) are shown in angstrom units next to the corresponding vertical arrows. For instance, the spectral line called "Lyman α," which comes about when an electron jumps from the first excited state to the ground state (emission) or vice versa (absorption), is 1216 Å, corresponding to a photon energy of just a little more than 10 eV.

trons. Similarly, if the electron system is initially in an excited state, it may fall back to the ground state (or to a lower excited state) by **emitting** a photon whose energy corresponds to the energy difference between the two states involved. The wavelengths of some photons that can be absorbed or emitted by hydrogen are indicated in Fig. C-2; see, in particular, the limiting wavelength of 912 Å (*continuum*) and "Lyman α" at 1216 Å. A wavelength of 912 Å corresponds to the minimal energy a photon must have in order to free an electron, that is, to ionize the hydrogen atom. The energy corresponding to a wavelength of 1216 Å moves the hydrogen atom from the ground state to the first excited state.

In a typical astronomical situation, billions of photons of all possible energies abound, so that atomic electrons are very seldom without photons suitable for

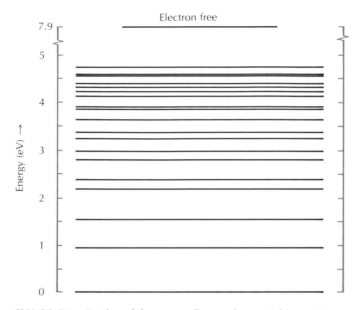

FIGURE C-3. Portion of the energy diagram for neutral iron. Note the numerous bound states, arranged in a very complex fashion.

absorption. However, whether an atom actually initiates such an absorption and, similarly, whether it actually emits a photon if it is in an excited state, depends on the structure of the atom and various other properties. Essentially, a specific **transition probability** is associated with every possible **transition** between any two states of any atomic system; these transition probabilities vary by orders of magnitude from one case to another. There are some transitions that are of great importance in astronomy in spite of the fact that they occur very seldom. They are commonly called **forbidden** transitions because they do not follow the usual transition patterns and have an extremely low probability.

Electrons in atomic systems can exchange energy with passing material particles such as free electrons, by absorbing some of their kinetic energy instead of absorbing photons. An atomic electron may also give off energy in such an **electron collision**. Obviously, the collision processes are much more likely to occur in dense gases; on the other hand, "forbidden" transitions involving photons usually take place only if the density of the gas is extremely low, because otherwise it is much easier to come by energy through the collision processes.

An atomic electron can be freed and its atom ionized if it receives an amount of energy equal to the appropriate ionization energy, say from a photon. But in this case, the photon need not have exactly the required energy. Any excess above the ionization energy simply becomes the kinetic energy of the freed electron. Similarly, if an ion captures a free electron with a certain kinetic energy in a **recombination** process, it emits a photon whose energy consists of the sum of the kinetic energy of the originally free electron and the ionization energy.

Thus, while transitions among the various excited states involve *discrete* amounts of energy, ionization and recombination involve a *continuous* range of energies above some minimum. Thus, the photons emitted or absorbed in transitions among excited states have discrete wavelengths; these wavelengths can be detected in the form of lines, and we say that they form **spectral lines**. The photons involved in ionization and recombination are not of individual wavelengths, but rather show a continuous distribution of wavelengths; they form a **continuum** in the spectrum, with a fixed lower boundary corresponding to the ionization energy.

Spectral Analysis. The principle of **spectral analysis** is now fairly obvious: A particular atom or ion, having its own very specific scheme of discrete energy levels, emits and absorbs a unique set of photons (in terms of energies or wavelengths) and so shows a unique set of spectral lines. Thus, if we observe the spectrum of a source and measure the wavelengths of the lines that appear in it, we can tell the **chemical composition** of the source, that is, of the atoms and ions (and molecules, for that matter) involved in the photon transitions. In Fig. C-2, for example, are the wavelengths of the photons generated in the more important transitions of hydrogen. Even hydrogen, with its very simple set of excited states, has a large number of possible characteristic wavelengths. We can, for example, compute a set of spectral lines for the iron atom from the differences between the pairs of discrete energy levels in Fig. C-3. Note, however, that the various combinations of energy differences, and hence the various transitions, will have vastly different transition probabilities.

By applying more detailed concepts of atomic physics, we can obtain even more information about a source from its spectrum. For instance, we can tell its temperature and density by measuring the shape or **contour** of its spectral lines, that is, by using the fact that even the discrete states of atomic systems allow for minute variations in energy values. Thus, depending upon the physical conditions, a collection of atoms in transition between the same excited states might emit photons of slightly different energies. Their wavelengths, in an actual example, may vary over a range of less than 1 Å in, say, the hydrogen line H_α at 6563 Å (Fig. C-2).

If a source moves with respect to us, we observe the Doppler effect in its spectrum. In that case, the whole spectrum, including the lines, is shifted from its rest value to a lower value if the source moves toward us, or to a higher value if it moves away. In the H_α example, the rest value is 6563 Å; it becomes 6565 Å if the source is moving away at 100 km/sec, and 6552 Å if moving toward us at 500 km/sec. The details of a spectral line are also altered in the presence of a magnetic field (the *Zeeman effect*); by measuring this change it is possible to find the actual magnetic-field strength at the position of the source.

The electron clouds of the atoms that make up a specific molecule combine in a manner characteristic of the molecule in question, and again show a specific set of discrete states. There are many more possible energy states in a molecule than even in the most complex atoms; they are grouped in clusters, so that the corresponding transitions show up as sets of spectral lines very close to each other, in what we call **bands**. Molecular bands can cover whole areas of the spectrum; they are prominent in cool stars (Section 7.5), and some of the interstellar radio lines are parts of specific bands (Section 16.2).

C.6 PLANCK'S LAW

While we have so far discussed mostly one atom colliding with one electron, or emitting and absorbing one photon, celestial sources are made up of billions and billions of systems continuously interacting with each other. Thus, in nature we are concerned with the *statistical properties* of large assemblies of systems.

In Section B.6 we defined *temperature* as a measure of the mean energy of a material; now we can say that some of this energy is vested in the kinetic energy with which the atoms and molecules of the material move about. In addition, some atoms and molecules will always be in excited states, or even ionized; their number, too, will be affected by temperature. The percentages of excited and ionized atoms and molecules are called the *degree of excitation* and *degree of ionization*.

Thus, at a given temperature and corresponding degrees of excitation and ionization, there is a continuous interplay of atoms with photons, some being absorbed and some emitted at all times. Wherever there are atoms or molecules that together make up a material body—a rock in a field or a star out in the universe—there are photons too, being emitted by one atom and absorbed by its neighbor, reemitted and reabsorbed, and so on.

Planck's Law.   It was established at the turn of this century that the total number of photons present in a source, and their energy distribution, are determined by the temperature of the source. This result is described quantitatively by **Planck's law** which is illustrated in Fig. C-4. Let us first look at one of the curves, say, the one labeled "5000°K." It gives in units, arbitrarily called "0" through "3," the number of photons present per cubic centimeter as a function of wavelength. As wavelengths increase (energies decrease) the number of photons suddenly rises, reaches a maximum at about 6000 Å, and then drops slowly toward long wavelengths.

If we compare these **Planck curves** for different temperatures, we find two things: first, for a particular wavelength, the number of photons present is larger at the higher temperature; second, the maximum number of photons tends toward shorter wavelengths (higher energy) as temperature increases. According to Planck's law, the total number of photons crossing a square centimeter of material, each multiplied by its energy, that is, the total **intensity** of the light source at a given temperature T is

$$I = aT^4$$

where a is a constant whose numerical value is 5.7×10^{-5} erg/cm$^2 \cdot$ sec $\cdot$ degree^4. Note the rapid increase of intensity with temperature predicted by the formula. Note also that the constant a does not depend on the type of material that is radiating. Finally, λ does not appear in the formula, since we account for photons of all wavelengths in computing the intensity I.

A fire that is really blazing in the fireplace is bright and has a bluish color; it gets dimmer and its color changes to yellow, then ultimately to red, with diminishing temperature. This corresponds to the decrease in total intensity and the shifting of the maxima of the Planck curves to longer wavelengths as temperature decreases; the many photons present at and near the wavelength of maximum intensity are the ones which determine the color impression recorded by our eyes.

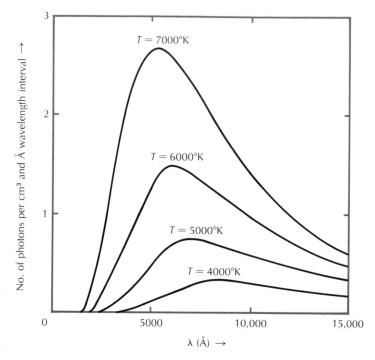

FIGURE C-4. Planck curves for 4000°K, 5000°K, 6000°K, and 7000°K. The vertical scale is plotted in arbitrary units.

Use in Astronomy. We have implied, in the foregoing discussion, the crucial point that allows us to apply Planck's law to astronomical situations, namely, that the photons emitted away from the surface of a material body at a certain temperature are not reabsorbed. When they are detected by an observer they have a wavelength distribution that approximately follows Planck's law for the same temperature of the body. The observer—that is, the astronomer—can then work backwards to determine the surface temperature of the body.

However, we must recall one complication, because it is central to some of our astronomical arguments: most astronomical sources do not have well-defined surfaces, but instead have layers from which most photons escape and then (more or less) follow Planck's law. In certain spectral ranges, particularly at the wavelengths corresponding to electron transitions with high probabilities, they come from beyond the "surface," where there is still some dilute gas present. The Planck curve followed by these photons will reflect the temperature in this outer gaseous area; this will, in general, result in spectral lines differing in intensity from those originating further down in the star, even if the individual transition probabilities are the same.

C.7 BREMSSTRAHLUNG AND SYNCHROTRON RADIATION

In the foregoing sections we summarized those interactions between matter and radiation that are of concern in astronomy. Implicit in these considerations was the premise that photons are emitted or absorbed by atomic, ionic, and molecular systems, whenever their electrons change energy configuration. However, there are some other ways of creating or absorbing photons; these involve free electrons, and they are of great importance in astronomy.

Bremsstrahlung. The first process we are concerned with is called **bremsstrahlung;** its name is a German word derived from a specific laboratory arrangement in which electrons are decelerated by atoms and emit photons (bremsstrahlung = deceleration radiation). The process, in our context, takes place whenever free electrons come near ions without being captured. Photons of all sorts of energies are emitted and absorbed by the free electrons, that is, bremsstrahlung results in a *continuum*. The number of high-energy photons emitted or absorbed is greater if the free electron has a high velocity relative to the ion. Bremsstrahlung photons are mostly observed in the radio range, and a great many astronomical sources owe the radio portions of their spectra to this mechanism. Among them are the solar corona (Section 7.5) and H II regions (Section 16.2).

Synchrotron Radiation. At still higher electron velocities, namely, close to the speed of light, another mechanism becomes predominant, producing more photons than the bremsstrahlung mechanism. This second mechanism requires the presence of magnetic fields, which actually exist practically everywhere in the universe to varying degrees. Relativistic electrons in magnetic fields emit and absorb photons ''by themselves,'' independently of the presence of ions, using their kinetic energies as reservoirs. This type of emission or absorption is called **synchrotron radiation;** the name originated with an earthly laboratory device called the synchrotron, which produces relativistic electrons.

The synchrotron radiation spectrum is quite distinct from that of bremsstrahlung, and the two can readily be distinguished. Both the magnetic-field strength, and the number of relativistic electrons and their energy distribution (or at least a combination of these data), can usually be extracted from the observed synchrotron spectrum. It can involve photons with energies all the way from the X-ray range to the radio range.

C.8 SOLIDS, LIQUIDS, AND GASES. DEGENERACY

The States of Matter. Let us summarize at this point the major difference between gases and solids, with the understanding that liquids occupy a place somewhere in between. A given amount of gas will fill any volume, whereas in the solid state the same number of atoms has a fixed volume. Of course, by lowering its temperature to a certain critical point (which depends on chemical composition and initial matter density), any gas can be transformed into a solid of one form or another.

In a solid the atoms and molecules are arranged in a fixed pattern, a **lattice,** with the temperature-specified motion largely vested in internal vibrations within this lattice. In metals at room temperature and atmospheric pressure, the atomic nuclei form the lattice. Just as the electron cloud of a single atom can occupy a large variety of discrete energy states, so the electron ''gas'' of the metal can assume discrete levels. The many electrons in the metal are distributed among these levels.

Degeneracy.   The *Pauli exclusion principle* states that no more than two electrons can be in the same energy state at the same time. Because the lowest energy states are the most appealing to electrons, they will always be filled. In a metal lattice, the electrons will actually seek out the low-energy states, up to a certain energy determined by the electron *density,* that is, the number of electrons per cubic centimeter. An electron in one of the higher filled states will be unable to lower its energy (for instance, by emitting a photon) if it cannot find an empty place lower on the energy scale. Then, in spite of a possibly large internal energy, the electrons are unable to expel energy by emitting photons. This physical situation is called **degeneracy:** the electrons are settled in a crystalline pattern, unable to change their energies or the volume they occupy.

Under "normal" conditions (the particle densities at the surface of the earth, room temperature, etc.) degeneracy occurs in metals, but not in elements such as hydrogen and helium. In the universe, however, there are objects in which vastly different physical conditions, in particular, much higher electron densities (say, in stellar interiors) prevail. Since the electron density determines whether the electrons become degenerate, that is, whether the lower electron states are filled, we would expect to find stellar objects in which the material is in the degenerate state; see, for instance, the white dwarfs of Section 13.5.

Finally, we mention that the exclusion principle holds for electrons but not for photons, for reasons that have to do with the basic properties of these particles. However, neutrons are subject to degeneracy, a fact which is crucial to an understanding of the mechanism behind neutron stars (Section 14.4).

D nuclei and their reactions

Some areas of astronomy, mainly those involved with the energy balance of stars, their evolution, and the mechanism of some of the more spectacular events, require a more detailed understanding of what goes on in atomic nuclei. Although nuclear physics is still not quite a settled field of knowledge, its applications to astronomy have been worked out and are fairly certain. Since our review is restricted to material which serves as background for the main body of the text, we present in this chapter an extremely biased selection from the principles of nuclear physics.

D.1 NUCLEAR FORCE AND BINDING ENERGY

Nuclear Force.   In Section C.3, we characterized the atomic nucleus as the central portion of the atom, containing almost all the mass in a minute volume, and being positively charged. We noted that each nucleus consists of electrically positive protons and electrically neutral neutrons, with the number of protons determining the position of the atom in the periodic table. Finally, we saw that each element may have several isotopes, differing from each other in the number of neutrons present in the nucleus.

We also noted that some of these isotopes are **stable,** and others are not. We shall now attempt to explain what this means — in particular, what changes take place in unstable nuclei. We first must determine what holds the protons and neutrons (collectively, **nucleons**) together in this extremely small volume called the nucleus. We know that protons repel each other through the Coulomb force acting among electrically charged particles, so that a very strong *attractive* force must be present to overcome this repulsion. Gravity certainly is not able to serve in this capacity. But there is a third, completely independent, force acting among material particles in the universe; whether this **nuclear force** is truly basic, as we think the Coulomb force is, or a derivative of some other independent force, is immaterial at the moment. It differs from the gravitational and Coulomb forces in that it is effective only if the particles are very close to each other; that is, the nuclear force decreases in strength with distance much more rapidly than either of the other forces. The nuclear force acts among protons and neutrons in the same manner and is always attractive.

Binding Energy.   We saw in Section B.5 that there is an energy associated with each type of force; the energy corresponding to the nuclear force is called nuclear **binding energy.** Every nucleus has a certain binding energy which we usually express in terms of a single nucleon; that is, we divide the total force per nucleus by the number of

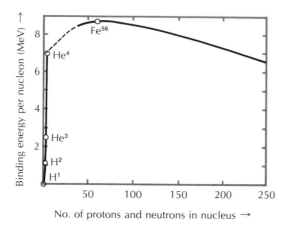

FIGURE D-1. Binding energy per nucleon versus element number.

protons and neutrons present. This **binding energy per nucleon** depends in a rather complex fashion on the relative numbers of protons and neutrons, but shows the trend pictured in Fig. D-1. It reaches a maximum in the neighborhood of iron, with the low values at the very light and very heavy nuclei. In the realm of intermediate nuclei, between He^4 and Fe^{56}, only an average curve (dashed in Fig. D-1) can be given, since the actual values scatter according to the ratio of protons to neutrons. Also note the binding energy per nucleon of the He^4 nucleus, about 7 MeV. As we saw in Section 7.2, binding four protons together into a He^4 nucleus results in an energy gain of about 27 MeV.

Fission and Fusion. A nucleon which is attracted to another and thus decreases their mutual distance is able to perform work, just as a stone or a meteorite falling to the surface of the earth can do work. Similarly, if we want to remove a nucleon from the neighborhood of others, we have to add energy to it. This energy is added to or removed from the energy reservoir vested in the mass of the nucleon — mass is transformed into energy, or vice versa. Energy E and mass m are related by **Einstein's formula**

$$E = mc^2$$

where c is the speed of light. If a nucleon moves into a nucleus, its mass decreases by an amount determined by the binding energy per nucleon from Fig. D-1 and this formula.

Thus, if we start with single nucleons (protons or neutrons) and combine them into complex nuclei, we end up with excess energy and slightly less mass. This process is called **fusion** and is the basis of the energy production of stars during most phases of their life. The opposite process, called **fission,** in which we break large nuclei such as U^{235} into smaller ones, also results in an energy gain, simply because the binding energy of the fragments, taken together, is larger than the binding energy of the original nucleus (see Fig. D-1). Nuclear-power reactors are based on fission processes. The big hydrogen bombs use both processes for good measure; a fission core starts the thing off, and its power is increased through hydrogen fusion.

Finally, the existence of a definite binding energy per nucleon implies a well-defined (discrete) energy state for nucleons. In fact, paralleling the case of electrons in the atoms, this binding energy defines the *ground state;* nucleons in a nucleus are able to occupy many *excited states* as well. Then, having some internal energy, they can undergo transitions among states; we shall return to this point presently.

D.2   SPONTANEOUS DECAY

The binding energy per nucleon depicted in Fig. D-1 is only a very crude measure of the physics of nuclei. In reality, there are significant differences among the isotopes of a given element. For instance, isotopes that contain a disproportionate number of protons or neutrons have much less tightly bound nuclei than isotopes containing protons and neutrons in roughly equal numbers or, in the case of heavy nuclei, in certain ratios. If excess neutrons could be converted into protons, or vice versa, the nuclei would go into energetically more advantageous states, that is, transform themselves into more tightly bound compounds. This, indeed, does occur, and we call this type of process **spontaneous decay.**

***β⁻* Decay (or Emission).**   A neutron can be transformed into a proton through the emission of an electron. The problem is to increase the total number of positive electric charges by one. This is accomplished by the creation of a pair of opposite charges and the emission of the negative one. The positive charge is retained within the nucleus, where it serves to transform a neutron into a proton. The negative charge is a conventional electron (in nuclear physics normally called a ***β⁻* particle**). For this process to be feasible, the nucleus must be capable of imparting to the electron its rest energy (mc^2, according to Einstein's formula) and whatever kinetic energy the electron takes along. For reasons that are not of concern here, another particle is emitted with the electron, a so-called **neutrino,** whose main properties are zero mass, zero electric charge, and some finite energy. Neutrinos almost never interact with other particles, so that the energy they remove from the nuclei is for all practical purposes lost forever.

***β⁺* Decay (or Emission).**   Protons can be transformed into neutrons through the emission of a ***β⁺* particle** and a neutrino. This *β⁺* particle, the **positron,** has all the properties of an electron except that its electric charge is positive; we can call the positron the mirror image of the electron. Positrons (at least in our corner of the world) are extremely short-lived: as soon as one comes near an electron, the two combine in a so-called **pair-annihilation process** and transform themselves—rest mass, kinetic energy, and all—into radiation of very short wavelength (γ-rays).

Before we continue this summary, we must mention that *every* type of particle— proton, neutron, or electron—has such a mirror image or **antiparticle;** and all anti-particles are extremely short-lived. However, all antiparticles have been produced in one way or another in the laboratory, and they play an important part in certain cosmological speculations.

α Decay.   Aside from β^- and β^+ emission, other possibilities exist for spontaneous changes in nuclear-energy balances. Most important is the ejection of a compound consisting of two protons and two neutrons bound together, in other words, a helium nucleus, usually called an **α particle**. In such an α decay, the chemical nature of the emitting element is changed, owing to the loss of the two protons. The nucleus that remains after α decay is often in one of the excited states mentioned at the end of Section D.1. It returns to the ground state via emission of high-energy photons of very short wavelength, which show up in the γ region of the spectrum.

Carbon Dating.   Again, the processes by which nuclei decay vary in their probabilities, resulting in vastly different average **lifetimes** for the transformed nuclei. Often a given nucleus can decay in several ways, only one of which is particularly probable. If only spontaneous decay processes occur in a mixture of elements, the most unstable nuclei will transform almost instantaneously; as time goes on, more and more of the most stable nuclei will appear. The relative abundances of the various isotopes after long periods of decay are used to determine the ages of earthly rocks, meteorites, fossils, and artifacts. In the case of fossils and artifacts, a particular unstable isotope of carbon (C^{14}) is the one whose history is most often traced; the process is then called **carbon dating.**

D.3   THERMONUCLEAR PROCESSES

Even more important in astronomy than the spontaneous decay processes are the **thermonuclear processes,** which take place at the temperatures of stellar interiors.

Assume that a nucleus performing some random motion in a gas comes so close to another nucleus that the attractive nuclear force pulls the two together to form a compound nucleus. Since both nuclei are positively charged, they will at first (that is, at greater distance) repel each other through the Coulomb force. However, if the relative speed of the nuclei is high enough to begin with, their kinetic energy may be sufficient to overcome the repulsive Coulomb force (or **Coulomb barrier**), so that they approach each other to the point where the nuclear force takes over. And if the temperature of the gas is high enough, some nuclei will indeed have sufficient speed, and thus kinetic energy, to initiate this fusion process.

If the original nuclei are relatively light, the formation of the compound nucleus releases energy. This energy can then be freed in a variety of ways: by direct emission of γ photons, by transformation of protons and neutrons into each other with simultaneous emission of β^+ or β^- particles and neutrinos, or even by the emission of α particles. This is the fundamental energy-production process for stars.

E astronomical instruments

We have already seen in our historical introduction that the invention of the *telescope* was one of the decisive steps forward into modern astronomy. Although we are, in this text, less concerned with the actual process of collecting data than with concepts and interpretations, we should discuss the major types of instrumentation, in particular those that are unique to astronomy.

E.1 TELESCOPES

The purpose of using a **telescope** (instead of, say, the human eye) is twofold: it increases the light-collecting area so that dim objects become clearly visible, and it gives us added resolving power, that is, we can separate two objects that might appear as one to the naked eye.

Collecting Power.   The first advantage of the telescope is that it increases the **light-collecting area,** so that even very small photon densities arriving from great distances can be utilized to form an image of the source. The increase in collecting area is easy to estimate. The diameter of the collecting area of the human eye is about 0.5 cm, the diameter of the biggest optical telescope in operation, the 200-inch telescope on Mount Palomar in California, is 5 m. Since the collecting area increases with the square of the diameter, we find that using the 200-inch telescope allows us to see objects that are less than one-millionth as strong as those we can see without it. Another way of looking at this situation is by recalling that the number of photons crossing a unit area decreases with the square of the distance from the source, so that the 200-inch telescope gives us the view of an observer who is 1,000 times closer to the source than we actually are. In practice, the full advantage of the telescope is realized when the eye is replaced by a man-made sensor, such as a photoelectric cell, a photon counter, or a photographic plate. The reason is not that the eye only responds to many photons (in fact, the reverse is true), but that the eye "forgets" the advent of photons after a very short time (a fraction of a second), whereas a photographic plate will sum all the photons arriving during hours or days to form the image. Needless to say, eyes are of no use at all in detecting radiation outside the visible range; in particular, in the radio range, only telescopic equipment, combined with the appropriate sensors, "sees" anything at all.

Resolving Power.   Owing to a basic property of light, the minimum distinguishable separation between two points depends on the size of the receiving area. Since many

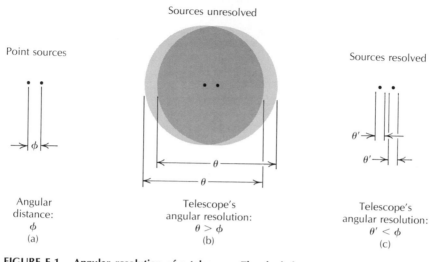

Point sources

Sources unresolved

Sources resolved

Angular
distance:
ϕ
(a)

Telescope's
angular resolution:
$\theta > \phi$
(b)

Telescope's
angular resolution:
$\theta' < \phi$
(c)

FIGURE E-1. Angular resolution of a telescope. The shaded areas indicate the minimum size of features distinguishable by the telescope. If $\theta > \phi$, the two sources are not resolved, and they would appear as one source spread over the large shaded area. If $\theta' < \phi$, the two sources are resolved, and they would appear as separate small discs.

of our sources are far away and thus have very small angular separation, we often need maximum **resolving power** to decide whether a light signal comes from a single source or several unresolved sources. The situation is illustrated in Fig. E-1. Assume that two point sources have an angular distance of ϕ from each other [Fig. E-1(a)]. If the resolving power of the measuring device is such that it can only distinguish between two sources with an angular separation of at least θ, with $\theta > \phi$, then the two sources are unresolved [Fig. E-1(b)]. If, on the other hand, the resolving power of the instrument is such that it can resolve within θ', with $\theta' < \phi$, then the sources are seen separated [Fig. E-1(c)].

Now, light moves in straight lines only as long as it does not impinge on a material body. If we force it through an opening, say a lens, it tends to spread out around the edges, a phenomenon we call **diffraction**. It is this phenomenon that limits angular resolution, for it results in extended images, the shaded areas in Figs. E-1(b) and E-1(c). If two objects are very close to each other, the extensions of their images will overlap. This diffraction behavior is a function of wavelength. For visible light, an opening of 10 cm (for instance, the mirror of a small reflecting telescope) allows for an angular resolution of about 1 arcsec. By contrast, the human eye, with its pupil of about 0.5 cm diameter, resolves only about 1 arcmin. We must mention here that the big modern telescopes do not do much better in this respect than a 10-cm instrument, for reasons that have to do with the earth's atmosphere rather than with their construction. Note, however, that atmospheric turbulence is of negligible importance in the radio range, so that radio telescopes can fully utilize the increased resolving power that results from greater instrument diameters.

Angular resolving power decreases proportionally as wavelength increases. Thus, the resolving power of a given telescope is almost twice as good in the violet part of the spectrum (3700 Å) as in the red (6500 Å). More important, between the visible range (5×10^{-5} cm) and a typical radio wavelength (5 cm), we lose five orders of magnitude in resolving power. If we wanted to see as clear a picture of the sky at radio wavelengths as we do with the naked eye, we would have to build a radio telescope of 500 m diameter! This, at present, is not quite feasible technically, so that the best radio maps of the sky show much less detail than even our eyes can make out in the visible range. A way out of this dilemma is discussed in Section E.4.

E.2 REFLECTORS AND REFRACTORS

Reflecting Telescopes.   There are two basic types of telescopes, **reflectors** and **refractors,** as well as a mixed version. The *reflector,* the more versatile and more basic, though newer type, consists of a mirror that collects (**focuses**) parallel or almost parallel rays of light into a point. Light gathered from two slightly different directions—say, from a double star—would then be focused into two images of corresponding angular separation (Fig. E-2). Of course, a point source should be seen as a point, or nearly so.

Surfaces of a variety of forms can be used as mirrors. However, not every surface will reproduce a point source exactly as a point image; the errors involved differ slightly from surface to surface. The simplest solution is to give the mirror the shape of a portion of a sphere, but in this case one of the more obnoxious errors is particularly great. Better quality is achieved by employing a mirror of **parabolic** shape, the result of rotating a parabola about its axis (see Fig. E-3). All the very large telescopes in use today are parabolic.

The surface at which the light is reflected is ground from a block of glass and then coated with a thin layer of silver or aluminum. Such a surface is reflective to all wavelengths down to X-rays. Radio waves are reflected in the same manner as visible light, except that, as we have seen, the resolving power is greatly reduced,

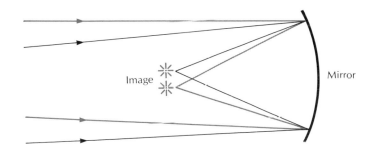

FIGURE E-2.   **Light paths in a reflecting telescope. The rays from the various points of an extended source (screened lines, solid lines) are focused at the corresponding points of the image. The construction assumes that the source points from which the photons arrive along the screened and solid rays are resolved (case $\theta' < \phi$ of Fig. E-1).**

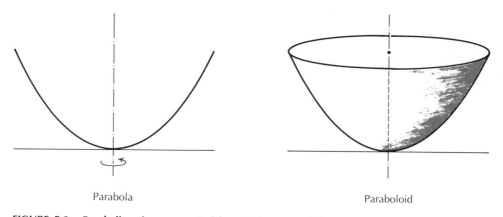

Parabola   Paraboloid

FIGURE E-3. **Parabolic mirror generated by rotating a parabola.**

and therefore very large mirrors must be built to achieve anything worthwhile. At radio frequencies, glass is not used; instead, the parabolic surface is formed of metal.

Astronomical telescopes track the apparent path of an object across the sky through **steering mechanisms**. Typically, modern optical telescopes are hung into a fork-type support which can rotate about its axis, while the telescope can be tilted inside the fork. Figure E-4 shows the 200-inch telescope in its mounting. Because of their huge mirrors, radio telescopes pose complex steering problems that limit their useful size. Figure E-5 shows the 300-foot steerable telescope of the National Radio Astronomy Observatory in Greenbank, West Virginia. If maximum size is desired, one can, of course, forgo steerability and move the sensor instead, which then limits use of the telescope to a relatively small area of the sky. If a radio telescope is not to be steerable, the mirror surface can be built into a natural depression or valley. Figure E-6 shows the nonsteerable radio telescope at Arecibo in Puerto Rico.

Refracting Telescopes. A different physical principle is used in building *refractors*. When light rays traverse dense material, they are bent away from their initial direction (**refraction**). Visible light behaves this way in glass; if we form a glass body with the right shape, we are able to bend parallel light rays so that they focus into a point. Such a **lens** is the main element of a refracting telescope or refractor. Figure E-7 shows the light path schematically.

Technical problems limit the maximum size of a refractor to about 1 meter in diameter; in addition, this type of telescope works only for photons that are not absorbed in the glass lens. Thus, reflectors have taken over most of the work once reserved for refractors. (Galileo's telescope was of the refractor type.) Figure E-8 shows the 36-inch refractor of the University of California's Lick Observatory.

Mixed Telescopes. For some 30 years now, mixed types of telescopes have also been used. The most common type is called the **Schmidt telescope** after its inventor. It has two main components, a reflector and a refracting element, and works this way: a spherical mirror is used to collect the light. But rather than being focused into an image that would be distorted because of the mirror, the light is reflected to a

FIGURE E-4. The 200-inch telescope in its dome on Mount Palomar in California. The mirror is at the lower right, the prime focus at the upper left. The huge tube system on the right is part of the mounting system. (*Hale Observatories*.)

correction plate, a sort of lens with a rather complex surface. This surface is constructed in such a manner that it removes most of the distortions introduced by the mirror, while focusing the light into an image. Figure E-9 shows the 48-inch Schmidt telescope on Mount Palomar in California.

E.3 SPECTROGRAPHS

We have spent a good deal of time in detailing the wealth of information contained in the spectrum of a light source. But if we are to extract any information, we have to be able to distinguish, and very finely, the many wavelengths that make up a spectrum. This is achieved with the aid of **spectrographs**.

Diffraction. In order to separate photons of different wavelengths, we must utilize phenomena whose physical behavior depends solely on wavelength. The two key processes were mentioned above in connection with telescopes. Again, we first consider *diffraction*, by which photons alter their direction of motion on meeting an

FIGURE E-5. **The 300-foot radio telescope of the National Radio Astronomy Observatory in Greenbank, West Virginia. The focus is at the end of the antenna mounting.** (*National Radio Astronomy Observatory.*)

"obstacle." By placing a row of obstacles (of the size of the photon's wavelength) in the path of a parallel beam of photons, it is possible to make the change in direction proportional to wavelength.

Figure E-10 shows schematically what happens to a mixture of "blue" and "red" photons impinging on the composite obstacle. What we have constructed is, in principle, known as a **diffraction grating,** the central element in a wavelength-separating device called the **grating spectrograph**.

Refraction. Another way of separating wavelengths makes use of the *refraction* of light in solids. A glass block of the appropriate shape will cause photons that enter it to leave at different angles, again depending on wavelength. The most common shape is the triangular **prism** shown in Fig. E-11, the central element of the **prism spectrograph**. Again, prism spectrographs can only be used to separate those wavelengths (mostly in the visible range) that are not absorbed by glass. Recent advances in the technology of gratings have made grating spectrographs quite versatile, so that prism spectrographs are seldom used nowadays. At any rate, it is now possible to separate photons whose wavelengths in the visible range differ by only 10^{-3} Å.

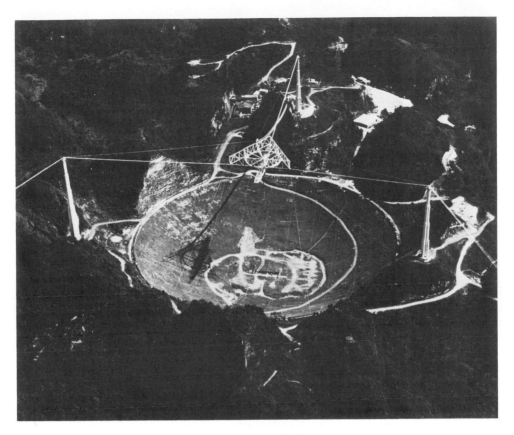

FIGURE E-6. **The Arecibo "telescope" in Puerto Rico. The diameter is about 1 km, the mirror surface is built into a natural depression and is lined with metal. The focus is at the symmetry point of the three antenna towers.** (*National Astronomy and Ionosphere Center, Cornell University.*)

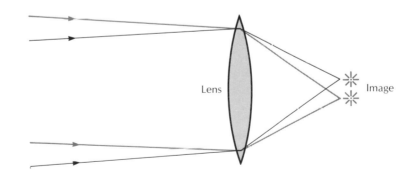

FIGURE E-7. **Light paths in a refracting telescope. The rays from the various points of an extended source (screened lines, solid lines) are focused at the corresponding points of the image. The construction assumes that the source points from which the photons arrive along the screened and solid rays are resolved (case $\theta' < \phi'$ of Fig. E-1).**

FIGURE E-8. The 36-inch refractor of the Lick Observatory on Mount Hamilton in California. The lens is mounted at the top right; the prime focus is at the lower end, where the observer stands. (*Lick Observatory.*)

FIGURE E-9. The 48-inch Schmidt telescope on Mount Palomar in California. The mirror is at the bottom of the main tube, the correction plate at the upper end. There are two small finder telescopes mounted on the tube. (*Hale Observatories.*)

Filters.   If only very crude wavelength separation is required, colored **filters**, which are cheap and easy to handle, are employed. Such filters—intrinsically no different from the stained glass in church windows—absorb all but a narrow range of wavelengths, and so give more or less monochromatic images of light sources.

Radio Range.   At radio frequencies, wavelength selectivity is achieved with elements which, in their general construction, are very similar to the tuners in radio and television sets. In the radio range it is comparatively easy to achieve extremely good resolution, and radio astronomy has provided very detailed information on the wavelength characteristics of the radiations of stars, interstellar matter, and distant extragalactic sources.

E.4   INTERFEROMETERS

It is possible to resolve two sources even if their angular distance is below the resolving power of a single telescope. This is done by using the phenomenon of **interference**, that is, the fact that photons emitted by two neighboring sources arrive at an observer's position via very slightly different paths and interfere with each other. Detection devices can be built to measure the degree of interaction. (Actually,

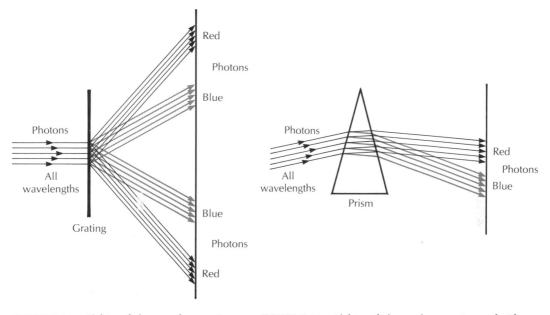

FIGURE E-10. **Light path in a grating spectrograph. The photons are deflected in the grating so that the deflection angle is proportional to the wavelength.**

FIGURE E-11. **Light path in a prism spectrograph. Photons of longer wavelength are deflected less than photons of shorter wavelength.**

a more detailed discussion of the workings of spectrographs in the last section would also have invoked the principle of interference.)

Suppose it is suspected that a source of radiation is actually a double source, but that the two objects involved cannot be resolved. If spectra are taken at opposite sides of the earth, they will be almost, but not quite, the same. If one spectrum is superimposed on the other, the "but not quite" will show up as an **interference pattern,** that is, strips of slightly increased or decreased intensity whose distance apart is a measure of the angular distance of the sources. This is the principle of the **interferometer.**

Although interferometry has been used at optical wavelengths—to obtain measures of the distances between very close binary systems of stars, or even of the diameters of single stars—its major application is in radio astronomy. The resolving power of a radio telescope is, as we have seen, so much lower than that of an optical telescope that almost any reasonable angular resolution requires interferometer techniques. Too, turbulence in the earth's atmosphere (or ionosphere) does not markedly limit the resolving power of radio interferometers. This makes it possible to measure much smaller angular distances. In the most recent applications, the telescopic elements of the interferometer were set up on different continents so that the distance between them was of the order of 10^4 km. The measurable angular distances were then of the order of 10^{-4} arcsec, or 1,000 times better than the best results obtainable with optical telescopes.

F names of celestial objects; catalogues

The names astronomers have given to celestial objects constitute what outsiders consider one of the more monumental confusions in scientific nomenclature; in rebuttal astronomers usually point to the systematic arrangement of the details. Throughout this text objects are identified by what astronomers usually call them, with an occasional short explanation of the origin of particular naming schemes. In the following, we list the various names once again, in one place, for reference. We do not claim that the name of a celestial object has an intrinsic value of itself, but on the whole the name simplifies identification of the object.

Fortunately, the naming of places on our earth is beyond the scope of this text. The moon is not much better off, with all its mountains, craters, and "oceans" without water (see Section 4.1 and, in particular, Fig. 4-3). The specific locations of features on planets are of interest to the specialist, and we have not bothered to list them in the text.

Of course, there are the planets themselves, and their names, derived from the gods of old whose personalities are known nowadays only to classics majors. Some of the asteroids have received names of the same type, but when too many were discovered, astronomers began to loosen the time-honored restrictions; hence, we have the asteroids Albert and Eva. For safety's sake, asteroids receive running numbers as well (see Table H-6).

The fate of the names of satellites of planets has not been much different, although lately the newcomers have been simply and prosaically numbered (see Table H-5). Comets, on the other hand, are named after their discoverers, which has led to a complicated scheme for establishing priorities; in addition, each comet receives a label consisting of the four digits of the year of perihelion passage and a running Roman number to distinguish among the several comets that might have come close to the sun in a particular year. Examples are found in Table H-7.

Relative to stars and celestial objects in general, we first mention the problem of defining the **constellations**. Originally the brightest stars in each area of the sky were grouped together and given the name of a mythological being or earthly object their outline or formation seemed to suggest. In modern astronomical usage the constellations are simply more or less gerrymandered areas on the celestial sphere (Figs. G-6 to G-9). Note that the constellation boundaries are simplified in the figures.

The brightest stars in a constellation are now named with letters of the Greek alphabet preceding the Latin designation of the constellation in genitive form; this is how δ Cephei in the constellation Cepheus gets its name. In addition, some stars have their own names, mostly badly mutilated Arab ones, such as Betelgeuse, otherwise known as α Orionis. Some of the stars of lesser brightness are identified by number and constellation name (like 40 Eridani, Section 13.4). Finally, a variable star is distinguished by one or more capital Roman letters preceding the constellation name, so we have, say, T Tauri (Section 12.1) and RR Lyrae stars (Section 15.1).

The large star catalogues prepared in the last 100 years or so arrange the many thousands of individual stars mostly according to their coordinates (right ascension and declination for a certain "epoch"; Section 3.1). Other catalogues specialize in bright stars, or stars within a certain distance of the sun (see Tables H-9 and H-10). Finally, in this connection, there is the monumental photographic atlas of the sky, the so-called *Palomar Sky Atlas* referred to on several occasions. This work is a collection of large-scale photographs of well-defined areas of the sky taken with the 48-inch Schmidt telescope. To specify a celestial object, astronomers will often use a reproduction of a small portion of one of these photographs; they simply mark the position of the object in question with an arrow (see Fig. 21-7).

There are also catalogues of the more "unusual" objects, such as gaseous nebulae and extragalactic systems. These usually list objects by running numbers. Here we mention Messier's classical catalogue from which we get the "names" M31, M33, etc., of bright galaxies; the later *New General Catalogue* (NGC); and the *Index Catalogue* (IC) (see Tables H-13 to H-15). Catalogues exist for practically every specialized class of objects.

Radio objects are listed in such catalogues as the *Cambridge* (England) *Catalogues*. Quasistellar objects and radio galaxies usually are quoted according to their designations in the third, fourth, and fifth editions as 3C, 4C, and 5C, followed either by a running number or a number based on celestial coordinates (see Table H-16). Finally, pulsars are named with respect to their coordinates, preceded by a letter designation from one or another partial list, such as CP or NP; the C stands for Cambridge, N for the National Radio Astronomy Observatory in West Virginia, and P for pulsar. As an example, NP 0532 is the Crab pulsar discussed in Section 14.7.

For comparison, we mention that in the days when only a few radio sources were known, they were simply identified by the name of the constellation followed by a capital Roman letter (for example, radio source Cyg A in Section 21.2); the same inadequate procedure is presently followed for X-ray and infrared sources (for example, Sco X-1 and Ori IR-A in Section 15.6). Before long, that will have to be changed again.

G visual observations and star charts

Our main interest in this text is to present the contemporary view of the universe, to explain its laws, and to extract from mountains of astronomical data those that tell us something new about the planets, stars, and galaxies.

But there is more to astronomy than that. The application of new ideas to the mysteries of a very old universe is motivation enough to keep the professional astronomer at his daily research chores. But then, on a clear night, it is the myriad of lights in the sky which brings back the first excitement of the unknown universe. After operating one of the big instruments from a console, or pushing a series of buttons to select a stellar object for photographing, or checking the latest computer results, we all, once in a while, just want to look, with the naked eye or a small backyard telescope.

This Appendix is a guide to what we can see in the skies, and its relation to some of the contemporary, highly technological results.

G.1   THE SOLAR SYSTEM

Sun.   Let us begin with the most obvious object in our sky: the sun. Aside from its apparent motion in the sky and its seasonal variation, little can be observed without telescopic aid. However, if a small field glass is used to project the sun's image onto a screen half a meter away (Experiment 2, Chapter 2), the sunspots are revealed. Their apparent motion across the disc, that is, the solar rotation, can be followed. Big groups of spots become visible—in projection—through so-called pinhole cameras, which can most easily be constructed by almost closing a venetian blind, until just a set of tiny openings remain in the corners. Each opening then will project a solar image on the opposite wall (Experiment 1, Chapter 8). Incidentally, the little round light spots we see through the leaves of trees in summer are pinhole-camera "pictures" of the sun; during a partial solar eclipse, at the stage where the sun appears as a crescent, the light spots, too, have the form of crescents.

In Section 4.3 we described the events observable during a total solar eclipse, a spectacle worth traveling quite a distance to watch. But even the much more frequently observable partial eclipses merit attention; the standard "instrument" to use is a dark glass filter which is specially prepared to protect the eyes from the intense solar radiation, in particular, the invisible ultraviolet portion of the spectrum. Through such a filter we can see the apparent motion of the moon in front of the sun; and if the partial phase is close to totality, we notice, without any instrumentation, the decrease in general illumination and the reaction of plants and animals to the sudden twilight.

Moon. The moon is one of the primary objects of observation with a small telescope. But even with a field glass we are able to distinguish the major surface features as outlined in Fig. 4-3. We can watch the shadows produced by the walls of the big craters and might even try to find the place where humans first set foot on a celestial object. There are, too, the lunar eclipses; during totality the moon glows an eerie red from scattered light in our planet's atmosphere. Again, we can follow the apparent motion of the moon in the sky, in particular, the seasonal change in rising and setting positions on the horizon.

Planets. The planets, aside from their apparent motions, offer hours of exciting observation to the owner of a small telescope. There are the phases of Venus (Section 5.1); the motions of the four big moons of Jupiter about their parent planet (Section 5.5), as well as Jupiter's more prominent surface features, such as the stratification and the Red Spot (Section 5.4); and finally the fascinating view of Saturn's ring. The amateur observer should try to distinguish the more easily seen planets—Venus, Mars, Jupiter, and Saturn—by their colors and brightnesses: Venus is whitish and very bright and, of course, always within about 45° of the horizon; Saturn is of about the same color, but not quite as bright, and observable anywhere along the ecliptic. Jupiter shows a yellow color to the naked eye and is, again, very bright, while Mars's color tends more to the red and is usually least bright. The positions of the planets during the year are shown in charts published by magazines such as *Sky and Telescope*, the outstanding publication for observers in this country.

Satellites and Other Objects. In recent years, artificial earth satellites have become an added attraction of the skies; many are visible with the naked eye. Satellites are readily distinguished from aircraft: their motions are slower and, of course, there are no blinking red and green lights. Satellites often do show some light variations because they become battered by meteoroids, and the amount of reflected sunlight varies in phase with their tumbling rotation.

Everybody has seen meteors or shooting stars, in particular during the periods when the earth crosses large groups (Section 6.1). The observation of comets (Section 6.3) is aided by a small telescope: the view of the tail above the horizon after sunset or before sunrise is one of the most exciting spectacles the heavens can offer.

At higher latitudes, auroras are visible a couple of days after the larger flare eruptions on the sun (Section 2.4). They are, of course, most likely to occur in the years of maximum solar activity; that is, we can expect auroras in greater numbers again in the years around 1980, 1990, etc. In areas with very clear skies and no pollution, we may be able to see the zodiacal light as a faint glow of conical shape, close to the western horizon along the ecliptic an hour or two after the sun sets. This is sunlight reflected in the dust cloud surrounding the sun in its equatorial plane, that is, very close to the ecliptic (Section 7.5).

G.2 THE CONSTELLATIONS

Throughout the text we locate objects in the sky by citing constellations, irregularly bordered areas of the celestial sphere with Latin names. The use of constellations to specify approximate positions, instead of citing right ascension and declination

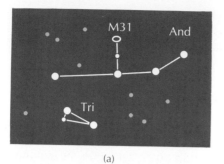

(a)

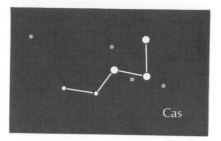

(d)

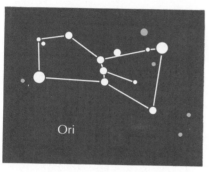

(b)

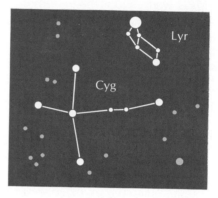

(e)

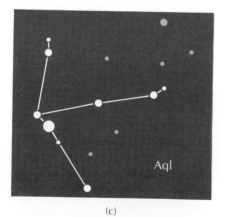

(c)

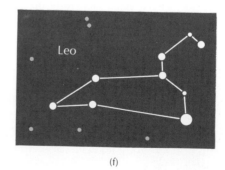

(f)

FIGURE G-1. **Finding charts for the major constellations of the northern sky. Shown are the constellations Andromeda (a); Aquila (c); Auriga (j); Bootes (k); Canis Major (h); Canis Minor (l); Cassiopeia (d); Corona Borealis (k); Cygnus (e); Gemini (l); Leo (e); Orion (b); Scorpius (i); Taurus (j); Triangulum (a); Ursa Major (g); and Ursa Minor (g).**

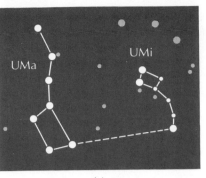

(g)

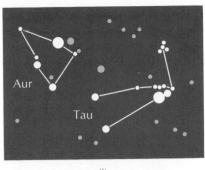

(j)

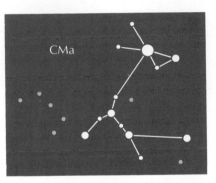

(h)

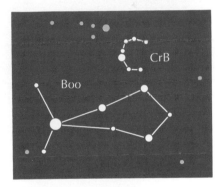

(k)

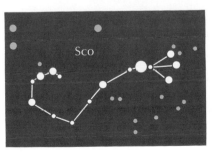

(i)

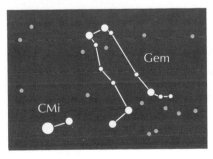

(l)

(Section 3.1), corresponds to defining the location of a town by giving the country it is in, instead of citing longitude and latitude. Table H-8 gives a complete list of all constellations with their Latin names, standard abbreviations, approximate right ascension and declination, and translations of the Latin names.

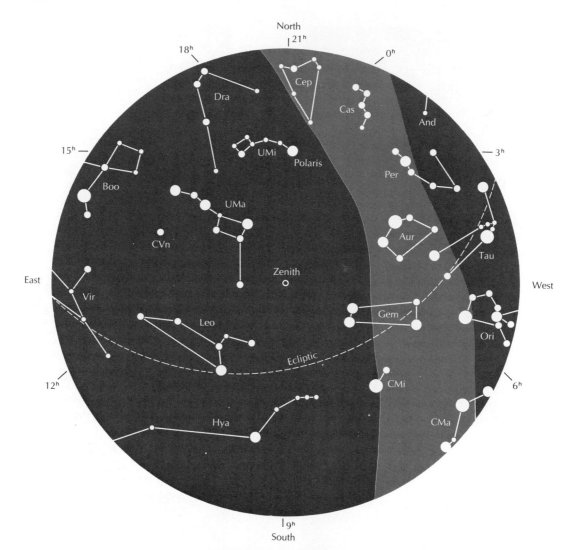

FIGURE G-2. Map of the sky as seen from a northern latitude at about 10 P.M. in March. Zenith is in the center of the chart. The lighter area outlines the Milky Way. North, west, south, and east, and right ascension (with respect to the celestial pole near Polaris in the constellation Ursa Minor) in steps of 3 hours are indicated at the outer circle. Also shown is the ecliptic near which the planets appear.

Recognizing the brightest stars of the major constellations is the observer's first task. To aid in this task, Fig. G-1 (a) to (l) gives simplified finding charts for the major constellations of the northern sky. The size of the star "disc" indicates the apparent brightness, and the objects shown in grey are not commonly used to outline the constellations. Locations in the sky are easily traced through the coordinates listed in Table H-8 and star charts G-6 to G-9.

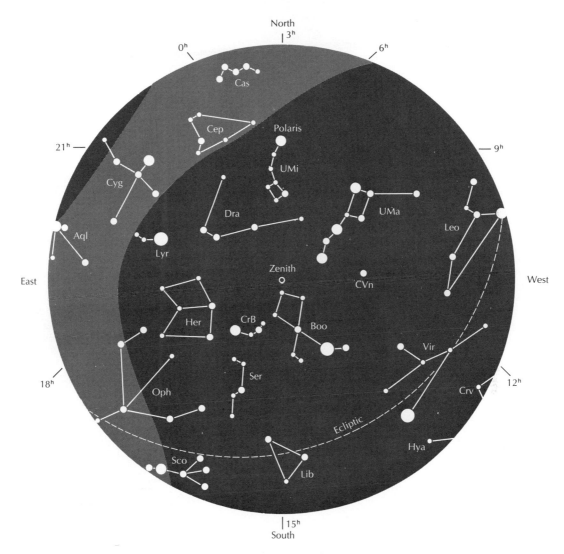

FIGURE G-3. Map of the sky as seen from a northern latitude at about 10 P.M. in June; for explanations, see Fig. G-2.

Figures G-2 to G-5 are maps of the sky as seen at about 10 P.M. from a northern latitude in spring (March 1), summer (July 1), fall (October 1), and winter (January 1), respectively. Again, the brightness of a star is indicated by the size of its image. The roster is not complete or uniform; instead, we have concentrated on those stars which are responsible for the characteristic appearance of a moderately clear sky. The major constellations are identified by their standard abbreviations as listed in Table H-8.

Also shown in Figs. G-2 to G-5 are the ecliptic and the Milky Way (lighter area). The zenith point in the center of each figure corresponds to a latitude in the northern tier of states. As always when a curved surface, such as the celestial sphere, is de-

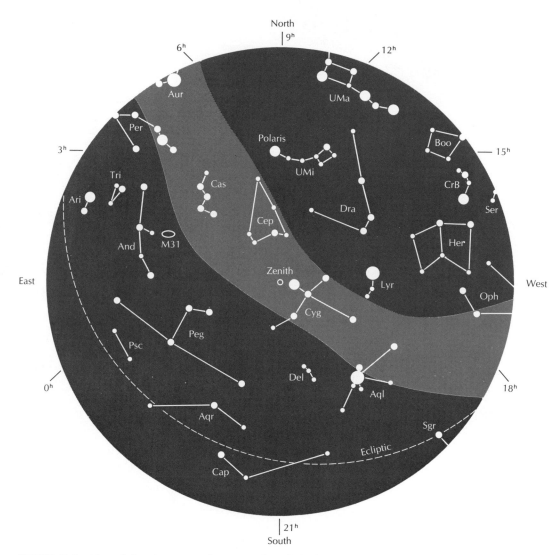

FIGURE G-4. Map of the sky as seen from a northern latitude at about 10 P.M. in September; for explanations, see Fig. G-2.

picted on a flat one, distortions occur. Thus, the constellations near the horizon appear much larger in extent than they actually are. The numbers at the edges of the figures mark the intersections of the great circles of right ascension with the horizon. Note the locations of the Pleiades and the Andromeda galaxy (M31).

G.3 STARS AND OTHER GALACTIC OBJECTS

Stars. We cannot resolve stellar radii, even with the largest telescopes, but we can observe some of their more obvious properties, even with the naked eye. We can easily observe some of the visual binary systems such as ζ Ursae Majoris and

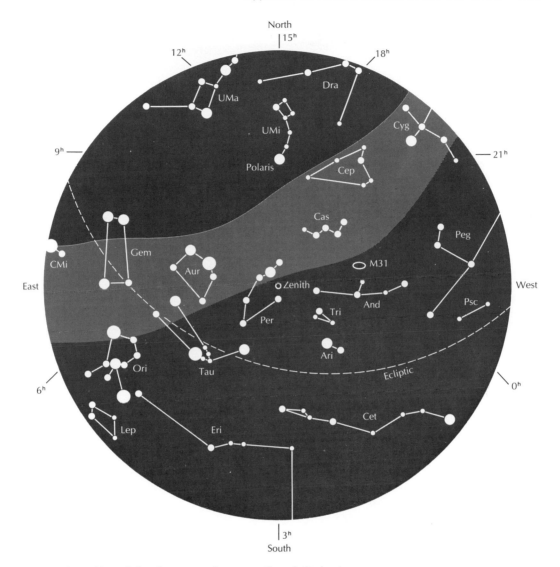

FIGURE G-5. Map of the sky as seen from a northern latitude at about 10 P.M. in December; for explanations, see Fig. G-2.

80 Ursae Majoris, or λ Orionis and φ¹ Orionis (Fig. 10-1). With a little patience one can see the light changes of periodic variables with large amplitudes, such as o Ceti, the star called Mira (Section 15.1).

Every observer should be able to point out some of the brighter examples of the different spectral classes. Among the main-sequence stars there is α Virginis or Spica (type B1V), α Canis Majoris or Sirius (type A1V), α Canis Minoris or Procyon (type F5V), and our closest neighbor in space, α Centauri (type G2V), which unfortunately is rather close to the horizon at the latitudes of North America. Of the cooler stars, because of their intrinsically lower brightness, only some of the giants can be easily seen: α Aurigae or Capella (type G2III), α Bootis or Arcturus (type K2III), and α Tauri

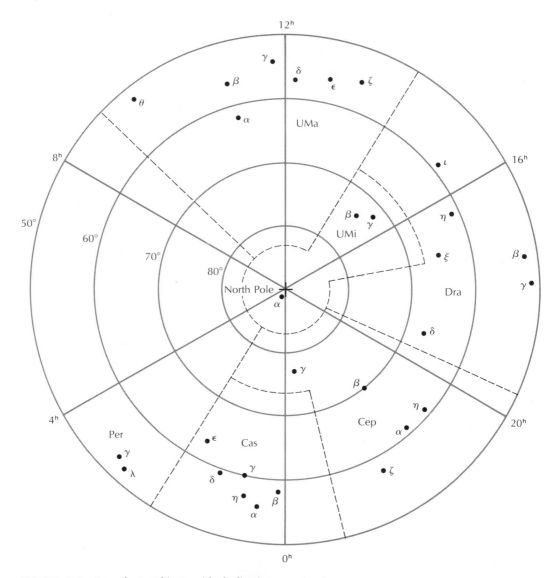

FIGURE G-6. Star chart. Objects with declinations greater than +50°, all right ascensions. The north pole is in the center; right ascensions are counted clockwise. The boundaries of the constellations are much simplified in this chart. All stars brighter than apparent magnitude 3ᵐ5 are listed (Table H-9).

or Aldebaran (type K5III). Finally, some supergiants of type M are visible: α Scorpii or Antares (type M1I), and α Orionis or Betelgeuse (type M2I). α Orionis is mentioned in Section 10.1 as a contrast to the nearby (in projection) O and B stars of the Orion association.

These individual stars are easily recognized in star charts G-6 to G-9, which show all stars brighter than magnitude 3ᵐ5 as listed in Table H-9 separated into four

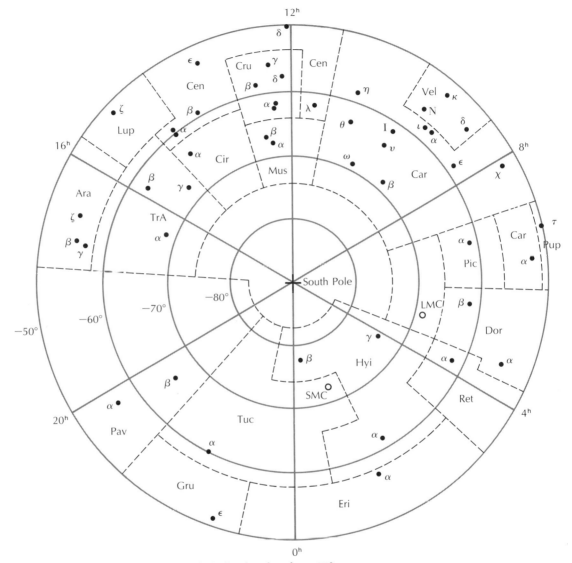

FIGURE G-7. Star chart. Objects with declinations less than −50°, all right ascensions. The south pole is in the center; right ascensions are counted counterclockwise. The boundaries of the constellations are much simplified in this star chart. All stars brighter than apparent magnitude 3ᵐ5 are listed (Table H-9).

parts: Fig. G-6 covers the area around the celestial north pole, down to declination +50°, and Fig. G-7 similarly shows the neighborhood of the celestial south pole, to declination −50°, both as polar projections. The intermediate area, between declinations +50° and −50°, is separated according to right ascension: Fig. G-8 shows the area bordered by right ascensions 0ʰ and 12ʰ; Fig. G-9 the area between 12ʰ and 24ʰ = 0ʰ. The stars are marked by their names (Table H-9), and arbitrary boundaries are introduced to distinguish the constellations; in reality, the boundaries are much more complex. Altogether, almost 300 stars are listed.

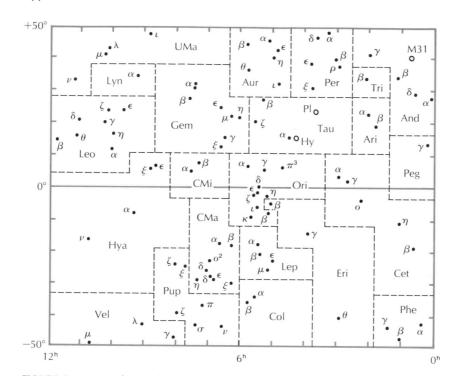

**FIGURE G-8. Star chart. Objects with declinations between +50°
and −50°, right ascensions between 0ʰ and 12ʰ. The boundaries of
the constellations are much simplified in this star chart. All stars
brighter than apparent magnitude 3ᵐ5 are listed (Table H-9).**

To use Figs. G-6 to G-9 to identify a star, find its approximate location in one of
the sky maps, Figs. G-2 to G-5; the choice of map is determined by the season and
the time of the night. The right-ascension marks, together with the location of Polaris
given in maps G-2 to G-5, make it easy to select the proper one of Figs. G-6 to G-9,
which are arranged by right ascension and declination. Finally, matching the observed position of the star in the constellation with the location on the chart yields
the star's name. Accurate coordinates can then be found from Table H-9.

All stars closer to us than 5 pc, that is, stars with a parallax exceeding 0.200
arcsec, are listed separately in Table H-10. Their positions in the sky can easily be
estimated from the right ascension and declination data given in Table H-10 and
charts G-6 to G-9. Finally, Table H-11 lists the stars mentioned in the text that are
neither brighter than 3ᵐ5 nor closer than 5 pc.

Most other objects in our galaxy, such as the ring nebula in the constellation
Aquarius (Section 13.1), a planetary nebula, are rather disappointing when observed
by people who are used to the blown-up photographs made with the aid of large
telescopes. The same is true for objects such as the Orion nebula (Section 16.1) and
the Crab nebula (Section 14.2).

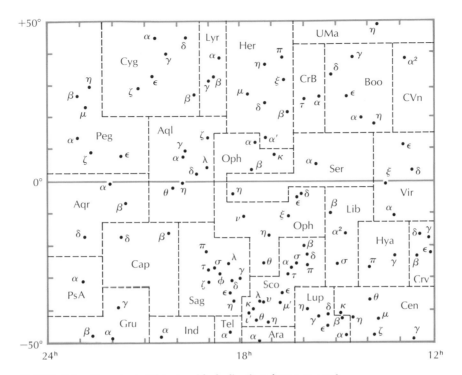

FIGURE G-9. **Star chart. Objects with declinations between +50° and −50°, right ascensions between 12ʰ and 24ʰ. The boundaries of the constellations are much simplified in this star chart. All stars brighter than apparent magnitude 3ᵐ5 are listed (Table H-9).**

The Milky Way. The luminous band of the Milky Way dominates the summer sky. Even a small telescope can resolve it into thousands of faint stars. With a good field glass one can make out star clusters such as the Pleiades (Section 11.2) which, even to the naked eye, shows a great concentration of stars in a small area of the sky. Both the Pleiades and the Hyades are marked in Fig. G-8.

The positions of galactic objects such as open clusters, supernovae, pulsars, and X-ray sources mentioned in the text are given in Table H-12, unless they are known by call numbers. These are given in Table H-13 (*Messier's Catalogue*), Table H-14 (the *New General Catalogue*), and Table H-15 (the *Index Catalogue*).

Finally, one of these days (or years, or centuries) a supernova will explode somewhere in our neighborhood. At that time the world will be treated to the most violent event that can be observed with the naked eye.

G.4 EXTRAGALACTIC OBJECTS

Only a very few extragalactic objects are clearly visible with the naked eye; of these, the two most obvious ones are in the southern hemisphere. They are the Large and the Small Magellanic Clouds (Section 19.2) which have the appearance of large luminous clouds. In the northern hemisphere we can see M31, the Andromeda system (Section 19.1), with the naked eye as a faint glow about the size of the full moon, but only on a clear night, with no city lights nearby and, of course, no moonlight. The view is not much more distinct with small telescopes. The light we receive now from M31 was emitted when the first protohumans ascended from their animal background on our planet. M31 and the two Magellanic systems are marked in Figs. G-8 and G-7, respectively.

Several of our own system's globular clusters (Section 18.1) are within reach of small telescopes.

The positions of other extragalactic objects mentioned in the text are listed in Tables H-13 to H-18. Table H-17, in particular, contains a list of galaxies commonly thought to be members of the local group.

H tables

TABLE H-1. GREEK ALPHABET

Name of letters	Lowercase symbols	Capital symbols
Alpha	α	A
Beta	β	B
Gamma	γ	Γ
Delta	δ	Δ
Epsilon	ϵ	E
Zeta	ζ	Z
Eta	η	H
Theta	θ	Θ
Iota	ι	I
Kappa	κ	K
Lambda	λ	Λ
Mu	μ	M
Nu	ν	N
Xi	ξ	Ξ
Omicron	o	O
Pi	π	Π
Rho	ρ	P
Sigma	σ	Σ
Tau	τ	T
Upsilon	υ	Υ
Phi	ϕ	Φ
Chi	χ	X
Psi	ψ	Ψ
Omega	ω	Ω

TABLE H-2. UNITS AND CONSTANTS

LENGTHS	*Metric system*	*United States system*	*Astronomical units*
	1 km = 10^3 m	1 in. = 2.54 cm	1 A.U. = 1.496×10^{13} cm
	1 m = 10^2 cm	1 ft = 12 in. = 30.5 cm	1 pc = 3.085×10^{18} cm
	1 mm = 10^{-1} cm	1 yd = 36 in. = 91.4 cm	1 kpc = 10^3 pc
	1 micron = 10^{-4} cm	1 (statute) mi = 1,610 m	1 Mpc = 10^6 pc
	1 Å = 10^{-8} cm		1 pc = 3.26 light-years

AREAS	*Metric system*	*United States system*
	1 km² = 10^6 m²	1 in.² = 6.45 cm²
	1 m² = 10^4 cm²	1 ft² = 929 cm²
	1 mm² = 10^{-2} cm²	1 yd² = 0.836 m²
		1 mi² = 2.59 km²

VOLUMES	*Metric system*	*United States system*
	1 km³ = 10^9 m³	1 in.³ = 16.4 cm³
	1 m³ = 10^6 cm³	1 ft³ = 2.83×10^4 cm³
	1 mm³ = 10^{-3} cm³	1 yd³ = 7.65×10^5 cm³

TIME		
	1 min = 60 sec	1 mean solar day = 1.0027 sidereal days
	1 h = 3,600 sec	1 sidereal day = 0.99727 mean solar day
	1 day = 8.64×10^4 sec	1 tropical year = 365.24 mean solar days
	1 year = 3.16×10^7 sec	

VELOCITY	
	1 km/h = 27.8 cm/sec
	1 mi/h = 1.47 ft/sec = 44.7 cm/sec

MASS*	
	1 kg = 10^3 g
	1 oz av. = 28.3 g
	1 lb av. = 454 g

ENERGY		
	1 joule = 10^7 erg	1 gram mass corresponds to an energy of
	1 eV = 1.602×10^{-12} erg	8.988×10^{20} erg
	1 keV = 10^3 eV	Gas particles at a temperature of 11,605°K
	1 MeV = 10^6 eV	have a mean energy of 1 eV
	1 kWh = 3.6×10^6 joule	
	1 15° calorie = 4.186 joule	
	1 BTU = 1.056×10^3 joule	

TEMPERATURE	
	Absolute zero: 0°K = −273.15°C = −459.67°F
	Freezing point of water: 273.15°K = 0°C = 32°F
	Boiling point of water: 373.15°K = 100°C = 212°F

*Strictly speaking the U.S. units are weight rather than mass units

TABLE H-2.   UNITS AND CONSTANTS (*continued*)

PHYSICAL CONSTANTS	Speed of light (c): 3.00×10^{10} cm/sec
	Gravitational constant (G): 6.67×10^{-8} dyn $\cdot$ cm^2/g^2
	Planck's constant (h): 6.625×10^{-27} erg $\cdot$ sec
	Electron charge (e): 4.803×10^{-10} c.g.s. unit $= 1.602 \times 10^{-19}$ coulomb
	Mass of proton (m_p): 1.672×10^{-24} g
	Mass of electron (m_e): 9.108×10^{-28} g
	Avogadro's number (N): 6.023×10^{23} particles per mole
	Boltzmann's constant (k): 1.380×10^{-16} erg/degree
	Radiation constant (a): 5.67×10^{-5} erg/cm^2 $\cdot$ sec $\cdot$ degree^4
	Bohr's radius (a_0): 0.529 Å
	Ionization energy of hydrogen: 13.60 eV
	helium: 24.58 eV
	calcium: 6.11 eV; Ca$^+$: 11.87 eV
	iron: 7.90 eV; Fe$^+$: 16.18 eV
	Fe^{++}: 30.64 eV
EARTH	Equatorial radius: 6,378.4 km
	Polar radius: 6,356.9 km
	Mass: 5.977×10^{27} g
	Surface gravity: 981 cm/sec^2
MOON	Radius: 1,738.0 km
	Mass: 7.38×10^{25} g
	Surface gravity: 162 cm/sec^2
	Mean distance from earth: 384,405 km
	Sidereal period: 27.322 days
	Synodic period: 29.531 days
SUN	Radius: 6.96×10^{10} cm
	Mass: 1.990×10^{33} g
	Surface gravity: 2.736×10^4 cm/sec^2
	Luminosity: 3.90×10^{33} erg/sec
	Effective temperature: 5780°K

TABLE H-3.   LIST OF ELEMENTS

Number of protons in nucleus	Name	Chemical symbol	Number of protons and neutrons in most important isotopes
1	Hydrogen	H	1
2	Helium	He	4
3	Lithium	Li	7
4	Beryllium	Be	9
5	Boron	B	11
6	Carbon	C	12
7	Nitrogen	N	14
8	Oxygen	O	16
9	Fluorine	F	19
10	Neon	Ne	20
11	Sodium	Na	23
12	Magnesium	Mg	24
13	Aluminum	Al	27
14	Silicon	Si	28
15	Phosphorus	P	31
16	Sulphur	S	32
17	Chlorine	Cl	35, 37
18	Argon	Ar	40
19	Potassium	K	39
20	Calcium	Ca	40
21	Scandium	Sc	45
22	Titanium	Ti	48
23	Vanadium	V	51
24	Chromium	Cr	52
25	Manganese	Mn	55
26	Iron	Fe	56
27	Cobalt	Co	59
28	Nickel	Ni	58, 60
29	Copper	Cu	63, 65
30	Zinc	Zn	64, 66
31	Gallium	Ga	69, 71
32	Germanium	Ge	70, 72, 74
33	Arsenic	As	75
34	Selenium	Se	78, 80
35	Bromine	Br	79, 81
36	Krypton	Kr	84, 86
37	Rubidium	Rb	85, 87
38	Strontium	Sr	88
39	Yttrium	Y	89
40	Zirconium	Zr	90, 92, 94
41	Niobium	Nb	93
42	Molybdenum	Mo	92, 95, 96, 98
43	Technetium	Tc	97, 98, 99
44	Ruthenium	Ru	101, 102, 103
45	Rhodium	Rh	103
46	Palladium	Pd	105, 106, 108
47	Silver	Ag	107, 109
48	Cadmium	Cd	112, 114
49	Indium	In	115
50	Tin	Sn	118, 120
51	Antimony	Sb	121, 123
52	Tellurium	Te	126, 128, 130

TABLE H-3 **LIST OF ELEMENTS** (*continued*)

Number of protons in nucleus	Name	Chemical symbol	Number of protons and neutrons in most important isotopes
53	Iodine	I	127
54	Xenon	Xe	129, 131, 132
55	Cesium	Cs	133
56	Barium	Ba	138
57	Lanthanum	La	138
58	Cerium	Ce	140
59	Praseodymium	Pr	141
60	Neodymium	Nd	142, 144, 146
61	Promethium	Pm	147
62	Samarium	Sm	153, 154
63	Europium	Eu	151, 153
64	Gadolinium	Gd	156, 158, 160
65	Terbium	Tb	159
66	Dysprosium	Dy	161, 162, 163, 164
67	Holmium	Ho	165
68	Erbium	Er	166, 167, 168
69	Thulium	Tm	169
70	Ytterbium	Yb	172, 173, 174
71	Lutecium	Lu	175
72	Hafnium	Hf	178, 180
73	Tantalum	Ta	181
74	Tungsten	W	183, 184, 186
75	Rhenium	Re	185, 187
76	Osmium	Os	190, 192
77	Iridium	Ir	191, 193
78	Platinum	Pt	194, 195, 196
79	Gold	Au	197
80	Mercury	Hg	200, 202
81	Thallium	Tl	203, 205
82	Lead	Pb	206, 207, 208
83	Bismuth	Bi	209
84	Polonium	Po	210
85	Astatine	At	219
86	Radon	Rn	222
87	Francium	Fr	223
88	Radium	Ra	226
89	Actinium	Ac	227
90	Thorium	Th	232
91	Protoactinium	Pa	231
92	Uranium	U	235, 238
93	Neptunium	Np	237
94	Plutonium	Pu	244
95	Americium	Am	243
96	Curium	Cm	247
97	Berkelium	Bk	247
98	Californium	Cf	249, 251
99	Einsteinium	Es	252
100	Fermium	Fm	252, 255
101	Mendelevium	Md	256
102	Nobelium	No	254
103	Lawrencium	Lw	257

TABLE H-4. THE PLANETS

Name	Radius (km)	Mass (in earth masses)	Rotation period (in earth units)	Semimajor axis of orbit (A.U.)	Eccentricity of orbit	Inclination of orbit to ecliptic	Revolution period
Mercury	2,440	0.055	59 days	0.39	0.206	7.0°	88 days
Venus	6,050	0.82	243 days	0.72	0.007	3.4	225 days
Earth	6,380	1.00	23^{h}56^m	1.00	0.017	0.0	365 days = 1 year
Mars	3,380	0.11	24^{h}37^m	1.52	0.093	1.9	1.88 years
Jupiter	71,350	318	9^{h}55^m	5.20	0.048	1.3	11.9 years
Saturn	60,400	95	10^{h}25^m	9.54	0.056	2.5	29.5 years
Uranus	23,800	14.5	10^{h}50^m	19.2	0.047	0.8	84.0 years
Neptune	22,200	17	15 hours	30.1	0.009	1.8	165 years
Pluto	?	?	6 days	39.4	0.250	17.2	248 years

TABLE H-5. PLANETARY SATELLITES

Name	Mean distance from planet (km)	Sidereal period (earth days)	Year of discovery
EARTH			
Moon	384,400	27.3	
MARS			
Phobos	9,400	0.32	1877
Deimos	23,500	1.26	1877
JUPITER			
V	181,000	0.50	1892
Io (I)	421,600	1.77	1610
Europa (II)	670,800	3.55	1610
Ganymede (III)	1,070,000	7.16	1610
Callisto (IV)	1,880,000	16.69	1610
VI	11,500,000	251	1904
VII	11,800,000	260	1905
X	11,800,000	264	1938
XII	21,000,000	631	1951
XI	22,500,000	693	1938
VIII	23,500,000	739	1908
IX	23,700,000	758	1914
SATURN			
Janus	60,000	0.75	1966
Mimas	185,000	0.94	1789
Enceladus	238,000	1.37	1789
Tethys	295,000	1.89	1684
Dione	377,000	2.74	1684
Rhea	527,000	4.52	1672
Titan	1,220,000	15.9	1655
Hyperion	1,480,000	21.3	1848
Iapetus	3,560,000	79.3	1671
Phoebe	12,950,000	550	1898
URANUS			
Miranda	125,000	1.4	1948
Ariel	192,000	2.52	1851
Umbriel	267,000	4.14	1851
Titania	438,000	8.71	1787
Oberon	586,000	13.46	1787
NEPTUNE			
Triton	353,000	5.88	1846
Nereid	5,560,000	360	1949

TABLE H-6. SOME WELL-KNOWN ASTEROIDS

Number designation	Name	Year of discovery	Diameter (km)	Semimajor axis (A.U.)	Eccentricity of orbit	Inclination of orbit to ecliptic	Period (years)
1	Ceres	1801	770	2.77	0.08	11°	4.6
2	Pallas	1802	490	2.77	0.24	35°	4.6
3	Juno	1804	190	2.67	0.26	13°	4.4
4	Vesta	1807	380	2.36	0.09	7°	3.6
433	Eros	1898	25	1.46	0.22	11°	1.8
944	Hidalgo	1920	35	5.71	0.65	43°	13.7
1566	Icarus	1949	1.5	1.08	0.83	23°	1.1

Source: G. F. Roth, *The System of Minor Planets*, New York: D. Van Nostrand Company, Inc., 1961

TABLE H-7. SOME WELL-KNOWN COMETS

Number designation	Name	Date of perihelion passage	Perihelion distance (A.U.)	Inclination of orbit to ecliptic	Periodicity
1868II	Winnecke	June 27	0.58	132°	Not periodic
1908III	Morehouse	Dec. 26	0.95	140°	Not periodic
1910II	Halley	April 20	0.59	162°	76 years
1911V	Brooks	Oct. 28	0.49	34°	Long period
1957III	Arend-Roland	April 08	0.32	120°	Not periodic
1957IV	Schwassmann-Wachmann	*	5.54	10°	16.1 years
1957V	Mrkos	Aug. 01	0.35	94°	Long period
1957VIII	Encke	Oct. 20	0.34	185°	3.3 years
1962VIII	Humason	Dec. 10	2.13	153°	Not periodic
1965VIII	Ikeya-Seki	Oct. 15	0.008	142°	Not periodic

*Under continuous observation

TABLE H-8. CONSTELLATIONS

Latin name (genitive)	Abbreviation	Approximate right ascension (hours)	Approximate declination (degrees)	Translation of Latin name
Andromeda *(Andromedae)*	And	01	35	Andromeda*
Antlia *(Antliae)*	Ant	10	−30	Pump
Apus *(Apodis)*	Aps	17	−75	Bird of Paradise
Aquarius *(Aquarii)*	Aqr	22	−05	Water Bearer
Aquila *(Aquilae)*	Aql	20	05	Eagle
Ara *(Arae)*	Ara	17	−55	Altar
Aries *(Arietis)*	Ari	02	20	Ram
Auriga *(Aurigae)*	Aur	05	40	Charioteer
Bootes *(Bootis)*	Boo	15	30	Herdsman
Caelum *(Caeli)*	Cae	05	−40	Chisel
Camelopardalis *(Camelopardalis)*	Cam	06	70	Giraffe
Cancer *(Cancri)*	Cnc	09	20	Crab
Canes Venatici *(Canum Venaticorum)*	CVn	13	40	Hunting Dogs
Canis Major *(Canis Majoris)*	CMa	07	−25	Big Dog
Canis Minor *(Canis Minoris)*	CMi	07	05	Little Dog
Capricornus *(Capricorni)*	Cap	21	−15	Goat
Carina *(Carinae)*	Car	09	−60	Ship's Keel
Cassiopeia *(Cassiopeiae)*	Cas	01	60	Cassiopeia*
Centaurus *(Centauri)*	Cen	13	−50	Centaur*
Cepheus *(Cephei)*	Cep	21	65	Cepheus*
Cetus *(Ceti)*	Cet	02	00	Whale
Chamaeleon *(Chamaeleonis)*	Cha	11	−80	Chameleon
Circinus *(Circini)*	Cir	16	−65	Compass
Columba *(Columbae)*	Col	06	−35	Dove
Coma Berenices *(Comae Berenices)*	Com	13	20	Berenice's Hair*
Corona Austrina *(Coronae Austrinae)*	CrA	19	−40	Southern Crown
Corona Borealis *(Coronae Borlelais)*	CrB	16	30	Northern Crown
Corvus *(Corvi)*	Crv	12	−20	Crow
Crater *(Crateris)*	Crt	11	−15	Cup
Crux *(Crucis)*	Cru	12	−60	Southern Cross
Delphinus *(Delphini)*	Del	21	15	Dolphin
Dorado *(Doradus)*	Dor	05·	−60	Swordfish
Draco *(Draconis)*	Dra	18	60	Dragon
Equuleus *(Equulei)*	Equ	21	10	Little Horse
Eridanus *(Eridani)*	Eri	03	−40	River Eridanus
Fornax *(Fornacis)*	For	03	−30	Furnace
Gemini *(Geminorum)*	Gem	07	25	Twins
Grus *(Gruis)*	Gru	22	−45	Crane
Hercules *(Herculis)*	Her	17	30	Hercules*
Horologium *(Horologii)*	Hor	03	−50	Clock
Hydra *(Hydrae)*	Hya	10	−10	Hydra*
Hydrus *(Hydri)*	Hyi	01	−70	Water Snake
Indus *(Indi)*	Ind	20	−50	Indian
Lacerta *(Lacertae)*	Lac	22	40	Lizard
Leo *(Leonis)*	Leo	10	20	Lion
Leo Minor *(Leonis Minoris)*	LMi	10	35	Little Lion
Lepus *(Leporis)*	Lep	05	−20	Hare
Libra *(Librae)*	Lib	15	−15	Balance
Lupus *(Lipi)*	Lup	15	−45	Wolf
Lynx *(Lyncis)*	Lyn	09	35	Lynx

*Proper names of mythological personalities and creatures

TABLE H-8. CONSTELLATIONS (continued)

Latin name (genitive)	Abbreviation	Approximate right ascension (hours)	Approximate declination (degrees)	Translation of Latin name
Lyra (*Lyrae*)	Lyr	19	35	Harp
Mensa (*Mensae*)	Men	06	−75	Table Mountain
Microscopium (*Microscopii*)	Mic	21	−35	Microscope
Monoceros (*Monocerotis*)	Mon	07	00	Unicorn
Musca (*Muscae*)	Mus	13	−70	Fly
Norma (*Normae*)	Nor	16	−55	Level
Octans (*Octantis*)	Oct	south pole		Octant
Ophiochus (*Ophiochi*)	Oph	17	−10	Snake Bearer
Orion (*Orionis*)	Ori	05	00	Orion*
Pabo (*Pavonis*)	Pab	20	−60	Peacock
Pegasus (*Pegasi*)	Peg	22	20	Pegasus*
Perseus (*Persei*)	Per	03	40	Perseus*
Phoenix (*Phoenicis*)	Phe	01	−45	Phoenix
Pictor (*Pictoris*)	Pic	07	−60	Easel
Pisces (*Piscium*)	Psc	00	00	Fishes
Piscis Austrinus (*Piscis Austrini*)	PsA	23	−30	Southern Fish
Puppis (*Puppis*)	Pup	07	−35	Ship's Stern
Pyxis (*Pyxidis*)	Pyx	09	−30	Ship's Compass
Reticulum (*Reticuli*)	Ret	04	−70	Net
Sagitta (*Sagittae*)	Sge	20	20	Arrow
Sagittarius (*Sagittarii*)	Sgr	18	−30	Archer
Scorpius (*Scorpii*)	Sco	17	−30	Scorpion
Sculptor (*Sculptoris*)	Scl	01	−30	Sculptor's Tools
Scutum (*Scuti*)	Sct	19	−10	Shield
Serpens (*Serpentis*)	Ser	16	00	Snake
Sextans (*Sextantis*)	Sex	10	00	Sextant
Taurus (*Tauri*)	Tau	05	20	Bull
Telescopium (*Telescopii*)	Tel	18	−45	Telescope
Triangulum (*Trianguli*)	Tri	02	35	Triangle
Triangulum Australe (*Trianguli Australis*)	TrA	16	−65	Southern Triangle
Tucana (*Tucanae*)	Tuc	22	−60	Toucan (tropical bird)
Ursa Major (*Ursae Majoris*)	UMa	11	50	Great Bear ("*Big Dipper*")
Ursa Minor (*Ursae Minoris*)	UMi	15	75	Little Bear ("*Little Dipper*")
Vela (*Velorum*)	Vel	09	−50	Ship's Sails
Virgo (*Virginis*)	Vir	13	00	Virgin
Volans (*Volantis*)	Vol	08	−70	Flying Fish
Vulpecula (*Vulpeculae*)	Vul	20	25	Fox

*Proper names of mythological personalities and creatures

TABLE H-9. STARS BRIGHTER THAN APPARENT MAGNITUDE 3ᵐ5

	Designation	Apparent magnitude	Right ascension 1900 (hours, minutes)	Declination 1900 (degrees arcminutes)	Remarks
ANDROMEDA, *And*	α	2.02	00 03	28 32	
	β	2.03	01 04	35 05	
	γ	2.28	01 58	41 51	
	δ	3.21	00 34	30 19	
AQUARIUS, *Aqr*	α	2.93	22 0l	−00 48	
	β	2.89	21 26	−06 01	
	δ	3.29	22 49	−16 21	
AQUILA, *Aql*	α	0.77	19 46	08 36	Altair
	γ	2.62	19 41	10 22	
	δ	3.36	19 20	02 55	
	ζ	2.99	19 01	13 43	
	η	3.50	19 47	00 45	
	θ	3.24	20 06	−01 07	
	λ	3.44	19 01	−05 02	
ARA, *Ara*	α	2.94	17 24	−49 48	
	β	2.84	17 17	−55 26	
	γ	3.33	17 17	−56 17	
	ζ	3.12	16 50	−55 50	
ARIES, *Ari*	α	2.00	02 02	22 59	
	β	2.65	01 49	20 19	
AURIGA, *Aur*	α	0.09	05 09	45 54	Capella
	β	1.90	05 52	44 56	
	ε	2.99	04 55	43 41	
	η	3.17	04 59	41 06	
	θ	2.69	05 53	37 12	
	ι	2.66	04 50	33 00	
BOOTES, *Boo*	α	0.06	14 11	19 42	Arcturus
	γ	3.03	14 28	38 45	
	δ	3.50	15 11	33 41	
	ε	2.70	14 41	27 30	
	η	2.69	13 50	18 54	
CANES VENATICI, *CVn*	α²	2.89	12 51	38 51	
CANIS MAJOR, *CMa*	α	−1.47	06 41	−16 35	Sirius
	β	1.98	06 18	−17 54	
	δ	1.84	07 04	−26 14	
	ε	1.50	06 55	−28 50	
	ζ	3.02	06 16	−30 01	
	η	2.40	07 20	−29 06	
	o²	3.04	06 59	−23 41	
	σ	3.46	06 58	−27 47	
CANIS MINOR, *CMi*	α	0.34	07 34	05 29	Procyon
	β	2.84	07 22	08 29	
CAPRICORNUS, *Cap*	β	3.07	20 15	−15 06	
	δ	2.83	21 42	−16 35	

Source: D. Hoffleit, *Catalogue of Bright Stars* (third ed.), New Haven, Conn.: Yale University Observatory, 1964

TABLE H-9. STARS BRIGHTER THAN APPARENT MAGNITUDE 3ᵐ5 (*continued*)

	Designation	Apparent magnitude	Right ascension 1900 (hours, minutes)	Declination 1900 (degrees, arcminutes)	Remarks
CARINA, *Car*	α	−0.73	06 22	− 52 38	Canopus
	β	1.67	09 12	−69 18	
	ε	1.85	08 20	−59 11	
	η	(−1.)	10 41	−59 10	Peculiar object, variable, infrared excess
	θ	2.76	10 39	−63 52	
	ι	2.24	09 14	−58 51	
	υ	3.15	09 44	−64 36	
	χ	3.46	07 54	−52 43	
	ω	3.31	10 11	−69 32	
	a	3.43	09 08	−58 33	
	I	3.40	09 42	−62 03	
CASSIOPEIA, *Cas*	α	2.24	00 35	55 59	
	β	2.25	00 04	58 36	
	γ	2.65	00 51	60 11	
	δ	2.68	00 19	59 43	
	ε	3.38	00 47	63 11	
	η	3.45	00 43	57 17	
CENTAURUS, *Cen*	α	0.33	14 33	−60 25	Multiple system. Second component 1.70
	β	0.59	13 57	−59 53	
	γ	2.16	12 36	−48 25	
	δ	2.88	12 03	−50 10	
	ε	2.30	13 34	−52 57	
	ζ	2.54	13 49	−46 48	
	η	2.35	14 29	−41 43	
	θ	2.05	14 01	−35 53	
	κ	3.12	14 53	−41 42	
	λ	3.12	11 31	−62 28	
	μ	3.47	13 44	−41 59	
CEPHEUS, *Cep*	α	2.41	21 16	62 10	
	β	3.18	21 27	70 07	
	γ	3.22	23 35	77 04	
	ζ	3.36	22 07	57 42	
	η	3.43	20 43	61 27	
CETUS, *Cet*	α	2.52	02 57	03 42	Menkar
	β	2.04	00 38	−18 32	
	γ	3.47	02 38	02 49	
	η	3.44	01 04	−10 43	
	o	(2.0)	02 14	−03 26	Mira, variable
CIRCINUS, *Cir*	α	3.17	14 34	−64 32	
COLUMBA, *Col*	α	2.63	05 36	−34 08	
	β	3.11	05 47	−35 48	
CORONA BOREALIS, *CrB*	α	2.23	15 30	27 03	
	T	2.0	15 56	26 12	Nova, 1866 and 1946

TABLE H-9. STARS BRIGHTER THAN APPARENT MAGNITUDE 3.5 (*continued*)

Designation		Apparent magnitude	Right ascension 1900 (hours, minutes)	Declination 1900 (degrees, arcminutes)	Remarks
CORVUS, *CrV*	β	2.66	12 29	−22 51	
	γ	2.60	12 11	−16 59	
	δ	2.95	12 25	−15 58	
	ε	3.00	12 05	−22 04	
CRUX, *Cru*	α	1.58	12 12	−62 33	Binary system. Second component 2.09
	β	1.24	12 42	−59 09	
	γ	1.62	12 26	−55 33	
	δ	2.82	12 10	−58 12	
CYGNUS, *Cyg*	α	1.26	20 38	44 55	Deneb
	β	3.24	19 27	27 45	
	γ	2.24	20 19	39 56	
	δ	2.92	19 42	44 53	
	ε	2.45	20 42	33 36	
	ζ	3.20	21 09	29 49	
DORADO, *Dor*	α	3.26	04 32	−55 15	
	β	3.40	05 33	−62 33	
DRACO, *Dra*	β	2.87	17 28	52 23	
	γ	2.22	17 54	51 30	
	δ	3.10	19 13	67 29	
	ζ	3.20	17 08	65 50	
	η	2.77	16 23	61 44	
	ι	3.26	15 23	59 19	
ERIDANUS, *Eri*	α	0.47	00 34	−57 45	Achernar
	β	2.80	05 03	−05 13	
	γ	2.96	03 53	−13 48	
	θ	3.42	02 54	−40 42	
GEMINI, *Gem*	α	1.99	07 28	32 06	Castor
	β	1.15	07 39	28 16	Pollux
	γ	1.93	06 32	16 29	
	ε	3.08	06 38	25 14	
	η	3.20	06 09	22 32	
	μ	2.97	06 17	22 34	
	ξ	3.37	06 40	13 00	
GRUS, *Gru*	α	1.73	22 02	−47 27	
	β	2.24	22 37	−47 24	
	γ	3.00	21 48	−37 50	
	ε	3.48	22 43	−51 51	
HERCULES, *Her*	α¹	3.10	17 10	14 30	
	β	2.83	16 26	21 42	
	δ	3.14	17 11	24 57	
	ζ	2.82	16 38	31 47	
	η	3.47	16 39	39 07	
	μ	3.35	17 43	27 47	
	π	3.15	17 12	36 55	

TABLE H-9. STARS BRIGHTER THAN APPARENT MAGNITUDE 3ᵐ5 (continued)

	Designation	Apparent magnitude	Right ascension 1900 (hours, minutes)	Declination 1900 (degrees, arcminutes)	Remarks
HYDRA, *Hya*	α	1.99	09 23	−08 14	
	γ	3.02	13 13	−22 39	
	ε	3.36	08 41	06 47	
	ζ	3.12	08 50	06 20	
	ν	3.12	10 45	−15 40	
	π	3.25	14 01	−26 12	
HYDRUS, *Hyi*	α	2.86	00 55	−62 03	
	β	2.79	00 2̄0	−77 49	
	γ	3.24	03 49	−74 33	
INDUS, *Ind*	α	3.10	20 31	−47 38	
LEO, *Leo*	α	1.36	10 03	12 27	Regulus
	β	2.14	11 44	15 08	
	γ	2.61	10 14	20 21	
	δ	2.55	11 09	21 04	
	ε	2.96	09 40	24 14	
	ζ	3.43	10 11	23 55	
	η	3.48	10 02	17 15	
	θ	3.31	11 09	15 59	
LEPUS, *Lep*	α	2.59	05 28	−17 54	
	β	2.85	05 24	−20 50	
	ε	3.18	05 01	−22 30	
	μ	3.28	05 08	−16 19	
LIBRA, *Lib*	α²	2.75	14 45	−15 38	
	β	2.61	15 12	−09 01	
	σ	3.30	14 58	−24 53	
LUPUS, *Lup*	α	2.30	14 35	−46 58	
	β	2.67	14 52	−42 44	
	γ	2.77	15 28	−40 50	
	δ	3.21	15 15	−40 17	
	ε	3.36	15 16	−44 20	
	ζ	3.40	15 05	−51 43	
	η	3.40	15 53	−38 07	
LYNX, *Lyn*	α	3.14	09 15	34 49	
LYRA, *Lyr*	α	0.04	18 34	38 41	Vega
	β	3.4	18 46	33 15	Close binary system
	γ	3.25	18 55	32 33	
MUSCA, *Mus*	α	2.71	12 31	−68 35	
	β	3.04	12 40	−67 34	
OPHIOCHUS, *Oph*	α	2.08	17 30	12 38	
	β	2.77	17 39	04 37	
	δ	2.72	16 09	−03 26	
	ε	3.24	16 13	−04 27	
	ζ	2.56	16 32	−10 22	
	η	2.44	17 05	−15 36	
	θ	3.28	17 16	−24 54	
	κ	3.31	16 53	09 32	
	ν	3.34	17 54	−09 46	

TABLE H-9. STARS BRIGHTER THAN APPARENT MAGNITUDE 3ᵐ5 (continued)

	Designation	Apparent magnitude	Right ascension 1900 (hours, minutes)	Declination 1900 (degrees, arcminutes)	Remarks
ORION, *Ori*	α	0.80	05 50	07 23	Betelgeuse
	β	0.08	05 10	−08 19	Rigel
	γ	1.04	05 20	06 16	Bellatrix
	δ	2.20	05 27	−00 22	
	ε	1.70	05 31	−01 16	
	ζ	2.05	05 36	−02 00	
	η	3.35	05 19	−02 29	
	τ	2.77	05 31	−05 59	
	κ	2.04	05 43	−09 42	
	π³	3.19	04 44	06 47	
PAVO, *Pav*	α	1.93	20 18	−57 03	
	β	3.42	20 36	−66 34	
PEGASUS, *Peg*	α	2.49	23 00	14 40	
	β	2.56	22 59	27 32	
	γ	2.83	00 08	14 38	
	ε	2.42	21 39	09 25	
	ζ	3.47	22 36	10 19	
	η	2.96	32 38	29 42	
	μ	3.50	22 45	24 04	
PERSEUS, *Per*	α	1.79	03 17	49 30	
	β	2.2	03 02	40 34	Algol, eclipsing binary
	γ	2.90	02 58	53 07	
	δ	2.99	03 36	47 28	
	ε	2.88	03 51	39 43	
	ζ	2.83	03 48	31 35	
	ρ	3.20	02 59	38 27	
	τ	3.09	02 47	52 21	
PHOENIX, *Phe*	α	2.39	00 21	−42 51	
	β	3.30	01 02	−47 15	
	γ	3.40	01 24	−43 50	
PICTOR, *Pic*	α	3.26	06 47	−61 50	
PISCIS AUSTRINUS, *PsA*	α	1.16	22 52	−30 09	Formalhaut
PUPPIS, *Pup*	ζ	2.25	08 00	−39 43	
	ν	3.17	06 35	−43 06	
	π	2.70	07 14	−36 55	
	π	2.88	08 03	−24 01	
	σ	3.24	07 26	−43 06	
	ξ	3.34	07 45	−24 37	
RETICULUM, *Ret*	τ	3.34	04 13	−67 43	
SAGITTARUIS, *Sag*	γ	2.98	17 59	−30 26	
	δ	2.70	18 15	−29 52	
	ε	1.84	18 18	−34 26	
	ζ	2.60	18 56	−30 01	
	η	3.12	18 11	−36 48	
	λ	2.84	18 21	−25 29	
	ρ	2.90	19 04	−21 11	
	σ	2.10	18 49	−26 25	

TABLE H-9. STARS BRIGHTER THAN APPARENT MAGNITUDE 3ᵐ5 (continued)

	Designation	Apparent magnitude	Right ascension 1900 (hours, minutes)	Declination 1900 (degrees, arcminutes)	Remarks
SAGITTARIUS, *Sag*	τ	3.32	19 01	−27 49	
(Continued)	φ	3.18	18 39	−27 10	
SCORPIUS, *Sco*	α	1.08	16 23	−26 13	Antares
	β¹	2.63	16 00	−19 32	
	δ	2.32	15 54	−22 20	
	ε	2.28	16 44	−34 07	
	η	3.33	17 05	−43 06	
	θ	1.88	17 30	−42 56	
	ι¹	2.98	17 41	−40 05	
	κ	2.41	17 36	−38 59	
	λ	1.62	17 27	−37 02	
	μ¹	3.14	16 45	−37 53	
	π	2.88	15 53	−25 50	
	σ	2.93	16 15	−25 21	
	τ	2.82	16 30	−28 01	
	υ	2.70	17 36	−37 13	
SERPENS, *Ser*	α	2.65	15 39	06 44	
	η	3.26	18 16	−02 55	
TAURUS, *Tau*	α	0.86	04 30	16 18	Aldebaran
	β	1.65	05 20	28 31	
	ζ	2.99	05 32	21 05	
	η	2.86	03 42	23 48	Alcyone, Pleiades group
	78	3.41	04 23	15 39	Hyades group
TELESCOPIUM, *Tel*	α	3.50	18 20	−46 01	
TRIANGULUM, *Tri*	β	3.00	02 04	34 31	
TRIANGULUM AUSTRALE, *TrA*	α	1.91	16 38	−68 51	
	β	2.84	15 46	−63 07	
	γ	2.88	15 10	−68 19	
TUCANA, *Tuc*	α	2.85	22 12	−60 45	
URSA MAJOR, *UMa*	α	1.79	10 58	62 17	
	β	2.36	10 56	56 55	
	γ	2.44	11 49	54 15	
	δ	3.31	12 10	57 35	
	ε	1.76	12 50	56 30	
	ζ	2.40	13 20	55 27	Mizar, companion 80 UMa
	η	1.86	13 44	49 49	
	θ	3.18	09 26	52 08	
	ι	3.14	08 52	48 26	
	λ	3.45	10 11	43 25	
	μ	3.04	10 16	42 00	
	ν	3.48	11 13	33 38	
URSA MINOR, *UMi*	α	2.50	00 23	88 46	Polaris
	β	2.08	14 51	74 34	
	γ	3.07	15 21	72 11	

TABLE H-9. STARS BRIGHTER THAN APPARENT MAGNITUDE 3ᵐ5 (*continued*)

	Designation	Apparent magnitude	Right ascension 1900 (hours, minutes)	Declination 1900 (degrees, arcminutes)	Remarks
VELA, *Vel*	γ	1.82	08 06	−47 03	
	δ	1.95	08 42	−54 21	
	κ	2.49	09 19	−54 35	
	λ	2.30	09 04	−43 02	
	μ	2.68	10 42	−48 54	
	N	3.12	09 28	−56 36	
VIRGO, *Vir*	α	0.96	13 20	−10 38	Spica
	δ	3.38	12 51	03 56	
	ε	2.81	12 57	11 30	
	ζ	3.36	13 30	−00 05	

TABLE H-10. STARS WITHIN 5 pc OF THE SUN

Catalogue number	Right ascension 1950	Declination 1950	Constellation	Parallax (arcsecs)	Spectral type	Apparent magnitude	Absolute magnitude	Remarks*
1	00 02	−37 36	Scl	.225	M4	8.58	10.35	
15A	00 16	43 44	And	.282	M1	8.08	10.33	Variable
15B	00 16	43 45	And	.282	M6e	11.04	13.29	Wolf 28, white dwarf
35	00 47	05 09	Psc	.239	F3	12.37	14.26	
65A	01 36	−18 13	Cet	.367	M6e	12.5	15.3	UV Cet, variable
65B	01 36	−18 13	Cet	.367	M4e	13.0	15.8	
71	01 42	−16 12	Cet	.277	G8	3.50	5.71	τ Cet
144	03 31	−09 38	Eri	.302	K2	3.73	6.13	ε Eri
166A	04 13	−07 44	Eri	.205	K1	4.43	5.99	
166B	04 13	−07 44	Eri	.205	A	9.53	11.09	40 Eri, white dwarf
166C	04 13	−07 44	Eri	.205	M4e	11.16	12.72	
191	05 10	−45 00	Pic	.256	M0	8.85	10.89	
234A	06 27	−02 46	Mon	.252	M4e	11.07	13.08	Ross 614
234B	06 27	−02 46	Mon	.252	?	14.4	16.4	
244A	06 43	−16 39	CMa	.377	A1	−1.46	1.42	Sirius, α CMa
244B	06 43	−16 39	CMa	.377	A5	8.3	11.2	White dwarf
273	07 25	05 23	CMi	.270	M4	9.82	11.98	
280A	07 37	21	CMi	.287	F5	0.37	2.66	Procyon, α CMi
280B	07 37	05 21	CMi	.287	F	10.7	13.0	White dwarf
380	10 08	49 42	UMa	.222	K7	6.59	8.32	
388	10 17	20 07	Leo	.206	M4e	9.43	11.00	AD Leo, variable
406	10 54	07 19	Leo	.429	M6e	13.53	16.69	Wolf 359, variable
411	11 01	36 18	UMa	.369	M2	7.49	10.48	
440	11 43	−64 33	Mus	.206	A	11.48	13.05	White dwarf
447	11 45	01 06	Vir	.301	M5	11.10	13.49	
473A	12 31	09 18	Vir	.231	M4e	12.46	14.28	Ross 128
473B	12 31	09 18	Vir	.231	M7	13.4	15.2	
526	13 43	15 10	Boo	.205	M4	8.46	10.02	Wolf 498
551	14 26	−62 28	Cen	.761	M5e	10.7	15.1	Proxima Cen, V645 Cen, nearest star, variable
559A	14 36	−60 38	Cen	.743	G2	−0.01	4.34	α Cen
559B	14 36	−60 38	Cen	.743	K0	1.33	5.68	
628	16 28	−12 32	Oph	.249	M4	10.12	12.10	

	RA	Dec						Remarks
674	17 25	−46 51	Ara	.216	M4	9.36	11.03	
682	17 33	−44 17	Sco	.213	M5	11.2	12.8	
687	17 37	68 23	Dra	.214	M4	9.15	10.80	
699	17 55	04 33	Oph	.548	M5	9.54	13.23	Barnard's star
725A	18 42	59 33	Dra	.284	M4	8.90	11.17	
725B	18 42	59 33	Dra	.284	M5	9.69	11.96	
729	18 47	−23 54	Sgr	.345	M4e	10.6	13.3	Ross 154, V1216 Sgr, variable
820A	21 05	38 30	Cyg	.296	K5	5.22	7.58	61 Cyg
820B	21 05	38 30	Cyg	.296	K7	6.03	8.39	
825	21 14	−39 04	Mic	.260	M0	6.68	8.75	
832	21 30	−51 04	Ind	.214	M1	8.68	10.33	
845	22 00	−57 00	Ind	.291	K4	4.69	7.01	ε Ind
860A	22 26	57 27	Cep	.253	M4	9.85	11.87	Krüger 60
860B	22 26	57 27	Cep	.253	M4e	11.3	13.3	DO Cep, variable
866	22 36	−15 35	Aqr	.305	M6e	12.18	14.60	
876	22 51	−14 31	Aqr	.209	M5	10.13	11.73	Ross 780
887	23 03	−36 08	PsA	.279	M2	7.36	9.59	
905	23 39	43 55	And	.318	M6e	12.29	14.80	Ross 248
9C6	01 57	12 50	Ari	.213	M5e	12.28	13.92	Variable

Source: R. Woolley et. al., *Catalogue of Stars Within Twenty-Five Parsecs of the Sun*, Herstmonceux: Royal Greenwich Observatory, 1970.
*If there is no entry "white dwarf" under *Remarks*, the star is of luminosity class V.

TABLE H-11.   OTHER STARS MENTIONED IN THE TEXT

Designation		Right ascension	Declination	Remarks
V603	Aql	18 47	00 31	Nova (outburst 1918)
ζ	Aur	04 55	40 56	Eclipsing binary
WW	Aur	32 26	32 32	Eclipsing binary
Z	Cam	08 14	73 26	Variable star
δ	Cep	22 25	57 54	Pulsating star
UV	Cet	01 36	−18 13	Flare star
R	CrB	15 44	28 28	Variable star
SS	Cyg	21 39	43 08	Variable star
40	Eri	04 11	−07 49	(o^2 Eri) White dwarf
U	Gem	07 49	22 16	Variable star
DQ	Her	18 07	45 50	Nova (outburst 1934)
RR	Lyr	19 23	42 40	Pulsating star
λ	Ori	05 30	09 52	Double star component
ϕ^1	Ori	05 29	09 25	Double star component
ϕ^2	Ori	05 31	09 14	Nearby star, not related to ϕ^1 Ori
GK	Per	03 28	43 44	Nova (outburst 1901)
T	Tau	04 16	19 18	Variable star, pre-main-sequence
ϕ	UMa	09 45	54 32	Visual binary
80	UMa	13 21	55 31	(Alcor) Double star component

TABLE H-12.   OTHER GALACTIC OBJECTS MENTIONED IN THE TEXT

	Designation	Right ascension	Declination	Constellation	Remarks*
Open clusters	h Persei	02 15	57°	Per	NGC 0869
	χ Persei	02 20	57°	Per	NGC 0884
	Hyades	04 20	15°	Tau	
	Pleiades	03 40	24°	Tau	
Supernovae	SN 1054	05 32	22 00	Tau	NGC 1952, Crab nebula
	SN 1572	00 22	64 15	Cas	Brahe's supernova
	SN 1604	17 28	−21 27	Oph	Kepler's supernova
	SN 1667	23 21	58 32	Cas	Radio source Cas A
Pulsars	CP 1133	11 34	16 08	Leo	
	NP 0532	05 32	21 59	Tau	Crab pulsar
	PSR 0833	08 34	45 00	Vel	
X-ray sources	Cyg X-2	21 43	38 05	Cyg	
	Cen X-4	15^h	−32°	Cen	
	Sco X-1	16 17	−15 31	Sco	

*In the case of extended objects such as open clusters, or where identification is uncertain, coordinates are approximate.

TABLE H-13. OBJECTS FROM MESSIER'S CATALOGUE MENTIONED IN THE TEXT

Messier number	Right ascension	Declination	Constellation	Remarks
M1	05 32	22 00	Tau	NGC 1952, Crab nebula, supernova remnant
M2	21 31	−01 02	Aqr	NGC 7089, globular cluster
M3	13 40	28 38	CVn	NGC 5272, globular cluster
M 5	15 16	02 17	Ser	NGC 5904, globular cluster
M11	18 48	−06 20	Sct	NGC 6705, open cluster
M20	17 59	−23 02	Sgr	NGC 6514, Trifid nebula, gaseous nebula
M27	19 58	22 35	Vul	NGC 6853, planetary nebula
M31	00 40	41 00	And	NGC 0224, Andromeda system, spiral galaxy
M32	00 40	40 36	And	NGC 0221, elliptical galaxy, companion of M31
M33	01 31	30 24	Tri	NGC 0598, spiral galaxy in local group
M42	05 33	−05 25	Ori	NGC 1976, main portion of Orion nebula
M43	05 33	−05 19	Ori	NGC 1982, northern portion of Orion nebula
M57	18 52	32 58	Lyr	NGC 6720, planetary nebula
M59	12 39	11 55	Vir	NGC 4621, parent galaxy of supernova event
M67	08 48	12 00	Cnc	NGC 2682, open cluster
M77	02 40	−00 14	Cet	NGC 1068, Seyfert galaxy
M81	09 51	69 15	UMa	NGC 3031, spiral galaxy
M82	09 52	69 57	UMa	NGC 3034, irregular galaxy
M87	12 28	12 44	Vir	NGC 4486, peculiar elliptical galaxy
M101	14 01	54 35	UMa	NGC 5457, spiral galaxy
M104	12 37	−11 21	Vir	NGC 4594, spiral galaxy

TABLE H-14. OBJECTS FROM NEW GENERAL CATALOGUE MENTIONED IN THE TEXT

NGC number	Right ascension	Declination	Constellation	Remarks
NGC 0147	00 30	48 15	Cas	Elliptical galaxy in local group
NGC 0185	00 36	48 05	Cas	Elliptical galaxy in local group
NGC 0188	00 39	85 03	Cep	Open cluster
NGC 0205	00 38	41 25	And	Elliptical galaxy, companion of NGC 0224
NGC 0221	00 40	40 36	And	M32, elliptical galaxy companion of NGC 0224
NGC 0224	00 40	41 00	And	M31, Andromeda system, spiral galaxy
NGC 0488	01 19	05 00	Psc	Spiral galaxy
NGC 0598	01 31	30 24	Tri	M33, spiral galaxy in local group
NGC 0869	02 15	57°	Per	h Persei, open cluster
NGC 0884	02 20	57°	Per	χ Persei, open cluster
NGC 1068	02 40	−00 14	Cet	M77, Seyfert galaxy
NGC 1300	03 17	−19 35	Eri	Galaxy (barred spiral)
NGC 1398	03 37	−26 30	For	Galaxy (barred spiral)
NGC 1952	05 32	22 00	Tau	M1, crab nebula, supernova remnant
NGC 1976	05 33	−05 25	Ori	M42, main portion of Orion nebula
NGC 1982	05 33	−05 19	Ori	M43, northern portion of Orion nebula
NGC 2682	08 48	12 00	Cnc	M67, open cluster
NGC 3031	09 51	69 15	UMa	M81, spiral galaxy
NGC 3034	09 52	69 57	UMa	M82, irregular galaxy
NGC 3242	10 22	−18 23	Hya	Planetary nebula
NGC 4151	12 08	39 41	CVn	Seyfert galaxy
NGC 4486	12 28	12 44	Vir	M87, peculiar elliptical galaxy
NGC 4565	12 34	11 43	Vir	Spiral galaxy
NGC 4594	12 37	−11 21	Vir	M104, spiral galaxy
NGC 4621	12 39	11 55	Vir	M59, parent galaxy of supernova event
NGC 4636	12 40	02 57	Vir	Parent galaxy of supernova event
NGC 5128	13 22	−42 45	Cen	Cen A, peculiar elliptical galaxy
NGC 5272	13 40	28 38	CVn	M3, globular cluster
NGC 5432 NGC 5435	14 01	−05 40	Vir	Pair of spiral galaxies
NGC 5457	14 01	54 35	UMa	M101, spiral galaxy
NGC 5866	15 05	55 57	Dra	Lenticular galaxy
NGC 5904	15 16	02 17	Ser	M5, globular cluster
NGC 6027	15 57	20 55	Ser	Peculiar group of galaxies
NGC 6166	16 27	39 40	Her	3C 3382, double galaxy
NGC 6514	17 59	−23 02	Sgr	M20, Trifid nebula, gaseous nebula
NGC 6705	18 48	−06 20	Sct	M11, open cluster
NGC 6720	18 52	32 58	Lyr	M57, planetary nebula
NGC 6751	19 03	−06 04	Aql	Planetary nebula
NGC 6822	19 42	−14 53	Sgr	Irregular galaxy in local group
NGC 6853	19 58	22 35	Vul	M27, dumbbell nebula, planetary nebula
NGC 6960	20 44	30°	Cyg	Veil nebula, portion of supernova remnant
NGC 6992	20 54	31 30	Cyg	Network nebula, portion of veil nebula
NGC 7089	21 31	−01 02	Aqr	M2, globular cluster
NGC 7293	22 27	−21 03	Aqr	Planetary nebula
NGC 7317 NGC 7318a,b NGC 7319 NGC 7320	22 34	33 42	Peg	Stephan's quintet of galaxies
NGC 7331	22 35	34 10	Peg	Parent galaxy of supernova event

TABLE H-15. OBJECTS FROM INDEX CATALOGUE MENTIONED IN THE TEXT

IC number	Right ascension	Declination	Constellation	Remarks
IC 434	05 39	−02 26	Ori	Horsehead nebula
IC 1613	01 03	01 52	Cet	Small galaxy in local group
IC 4182	13 04	37 52	CVn	Parent galaxy of supernova event

TABLE H-16. OBJECTS FROM THE CAMBRIDGE RADIO SOURCE CATALOGUES MENTIONED IN THE TEXT

Catalogue number	Right ascension	Declination	Constellation	Remarks
3C 120	04 31	05 15	Tau	Seyfert galaxy
3C 147	05 39	49 50	Aur	Quasar
3C 273	12 27	02 20	Vir	Quasar
3C 338	16 27	39 40	Her	NGC 6166, double galaxy
3C 405	19 58	40 36	Cyg	Cyg A, D type galaxy
4C 05.34	08 05	04 41	CMi	Quasar

TABLE H-17. THE LOCAL GROUP OF GALAXIES*

Designation	Classification	Right ascension	Declination	Constellation
Our galaxy	Sb			
NGC 0147	Ell	00 30	48 15	Cas
NGC 0185	Ell	00 36	48 05	Cas
NGC 0205	Ell	00 38	41 25	And
NGC 0221	Ell	00 40	40 35	And
NGC 0224	Sb	00 40	41 00	And
NGC 0598	Sc	01 31	30 25	Tri
NGC 6822	Irr	19 42	−14 55	Sgr
IC 1613	Irr	01 03	01 50	Cet
LMC	Irr	05^h	−69°	Dor
SMC	Irr	01^h	−73°	Tuc
Draco	Ell	17 19	58 00	Dra
Fornax	Ell	02 38	−34 45	For
Leo I	Ell	10 06	12 35	Leo
Leo II	Ell	11 11	22 25	Leo
Sculptor	Ell	00 58	−34 00	Scl
Ursa Minor	Ell	15 08	67 20	UMi
Maffei 1	(Ell)	02 33	59 25	Per
Maffei 2	(Ell)	02 38	59 25	Per

*Several other suspected members are not listed

TABLE H-18. CLUSTERS OF GALAXIES

Name	Right ascension	Declination	Constellation
Coma cluster	12 30	15°	Com
Virgo cluster	12 40	30°	Vir

l glossary

Absorption *of photons (of light, radio waves, etc.):* assimilation of photons by atoms, molecules, solid particles, etc.; the absorbed photon energy increases the internal energy of the absorber. **Absorption** *lines:* narrow regions in the spectrum of a light source in which *fewer* photons show up than in neighboring wavelength regions.

Activity, *solar:* increased temperature, strongly enhanced magnetic fields, etc., in localized areas of the sun. **Activity** *stellar:* postulated phenomenon in stars equivalent to solar activity

Altitude: angular distance from the horizon.

Amplitude: maximum extent, usually of a fluctuating quantity such as stellar brightness, with respect to the average.

Angular *diameter:* angle subtended by the diameter of an object such as a planet or a galaxy, as seen from the earth. **Angular** *distance:* angle subtended by two objects, such as the two components of a double star or two markings on a planetary surface, as seen from the earth.

Association, *star:* group of stars that physically belong together because they were formed at about the same time close to each other in space.

Atmosphere, *earth:* gases surrounding the solid body of the earth. **Atmosphere,** *solar (stellar):* outer portion of the sun (star), comprising the layers from which we receive photons.

Bands, *molecular:* arrangement of spectral lines in groups, the result of emission or absorption by molecules.

Binary star: twin star; two stars, presumably formed together and gravitationally bound to each other.

Black body: idealized light source; the energy distribution inherent in its radiation spectrum is described by a specific relation between brightness, temperature, and wavelength (Planck's law).

Closed system: one that has negligible interaction with its surroundings.

Cloud, *interstellar:* localized volume in which gas and dust are denser than elsewhere in the universe.

Cluster, *open* and *globular:* group of stars, presumably formed at about the same time from one large cloud of uncondensed material; open and globular clusters differ in spatial arrangement, age, and other characteristics. **Cluster** *of galaxies:* grouping of galaxies presumably bound together by gravitational interaction.

Color: term referring to and resulting from the wavelengths of light photons. Because of the relation between the surface temperature of, say, a star and the wavelengths at which most photons are emitted from its surface, the color is indicative of the temperature of the light source.

Compound nucleus: nucleus resulting from a fusion process, usually either in an excited state or unstable.

Condensation *of a star:* formation of a star from dilute material present in the universe.

Conduction *of heat:* transport of heat energy by individual atoms and molecules.

Configuration, *electron:* arrangement of electrons in an atom, corresponding to a specific internal energy.

Conservation *of energy (momentum):* the energy (momentum) of a closed system cannot change.

Constellation: gerrymandered area on the celestial sphere, used to identify the approximate position of celestial objects. The term originally referred to sets of bright stars which were thought to outline mythological beings or animals in the sky.

Continuum: photons of many different energies or wavelengths making up a more or less uniform spectral background. Contrast with *spectral lines.*

Convection: transport of heat energy through the motion of bubbles of gas or liquid.

Core, *solar (stellar):* innermost region of the sun (star).

Cosmology: study of the universe at large, its structure, and its development.

Degeneracy: particular state of matter, at great densities, in which component parts such as electrons or neutrons are fixed in their lowest energy states.

Density, *electron (ion):* number of electrons (ions) per unit volume. **Density** *(of matter):* mass per unit volume.

Disc, *solar:* projection of the sun onto the celestial sphere. **Disc,** *galactic:* the flattened portion of our star system (Galaxy).

Discrete energy levels *of an atom (molecule, ion):* very narrowly defined ("discrete") energy values which can be taken on by the electrons in an atom (molecule, ion).

Double *star:* two stars which appear very close to each other on the celestial sphere; most such stars are unrelated, their closeness being a consequence of the projection effect.

Dust: interstellar mixture of very small solid grains, such as ice crystals, metal particles, graphite.

Dwarf: designation for stars that are significantly smaller than some comparison group.

Eccentricity *(of an ellipse):* a number describing how much the shape of an ellipse departs from circularity.

Element: a specific configuration of neutrons, protons, and electrons to form an atom and result in a specific set of physical properties. There are about 100 different elements known (see Table H-3).

Emission *of photons:* creation and explusion of photons by atoms, molecules, etc.; the photons carry away a portion of the internal energy of the system in which they originated. **Emission** *lines:* narrow regions in the spectrum of a light source in which *more* photons show up than in neighboring wavelength regions.

Energy: quantity that describes the ability of a system to do work. **Energy,** *gravitational:* energy vested in the position of a body with respect to others with which it interacts through gravity. **Energy,** *kinetic:* energy vested in the motion state of a system. **Energy,** *magnetic:* energy vested in magnetic fields.

Envelope: gas cloud surrounding a star, a star system, a galaxy, etc.

Epoch: a specific date, written as, say, 1950 January 1; a term usually used in celestial mechanics.

Equilibrium, *thermodynamic:* state of a physical system in which all its internal-energy forms can be defined by one number, its temperature. **Equilibrium,** *hydrostatic:* situation in which the structure of an object such as a star is determined by a balance of the internal pressure and the gravitational force.

Excitation *(of an atom):* change in the arrangement of electrons in an atom to one with greater internal energy, usually accomplished by the absorption of photons.

Extragalactic object: one whose position is *outside* our star system (galaxy).

Field: *(electric, gravitational, magnetic, etc.):* the presence of (electric, gravitational, magnetic, etc.) forces. **Field,** *radiation:* the presence of photons. **Field strength:** a measure of the amount of force acting at a particular position.

Fission: break up of large atomic nuclei into smaller units.

Flare, *solar:* multifaceted phenomenon in the solar atmosphere. **Flare,** *stellar:* postulated phenomenon in stellar atmospheres corresponding to solar flare.

Flux, *energy (radiation):* amount of energy (radiation) passing through a unit surface area per unit time.

Focus *(of a telescope):* point of convergence of light photons after reflection by a mirror, or after passage through a lens. **Focus** *(of a conic section):* reference point of a conic section.

Forbidden transition: change in the atomic-energy state that has a very low probability of occurring. **Forbidden line:** the spectral line resulting from a forbidden transition.

Force: agent able to change the motion state of a physical system.

Frequency: a number proportional to the energy of a photon.

Galaxy: very large group of stars tied together by mutual gravitational interaction, usually with a very complex structure. All stars visible to the naked eye belong to a small portion of our galaxy. **Galactic rotation:** rotation of galactic material about some axis, that is, some imaginary line through the system.

Giant: designation for stars that are significantly larger than some comparison group.

Globular cluster: specific type of star cluster, characterized by highly symmetrical structure.

Globule: small, dense area in an interstellar cloud involved in star formation.

Granulation: fine structure of the solar atmosphere due to convection.

Halo: spherical space surrounding a galaxy, populated by globular clusters, cosmic rays, etc.

Inclination, *angle of:* angle between two planes, for instance, the plane of the earth's orbit about the sun and the plane through its equator.

Intensity, light: brightness; proportional to the number of photons passing through a unit area of a light source per unit time.

Light: form of energy vested in photons. Some light is visible to the human eye, other "light" is not (ultraviolet, infrared, X-rays, etc.).

Limb, solar: edge of the solar disc.

Line of sight: line connecting an object with the observer.

Linear distance: distance between two objects measured in units of length. Contrast with *angular distance.*

Magnitude *of a star:* brightness. **Magnitude number:** brightness expressed as a numerical value according to a specifically defined logarithmic scale. **Magnitude,** *apparent:* observed brightness. **Magnitude,** *absolute:* brightness an object would have if it were at a distance of 10 pc from the earth.

Mass: a quantity of matter; also a form of energy. Gravitational forces act among masses.

Momentum: product of mass and velocity, provided the absolute value of the velocity is much smaller than 300,000 km/sec (*speed of light*).

Nebula: gas cloud, visible to the naked eye or detectable in visible light by means of telescopes.

Nucleus, *atomic:* central region of an atom, contains almost all the atom's mass in the form of protons and neutrons. **Nucleus** *of a galaxy:* innermost portion of a galaxy, often not resolvable even with large telescopes.

Oblateness: flattening of a celestial object, such as a planet or a star, due mostly to its rotation.

Open cluster: star cluster located in a spiral arm of a galaxy.

Orbit: path of a celestial object.

Particle: small entity of not otherwise defined properties, such as "dust" particles. **Particle,** *elementary:* least complex building block of matter.

Perturbation *of an orbit:* deviation of the path of a celestial object from an idealized form.

Potential, gravitational: gravitational energy content of a body by virtue of its position with respect to another body.

Projection *effect:* two objects appearing very close to each other on the celestial sphere, when their directions from the earth are almost the same; they may be at very different distances from us.

Prominence: relatively cool, dense gas suspended in magnetic fields in the solar corona.

Proper motion: change in position of an object on the celestial sphere, that is, the component of the object's motion at right angle to the line connecting the object with the observer (the *line of sight*); measured in angular units per unit time.

Radial velocity: component of the velocity of an object along the line connecting the body with the observer (the *line of sight*).

Radiation: visible or invisible light.

Radical, free: molecule consisting of very few atoms, normally not stable under the conditions prevailing in the earth's atmosphere.

Rays, cosmic: high-energy particles such as electrons, or protons, or high-energy photons. **Rays, X:** high-energy photons of typically 10 Å wavelength. **Rays, gamma:** high-energy photons typically of wavelength 0.1 Å.

Relativistic: very energetic. Relativistic particles move with speeds close to 300,000 km/sec (*speed of light*).

Relativity, *theory of general:* theory describing the behavior of physical quantities in very strong gravitational fields. **Relativity,** *theory of special:* theory describing the space and time behavior of physical quantities; includes the exchange of mass and energy forms.

Resolution, angular: ability to distinguish two objects separated by a very small *angular distance*. **Resolution, spatial:** ability to distinguish two objects separated by a very small *linear distance*. **Resolution, spectral:** ability to distinguish two features with a very small *wavelength difference*.

Revolution: periodic motion of a body about another, such as the earth's motion about the sun.

Rotation: spin. **Rotation,** *differential:* state of motion in which the parts of a system spin at different speeds. Contrast *rigid-body rotation*. **Rotation,** *rigid-body:* spinning of a body such that all parts of the body remain in the same positions relative to each other.

Satellite *of a planet:* a moon bound to a planet by gravity. **Satellites** *of earth;* the moon and man-made bodies in orbit about the earth.

Scattered light: light deflected at more or less random angles without a significant change in energy content.

Shell, *circumstellar:* cloud of gas or dust of relatively small radial extent surrounding a star. **Shell source:** spherical region of relatively small radial extent surrounding the center of a star and undergoing nuclear reactions.

Shock wave: explosion wave, moving away from an explosion with a speed greater than the speed of sound.

Shower, meteor: collision of a *group* of meteoroids with the earth's atmosphere.

Source *(of radiation):* place of origin of photons.

Spectrum: a list (usually a chart) of the number of photons radiated as a function of wavelength. **Spectrum, visible:** the distribution of photons with energies corresponding to the range of sensitivity of the human eye. **Spectrum, radio:** the distribution of photons with wavelengths larger than about 1 millimeter. **Spectral line:** very narrow range of wavelengths in which photons are absorbed or emitted, mostly by one particular energy state of a specific atom or molecule.

Subsonic speed: a speed below the speed of sound.

Supersonic speed: a speed above the speed of sound.

Transition, *electron:* a change in the internal energy content of atomic electrons, mostly by absorption or emission of photons.

Unit: basis for physical measurements. **Unit length:** 1 cm. **Unit time:** 1 sec. **Unit area:** 1 cm². **Unit volume:** 1 cm³.

Variable star: a star which undergoes changes in one or more of its properties (brightness, surface temperature, radius, etc.).

Visual binaries: twin stars which are detectable with the eye or on photographs.

Wind, *solar (stellar):* material of the outermost atmosphere of the sun (star) which is continuously streaming away from the sun (star).

index

Page numbers in boldface refer to principal discussion or basic definition.